Spirit Baptism

Spirit Baptism
A Pentecostal Alternative

HAROLD D. HUNTER

WIPF & STOCK · Eugene, Oregon

SPIRIT BAPTISM
A Pentecostal Alternative

Copyright © 2009 Harold D. Hunter. All rights reserved. Except for brief quotations in critical publications or reviews, no part of this book may be reproduced in any manner without prior written permission from the publisher. Write: Permissions, Wipf and Stock, 199 W. 8th Ave., Suite 3, Eugene, OR 97401.

Wipf and Stock Publishers
199 W. 8th Ave., Suite 3
Eugene, OR 97401

www.wipfandstock.com

ISBN 13: 978-1-55635-930-9

Manufactured in the U.S.A.

Contents

Acknowledgements / vii

Preface / ix

1. Introduction / 1
2. The Pauline Corpus / 37
3. Luke-Acts / 73
4. The Johannine Literature / 104
5. Patristic Literature / 122
6. Selected Literature from 600–1900 / 139
7. The Doctrine of Salvation / 202

   Conclusion / 221

   Bibliography / 233

Acknowledgements

WHEN THIS MANUSCRIPT WAS published in 1983, it envisioned future expansion. This has been realized through various means, including: continued biblical, historical, and theological research on the subject; additional publications and specialized studies in the area; use of the book in classrooms and scholarly conferences spread across five continents; responses by friends; reviews in journals.

One result of further submersion in the subject is seen both in the revision of earlier editions and the willingness to leave the majority of the text as originally published. The more substantial updating involves bibliographic data and the introductory chapter. Despite these multifaceted influences, it is the author alone who assumes responsibility for the contents. Considering the diversity of Scripture and current ecclesiastical fragmentation, this work is seen as most relevant to the current generation of classical pentecostals in the West.

One noticeable difference between this revised edition and the original is that some sections have been removed due to space limitations, but the most significant loss is the original addendum. That addendum reproduced the following article: "Tongues-Speech: A Patristic Analysis," in the *Journal of the Evangelical Theological Society* 23:2 (June 1980), 125–37. This has been perhaps the most widely quoted article that I have written. Another gap is an excursus that was published as "Spirit Christology: Dilemma and Promise," *Heythrop Journal* 24:2 (1983) continued in 24:3 (1983).

On the other hand, this manuscript has been revised up through 1998. This accounts for the absence of dialogue partners that have emerged since then. However, I have stayed current with the literature in the field and have yet to be persuaded to change course in any matter of substance in this study. The opening chapter has been updated and expanded as "Orphans or Windows: Seeing Through A Glass Darkly," *Cyberjournal for*

Pentecostal-Charismatic Research #17 (2008). The bibliography is taken from the first edition.

A word of appreciation to Wipf and Stock for bringing this volume back into the ongoing discussion of Classical Pentecostal distinctives. Special mention must be made of Robert W. Graves and The Foundation for Pentecostal Scholarship (www.tffps.org) who addressed technical issues like formatting and paid for typesetting thus making the manuscript fully ready for publication.

I remain most grateful to my wife, Sondra, for a variety of contributions she has made to this project. This extends to typing and proofreading portions of the original publication. Most of all, her steadfast love has been evident through the doctoral project, the outworking of that commitment and further forward steps. I pray to be able to return the love she has shared with me.

Preface

CLASSICAL PENTECOSTAL DISTINCTIVES HAVE been called into question by a wide range of writers and at times have had unexpected support. The dissertations turned books by J. D. G. Dunn and F. Dale Bruner dissuaded some seminarians from their pentecostal heritage and entrenched opponents in their resistance to pentecostal teachings on Spirit baptism. The issue has not gone away which is apparent from the continuing influence of the pentecostal point of view through various media and particularly seen in dissertations on the subject by Donald Wheelock and Henry Lederle. Larry Hart completed a dissertation independent from me at the same time but further work led him to espouse a view different than that defended in his dissertation. A later volume of some influence is *Christian Initiation and Baptism in the Holy Spirit* by Kilian McDonnell and George Montague.

Another barometer of the importance of this issue is that J. Rodman Williams dedicated the 1984 annual conference of the Society for Pentecostal Studies to this theme. The papers are available in a collection entitled *Toward a Pentecostal/ Charismatic Theology: Baptism in the Holy Spirit*. Many of those papers responded to the first edition of this book. The first edition of this book was noted in various journals—including *Gregorianum* and the *EPTA Bulletin*—with reviews in the *Scottish Journal of Theology* 38:1, the *Evangelical Quarterly*, *Religious Studies Review* 12:1, and *Paraclete* 21:2.

It is the purpose of this study to examine the essence of Pentecostal Spirit baptism theology—namely, that there is a distinct work of the Spirit which effects charismatic activity in the life of the believer. Is this a historically contrived novelty? Exegesis of selected passages from the Pauline Corpus, Lucan Writings and Johannine Literature will be used to see if these texts expose an identifiable work of the Holy Spirit which is charismatic in nature. This will be followed by a historical survey of many prominent Christians to see if the essence of this pentecostal distinctive is limited to the current century. The work then concludes with an attempt to assimilate the canonical and historical data and relate them to traditional Protestant ordo salutis formulas.

The reading for this research project is extensive and spans the theological spectrum. I believe there is much to be learned from authors of various traditions and of varying quality. I hope they have been represented fairly and that their contribution is evident. I also desire that the pentecostal movement not be judged on this issue alone. My 1984 presidential address to the Society for Pentecostal Studies delivered at Gordon-Conwell Theological Seminary sought to interpret the movement as combining basically orthodox propositions with a distinct but not unknown ethos. Thus those who evaluate the movement in light of this book alone will not be sufficiently introduced to the most significant dimension of pentecostal identity.

1

Introduction

THE ISSUE

THE TWENTIETH CENTURY WITNESSED the birth and phenomenal growth of what is known in North America as the Classical Pentecostal Movement. Reaction in the first half of this century was almost unanimously negative by traditional church leaders, theologians, psychologists, and sociologists. Many judged Pentecostals to be emotionally disturbed, mentally limited, inherently sociologically deprived and/or concluded that the pneumatic unction claimed by the Pentecostalist was not genuine. Those views have not been abandoned by many and yet the ecclesiastical landscape has been sufficiently rearranged that many traditions have re-evaluated their opposition to the movement. This is due in no small part to the metaphorphasis of the movement itself and the fact that it has figured in spreading its influence to much of world-wide Christianity. The surprise for many people in the 1960's was that this expanse included mainline Protestant churches and the Roman Catholic Church. Many center and right-wing evangelicals found increasing numbers of Classical Pentecostals pliable to much of their theological agenda.[1]

Another reason that the wider Christian community has had to reckon more seriously with Pentecostalism is because of the dramatic increase in the size of the movement. It seemed to startle some when David Barrett's *World Christian Encyclopedia* (1982) determined that Classical Pentecostalism now constituted the largest unit in the Protestant

---

1. It is clear that a similar pattern emerged as the Pentecostal–Charismatic Movement burgeoned in Non-Western Countries. See Joseph Osei-Bonsu, "The Spirit as Agent of Renewal: the New Testament Testimony," *The Ecumenical Review* 41:3 (July 1989): 459f. Cf. Kenneth J. Archer, "Pentecostal Hermeneutics: Retrospect and Prospect," *Journal of Pentecostal Theology* 8 (1996): 74f.

family. He showed also that four—including the top three—of the world's largest congregations were Pentecostal. His figures for 1985 identified 168,000,000 persons as pentecostal or charismatic.[2]

Most impressive has been the impact on theological inquiry. Although studies of pneumatology preceded this century, some periods have been characterized as "Benign Neglect." The trickle of research on this subject has turned into a flood. There are now lengthy bibliographies devoted solely to the Holy Spirit. Pentecostal studies are now featured at previously unheard of places like Harvard University (USA), the University of Cambridge (England), the University of Amsterdam (Holland), the University of South Africa (UNISA), and Trinity College (Singapore).

A telling state of affairs was revealed in the adoption of the theme "Come, Holy Spirit" for the Seventh Assembly (1991) of the World Council of Churches (WCC). Emilio Castro, initiator of this theme when General Secretary of the WCC, participated in the 1992 edition of Encuentro Pentecostal Latinoamericano. Some North American Pentecostals will have to adjust their thinking when they read the following in the officially prepared document for the Seventh Assembly:

> The transformation that the Spirit brings restores our communion with God and one another. We are built up through the gifts of the Spirit into a people empowered to do God's will, to share the good news, and to become a community of sharing.[3]

---

2. The numbers should not be overplayed for several reasons including the fact that many Pentecostal denominations are not experiencing genuine growth in the USA. The Assemblies of God have taken in several Charismatics and, like many other Pentecostal denominations, have various affiliations in the USA and abroad. For other points of caution see Peter Hocken's presidential address to the 1986 edition of the Society For Pentecostal Studies, "One Body and One Spirit," *Azusa St. Revisited*, ed. by Edith Waldvogel Blumhofer (Costa Mesa: Society for Pentecostal Studies, November 13–15, 1986), 17; a response to Vinson Synan by Barbara Zikmund at the consultation on Pentecostalism sponsored by the Commission on Faith and Order of the NCCCUSA held at Fuller Theological Seminary during October 22–24, 1986. The idea (cited by Virgil Elizondo, "Healing and Deliverance: The Response of Liberation Theology," *Concilium* (3/1996): 53, edited by Jürgen Moltmann and Karl-Josef Kuschel) that by 2000 one in four Christians will be pentecostal is an exaggeration.

3. This quotation is taken from *Come, Holy Spirit: Renew Thy Whole Creation* (New York: Friendship Press, 1989), 8. Of greater fascination to scholars is "Come, Holy Spirit," *The Ecumenical Review* 41:3 (July 1989). Cf. Watson E. Mills, *The Holy Spirit: A Bibliography* (Peabody: Hendrickson Press, 1988).

It has become increasingly clear that informed theologians cannot make the Holy Spirit a mere addendum to their systems.[4] As rightly affirmed by a Greek Orthodox theologian, "Trinitarian theology is rediscovered as the heart of authentic Christian theology."[5]

Judging by the textbooks used for most USA seminary classes on Church History and Historical Theology, most western historians think of Christianity through the centuries as having two primary components. There is, of course, no unanimity on particulars, but to partially elucidate what is in view it might be said that one stream is Anglo-Catholic-Orthodox and the other magisterial Protestantism.

The following is a North American pentecostal paradigm on church history.

	APOSTOLIC	
Succession	Teaching	Restoration[6]
Catholic	Magisterial Reformation	Enthusiastic Pneumatomania[7]
Orthodox	Lutheran	Believer's Church[8]
Anglican	Presbyterian	Landmark, Missionary Baptists
	American Baptists	Wesleyanism[9]

---

4. Consider Jürgen Moltmann as the keynote speaker for the Theological Stream of Brighton '91, the first global conference of Pentecostal scholars. See his address, "The Spirit of Life: Spirituality and New Vitality" in *All Together In One Place*, ed. by Peter D. Hocken and Harold D. Hunter (Sheffield: Sheffield Academic Press, 1993) and *The Spirit of Life* (Philadelphia: Fortress, 1992). Consider also Michael Welker, *God the Spirit* (Philadelphia: Fortress, 1995); Michael Welker, "'Word and Spirit Spirit and Word': A Protestant Response," *Concilium* (3/1996) [London:SCM/Maryknoll: Orbis] 76–84, edited by Jürgen Moltmann and Karl-Josef Kuschel dedicated to the theme "Pentecostal Movements As An Ecumenical Challenge"; T. W. Gillespie, *The First Theologians: A Study in Early Christian Prophecy* (Grand Rapids: Eerdmans, 1994). Harvey Cox looks at Pentecostalism in his *Fire From Heaven: The Rise of Pentecostal Spirituality and the Reshaping of Religion in the Twenty-first Century* (Reading: Addison-Wesley Publishing Company, 1994), but in a way that his mentor Paul Tillich would applaud.

5. Emmanuel Clapsis, "The Holy Spirit in the Church," *The Ecumenical Review* 41:3 (July 1989): 339. Clapsis quotes Kilian McDonnell approvingly for chiding those who have relegated pneumatology to a decoration. See Konrad Raiser, "The Holy Spirit in Modern Ecumenical Thought," *The Ecumenical Review* 41:3 (July 1989): 375ff. Late in 1992, Professor Raiser accepted the position of General Secretary of the World Council of Churches.

On closer inspection it is apparent that several eminent historians realize that among those Christians who do not fit neatly into these groupings there is one lineage in particular that has many shared attributes. Some might consider the label "Enthusiasts" appropriate. It is true that most of the major groups dealt with in the classic by R. A. Knox are in view here. Ultimately, it seems, there are significant points of divergences which warrant this particular appellation. Some of this would be evident by comparing Knox to the material that follows.

Historians are most often inclined to used labels like heretics, sects, mystics, and revivalists to describe the groups treated here. This reflects, first of all, the fact that Enthusiastic Pneumatomania are rarely identified with the mainstream of Christendom. Not surprisingly, then, mainstream historians find it easy to blur the line between sects and cults. The groups classed here as Enthusiastic Pneumatomania can be rightly called sects, but no cult is knowingly included.

---

6. See Garry Dale Nation, "The Hermeneutics of Pentecostal-Charismatic Restoration Theology: A Critical Analysis," unpublished Ph.D. dissertation, Southwestern Baptist Theological Seminary, December, 1990, 1ff., 16, 19, 28, 30; *Variety of American Evangelicalism*, 113ff., 35, 42, 64, 67, 70. Nation notes (p. 97) that current restorationists identify with Paulicians, Bogomites, Albigenses, Waldensians, etc. He himself rules out Montanists in this category. Cf. Edith L. Blumhofer, *Restoring the Faith: The Assemblies of God, Pentecostalism, and American Culture* (Urbana: University of Illinois Press, 1993); Edith L. Blumhofer, "Restoration as Revival: Early American Pentecostalism," *Modern Christian Revivals* (Urbana: University of Illinois Press, 1993), edited by Edith L. Blumhofer and Randall Balmer.

7. This is my current alternative to the general term Spirit Movement. I used Spirit Movement for several years before discovering that Martin Marty appropriated it in a similar way when addressing the 1973 session of the Society for Pentecostal Studies. See Martin Marty, "Pentecostalism in the Context of American Piety and Practice," *Aspects of Pentecostal-Charismatic Origins*, ed. by Vinson Synan (Plainfield: Logos, 1973), 200. The term is found also in the 1974 Tübingen dissertation by John J. McNamee, "The Role of the Spirit in Pentecostalism: A Comparative Study," unpublished Ph.D. dissertation (University of Tubingen, 1974).

8. See Donald F. Durnbaugh, *The Believers' Church* (Scottsdale: Herald Press, 1985); Paul Gritz, "'Church' in the History of Pentecostalism," paper read to 1991 Pentecostal-NCC Faith & Order Dialogue, 2; Eric H. Ohlmann, "Baptists and Evangelicals," *Variety of American Evangelicalism*, 149. Nation, "Restoration Theology," agrees [117, 61, 7, 95], but is quick to remind that not all believers' churches are restorationists.

9. See Durnbaugh, *Believers' Church*, ch. 5; Gritz, "'Church' in the History of Pentecostalism," 2ff.; Richard T. Hughes, "Are Restorationists Evangelicals?" *Variety of American Evangelicalism*, 112. Dick Iverson connects Luther, Mennonites, Baptists, Wesley and A. B. Simpson in restoration according to Nation, "Restoration Theology," 100f.

Classical Pentecostalism in North America has rightly been described as an expression of popular religiosity. A social history of Church of God by Mickey Crews casts the populist shadow over the early years. Specializing in various facets of turn of the century indigenous Appalachian religiosity, Deborah McCauley enumerates the particulars of oral religious tradition as worship—preaching, singing, and prayer, along with conversion narratives—testimonies, visions, dreams, and trances.

Spirit Possession and Popular Religion by Clarke Garrett shows the prevailing mass appeal of the Great Awakening. Paul Gritz from Southwestern Baptist Theological Seminary outlines an overlap of Baptist and pentecostal traditions which surfaces the popular religious perspective. It is no small wonder that the WCC would publish Sepulveda's treatment of pentecostalism as popular religion inasmuch as non-credalism has remained a constant agitation in putting together the *BEM* document and the reinterpretation of the Nicene-Constantinopolitan Creed (e.g., *Confessing The One Faith*).[10]

Enthusiastic Pneumatomania produce groups most likely to earn the title, "Sacred theater of the spirit possessed." Further, twentieth century restorationists include those Pentecostals known collectively in North

---

10. See Deborah Vansau McCauley, "Appalachian Mountain Religion," 3, 377, Ph.D. dissertation, Columbia University, 1990 published as *Appalachian Mountain Religion: A History* (Urbana: University of Illinois Press, 1995); Peter W. Williams, *Popular Religion In America* (Urbana: University of Illinois Press, 1989), 5f., 144; Clarke Garrett, *Spirit Possession and Popular Religion* (Baltimore: John Hopkins Press, 1987); Gritz, "'Church' in the History of Pentecostalism,"; Michael Kinnamon, *Truth and Community* (Grand Rapids: Eerdmans, 1988), 94; Juan Sepulveda, "Pentecostalism As Popular Religiosity," *International Review of Mission* 78:309 (Jan 1989): 80–88; Jim Manney, "The People's Movement at Age 25," *New Covenant* (Feb 92): 7–13; Anton Houtepen, "Toward An Ecumenical Vision of the Church," *One in Christ* 3 (1898): 226, 230–33; Everett A. Wilson, "Passion and Power: A Profile of Emergent Latin American Pentecostalism," *Called and Empowered: Global Mission in Pentecostal Perspective*, ed. by Murray A. Dempster, Byron D. Klaus, and Douglas Petersen (Peabody: Hendrickson, 1991), 68, 73, 83, 85; David Stoll, *Is Latin America Turning Protestant?* (Berkeley: University of California Press, 1990), 318f.; David Martin, *Tongues of Fire* (Cambridge: Basil Blackwell, 1990); Christian Lalive d'Epinay, *Haven of the Masses* (London: Lutterworth Press, 1969); Randall Balmer, "Local Religion In America," American Academy of Religion (11-19-90); Donald W. Dayton, "Yet Another Layer of the Onion: or Opening the Ecumenical Door to Let the Riffraff in," *The Ecumenical Review* 40:1 (January 1988): 88, 94–96; Steven J. Land, "Pentecostal Spirituality: Living in the Spirit," *Christian Spirituality III* (New York: Crossroads, 1989), 485.

America as Apostolics who have a particular twist on the subject that requires a reshaping of most proposals put forward.[11]

Enthusiastic Pneumatomania do not manifest the same kind of continuity known to the two principal traditions, and it is intrinsic to their nature that very little is known about any one of them. Each new manifestation struggles to identify a heritage and established historians usually are not willing to acknowledge any legitimate pedigree thus treating each new manifestation as a novelty if not a complete aberration. The designation by Bishop Lesslie Newbegin (1954) and Henry P. Van Dusen (195) of Classical Pentecostalism being the Third force in Twentieth Century Christianity reflects Newbegin's paradigm[12] of order (Roman Catholic), faith (Protestant), and experience (Pentecostal).

It is not surprising to discover that from the Azusa St. Revival onwards, modern day Enthusiastic Pneumatomania have published lists of persons and groups considered predecessors, and the names most common among them quite properly belong to the Enthusiastic Pneumatomania category. When early North American Pentecostals described their origins as "Suddenly from Heaven," they did not mean they were a historical novelty, but that no one individual masterminded the agenda.

---

11. Pentecostalist Richard Riss, *A Survey of 20th Century Revival Movements in North America* (Peabody: Hendrickson, 1988) counts the Pentecostal and Charismatic Movements among varying revival movements. Early Pentecostal self-perception is clearly revealed in names and phrases used with such frequency: The Apostolic Faith, The Church of God, The Promise Fulfilled, With Signs Following, The Latter Rain. Cf. James R. Goff, Jr., *Fields White Unto Harvest* (Fayetteville: University of Arkansas Press, 1988), 5; J. Edwin Orr, *The Flaming Tongue* (Chicago: Moody, 1975); Lemmer DuPlessis, "A Proprium For Pentecostal Theology," *What Is Distinctive About Pentecostal Theology?* (Pretoria: University of South Africa, 1989), 144.

Regarding Oneness Pentecostalism, see David K. Bernard, "Essentials of Oneness Theology" and Dan Lewis, "The Theology of the Baptism in the Holy Spirit in the United Pentecostal Church," in papers presented to *The First Occasional Symposium on Aspects of the Oneness Pentecostal Movement* (Cambridge: Harvard Divinity School, July 5–7, 1984), *Symposium on Oneness Pentecostalism: 1988 and 1990* (Hazelwood: World Aflame, 1990) and *Spiritus: Estuidios Sobre Pentecostalism* (Mexico City: 1985 onward) edited by Manuel J. Gaxiola-Gaxiola.

12. McNamee, "Role of the Spirit in Pentecostalism," 52f. See also Carter Lindberg, *The Third Reformation? Charismatic Movements and the Lutheran Tradition* (Macon: Mercer University Press, 1983). Karl Barth is reported to have said to David du Plessis that a renewed Roman Catholicism and a mature Pentecostalism could bring Christianity closer together. Watching events unfold at Canberra 1991, Fr. Ioan Sauca, Executive Secretary for Orthodox Studies and Relationships in Mission at the WCC, reflected aloud that Pentecostalism could help heal the schism between East and West.

This is not to suggest that some early Pentecostal historians did not think in a similar way. More than one Pentecostal writer suggested that a founder was absent. This was thought to give added credence to the claim that the movement was uniquely born of God and especially attached to the early church. This theory was kept alive for some time because Parham and Seymour quickly lost their place of prominence.[13]

This point is not negated by the fact that many Pentecostal pioneers propagated a restorationist view of history. Some light is shed on this subject by looking at the writings of A. J. Tomlinson, first general overseer of the Church of God. A. J. Tomlinson demonstrated his thoroughgoing commitment to restorationism in many of his writings.[14]

Yet he was among the first to publish a history of North American Pentecostalism. Influenced by the canonical Acts of the Apostles and a Quaker orientation, he recorded then published the minutes of the January 26–27, 1906, meeting at Camp Creek, North Carolina that is reckoned to be the first General Assembly of the Church of God. By this time, he had begun a journal that later showed clear marks of being written with a view to being published. His own search in church history shows up in his published sermons and annual addresses delivered at general assemblies.

By 1913, Tomlinson published the *Last Great Conflict* which includes two chapters on Pentecostal history. Although limited in scope, this anticipates, somewhat, B. F. Lawrence's 1916 *The Apostolic Faith Restored*.[15] Then an unsigned history of the Pentecostal Movement is published in the *Faithful Standard* (1922). Printed by the Church of

---

13. See Goff, *Harvest*, 9ff. Paul A. Pomerville, *The Third Force in Missions* (Peabody: Hendrickson, 1985), disputes the claim that the historical roots of global pentecostalism are yet clearly known. An effort to make progress in this regard was undertaken by the Theological Stream of Brighton 1991 with an entire session devoted to this concern. See papers by Robeck, Goff, and Lapoorta in *All Together in One Place*, ed. by Harold D. Hunter and Peter D. Hocken (Sheffield: Sheffield Academic Press, 1993).

14. See Grant Wacker, "A Profile of American Pentecostalism," *Pastoral Problems in the Pentecostal-Charismatic Movement*, ed. by Harold D. Hunter (Cleveland: Society for Pentecostal Studies, 1983), 25f.; Harold D. Hunter, "Church of God of Prophecy," *DPCM*, 208; Blumhofer, *Assemblies of God* 1:120.

15. Several Pentecostal magazines printed portions of the Pentecostal story. However, this 1913 publication is distinguished from them in that this was not a series of testimonies, but a deliberate attempt to put Pentecostal events in historical perspective. On the other hand, Grant Wacker, "Bibliography and Historiography of Pentecostalism (US)," *DPCM*, 69, rightly points out that no published work preceded Lawrence's attempt in terms of its scope. Cf. Blumhofer, *Assemblies of God* 1:13.

God, A. J. Tomlinson is listed as the editor while much of the work was actually done by Homer Tomlinson. Although various writers were used throughout the short life of the magazine, cumulative evidence suggests that A. J. Tomlinson had an editorial hand in the history. In any event, his publication of this six part series in 1922 illustrates well the juxtaposition of restorationism and search for historical roots and parallels that was widespread in the movement.[16]

Tomlinson kept alive the restorationist impulse and a commitment to history throughout his life. This shows that early Pentecostal restorationism was not ahistorical in the sense that history was not read, recorded and considered. However, it would be true in the case of Tomlinson and other restorationists, that theological judgments were most influenced by their understanding of how to restore "the early church." Many Christian traditions do exhibit tendencies not unlike this. Yet, it would obviously be more typical of restorationists to operate in a fashion that traditional church history meant little of substance to them. When, however, one considers the ignorance of Orthodox history displayed by Protestant scholars in the West, the situation may be viewed somewhat differently.

It seems imperative, not only in light of the historical reality but also in view of the growing influence of three current Enthusiastic Pneumatomania, for some histories to be rewritten. A few historians have drawn considerable attention to this stream. The most detailed account is that given in the classic work by a Roman Catholic prelate, R. A. Knox, titled simply *Enthusiasm*. Knox connects the following groups: Montanists, Circumcellions, Waldensians, Catharists, Fraticelli, Beguins, Apostolics, Brotherhood of the Free Spirit, Anabaptists, Quakers, Jansenism, Quietism, Prophets of the Cevennes, Convulsionaries, Moravians, Cathari, and Shakers. Another classic, authored by a 19th century Cambridge professor, focused on the very first Enthusiastic Pneumatomania. John DeSoyres' *Montanism* connected the following groups: Novatians, Donatists, Cathari, Waldenses, Fraticelli, Brothers of

---

16. This series taken together constitutes one of the most significant contributions to this subject at that time. It also predates by three years the publication of Frank Bartleman's *How "Pentecost" Came to Los Angeles—How It Was in the Beginning*. See *The Faithful Standard* 1:3 (June 1922): 6ff.; *The Faithful Standard* 1:4 (July 1922); *The Faithful Standard* 1:5 (August 1922): 6ff.; *The Faithful Standard* 1:6 (September 1922): 6ff.; *The Faithful Standard* 1:7 (October 1922): 9ff.; *The Faithful Standard* (November 1922): 8ff. This places a question mark beside the often repeated thesis of Grant Wacker, "The American Quest for the Primitive Church," 200f.

the Free Spirit, Flagellants, Joan of Arc, Savonarola, Anabaptists, Boehue, Petersen, Quakers, Labadie, Quietism, Quirinus Kuhlmann, Zinzendorf, E. Von Butler, Swedenborg, Schonherr, Mormonism, Irving, Simmons. The esteemed historian Philip Schaff observed first hand Enthusiastic Pneumatomania of the 19th century. His list of like groups included: Novatians, Donatism, Franciscans, Anabaptists, Camisards, Puritanism, Quakerism, Quietism, Pietism, Second Adventism, Irvingism, etc.[17]

When looking at the records of related activity prior to the Twentieth Century, it is evident that this was widespread in many Christian communities into the Fourth Century and especially crystallized in the Montanists. In sketching the subsequent centuries, the following persons and groups would come under the category of Catholic Enthusiastic Pneumatomania: St. Hildegard; Elizabeth of Schonau; St. Dominic; Franciscans; Richard Rolle; St. Vincent Ferrer; Spiritual Franciscans; Beguines; Francis Xavier; St. Louis Betrand; Jansenists. In the lineage of what is today referred to as Protestant would be the following: Cathari/Albigenses; Waldensians; Apostolic Brethren; Brethren of the Free Spirit; some Anabaptists; Camisards; Kylysty; Ranters; Convulsionaries; Shakers; Catholic Apostolic church; the Readers; Russian and Armenian Molokans; Gift People. There are other persons and groups that could be noted and other categories utilized.

The records pertaining to these things call upon the master skills of any researcher in deciphering the unwieldy, complex data available, while trying to reckon with materials no longer extant. Yet it must be said that pertinent sources are no less useful than most those utilized in traditional

---

17. Additional samples include: E. H. Klotsche, *The History of Christian Doctrine* (Grand Rapids: Baker, 1945), 39—Novatians, Donatists, Anabaptists, Chiliastic Enthusiasts, Irvingites, Adventists; Otto W. Heick, *A History of Christian Thought* (Philadelphia: Fortress, 1965), 1:79—Novatians, Donatists, Waldensians, Mennonites, Holiness; Stanley Burgess, *The Spirit and The Church: Antiquity* (Peabody: Hendrickson, 1984), 53–Novatians, Donatists, Waldensians, radicals of Reformation, Wesleyan Revivalists, Modern Holiness. Many of these same groups have been cited by Pentecostal historians who wrote at the midpoint of this century. Bresson, Brumback, Kendrick, Conn, Nichol and Campbell will be cited here from time to time. An accessible summary of their lists is given by Synan in "Mystical Tradition," 195f. It is interesting also to see other writers connect these groups for related reasons. This is done, for example, in the compelling defense of divine healing by A. J. Gordon in his *The Ministry of Healing* (Harrisburg: Christian Publications, Inc., 1882). See also Lawrence, *The Apostolic Faith Restored*, 33ff.; W. H. Turner, *Pentecost and Tongues* (Franklin Springs: Advocate Press, [1939] 1968), 53ff.

church histories. This does not, however, suggest that everything that is reported actually happened as recorded. The eccentric stories that abound in this lineage are more intelligible when studied in their historical contexts. This includes socioeconomic, ethnic, national, etc., elements that make up the multiplex reality of life. It is hardly accidental that church historians of various periods have treated these groups as though they were meaningless, when in fact they were then most visible. These groups have also illustrated that some scholars of all generations are given to propaganda. If these scholars would apply the same kind of historiography to their own tradition, they would be less inclined to publish their findings and less likely to secure influential publishing venues.[18]

When judging the quality and contents of the sources related to Enthusiastic Pneumatomania, it is helpful to remember that the participating historians did not establish a continuous lineage of historians. The numerous gaps raises several questions. A primary problem is determining the accuracy of the assorted claims. For now, we often have to be content with the fact that something reported to have happened must be processed even if the story is fictional. Those inclined to unilaterally condemn these exaggerations might do well to remember that such is not absent from an ecclesiastical lineage including those called "the mainstream."

There is a certain irony in the scholarly disdain heaped on the myths that are part of the fabric of Enthusiastic Pneumatomania. Many of these same scholars esteem highly sections of canonical materials they judge to be mythical. The inconsistency of valuing one set of myths while unilaterally condemning all such things when associated with Enthusiastic Pneumatomania may at times reflect a socioeconomic bias. Further, it may demonstrate a highly ethnocentric view of reality. The scholarly study of popular religion is gaining ground in some academic circles. However, the analysis of the belief systems of ordinary people has often been held in disrepute by intellectuals and always provided an easy target for ridicule. On the other hand, a remaining peril of the affirmation of the

---

18. Yves Congar, *I Believe in the Holy Spirit* (New York: Seabury Press, 1983), 1:148n16, can describe Knox's treatment of the Quakers as "mainly anecdotes" which stress "eccentricities." Meanwhile, Lovelace, "Evangelical," 209, quotes J. S. Whale's snappy anecdote that "the inner light is often the shortest pathway to the outer darkness." Garrett, *Spirit Possession*, 11, casts groups of this nature as "the religious 'underside' of the sacred theater of trance and possession."

extraordinary by Roman Catholicism and Enthusiastic Pneumatomania is being riddled with unbelievable and unacceptable stories.[19]

The label Enthusiastic Pneumatomania is not intended to be value laden. That is, this does not assume that all persons placed in this grouping were Christians or "orthodox" Christians. If tongues-speech was the only criterion the lineage would be quite crooked.[20] This point has been pressed by Richard Lovelace, among others. Lovelace advances the view that the truest ancestral line for contemporary Pentecostals and Charismatics is found in those who acknowledge "the manifest presence of the Holy Spirit in renewing power...."[21] In his view, the lineage that best fits this criterion is the Evangelical awakenings.

The convergences and divergences of Enthusiastic Pneumatomania and Renewal Movements can be noted by comparing my list which follows shortly with the marks of Renewal Movements as embodied in Pietism,

---

19. Cf. Pomerville, *Third Force*, 25. Attempting to bridge the gap between Roman Catholics and Classical Pentecostals, Vinson Synan ["Mystical Tradition," 199f.] unconsciously provides a summary of stories that border on the ludicrous:

> Parallels to most of the miracles attributed to Catholic saints are not to be found in the literature of the modern pentecostal-charismatic movement. In my studies, I have found no examples among Pentecostals of the following mystical phenomena: stigmata, tokens of espousal, telekinesis, luminous phenomena, the ocour of sanctity, incorruption, the absence of cadaveric rigidity, blood prodigies, living without eating, and multiplication of food. There are examples in Pentecostal literature, however, of the following phenomena: levitation, human salamanders, incendium amoris, seeing without eyes, bodily elongation and miraculous oil.

This context for the absurd continued in the 1980s with the Roman Catholic infatuation with Marian apparitions at Medjogorge and the Charismatic preoccupation with the 'healing hands' of Oral Roberts' City of Faith. Of course, steady competition is provided by various pilgrimages undertaken by Evangelicals and Liberals. One can only hope that events will coincide when Evangelicals find Noah's Ark and Liberals find Utopia. See Russell P. Spittler, "Pentecostal and Charismatic Spirituality," *DPCM*, 806; Garrett, *Spirit Possession and Popular Religion*, 1f.

20. Garrett, *Spirit Possession and Popular Religion*, 2, documents that the same would be true of the trail of spirit possession.

21. Richard Lovelace, "Baptism in the Holy Spirit and the Evangelical Tradition," *Faces of Renewal*, ed. by Paul Elbert (Peabody: Hendrickson, 1988), 209. This article was originally presented as a paper to the 1984 session of the Society For Pentecostal Studies held at Gordon Conwell Theological Seminary. The perspective of Professor Lovelace is surely informed by his particular evangelical context.

Moravanism, Brethren and early Methodism according to Howard A. Snyder: a dynamic of the Christian faith is rediscovered; an ecclesiola is formed; small-group structures are utilized; a structural link exists with the institutional church; the renewal structure is committed to the unity, vitality, and wholeness of the larger church; mission orientation; distinct, covenant-based community emerge; new forms of ministry and leadership are formed and exercised; close daily contact is maintained with society; emphasis is placed on the Spirit and Word as the basis of authority.

The priority of oral tradition and focus on praxis in the Classical Pentecostal Movement illustrates well the problem any manifestation of Enthusiastic Pneumatomania encounters in defining their own identity. Perhaps all the scholarly work published in the first half of the 20th Century relative to Pentecostalism was generated by those who did not participate in such things. This becomes increasingly problematic because from at least the time of G. B. Cutten, the treatments are almost uniformly negative and semi-informed at best.

This sort of thing is not difficult to document. It takes little more than quick scans of commentaries and church histories produced in the nineteenth Century to realize the great divide from later commentators and historians relative to Pentecostal distinctives.[22] Consider the Gospel of Luke as dealt with in the following: *International Critical Commentary* (1896), *New International Commentary on the New Testament* (1951), and *Word Biblical Commentary* (1989). The tide is now turning.

While it is obvious that contemporary Enthusiastic Pneumatomania reflect numerous influences, it is misleading to align too closely even North American Classical Pentecostals with Evangelicals of any generation. To do so might remove some of the venom from the sting of criticism directed toward Pentecostals constantly flowing from bastions of right-wing Evangelicals in the West, but it would not be a faithful historical reckoning.

The following is a list of succinctly described attributes often characteristic of Enthusiastic Pneumatomania personnel. This list is not prioritized nor is it exhaustive and does not mean to imply that all groups have all these characteristics or that such are limited to Enthusiastic Pneumatomania. Most of the categories and data provided here reflect

---

22. Consider the volumes dedicated to the Gospel of Luke in the following series: *International Critical Commentary* (1896), *New International Commentary on the New Testament* (1951), *Word Biblical Commentary* (1989).

original research. The first related scheme brought to my attention was that developed by the eminent historian Reinhold Seeberg. The single most important advance in this for me has been the exhausting yet magnificent *Enthusiasm* by R. A. Knox. Knox's collection of pertinent data—if not always his interpretations—is second to none known in English. Clarke Garrett speaks for many when he commends the book for today's audience, but judges it to be "wrongheaded." Garrett describes Knox's insistence that religious enthusiasm represents a persistent irrational deviation from the path of orthodoxy "as not very useful for a historical understanding of religious developments."[23]

1. A limited eschatology that often advocates an imminent return of the Lord.

2. A specialized pneumatology that focuses on the charismatic dimension of the Holy Spirit.

3. Strict moral codes.

4. Spectacular charisms are a centerpiece in their expression of Christianity. This includes speaking in tongues and/or prophesying accompanied by particular kinds of healings, exorcisms, visions et al.

5. They are orthodox on matters fundamentals to soteriology [thus they are Christians] and some heterodoxy is usually evident.

6. Enthusiastic worship.

7. Women are prominent, often including leadership positions if not always concomitant authority.

8. For a variety of reasons they often form their own distinct identity.

9. Their early years usually include dramatic spiritual experiences and rapid growth.

---

23. Garrett, *Spirit Possession and Popular Religion*, 2. See Seeberg in F. Dale Bruner, *Theology of the Holy Spirit* (Grand Rapids: Eerdmans, 1970), 36; R. A. Knox, *Enthusiasm* (Oxford: At the Clarendon Press, 1954); Gordon W. Wakefield, "Renewal in Past Ages," *Open to the Spirit*, ed. by Colin Craston (London: Church House Publishing, 1987), 139–50; Küng, *The Church*, 97. Cf. John Yoder in Morris A. Inch, *Saga of the Spirit* (Grand Rapids: Baker, 1985), 234–36; Peter Hocken, "Charismatics and Mystics," *Theological Renewal* #1, 11f.; Mathew S. Clark, Henry I. Lederle, et al., *What is Distinctive About Pentecostal Theology?* (Pretoria: University of South Africa, 1989), 7ff.

10. Many times they perceive themselves as evidence of the dawning of a new spiritual era.
11. Frequently there is considerable focus on things apocalyptic.
12. An ethos involving absolute sincerity, humility, deep love, total personal involvement, etc.
13. A sociological profile would run the gamut with perhaps the majority of a either the working poor or those financially stable.
14. They have been willing to allegorize as it suits their purpose(s) and yet often be woodenly literal with numerous texts.
15. Their leaders cannot usually be described as knowingly anti-rational or irrational, but seeking to be transrational.
16. Their ecclesiologies have included theocratic teachings, priesthood of believers, feet washing, immersion for water baptism and symbolic eucharist.
17. Things miraculous are often expected to be commonplace.
18. Many of the participants become so sensitized to the guidance of the Holy Spirit that when this is coupled with various charismatic phenomena they appear to equal themselves in a metaphysical sense with the Holy Spirit.

No Enthusiastic Pneumatomania prior to this century has survived in anything but distant echoes of the original sound. Current groups like the Waldensians, Molokans, and Irvingites may trace their ancestry to the founders, but they are theologically distant heirs at best.[24] No one formula encapsulates adequately this reality but among the pertinent attempts are the following schemes: pilgrims, settlers, landed aristocracy; man, men, movement, machine, monument; born, complex issues, hated sect, tolera-

---

24. Waldensians of the Twentieth Century are reported to have persecuted pentecostals in Italy. So McNamee, "The Role of the Spirit in Pentecostalism," 31. While staying at the Waldensian Church retreat center, Foresteria Valdese, in Tore Pellice, Italy (May 15–20, 1996), Aldo Comba told me that no such events transpired. Nevertheless, the change in posturing when representatives of "various Pentecostal denominations, "Valdese (Waldensian), Baptist, Apostolic, and Orthodox Churches" joined unity efforts of the Catholic Charismatic Renewal, was deemed newsworthy. See 1992 newsletter from International Catholic Charismatic Renewal Office (ICCRO). Meanwhile, the Catholic Apostolic Church in England has not identified in any way with the pentecostal denominations in England.

tion to acceptance, popularity, increasing centralization, and institutionalization. These are helpful, but perhaps the most useful categories may be the following: experience, reflection, and integration.[25]

There may be some difference relative to whether a given movement is in the Roman Catholic tradition and/or whether it is centered in a church environment like that currently found in Europe as opposed to America. Although not limited to Roman Catholics, it is possible that Catholic oriented Enthusiastic Pneumatomania may have had fewer groups which have completely broken away. On the other hand, it seems that environments similar to the church fragmentation which characterizes America is most conducive to eventual schism. However, even if an Enthusiastic Pneumatomania does not break fellowship with its tradition, none to my knowledge have outlasted the third phase.

Among the factors which could account for an unexpected longevity of the Classical Pentecostal Movement in the USA are the following. First, the Pentecostal message is going through an early stage in many countries around the world and combined with global miniaturization, this strengthens and sometimes renews the movement in America. Second, the Charismatic movement in the Protestant tradition and Roman Catholic church serves as a revitalizing influence on Classical Pentecostalism.

A concise definition of Classical Pentecostalism remains elusive. In contrast to the sometimes perceived monolithic character of the movement, it is the considerable diversity that complicates this process. Even when the focus is narrowed to the USA, the interpreter must some how assimilate far ranging opinions on issues like the sacraments, ecclesiology, pneumatology, and eschatology. Despite these considerable challenges, a few gallant attempts have surfaced. However, social upward mobility, such as that unveiled in Dan Morgan's *Rising in the West*, may have the final word.[26]

---

25. The last description was originally used by Professor John Westerhoff of Duke University to trace the spiritual development of an individual. This according to David Reed who has his own application in "Oneness Pentecostalism: Tracing the Emergence of an American Religious Movement," *The First Occasional Symposium on Aspects of the Oneness Pentecostal Movement* (Harvard Divinity School, July 5–7, 1984). The others are found in the following sources: Vinson Synan, "Worldwide Charismatic Revival," *Charisma* (August 1985): 44; Findley B. Edge, Professor Emeritus at the Southern Baptist Theological Seminary, interview in 1987.

26. Dan Morgan, *Rising in the West: The True Story of an 'Okie' Family in Search of the American Dream* (New York: Vintage Books, 1992).

In 1982 David Barrett would define Pentecostalism thus:

> ... a Christian confession or ecclesiastical tradition holding the distinctive teaching that all Christians should seek a post-conversion religious experience called the Baptism with the Holy Spirit, and that a Spirit baptized believer may receive one or more of the supernatural gifts known in the early church: instantaneous sanctification, the ability to prophesy, practice divine healing, speak in tongues (glossolalia), or interpret tongues."[27]

A later summary runs for pages and uses distinctions like Prepentecostals, Indigenous radical-pentecostals, Postpentecostals, Radio/television charismatics, and Third-Wave Black/Non-White Evangelicals.[28]

Parenthetically it should be noted that skepticism over the accuracy of Barrett's figures have arisen in direct proportion to his marked increase of Pentecostal-Charismatic totals. By July, 1989, his count of Pentecostals and Charismatics had already soared to 351 million.[29] One area of weakness in his computation receiving attention is the failure to adequately segment the conglomeration of 30 million people who makes up the African Instituted Churches. Dean S. Gilliland has shown that one, at best parts of two, out of four broad categories properly deserve the label Pentecostal. Similarly an investigation of a group known as the United Orthodox Independent Zion Churches of Kenya listed by Barrett in his *Rise Up and Walk!* proved conclusively these people were not Pentecostals. This group has earned Hollenweger's label of Messianic sect.[30]

---

27. David B. Barrett, ed., *World Christian Encyclopedia* (Oxford: Oxford University Press, 1982), 838.

28. David B. Barrett, "Global Statistics," *Dictionary of Pentecostal and Charismatic Movements*, ed. by Stanley M. Burgess and Gary B. McGee (Grand Rapids: Zondervan, 1988), 810–30. Hereafter listed simply as *DPCM*.

29. Among the helpful correctives is Paul B. Tinlin and Edith L. Blumhofer, "Decade of Decline or Harvest? Dilemmas of the Assemblies of God," *The Christian Century* 108:21 (July 10–17, 1991): 684–87. Minutes of late 1980s general assemblies of the Church of God of Prophecy show a numerical decline in North America.

30. Dean S. Gilliland, "How 'Christian' Are African Independent Churches?" *Misology: An International Review* 14:3 (July 1986): 259; David Barrett and T. J. Padwick, *Rise Up and Walk! Conciliarism and the African Indigenous Churches, 1815–1987* (Nairobi: Oxford, 1988): Appendix III; Harold D. Hunter interview (3-17-89) with leaders from the United Orthodox Independent Zion Churches of Kenya outside Nairobi; Peter Wagner, "Church Growth," *DPCM*, 182; Walter J. Hollenweger, *The Pentecostals* (Minneapolis: Augsburg, 1972), 150; Russell P. Spittler, "Maintaining Distinctives: The Future of Pentecostalism," *Pentecostals From the Inside Out*, ed. by Harold B. Smith (Wheaton: Victor Books, 1990),

The ubiquity of the movement as it launches into the Twenty-First Century out-distances attempts to offer a brief summary. For the purposes of this study, it will be sufficient to identify the Classical Pentecostal Movement in North America by its relation to the events at the Bethel Bible School (1901) and the Azusa St. Revival which started in 1906. The most prominent fabric woven into this tapestry is the doctrine of the Spirit baptism[31] and its relationship to tongues-speech. In 1970, Dale Bruner said flatly that Pentecostals were pneumobaptistocentric.[32] Although this distinctive does not define the movement, it remains a continual focus of participants and onlookers alike. Evidencing the considerable importance of these subject areas, the study that follows will reckon most with the North America Classical Pentecostal distinctives. The extended analyses

---

121. Leaders from the United Orthodox Independent Zion wanted me to meet The First Most Nabii Jathan Muranga who was living in the Kenyan desert. However, I endorse the perimeters set by the World Council of Churches which excludes a group with an African Christ from the circle of Christian churches.

31. Use of the term Spirit baptism as an alternative to the elongated phrase 'baptism in/with/of the Spirit' became prominent in the 1970s. Consider the following entries from that decade using the term Spirit baptism in the text: John A. Schep, *Baptism in the Spirit* (London: Fountain Trust, 1969); J. D. G. Dunn, *Baptism in the Holy Spirit* (London: SCM Press Ltd., 1970); McNamee, "The Role of the Spirit in Pentecostalism." The term was used earlier by A. M. Hills, *Pentecostal Rejected and the Effect on the Churches* (Cincinnati: God's Revivalist Office, 1902), 7. Unknown is the origin of a church listed in the Indianapolis, Indiana telephone directory (December 1990) as the Free Spirit Baptism Church, 877 Collier, 247-0580.

32. Cf. Bruner, *Theology of the Holy Spirit* (241, 313, 239) plus his disappointing *The Holy Spirit: Shy Member of the Trinity* (Minneapolis: Augsburg, 1983) authored with W. Hordern; Dunn, *Baptism in the Holy Spirit*, 171; J. D. G. Dunn, "Spirit-baptism and Pentecostalism," *SJT* (Nov., 1970): 406; J. D. G. Dunn, "Pneuma," *NIDNTT* 3:701ff.; Juan Sepulveda, "Born Again: Baptism and the Spirit: A Pentecostal Perspective," *Concilium* (3/1996): 104–9, edited by Jürgen Moltmann and Karl-Josef Kuchel; Anthony A. Hoekema, *Holy Spirit Baptism* (Grand Rapids: Eerdmans, 1972), 81; John Stott, *Baptism and Fullness* (Downer's Grove: InterVarsity Press, 1977), 50 et passim; O. J. Smith, *The Spirit-Filled Life* (New York: Christian Alliance Publishing Co., 1926), 21; Robert H. Culpepper, *Evaluating the Charismatic Movement* (Valley Forge: Judson Press, 1977), 67; L. S. Chafer, *He That is Spiritual* (Grand Rapids: Zondervan, 1967); Tak-Ming Cheung, "Understandings of Spirit-Baptism," *Journal of Pentecostal Theology* 8 (1996), 115–28; René Pache, *The Person and Work of the Holy Spirit* (Chicago: Moody, 1954); Richard B. Gaffin, Jr., *Perspectives on Pentecost* (Phillipsburg: Presbyterian & Reformed Publishing Co., 1979); W. A. Criswell, *Great Doctrines of the Bible: Pneumatology* (Chicago: Moody, 1984); T. R. Edgar, *Miraculous Gifts* (Neptune: Loizeaux Brothers, 1983); J. I. Packer, *Keep in Step With the Spirit* (Old Tappan: Revell, 1984).

of these areas do not intend to negate efforts of broadening the theological base of the movement.

In view of the inability to provide a definitive definition, a historical introduction of the Classical Pentecostal Movement in North America will be advantageous. Also of value will be brief historical introductions to the Mainstream Charismatic Movement and the Roman Catholic Charismatic Movement as known in the USA.

VARIOUS APPLICATIONS OF SPIRIT BAPTISM: CLASSICAL PENTECOSTALISM

North American Classical Pentecostal denominations were formed in and around the turn of the Twentieth Century. All of the major denominations have been influenced in varying degrees by Charles Parham and W. J. Seymour.[33] The general theological heritage of this movement is quite broad and includes distant groups like the Pietists along with recent millenniarians and the Nineteenth Century healing movement. Among the most telling theological roots are the related Holiness and Keswick Movements.[34]

33. Pomerville, *Third Force*, 47ff., rightly disavows the "Jerusalem-Centrifugal" theory. As will be demonstrated later, he says such histories (p. 48) "overlook other significant, previous and simultaneous, Pentecostal outpourings around the world which have no historical-casual linkage to the American revival." See also Harold D. Hunter, "Aspects of Initial Evidence Dogma: A European-American Holiness Pentecostal Perspective," *Asian Journal of Pentecostal Studies* 1:2 (1998): 185–202.

34. I have drawn attention to these and other influences since first teaching a historical theological course on Pentecostal/Charismatic origins at Melodyland School of Theology in 1978. This same course has been subsequently taught at the Church of God School of Theology and ORU School of Theology. See entries in *Dictionary of Christianity in America* (Downer's Grove: InterVarsity Press, 1990) and *Twentieth Century Encyclopedia of Religious Knowledge* (Grand Rapids: Baker, 1991). Among the important contributions to this area of research are the following works: Edith Waldvogel, "'The Over-Coming Life': A Study in the Reformed Evangelical Origins of Pentecostalism," (Cambridge: Harvard University, April, 1977); Donald W. Dayton, *Theological Roots of Pentecostalism* (Grand Rapids: Zondervan, 1987); Charles E. Jones, "Tongues-Speaking and the Wesleyan-Holiness Quest for Assurance of Sanctification," *Wesleyan Theological Journal* 22:2 (Fall 1987); David Bundy, "European Pietist Roots of Pentecostalism," *DPCM*, 279–81; Larry Hart, "A Critique of American Pentecostalism," (Louisville: Southern Baptist Theological Seminary, 1978), 53ff., 58ff.; Schaff, *History* 1:2:190; Knox, *Enthusiasm*, 206, etc.; Lindberg, *Third Reformation*; Congar, *Holy Spirit* 1:144; Reed, "Oneness," 13ff.; Christian Duquoc, "Theological Roots," *Charisms in the Church* (New York: Seabury, 1978), 33f., 47ff.; Paul Tillich, *A History of Christian Thought* (New York: Simon and Shuster, 1968), 286; Hans Küng, *The Church* (New York: Sheed and Ward, 1967), 195.

These and other considerations surface three major segments of the Classical Pentecostal Movement in the USA: Holiness—Church of God in Christ, International Pentecostal Holiness Church, Church of God (Cleveland), etc.; Keswick—Assemblies of God, International Church of the Foursquare Gospel, Pentecostal Church of God, etc.; Oneness—Pentecostal Assemblies of the World, United Pentecostal Church International, etc. The first two divisions are based primarily on the respective doctrines of sanctification while a distinctive view of the divine nature accounts for the final category.[35]

35. This threefold division was used in "History of Pentecost," *The Faithful Standard* 1:8 (November 1922): 14. Works which deal with the international Pentecostal Movement as a whole include Hollenweger, *The Pentecostals* (1972). This was reprinted without changes by Hendrickson in 1988. This book is condensed from the author's exhaustive ten volume doctoral dissertation, "Handbuch der Pfingstewegung," (Geneva: 1965-1967). Other works which describe Classical Pentecostalism in the USA are: Arthur C. Piepkorn, *Profiles in Belief*, Volume 3, Holiness and Pentecostal (New York: Harper & Row, 1979); D. E. Harrell, *All Things Are Possible* (Bloomington: Indiana University Press, 1975); John T. Nichol, *The Pentecostals* (Plainfield: Logos, 1971); Vinson Synan, *The Holiness-Pentecostal Movement* (Grand Rapids: Eerdmans, 1971); Nils Bloch-Hoell, *The Pentecostal Movement* (New York: Humanities Press, 1964); Goff, *Harvest*; *Dictionary of Pentecostal and Charismatic Movements*, edited by Stanley M. Burgess and Gary B. McGee (Grand Rapids: Zondervan, 1988); *Encyclopedia of Religion in the South*, ed. by Samuel S. Hill (Macon: Mercer University Press, 1984); Daniel Reid, ed., *Dictionary of Christianity in America* (Downer's Grove: InterVarsity Press, 1989); Richard M. Riss, *A Survey of 20th Century Revival Movements in North America* (Peabody: Hendrickson, 1988); Randall Balmer, *Mine Eyes Have Seen the Glory: A Journey Into the Evangelical Subculture in America* (Oxford: Oxford University Press, 1989); Wardell Payne, ed. *Directory of African American Religious Bodies* (Washington, D. C.: Howard University Press, 1991); Vinson Synan, *In the Latter Days* (Ann Arbor: Servant Books, 1984); Vinson Synan, *The Twentieth-Century Pentecostal Explosion* (Altamonte Springs: Creation House, 1987); James C. Richardson, Jr., *With Water and Spirit* (Washington, D.C.: Spirit Press, 1980); Stanley Frodsham, *With Signs Following* (Springfield: Gospel Publishing House, 1946); Steve Durasoff, *Bright Wind of the Spirit* (Englewood Cliffs: Prentice-Hall, 1972); Gordon Atter, *The Third Force* (Peterborough: College Press, 1970); David W. Faupel, *The American Pentecostal Movement* (Wilmore: Asbury Theological Seminary, 1972); *Perspectives on the New Pentecostalism*, ed. by Russel P. Spittler (Grand Rapids: Baker, 1974); *Aspects of Pentecostal-Charismatic Origins*, ed. by Vinson Synan (Plainfield: Logos, 1975); Prudencio Damboriena, *Tongues As of Fire: Pentecostalism in Contemporary Christianity* (Washington: Corpus Books, 1969); Leonard Lovett, "Black Holiness Pentecostalism: Implications for Ethics and Social Transformation," Unpublished Ph.D. dissertation, (Emory University, 1979); R. F. Martin, "The Early Years of American Pentecostalism, 1900-1940: Survey of A Social Movement," Unpublished Ph.D. dissertation (University of North Carolina, 1975); A. E. Paris, *Black Pentecostalism* (Amherst: University of Massachusetts Press, 1982); Everett P. Fulton, "An Investigation of the Changing Theological Concepts of the Ministers of the Open Bible Standard Churches," Unpublished M.A. thesis (Drake University,

Keswick[36] Pentecostals are most like traditional Protestantism since

---

June 1964); Irvine John Harrison, "History of the Assemblies of God," Unpublished Th.D. dissertation (Berkeley Baptist Divinity School, June 4, 1954); Ray T. Geiger, "A Bibliographic History of Pentecostal Denominations," Unpublished dissertation; Richard Crayne, *Pentecostal Handbook* (Morristown: By the author, 1989). For the perspective from individual churches see the following: KESWICK: Assemblies of God—Edith L. Blumhofer, *The Assemblies of God* (Springfield: Gospel Publishing House, 1991) 2 volumes; William Menzies, *Anointed to Serve* (Springfield: Gospel Publishing House, 1971); Klaude Kendrick, *The Promise Fulfilled* (Springfield: Gospel Publishing House, 1961); Carl Brumback, *Suddenly From Heaven* (Springfield: Gospel Publishing House, 1961); Irwin Winehouse, *The Assemblies of God* (New York: Vantage Press, 1959); Edith Waldvogel Blumhofer, *The Assemblies of God: A Popular History* (Springfield: Radiant Books, 1985); Foursquare—Raymond Cox, *The Foursquare Gospel* (Los Angeles: Heritage Committee, 1969). Open Bible Standard Churches—Robert B. Mitchell, *Heritage and Horizons* (Des Moines: Open Bible Publishers, 1982). Pentecostal Church of God-Elmer L. Moon, *The Pentecostal Church* (New York: Carlton Press, 1966). HOLINESS: Church of God in Christ-Ithiel C. Clemmons, *Bishop C. H. Mason and the Roots of the Church of God in Christ* (Bakersfield: Pneuma Life Publishing, 1996); J. O. Patterson, G. R. Ross & Julia Mason Atkins, *History and Formative Years of the Church of God in Christ with Excerpts from the Life and Work of Its Founder-Bishop C. H. Mason* (Memphis: Church of God in Christ Publishing House, 1969); Church of God (Cleveland)-Charles W. Conn, *Like A Mighty Army* (Cleveland: Pathway, 1977); Mickey Crews, *The Church of God: A Social History* (Knoxville: University of Tennessee Press, 1990); E. L. Simmons, *History of the Church of God* (Cleveland: Church of God Publishing House, 1938); International Pentecostal Holiness Church—Vinson Synan, *The Old-Time Power* (Franklin Springs: Advocate Press, 1973); Joseph E. Campbell, *The Pentecostal Holiness Church* (Franklin Springs: Publishing House of the Pentecostal Holiness Church, 1951); A. D. Beacham, Jr., *A Brief History of the Pentecostal Holiness Church* (Franklin Springs: Advocate, 1983); Church of God of Prophecy—C. T. Davidson, *Upon This Rock*, 3 volumes (Cleveland: White Wing Publishing House, 1973-76); James Stone, *Church of God of Prophecy: History and Polity* (Cleveland: White Wing Press, 1977); United Holy Church of America—*Standard Manual and Constitution and By-Laws of United Holy Church of America, Inc.* (Washington, D. C.: Middle Atlantic Regional Press, 1982); Pentecostal Free Will Baptist-*History of the Pentecostal Free Will Baptist Church, Incorporation* (Dunn: n.d.); Apostolic Faith-*The Apostolic Faith* (Portland: Apostolic Faith Publishing House, 1969). ONENESS: United Pentecostal Church-Arthur L. Clanton, *United We Stand* (Hazelwood: Pentecostal Publishing House, 1970); Frank J. Ewart, *The Phenomenon of Pentecost* (Hazelwood: World Atlantic Press, 1975); Fred J. Foster, *Think It Not Strange* (St. Louis: Pentecostal Publishing House, 1965); Pentecostal Assemblies of the World—M. E. Golder, *History of the Pentecostal Assemblies of the World* (Indianapolis: by the author, 1973); James L. Tyson, *The Early Pentecostal Revival* (Hazelwood: World Aflame Press, 1992).

36. I have stayed with the term Keswick to describe this view of sanctification while others have used Reformed and Baptistic. All concerned are attempting to indicate that a Reformed version of Holiness theology is in view. The term Keswick is more appropriate because there are actual historical connections—Robert Pearsall & Hannah Whital Smith, W. E. Boardman, Andrew Murray, James Elder Cumming, F. B. Meyer then A. J. Gordon, R. A. Torrey and A. B. Simpson—between the original Keswick conventions and

they speak of sanctification beginning in the initial salvific experience and progressing throughout one's lifetime. Holiness Pentecostals, on the other hand, have traditionally referred to sanctification as a "second definite work of grace whereby the Adamic nature is eradicated." This purification is effected subsequent—both logically and temporally—to the initial salvation-event. Both groups conceive of Spirit baptism as an independent member of the ordo salutis. Thus Keswick Pentecostals often postulate Spirit baptism to be a "second work of grace" while Holiness Pentecostals have spoken of it as a "third work of grace."[37]

Keswick Pentecostalism as well as many obvious theological similarities. This is qualified by the 'Americanization' of the original conventional formulas and yet this is still one of the most influential sources for this segment of Pentecostalism. Contra Henry Lederle, "An Appraisal of Some Aspects of the Theology of the Charismatic Movement," (Pretoria: University of South Africa, 1985), 26–28. Among many available sources one should consult at least the following: Robert Mapes Anderson, *Vision of the Disinherited* (New York: Oxford University Press, 1979), 43, 112; Faupel, *American Pentecostal Movement*, 12; Joe Creech, "Visions of Glory: The Place of the Azusa Street Revival in Pentecostal History," *Church History*, 419; David D. Bundy, *Keswick: A Bibliographic Introduction to the Higher Live Movements* (Wilmore: Asbury Theological Seminary, 1975); William Menzies, "The Holy Spirit in Christian Theology," *Perspectives on Evangelical Theology*, ed. by K. S. Kantzer and S. N. Gundry (Grand Rapids: Baker, 1979), 75f.; Menzies, "Non-Wesleyan Origins," David D. Bundy, "Keswick Higher Life Movement," *DPCM*, 518f.; *DIALOGUES with The Evangelical Free Church of Finland and Finnish Pentecostal Movement* (Helsinki: Church Council for Foreign Affairs, Ecclesiastical Board, 1990), 61. The discussion has often centered on William H. Durham's 1910 formulation of the 'finished work' doctrine. Yet Durham was no more and no less than a catalyst. It is true that the Parham-Seymour version of Spirit baptism incorporated a Holiness view of sanctification, however, Durham's 1910 declaration and the 1914 Hot Springs conference show that a great number were not Holiness. The most visible wing of Pentecostalism has not been Holiness. Further, few churches started as Holiness Pentecostal churches but were already churches existing as Holiness organizations that added Pentecostal Spirit baptism to their beliefs. See *Upper Room* 2:5 (May, 1911); *The Faithful Standard* (November 1922); Edith Blumhofer, "The Finished Work of Calvary," *AG Heritage* 3:3 (Fall, 1983); Roland Wessels, "The Doctrine of the Baptism in the Holy Spirit Among the Assemblies of God," unpublished Th.D. dissertation (Berkeley, Pacific School of Religion, May, 1966), 100ff.; Grant Wacker, "Assemblies of God," *Encyclopedia of Religion in the South*, ed. by Samuel S. Hill (Macon: Mercer University Press, 1984), 72–75; Allen Clayton, "W. H. Durham," *Pneuma* 1:2 (Fall 1979). The 'success' of pentecostalism is such that holiness scholars like Donald Dayton, M. E. Deiter and C. E. Jones are suggesting that Wesleyan thought is the basis for that which is constructive about pentecostalism. Cf. Goff, *Fields*, 7–9. Cf. Henry H. Knight III, "From Aldersgate to Azusa: Wesley and the Renewal of Pentecostal Spirituality," *Journal of Pentecostal Theology* 8 (1996): 82–98.

37. See Kevin Ranaghan, "Rites of Initiation in Representative Pentecostal Churches in the U.S., 1901–72," Unpublished Ph.D. dissertation (South Bend: University of Notre Dame, 1974); C. E. Jones, *A Guide to the Study of the Pentecostal Movement* (Metuchen:

North American Pentecostals who label themselves Apostolic explicitly repudiate the term unitarian. One reason seems to be that while much present day American Unitarianism is at best left wing Christianity, at worst not Christian at all, Apostolics comprise the most conservative branch of Pentecostalism (much less Christianity at large). Also, apologists from this sector claim to acknowledge diversity within the Godhead without impinging on the oneness of God. The beliefs of these saints are due cause for a chapter to be added to the historical analyses of Unitarianism. While traditional American Unitarianism has emphasized a unity of the Godhead which denies the deity of Christ and the Holy Spirit, Oneness Pentecostals see the fullness of divinity in Jesus Christ.[38]

Up until the 1940s, there was limited formal cooperation between Holiness and Keswick Pentecostals. Then came the National Association of Evangelicals (NAE) and the Pentecostal Fellowship of North America

---

Scarecrow Press, 1983); Watson Mills, *Charismatic Religion in Modern Research* (Macon: Mercer University Press, 1984); Faupel, *American Pentecostal Movement*, 16; Menzies, "Non-Wesleyan Origins," 86–98; Menzies, "The Holy Spirit in Christian Theology."

38. See David K. Bernard, *The Oneness of God* (Hazelwood: Word Aflame, 1983); *Symposium On Oneness Pentecostalism: 1988 and 1990* (Hazelwood: Word Aflame, 1990); David Reed, "Origins and Development of the Theology of Oneness Pentecostalism in the United States," Unpublished Ph.D. dissertation (Boston: Boston University, 1978); David Reed, "Aspects of the Origins of Oneness Pentecostalism," *Aspects of Pentecostal-Charismatic Origins*, ed. by Vinson Synan, 145–68; Clanton, *United We Stand*, 143; Everett L. Moore, "Handbook of Pentecostal Denominations in the United States," unpublished M.A. thesis (Point Loma College, June, 1954). With regard to the doctrine of sanctification, Oneness Pentecostals have churches that are Holiness, but the majority are Keswickian. These pentecostals have kept many characteristics of the early days of the movement and seemingly their doctrinal distinctive centers more on the power of the name of Jesus than an exact theological formula pertaining to the Godhead. Those who use the prejudicial "Jesus Only" should trade this in for "Jesus Name" Pentecostals. There has been mutual isolation of Oneness Pentecostals from all the others, but signs of change are now evident. One such thing was Manuel Gaxiola-Gaxiola becoming president of the Society for Pentecostal Studies in 1990 and another can be seen in The First Occasional Symposium on Aspects of the Oneness Pentecostal Movement held at Harvard Divinity School, July 5–7, 1984. Also: J. L. Hall, *The United Pentecostal Church and the Evangelical Movement* (Hazelwood: Word Aflame, 1990); Kenneth D. Gill, "The New Issue Reconsidered," *Continuity and Change in the Pentecostal and Charismatic Movements*, ed. by Murray W. Dempster (Dallas: Society For Pentecostal Studies, 1990); David K. Bernard, "The Oneness View of Jesus," *Old and New Issues in Pentecostalism*, ed. by Manuel Gaxiola-Gaxiola (Fresno: Society For Pentecostal Studies, 1989); Manuel Gaxiola-Gaxiola, "The Unresolved Issue: A Third-World Perspective on the Oneness Question," *Probing Pentecostalism*, ed. by Donald Dayton (Virginia Beach: Society For Pentecostal Studies, 1987).

(PFNA). It was not until the 1980s that the Society for Pentecostal Studies intentionally sought to bridge the gap between Oneness Pentecostals and the rest of the lot. It is now conceded that both sides have exaggerated their positions with trinitarian pentecostals often talking like tritheists while some Oneness have sounded like Unitarians. But now it is said that trinitarians have emphasized the diversity of the Godhead while Apostolics have stressed the unity of the Godhead, but both acknowledge both dimensions.[39] 1993–94 saw the launching of a racially integrated body with the name Pentecostal Charismatic Churches of North America (PCCNA).

Traditional denominations from all three segments of the North American Classical Pentecostal Movement continue to agree on the basic issue, namely that Spirit baptism is to be understood as a work of the Spirit which is distinct from and can be subsequent to regeneration, et al. The substance of this experience is power as distinct from purity. The most influential version of the Spirit baptism formula in the USA designated speaking in tongues as the initial evidence. Although there has never been complete uniformity on the particulars of this dogma, it clearly was the catalyst for the manner in which Classical Pentecostalism developed in the North America.[40] Although this logion has been written into all the North American Pentecostal denominational creeds, tongues-speech as the initial evidence has never enjoyed complete acceptance in the USA much less around the world. Grant Wacker accurately describes this restricted formula as "the litmus test of orthodoxy among [U.S.] Pentecostals or at least among white ones after World War I."[41] T. B. Barrett and George Jeffreys, two important Pentecostal pioneers in Europe, did not insist on tongues-speech as the initial evidence of Spirit baptism. The Mühleim

---

39. See Manuel Gaxiola, Presidential Address to the Society for Pentecostal Studies; Daniel L. Scott, Jr., *Family Reunion and Confession of Faith* (Nashville: Global Christian Ministries, Inc., n.d.); J. L. Hall, *The United Pentecostal Church and the Evangelical Movement* (Hazelwood: Word Aflame, 1990); David Bernard, *The Oneness of God*.

40. Even a British Pentecostal, Canty, *Pentecost*, 104, says that without this formula there would be no Pentecostal Movement.

41. Grant Wacker, "Bibliography and Historiography of Pentecostalism (U.S.)," *DPCM*, 72. More recently, Wacker, "Wild Theories and Mad Excitement," *Pentecostals From the Inside Out*, ed. by Harold B. Smith (Wheaton: Victor Books, 1990) continues: "There is, however, at least one conviction that all Pentecostals share, virtually by definition. Conversion to Christ must be followed by another life-transforming event known as baptism, or filling, by the Holy Spirit," See also Grant Wacker, "Playing for Keeps: The Primitivist Impulse in Early Pentecostalism," *The American Quest for the Primitive Church* (Chicago: University of Illinois, 1988), 196f.

Association of Christian Fellowship not only has rejected tongues as the sole evidence, but has not made the usual distinction between the initial salvific event and Spirit baptism.[42] The further one moves geographically, the more extensive becomes the list of varying Spirit baptism formulas among those identified as Pentecostal.

It is difficult to ascertain when the North American version of the Classical Pentecostal doctrine of Spirit baptism emerged. Despite examples of a mixture of Spirit baptism doctrine and the presence of tongues-speech before 1900, it remains most likely that Pentecostal historians are reading their own theology into past events when it is stated that the theology of these groups is congruent with that of present day Pentecostalism.[43]

An exhaustive research for records of tongues-speech suggests there may not be a major period of church history without this phenomenon occurring among Christians.[44] In light of this, it is not surprising to find tongues-speech being practiced in the Nineteenth Century. Further, "Pentecostal terminology" (baptism in the Spirit, fullness of the Spirit, et al.) became more pronounced after the Reformation, gained momentum in the Nineteenth Century and exploded in the Twentieth Century. The pneumatology formulated by Edward Irving (1793–1834) seems to run parallel to present day Pentecostalism. It has sometimes been argued that Irving understood tongues-speech as the "initial evidence" of Spirit baptism. However, such a position must reckon with: (1) Irving associating prophecy as well as tongues with the initiation of Spirit baptism and (2)

---

42. Hollenweger, *Pentecostals*, 236, 335; Atter, *Third Force*, 149; James Tinney, "Exclusivist Tendencies in Pentecostal Self Defense," unpublished paper presented to the Society for Pentecostal Studies (Valley Forge: December 2, 1978); John R. Rice, *The Charismatic Movement* (Murfreesboro: Sword of the Lord, 1976), 90. For a representative reading of the Pentecostal view in America that glossolalia is the invariable evidence of Spirit baptism, see these works: HOLINESS—Ray Hughes, *What is Pentecost?* (Cleveland: Pathway, 1966); *The Glossolalia Phenomenon*, ed. by Wade Horton; John Sims, *Power With Purpose* (Cleveland: Pathway, 1984). KESWICK—Harold Horton, *Baptism in the Holy Spirit* (London: Assemblies of God, 1961); Aimee Semple McPherson, *The Four-Square Gospel* (Los Angeles: Foursquare Publications, 1969); G. P. Duffield and M. M. Van Cleave, *Foundations of Pentecostal Theology* (Los Angeles: LIFE Bible College, 1983); Carl Brumback, *What Meaneth This?* (Springfield: Gospel Publishing House, 1947). ONENESS—J. T. Pugh, *How to Receive the Holy Ghost* (Hazelwood: Pentecostal Publishing House 1969); Kenneth V. Reeves, *The Holy Ghost with Tongues* (1966).

43. Contra Frodsham, *Signs*, 10ff and Brumback, *Suddenly*, 13ff.

44. Harold D. Hunter, "Pentecostal Pneumatology," V:C:2, Unpublished lectures.

that Irving himself would not have been a recipient of this pneumatic experience in view of the fact that there is no record of his having spoken in tongues.[45]

The term Spirit baptism as it is currently employed by North American Classical Pentecostals has often been traced back to Charles Fox Parham's Bethel Bible College in Topeka, Kansas. The experience of 30 year old Agnes Ozman on January 1, 1901, is central to such inquiries.[46] It is also clear that Parham's exposure to tongues at Frank Sandford's Shiloh at least helped ferment such a concept. What has yet to be adequately researched is whether the Doughty connection from Sandford to the Gift Adventists to a Doughty patriarch actually pushes this question to an earlier time. This research project looks also at B. H. Irwin and a short-lived community in Bradley County, Tennessee once known as Beniah.[47] James

---

45. Edward Irving, "On the Gifts of the Holy Ghost," *The Collected Writings of Edward Irving*, ed. by Caryle (London: Alexander Strahan Publisher, 1866), 5:539, 559, 544–46, 524; Irving, "The Sealing Virtue of Baptism," Homilies on Baptism 2, *Writings* 2:277f.; A. L. Drummond, *Edward Irving and his Circle* (London: James Clark and Co. Ltd., 1871), 164; Larry Christenson, *A Message to the Charismatic Movement* (Minneapolis: Dimension Books, 1972), 56; Gordon C. Strachan, *The Pentecostal Theology of Edward Irving* (London: Darton, Longman & Todd, 1973), 130, 19, 127; McNamee, "The Role of the Spirit in Pentecostalism," 31; Bernard L. Bresson, *Studies in Ecstasy* (New York: Vantage Press, 1966), 96; George J. Williams and Edith Waldvogel, "A History of Speaking in Tongues and Related Gifts," *The Charismatic Movement*, ed. by M. P. Hamilton (Grand Rapids: Eerdmans, 1975), 86; David W. Dorries, "Edward Irving and the 'Standing Sign' of Spirit Baptism," *Initial Evidence*, ed. by Gary McGee (Peabody: Hendrickson Press, 1991), 48–53; G. B. Cutten, *Speaking With Tongues* (New Haven: Yale University Press, 1927), 100; Damboriena, *Tongues*, 189n48; Martin Parmentier, "Two Charismatic Movements: Montanism and Messalianism," *Theological Renewal* 3 (June/July, 1976): 19n15; Dave MacPherson, *The Incredible Cover-Up* (Plainfield: Logos, 1975), 29; Nichols, *Pentecostals*, 24. Atter, *Third Force*, 35, says that Irvingites who came to Canada in the nineteenth century exercised charismatic phenomena but did not teach Spirit baptism as subsequent nor tongues as initial evidence.

46. There is minor confusion regarding the actual time this occurred. Mrs. Parham, *Charles Fox Parham* (Baxter Springs, 1969) gives two differing accounts. Mrs. Parham's sister may have remembered the day as being December 31, 1900, (p. 59) but Agnes is quoted (p. 66) as singling out January 1, 1901. Agnes repeats this date in her own book, Agnes N. O. LaBerge, *What God Hath Wrought* (Chicago: Herald, n.d.), 28f. See Goff, *Fields*, 69, 197n15; Ethel E. Goss, *The Winds of God* (Hazelwood: World Aflame Press, 1977); Synan, *Old-Time Power*, 104.

47. See Harold D. Hunter, "Beniah At The Apostolic Crossroads: Little Noticed Crosscurrents of Irwin, Sandford, Parham, and Tomlinson," *Memory and Hope*, edited by Grant Wacker (Wycliffe College, Toronto: Society For Pentecostal Studies, March 8, 1996). This was revised and published in the *Cyberjournal for Pentecostal-Charismatic Research* (www.pctii.org/cybertab.html).

Goff has already made a compelling case about how the Frank Sandford exposure absorbed by the B. H. Irwin theory produced in Parham the concept of missionary tongues as the reason for a distinct baptism of the Spirit. The only thing left, says Goff, was moving Bethel students squarely into his camp.[48]

A chronology of events in Topeka is not without some dispute. Mrs. Parham's account of her husband, entitled simply *Charles Fox Parham*, perpetuates that story that the Topeka formula was agreed upon prior to Miss Ozman's experience. Mrs. Goss, the wife of a minister friend of Mr. Parham, passes on much of the same story uncritically in her *The Winds of God*. Agnes' personal account, published under the title *What God Hath Wrought* and released earlier than these works, may confirm such a process. Entitled *Baptism with the Holy Ghost and The Gift of Tongues and Sealing of the Church and Bride*, Charles Parham's 1902 article published in November, 1906 in conjunction with W. F. Carother's *The Baptism with the Holy Ghost and the Speaking in Tongues*, sounds a cautious note on prior teaching. Dr. G. B. Cutten, Baptist pastor and later professor at Yale University, wrote in 1908 that the Apostolic Faith Movement started in Kansas in 1900 and declares "that speaking with tongues is the only Bible evidence of the baptism of the Holy Spirit."[49] The account given in the earliest history of the movement, namely B. F. Lawrence's *The Apostolic Faith Restored*, first published in 1916, must be consulted. Lawrence suggests that study by the Bethel students plus the experience of Agnes cemented tongues as "the" evidence. The cryptic account in the first published Azusa St. version of Topeka entitled "Pentecost Has Come" published September, 1906, Seymour's inaugural *The Apostolic Faith*, acknowledges study then points to Agnes as exemplifying the erasing of the Holiness equation of Spirit baptism and sanctification.[50]

---

48. Goff, "Parham," 64; Goff, *Fields*, 74f.

49. G. B. Cutten, *The Psychological Phenomena of Christianity* (New York: Charles Scribner's, 1908) 57. Cutten proceeds to tell about attending a service from this tradition where people manifested glossolalia. Cutten cites S. A. Manwell's "Speaking with Tongues" run in *The Wesleyan Methodist* (February 20, 1907) 8f. This periodical ran a series of articles on the subject by Manwell and P. B. Campbell up through an issue dated March 6, 1907.

50. See also *The Apostolic Faith* 1:2 (October, 1906): 1; Anderson, *Disinherited*, 34-36, 54f.; Waldvogel, *Assemblies of God*, 25f.; Irvine John Harrison, "A History of the Assemblies of God." Contra William M. Menzies, "The Methodology of Pentecostal Theology," *Essays on Apostolic Themes*, ed. by Paul Elbert (Peabody: Hendrickson, 1985),

The priority of this circuit has been contested because of an interpretation of over 100 persons who spoke in tongues following an 1896 revival in Cherokee County, North Carolina. Various members of this group, especially W. F. Bryant, eventually became part of the Church of God (Cleveland). Adjuring this as evidence for 1896 being the actual start of the Pentecostal Movement, does not seem to reckon adequately with the fact that there are no documents contemporary to the 1896 event which explicitly designate the phenomenon as completely congruent with the developed North American Pentecostal doctrine of Spirit baptism with glossolalic initial evidence.[51] A. J. Tomlinson, the first general overseer of the Church of God, wrote in 1913 of learning about Spirit baptism as evidenced by tongues in January, 1907. It appears that he credits W. J.

2n3. Harrison, 62, goes so far as to suggest that Parham did not even return from his trip until twelve students had already spoken in tongues. However, Agnes recounts Parham laying hands on her.

51. Until September 1998, Ray H. Hughes was the chair of the Pentecostal World Conference which planned its 2001 conference held in the USA in celebration of the Classical Pentecostal centennial. Synan, *Old Time Power*, 91n21, notes that the three evangelists and Sarah Smith were affiliated with the Tennessee chapter of the Fire-Baptized Holiness Association. Synan's source is Clyde S. Bailey, *Pioneer Marvels of Faith* (Morristown, TN, n.d.). B. H. Irwin's multiple Spirit reception scheme was not identical to initial evidence Spirit baptism. Only after the Azusa Street revival did the Fire-Baptized Holiness Church officially adopt the Pentecostal doctrine of Spirit baptism. Agnes Ozman Laberge eventually joined this tradition [Campbell, *Pentecostal*, 208]. An article entitled "History of Pentecost" in the September, 1922 edition of the *Faithful Standard* (p. 6) claims these early leaders did not make tongues a prerequisite of the fullness of the Spirit.

Seymour with having first formulated the doctrine.[52] More importantly, the Beniah, Tennessee story pulls together many of the threads.[53]

All Pentecostal historians agree that the theology activated in Topeka is directly linked to the events that transpired in Los Angeles and is, therefore, of considerable importance. The debate among those who launched PCCNA centers on whether Parham or Seymour should be designated founder of the U.S. movement. The distinct U.S. Pentecostal pneumatol-

---

52. Charles W. Conn, *Our First 100 Years: 1886-1986* (Cleveland: Pathway Press, 1986), 17, ascribes importance to the events of 1896 in North Carolina because they "prepared the way for the universal outpouring that followed ten years later." This is a welcome appraisal in light of an earlier judgment often bound up in the North American church's self-perception, namely [Charles W. Conn, *Like A Mighty Army* (Cleveland: Pathway Press, 1977), 25]: "... this was the first general outpouring that would continue unabated until it encompassed the Christian world." The re-evaluation process can be followed in Charles W. Conn, *Cradle of Pentecost* (Cleveland: Pathway, 1981), 17, "If it was not the beginning of the modern Pentecostal Awakening, it was certainly the greatest prelude to it." Then "Church of God" by Charles W. Conn in *Encyclopedia of Religion in the South*, ed. by Samuel S. Hill (Macon: Mercer University Press, 1984), 160, calls this an "extraordinary event" "without precedent in the region." On the other hand, Conn's entry in the same volume on "A. J. Tomlinson," repeats the older view espoused in *Army*. Conn's piece on the revival in *DPCM*, 161, says the group "formulated no doctrine about it. They simply thanked God for the 'blessing'..." He opens the article by calling this "one of the earliest known outpourings of the Holy Spirit in America" in contrast to the closing statement that the "universal outpouring would begin ten years later, 1906, in far away California." Also see Marcia Ford, "Church of God Celebrates Anniversary," *Charisma* (August 1996): 28-34. Cf. E. L. Simmons, *History of the Church of God* (Cleveland: Church of God Publishing House, 1938), 11f.

53. It is possible that Tomlinson heard tongues-speech in Shiloh at least by 1901. There are a variety of other considerations including the following: (1) The Church of God did not officially accept the doctrine in formal session until 1911. The August 15, 1910 edition of the *Evening Light and Church of God Evangel* listed major teachings and number nine was tongues as part of Spirit baptism. These teachings were adopted by the general assembly in 1911 with only slight revision and published with the 1922 minutes, the first set of minutes to be printed. See *General Assembly Minutes, 1906-1914, photographic reproductions* (Cleveland: White Wing Press, 1992), 91, 150f.; *Book of Minutes of the Church of God* (Cleveland: Church of God Publishing House, 1922), 47, 129; *Cyclopedic Index of Assembly Minutes and Important Business Acts of the Church of God of Prophecy, 1906-1974* (Cleveland: White Wing Publishing House, 1975), 337, 216; Conn, *Army*, 119. (2) No one credits them with this doctrine, or says they borrowed it from them whereas there is considerable evidence of the influence of Azusa on Cleveland. (3) The doctrine of initial evidence became prominent in the 1908 general meeting of the emerging Church of God. The next year a pastor left in charge of the Cleveland church by A. J. Tomlinson denied initial evidence and was able to lead out a group that concurred with that view. A detailed discussion of this can be found in my article entitled "Spirit-Baptism and the 1896 Revival in Cherokee County, North Carolina," *Pneuma* 5:21 (Fall 1983).

ogy was apparently cemented by Parham, but it was the implementation of this by Seymour coupled with a fellowship that transcended racial and other barriers, publication of a periodical and the resulting media attention that made the teaching a global phenomenon.[54]

It is interesting to note that Miss Ozman's initial experience in Topeka was said to have involved speaking in Chinese. Parham never modified the understanding that tongues-speech was to be xenolalic,[55] neither have his theological heirs the Apostolic Church.[56] The 1901 Topeka and the 1906 Azusa St. revivals included reports of xenolalia.[57] Among other leaders the claim of xenolalia in the initial experience of Spirit baptism was made by Florence Crawford, T. B. Barrett and A. J. Tomlinson.[58] Also, many new Pentecostals went outside the USA with the expectation of being supernaturally endowed with the appropriate language.[59] There are other stories of xenolalia among Classical Pentecostals that need not be recounted here,[60] but it is interesting to note that similar reports marked

---

54. See also Douglas Nelson, "For Such a Time As This," Unpublished Ph.D. dissertation (University of Birmingham, England, 1981); James S. Tinney and Stephen N. Short, *In the Tradition of William J. Seymour* (Washington, D.C.: Spirit Press, 1978); Goff, *Fields*; E. Myron Noble, "Genesis of W. J. Seymour in Perspective," *MAR Gospel Ministries Newsletter* 1:1 (Spring-Summer, 1990): 4-8.

55. Harold D. Hunter, "Pentecostal Pneumatology," V:B:12.

56. Article 7 of the By Laws of the Apostolic Faith Bible College, Inc., as published in *Apostolic Faith Report* 38:4-6 (April–June 1992): 12, depicts Spirit baptism as "evidenced by the speaking in other languages." Much good original material has been collected by Lyle Murphy and published under the title "Beginnings at Topeka," *Calvary Review*, (Spring 1974): 2–4. Early original sources are also quoted in: Charles W. Shumway, "A Critical History of Glossolalia," Unpublished Ph.D. dissertation (Boston University, 1919), 11f., 60, 43; Harrison, "A History of the Assemblies of God," 63f. Also helpful are: LaBerge, *What God Hath Wrought*, 29f.; Parham, *Charles Fox Parham*; Anderson, *Vision of the Disinherited*, 54f., 90f.; William G. MacDonald, "Pentecostal Theology: A Classical Viewpoint," *Perspectives on the New Pentecostalism*, ed. by Russell P. Spittler (Grand Rapids: Baker, 1976), 59.

57. Brumback, *Suddenly*, 24f.; Synan, *Pentecostal*, 110f.; Bloch-Hoell, *Pentecostal Movement*, 42f., 87.

58. *A Historical Account of the Apostolic Faith* (Portland: 1965), 45, 59; Nichols, *Pentecostals*, 41f.; Bloch-Hoell, *Pentecostal Movement*, 87; Tomlinson, *Last Great Conflict*, 177f.; Conn, *Army*, 85; *Book of Doctrines*, 48f.

59. There are a variety of records that verify this including the early editions of *The Apostolic Faith* published at Azusa St. during 1906. Also see Anderson, *Disinherited*, 90f.; Atter, *Third Force*, 293; Brumback, *Suddenly*, 42; *Cyclopedic Index . . . of the Church of God of Prophecy*, 334; Drummond, *Irving*, 147.

60. See Durasoff, *Bright Wind*, 62; Synan, *Pentecostal*, 102, 104, 110f.; Frodsham, *Signs Following*, 35, 39f.; Bloch-Hoell, *Pentecostal Movement*, 42f., 47f., 87; Conn, *Army*, 85;

the early years of both the Protestant Charismatic Movement and the Roman Catholic Charismatic Movement.[61] While there have been several written documentaries on this phenomenon, to my knowledge there has not been a positive verbal identity made by language experts in a controlled environment.[62]

VARIOUS APPLICATIONS OF SPIRIT BAPTISM: MAINSTREAM CHARISMATICS

Originally called Neo-Pentecostals, the word charismatic is better suited to describe this group. The word charismatic shows that while there is a common denominator with Classical Pentecostalism, there are also differences. As the term implies, one of the early major differences was the preference of this group for Paul over Luke.[63] An important histori-

---

Horton, *Glossolalia Phenomenon*, 192, 151f., 210ff.; Brumback, *Suddenly*, 24f., 42; Atter, *Third Force*, 293; Goss, *Winds*, 34ff., 54, 57f., 85ff.; *Touched by the Spirit*, ed. Warner, 90.

61. Included among the Protestant charismatics are Pat Robertson, Harald Bredesen, Donald Pfotenhauer, Larry Christenson and Ken Pagard. Writing about a similar phenomenon, Edward D. O'Conner, *The Pentecostal Movement* (Notre Dame: Ave Marie, 1974), 48, seems cautious. However his remark on page 57 may indicate otherwise. Cf. Kevin and Dorothy Ranaghan, *Catholic Pentecostals* (Paramus, N. J.: Paulist Press, 1969), 44; René Laurentin, *Catholic Pentecostalism* (New York: Doubleday, 1977), 67ff., 95f.

62. See Harold D. Hunter, "Pentecostal Pneumatology," V:B:12. This could be done by having a tape recording submitted to recognized language authorities. All previous analysis that has been done outside the worship context has been negative. See Anderson, *Disinherited*, 16f.; Cyril G. Williams, *Tongues of the Spirit* (Cardiff: University of Wales Press, 1981), 34f.; J. D. G. Dunn, *Jesus and the Spirit* (London: SCM, 1975), 151, 399n84; Knox, *Enthusiasm*, 553. Alma White, *Demons and Tongues* (Zarephath, New Jersey: Pillar of Fire Publishers, 1949), 119-22, claims to have visited the Azusa St. Revival in 1909 and was alarmed at claims of xenolalia. When someone asked her if she spoke in tongues, she cited Paul's reference to many tongues and promptly spoke in Latin. She claims the people around her believed the phenomenon to be xenolalia, whereupon it confirmed her conviction that the revival movement as a whole lacked integrity. The August 13, 1905 edition of *The Houston Chronicle* includes a report that "20 Chinese dialects" were verified by "government interpreters" at a Parham meeting. However, Charles W. Shumway completed a doctoral dissertation entitled "A Critical History of Glossolalia" at Boston University in 1919 and he disputes this record. He says that he wrote the authorities in Houston and could find no knowledge or record of any such confirmation. Shumway tells (p.60) about a priest who heard an ex-catholic burst out with a verbal barrage that included: "In truibo ad altare Dei, Ad Deum que laetificat juventutum meum." The priest reported that these were words from the Roman mass that had been pulled from the person's latent memory. He recounts also the folly of A. G. Garr leaving Azusa in 1906 for a mission field because of his perceived experience with xenolalia.

63. Fr. Peter Hocken, "The Pentecostal-Charismatic Movement as Revival and Renewal," *Pneuma* 3:1 (Spring, 1981) 31–47, addresses the reasons for this development

cal point of reference for formation of the North American Protestant Charismatic Movement is the 1960 expulsion of Dennis Bennett from St. Mark's Episcopal Church in Van Nuys, California. There were others of a similar theological persuasion and experience who preceded Fr. Bennett, within historical churches and many factors including the work of the Full Gospel Business Men's Fellowship International, aided in consolidation. Yet it appears that the national publicity given Bennett's activities by the press in addition to the birth of *Trinity* magazine was responsible for isolated groups learning of one another and others taking the phenomena more seriously.[64]

Leaders in the North American Protestant Charismatic Movement have generally agreed that Spirit baptism is a work of the Spirit which can be distinguished from regenerating work, but opinions vary with regard to the issues of subsequence and evidence.[65] Included under the label Mainstream Charismatic are two major sections: (1) Those 'charismatic' members of established traditions known as Presbyterian, Episcopalian, Methodist, United Church of Christ, Baptist and Lutheran as well as those

---

in his discussion of the applicability of the terms revival and renewal to the current Spirit movements. cf. W. W. Menzies, "A Taxonomy of Contemporary Pentecostal-Charismatic Theologies," unpublished paper addressed to the Society for Pentecostal Studies (Valley Forge: December 1, 1978). One trend in the 1980's was watching pentecostals and charismatics reverse doctrinal positions.

64. For this and related questions, see the following: "What did Happen at St. Mark's Episcopal Church?" *Trinity* 1:2 (Charismastide, 1961–62): 2–5; *Acts* 1:1 (July/August, 1967): 10ff.; Peter D. Hocken, "Charismatic Movement," *DPCM*, 130–32; Richard Quebedeaux, *The New Charismatics* (Garden City: Doubleday, 1976) now revised, *The New Charismatics II* (1983); Charles E. Hummel, *Fire in the Fireplace* (Downers Grove: InterVarsity Press, 1978); Michael Harper, *As At the Beginning* (Plainfield: Logos, 1965); Erling Jorstad, *Bold in the Spirit* (Minneapolis: Augsburg, 1974); David DuPlessis, *The Spirit Bade Me Go* (Plainfield: Logos, 1970); John L. Sherrill, *They Speak With Other Tongues* (Old Tappen: Fleming H. Revell, 1965). Cf. Peter Hocken, "The Significance and Potential of Pentecostalism," *New Heaven? New Earth?* (Springfield: Templegate Publishers, 1976), 43.

65. Oddly some have thought that they escape criticism due Classical Pentecostalism by saying that tongues are not the sign of Spirit baptism but the "consequence" of it. Cf. Stanley Wayne, "The Tongues Debate," *Agora* 2:2 (Fall 1978): 12, 15. Mr. Wayne unfortunately makes some factual errors in this brief analysis. See also Kenneth S. Kantzer, "Charismatic Renewal: Threat or Promise?" *Theology and Mission*, ed. by D. J. Hesselgrave (Grand Rapids: Baker, 1978), 17–37. The endnotes are the strength of this contribution. An article by Paul D. Feinberg on Spirit baptism follows that of Kantzer's, but it demonstrates the lack of first hand acquaintance with the issues.

aligned with the holiness movement, Greek Orthodoxy and Mennonites.[66] Distinctive organizations serve all these constituencies. (2) Charismatics who are not denominationally aligned, but are in the process of various forms of institutionalization. This includes many prominent members of the electronic church like Kenneth Copeland, increasing numbers of mega-churches like Billy Joe Daughtery's Victory Christian Center, para-church organizations, schools like Oral Roberts University and fledgling denominations like Maranatha Christian Churches, Calvary Chapels, Covenant Churches, Churches on the Rock, etc. An increasingly visible segment of this section can be called the Word/Faith Movement and is known by the ministries of Kenneth Hagin, Fred Price, Robert Tilton, and Jerry Savelle, etc.[67]

One of the trademarks of the American Protestant Charismatic Movement has been its claim to ecumenism. In reality, however, most Protestant Enthusiastic Pneumatomania, like the Classical Pentecostal Movement itself, results in new Christian organizations and churches.[68]

---

66. See earlier paradigm using the apostolic motif. However, for purposes of this study it is not inappropriate to lump these groups together since this is the practice of NARSC in their national conferences.

67. See these works: Thomas A. Smail, *Reflected Glory* (Grand Rapids: Eerdmans, 1975); J. Rodman Williams, *Renewal Theology*, Volume 2 (Grand Rapids: Zondervan, 1990; J. Rodman Williams, *The Gift of the Holy Spirit Today* (Plainfield: Logos, 1980); J. Rodman Williams, *The Pentecostal Reality* (Plainfield: Logos, 1972); Howard Ervin, *Conversion-Initiation and the Baptism in the Holy Spirit* (Peabody: Hendrickson, 1984); Dennis Bennett, *How to Pray for the Release of the Holy Spirit* (South Plainfield: Bridge, 1985); Paul S. Fiddes, "The Theology of the Charismatic Movement," *Strange Gifts? A Guide to Charismatic Renewal*, ed. by J. Maston and P. Muller (Oxford: Basil Blackwell, 1984), 19ff.; Howard M. Ervin, *These Are Not Drunken as Ye Suppose* (Plainfield: Logos, 1968); Larry Christenson, *The Charismatic Renewal Among Lutherans* (Minneapolis: Lutheran Charismatic Renewal Services, 1976); Oral Roberts, *Baptism in the Spirit and You* (Plainfield: Logos, 1971); John A. Schep, *Baptism in the Spirit* (Plainfield: Logos, 1972); John Rea, *The Layman's Commentary on the Holy Spirit* (Plainfield: Logos, 1971); Michael Green, *I Believe In The Holy Spirit* (Grand Rapids: Eerdmans, 1975); Don Basham, *A Handbook on Holy Spirit Baptism* (Monroeville: Whitaker Books, 1969); Catherine Marshall, *Something More* (New York: Avon Books, 1976). The now defunct Logos was the most prominent publisher of Protestant Charismatic literature. Several churches have responded to charismatics by offering theological analyses. The most significant documents for Protestant Charismatics and Roman Catholic Charismatics are neatly arranged with helpful introductions by Kilian McDonnell in his three volume *Presence, Power, Praise* (Collegeville: The Liturgical Press, 1980).

68. Heribert Mühlen makes much the same point in his "A Church in Movement-Not A Movement in the Church," *Theological Renewal* 9 (June/July, 1978) 15–20. Peter

One aspect of the movement that was to have substantiated this claim is that many prayer meetings had a variety of denominations and organizations represented. But this is only a familiar pattern. Aimee Semple McPherson, for example, could boast of a great number of organizations present during her crusades, yet she also founded a denomination and in doing so successfully encouraged some church members and leaders to join her organization. The same thing is happening today as, among other things, the central concerns associated with the various nuances of Charismatic Spirit baptism theology becomes a rallying point more crucial than their denominational allegiance. Thus these small independent prayer groups have spawned local churches; some local churches are loosely organized thus preparing the way for a complete denomination and a large body of written material, seminars, conventions, and special organizations facilitate this process.[69]

Hocken, "The Charismatic Movement and the Church: A Response to Heribert Mühlen," *Theological Renewal* 31 (October, 1979) 22–29, responds with some helpful qualifications. Part of the problem is the earlier noted different impact of Enthusiastic Pneumatomania in the Protestant tradition as opposed to the Catholic tradition and movements in America as opposed to Europe in particular. Roman Catholic Charismatics are not free of problems here, sometimes because of their ecumenism, but this is not the largest factor. cf. Kilian McDonnell, *The Charismatic Renewal and Ecumenism* (New York: Paulist Press, 1978); Peter Hocken's doctoral dissertation "'Baptized in the Spirit': The Origins and Early Development of the Charismatic Movement in Great Britain," (University of Birmingham, 1984), published in 1986 by Paternoster Press under the title *Streams of Renewal*. My primary concern is for North American Protestant Charismatics. This is not limited to the USA, however, as can be seen in Thomas Smail's re-evaluation of the European Protestant Charismatic movement in his *The Forgotten Father* (Grand Rapids: Eerdmans, 1980) and then *The Giving Gift* (London: Hodder and Stoughton, 1988).

69. Ecumenism needs to reckon with the kind of pragmatic identity pushed by the Charismatics and their ability to bring local groups together, but the Charismatics need to cope with genuine theological dialogue. In the 1970s and 1980s, Classical Pentecostals have been involved in dialogue with the Roman Catholic Church, the National Council of Churches, and the World Council of Churches. 1996 saw the start of an International Pentecostal-World Alliance of Reformed Churches Dialogue. Further, the Society of Pentecostal Studies has increasingly sought to become more inclusive. For a sample of such things consult these important studies: Cecil M. Robeck, "Pentecostals and Ecumenism: An Expanding Frontier," *Conference on Pentecostal and Charismatic Research in Europe*, ed. by Jean Daniel Plüss (Kappel: July 3–6, 1991); Arnold Bittlinger, ed., *The Church is Charismatic* (Geneva: World Council of Churches, 1981); Jerry L. Sandidge, "Roman Catholic/Pentecostal Dialogues (1977–82): A Study in Developing Ecumenism," (Katholiete Univessiteit Te Leuven, 1985); Cecil M. Robeck, "Name and Glory: The Ecumenical Challenge," *Pastoral Problems in the Pentecostal/Charismatic Movement*, ed. by Harold D. Hunter (Cleveland, TN: Society For Pentecostal Studies, 1983); Rex

VARIOUS APPLICATIONS OF SPIRIT BAPTISM: ROMAN CATHOLIC CHARISMATICS

1992 saw various conferences celebrating 25 years of renewal. A lead article in *New Covenant* trumpeted "The People's Movement at Age 25."[70] The movement had matured in many ways, but it has also fragmented. The Roman Catholic tradition includes a rich mixture of many different ingredients, but the specific point of reference in the American Roman Catholic church as it relates to a pentecostal infusion centers on events in 1967 at Duquesne University in Pittsburgh, a Catholic University under the direction of the Fathers of the Congregation of the Holy Spirit. Among early influences too large to overlook are Vatican II and the Cursillo Movement.[71]

Roman Catholic Charismatics have often paralleled their pneumatic experiences and tongues-speaking to that of the Classical Pentecostal, but none of the participating scholars supports the traditional Pentecostal formulas. While there is no unanimity among Catholic thinkers, the prevailing opinion seems to be that regardless of any separation in time, Spirit baptism is theologically tied to Christian initiation. Some writers single out water baptism, others confirmation and others are less

---

Davis, *Locusts and Wild Honey* (Geneva: World Council of Churches, 1978); "Agora Talks to David duPlessis," *Agora* 2:1 (Summer, 1978); W. J. Hollenweger, "The Pentecostal Movement and the World Council of Churches," *Ecumenical Review* 18:3 July, 1966).

70. Jim Manney, "The People's Movement at Age 25," *New Covenant* (2-92) 7ff. Also see Julia Dunn, "Catholics on the Pentecostal Trail," *CT* (6-22-92) 24ff.

71. James T. Connelly, "Neo-Pentecostalism: The Charismatic Revival in the Mainline Protestant and Roman Catholic Churches in the U.S.: 1960–1971," Unpublished Ph.D. dissertation (University of Chicago, 1977); Kevin and Dorothy Ranaghan, *Catholic Pentecostalism*, newly revised and published under the title *Catholic Pentecostals Today* (South Bend: Charismatic Renewal Services, 1984); Edward D. O'Connor, *The Pentecostal Movement in the Catholic Church*; F. A. Sullivan, "The Pentecostal Movement," *Gregorianum* 53:237ff.; Laurentin, *Catholic Pentecostalism*; Francis A. Sullivan, *Charisms and Charismatic Renewal* (Ann Arbor: Servant Books, 1982), 56f.; Kilian McDonnell, ed., *Open The Windows: The Popes and the Charismatic Renewal* (South Bend: Greenlawn Press, 1989); R. J. Bord and J. E. Faulkner, *Catholic Charismatics* (University Park: Pennsylvania State University Press, 1983); Ralph Martin, *The Spirit and the Church* (New York: Paulist Press, 1976); Meredith B. McGuire, *Pentecostal Catholics* (Philadelphia: Temple University Press 1982). It is interesting to note how often the participants refer to themselves as Pentecostal Catholics. *CT* (November 7, 1986): 33, reports that many Catholics leave their tradition to become Classical Pentecostals. Yet there are Classical Pentecostals who became Roman Catholic Charismatics like Stephan Barham and Marilynn Kramar.

specific. Yet none intend to permit any thought parallel to the Classical Pentecostal teaching of a "second work of grace." Also, although a doctrine of tongues-speech as initial evidence of Spirit baptism would be repudiated by Roman Catholic Charismatics, pragmatically speaking it seems that tongues-speech is treated by many as being a normative part of their Spirit baptism.[72]

This movement has become as large as it is diverse. It has enjoyed unusual ecclesiastical encouragement from the 1969 report by the Committee on Doctrine submitted to the Catholic Bishops of the USA up to and including the responses of Pope John Paul II. It seems that in the early stages there was a considerable Protestant influence on many participants, but that is increasingly moving the other way.[73] Yet Roman Catholic organizations continue to thrive with which Protestants and Pentecostals should be able to identify. Among such groups would be: FIRE, SHARE, Lamp Ministries, Calix, Centurions, Families in Christ.

The unique blend of caring for the poor and charismatic expectations has been seen in the ministry of Fr. Rick Thomas to Juarez, Mexico. He constantly works with the poor and has several stories of food being miraculously provided as masses were served. One story in particular includes having calculated precise servings, but ending up feeding three times as many as planned. He is in no way limited to working in a large

---

72. For additional help in these matters see the following works of interest: Kilian McDonnell and George T. Montague, *Christian Initiation and Baptism in the Holy Spirit* (Collegeville: Liturgical Press, 1991); Stephen B. Clark, *Baptized in the Spirit* (Pecos: Dove Publications, 1976); Donald L. Gelpi, *Charism and Sacrament* (New York: Paulist Press, 1976); Simon Tugwell, *Did You Receive the Spirit?* (Notre Dame: Avia Maria, 1975); Piet Schoonenberg, "Le Bapteme d'Esprit-Saint," *L'EXPERIENCE DE L'ESPRIT* (Paris: Beachesne, 1976); Peter Hocken, "Catholic Pentecostalism: Some Key Questions"-1, *Heythrop Journal* 15:2 (April, 1975): 131–38; George T. Montague, *The Holy Spirit* (New York: Paulist Press, 1976); F. A. Sullivan, "Baptism in the Holy Spirit," *Gregorianum* 5 (1974): 49ff.; Robert Wild, *Enthusiasm in the Spirit* (Notre Dame: Avia Maria, 1975); Richard J. Pettery, *In His Footsteps* (New York: Paulist Press, 1977).

73. See J. Massyngberde Ford, *Which Way for Catholic Pentecostals?* (New York: Harper & Row, 1976); Nick Cavnar, "Why Are Catholic Charismatics Getting So 'Catholic'?" *Charisma* (April, 1985) 56–60; Robert Wild, *The Post-Charismatic Experience* (Locus Valley: Living Flame Press, 1984); *New Covenant* especially since 1982. This was evident in the diversified Roman Catholic presence at the 1987 Congress on the Holy Spirit and World Evangelization in New Orleans as compared to the related conference held in Kansas City in 1977.

theater. He works personally with the poor, has a ranch called the Lord's Ranch, has a medical clinic at the dump curing people of TB.[74]

THE APPROACH

It will be the purpose of this study to examine evidence related to the essence of the Classical Pentecostal doctrine of Spirit baptism. That is, may one speak of a distinct work of the Spirit which is "charismatic" in nature and which may become operative at a time subsequent to one's Christian beginnings? The starting point will be a biblical investigation. Ecclesiastical records will then be consulted with a view to seeking assistance in the interpretation of the biblical data. The final analysis will seek to relate these findings to traditional Protestant dogmatic treatments of the doctrine of salvation.

This book is not premised on the view that the theological conclusions reached here will be directly usable by non-Pentecostal traditions. Such an admitted limitation reflects, among other things, that the diversity of Scripture does not leave one formula for all the questions raised by varying traditions.[75] However, as the spaceship Earth races through the cosmos, this menu might help the passengers better digest the shrinking supply of vital sources.

---

74. Elizabeth Farrell, "Food Miracles in Juarez, Mexico," *Charisma* (Dec 92): 48f.

75. In this regard I am willing to note specific support for two articles in *Strange Gifts?* edited by D. Martin and P. Mullen. The first is by J. D. G. Dunn and entitled "Models of Christian Community in the New Testament," and the second uses the title "Pentecostal Theology and the Charismatic Movement," (especially 200ff.) and was written by Julian Ward.

2

The Pauline Corpus

INTRODUCTION

THE INTRODUCTORY CHAPTER ESTABLISHED the centrality of the doctrine of Spirit baptism to the Pentecostal Movement. At this point, it might be well to point out the manner in which Pentecostals have come to advocate certain teachings. Among the contributions to this subject by Pentecostals, few surpass the elocution of Jean-Daniel Plüss' *Therapeutic and Prophetic Narratives in Worship*. Dr. Plüss applies to the movement the type of analysis forged by Vladimir Propp and Antti Aarne and taken up in different forms by J. B. Metz, C. Schillebeeckx, Ian Ramsey, H. G. Gadamer, among others.

Exhibiting patience characteristic of the European scholarly community, Plüss draws attention to the concurrent emergence of Propp's and Aarne's work with the Pentecostal Movement. Plüss easily documents that oral language is not relegated to the past and is not absent from Europe today. This, naturally, contrasts to the conceptual empires constructed in a high literary tradition which accompanies most theologies produced by Protestants and Roman Catholics in Europe. This tension cannot be easily resolved. Plüss seeks some common ground by arguing that at issue is not "a new theology, but rather a way of doing theology that is familiar with the relationship between faith and experience."[1]

This fundamental mark of the Pentecostal Movement need not be forgotten. The treatment of the theological issue here will seek to engage advanced levels of work on the subject. However, in so doing the find-

---

1. Jean-Daniel Plüss, *Therapeutic and Prophetic Narratives in Worship* (Frankfurt am Main: Verlag Peter Lang, 1988), xxvii. See also Clark, Lederle, et al., *What Is Distinctive About Pentecostal Theology?*

ings here will be distant to many Pentecostals. This is certainly true of the Third World community, but found extensively also in Europe and North America.

To many theologians it is axiomatic that if Pentecostal Spirit baptism theology has a biblical foundation it is in the writings of Luke, certainly not in Pauline or Johannine literature.[2] Pentecostals can blame themselves for this criticism. What little theological work they have produced until the 1980's on the subject of Spirit baptism has generally been an exposition of Lucan theology with only casual interest in Pauline (Ephesians 5:18) and Johannine (John 7:37–39) writings. There are at least two reasons for this development: (1) The fact that Pentecostals did not produce a major theological treatise on the subject of Spirit baptism for seven decades reflects their praxis orientation. That is, it has been this combined with an immense eschatology devaluated attempts to write a major work about pneumatology, much less a Pauline perspective on such. (2) The second major problem is the improper application of the hermeneutical principal known as the analogia fidei. Most Pentecostals have been convinced that their case is proven in Luke-Acts and when dealing with Pauline literature many often did not concern themselves with an analysis of Paul's pneumatology but considered their position verified when a Pauline text could be found which dealt with tongues-speech. Those North American Pentecostals who have concluded that Acts presents tongues-speech as the initial sign of Spirit baptism, then the Pauline approval of tongues-speech is a priori assumed to be confirmation of their doctrine of Spirit baptism. This is a case of incomplete research, for the Pentecostal question must be decided on the basis of the pneumatology of Luke and Paul as well as other canonical writers.

Limitations of space have meant that the research will center on literature traditionally ascribed to Luke, Paul and John. Robert Mansfield's *Spirit and Gospel in Mark* along with other important contributions made to biblical theology by Pentecostal scholars show how restrictive is this choice.[3]

---

2. Walter J. Hollenweger, *Pentecostals*, 337ff., argued that the Pentecostal position can be established by exegeting the writings of Luke. He adds, however, that the traditional Protestant position is soundly based on the Pauline literature. One's theology, therefore, is determined by whether priority is given to Luke or Paul. This issue is addressed in the next chapter.

3. M. Robert Mansfield, *Spirit and Gospel in Mark* (Peabody: Hendrickson, 1987); Charles L. Holman, "A Lesson from Matthew's Gospel for Charismatic Renewal," *Faces*

In conformity with the prevailing opinion of New Testament scholarship, the Pauline corpus will be dealt with first. Following James D. G. Dunn, it will not be considered necessary to determine the dating and authorship of those New Testament epistles which have been traditionally attributed to the apostle Paul. As a matter of convenience, the sequence of epistles suggested by W. G. Kümmel will be followed.

רוח IN THE HEBREW CANON

A determination of the written usage of רוח by ancient Israel will serve as an important foundation for the investigation into the pertinent pneumatologies espoused by Paul, Luke, and John. The following analysis of רוח will be treated under a fourfold division.[4]

רוח as Wind

It is not possible for us to know the original meaning of *rûaḥ*. The debate has centered on the priority of "wind" or "breath" (from "air in motion"). The criteria of scholars like W. R. Shoemaker, Paul Volz, E. D. Burton, H. Wheeler Robinson, Robert Koch, Ludwig Koehler, G. Gerleman, Paul Younger, and Walter Eichrodt which favor the priority of "wind" may outweigh the dissenting opinions expressed by David Hill, Irving F. Wood, and G. E. Whitlock.

The translation of *rûaḥ* as "wind" seems to be the numerical favorite. Putting together the verb and noun forms of *rûaḥ*, Charles Briggs counts 378 instances and Leon Wood counts 388 cases in the Hebrew Bible. Out

---

of *Renewal*, Elbert, 48–63; John Christopher Thomas, "Discipleship In the Synoptic Gospels," *Pastoral Problems in the Pentecostal-Charismatic Movement*, Harold D. Hunter; John Christopher Thomas, "Discipleship in Mark's Gospel," *Faces of Renewal*, Elbert, ed., 64-80. See the review of Mansfield's book by Gordon D. Fee in *CT* (8-12-88): 69.

4. The divisions used are a modification of those given by the following: James D. G. Dunn, "The Understanding and Role of the Spirit in the Religion of Israel and Early Judaism," (Pasadena: Fuller Theological Seminary, January 12, 1976); Schweizer, "πνεῦμα," *TDNT* 6:360; George Johnston, "Spirit," *A Theological Word Book of the Bible*, ed. by Alan Richardson (New York: Macmillan, 1950), 234; David Hill, *Greek Words and Hebrew Meanings* (Cambridge: At the University Press, 1967), 205ff.; Walter C. Wright, Jr., "The Use of Pneuma in the Pauline Corpus with Special Attention to the Relationship Between Pneuma and the Risen Christ," unpublished Ph.D. dissertation (Pasadena: Fuller Theological Seminary, May, 1977), 16; J. W. Simpson, Jr., "Spirit," *ISBE* 4:599f.; T. S. Caulley, "Holy Spirit," *Evangelical Dictionary of Theology*, ed. by W. A. Elwell (Grand Rapids: Baker, 1984), 521f. Cf. Leon J. Wood, *The Holy Spirit in the Old Testament* (Grand Rapids: Zondervan, 1976), 16.

of these Leon Wood counts 101 of them as "wind," and Charles Briggs counts 117 such instances. This compares, for instance, to Leon Wood's count that 84 are used for an aspect of humans and 97 refer to an aspect of God.

Pervasive through all strata of the Hebrew canon is the *rûaḥ* blowing upon the earth and connoting violence or force. The power is manifest in the ability to move objects from one place to another (Ez 5:2, Isa 41:16, et al.), breaking down walls (Ez 13:11–13) and destroying ships at sea (Ez 27:26). All of this was under the superintendence of Yahweh (Ps 107:25, 148:8, et al.).[5]

רוח *as breath*

E. D. Burton is of the opinion that *rûaḥ* did not connote "breath" until the exilic period. By contrast, Donald L. Gelpi breaks new ground when he consistently translates *rûaḥ* as "breath."[6] Burton's thesis cannot bear the weight of the following passages:

> The bed of the seas was revealed,
> The foundations of the world were laid bare
> at Yahweh's muttered threat,
> at the blast (*neshemah*) of his nostrils' breath (*rûaḥ*).
> 2 Samuel 22:16

> A blast (*rûaḥ*) from your nostrils and the waters piled high;
> the waves stood upright like a dyke
> in the heat of the sea the deeps came together.
> Exodus 15:8

---

5. This section was summarized from Walter Wright, "Pneuma in the Pauline Corpus," 10ff., who offers a great deal more. See also Schweizer, "πνεῦμα," 360; Dunn, "Role of the Spirit"; Eichrodt, *Old Testament* 2:46; Rudolf Bultmann, *The Gospel of John* (Philadelphia: Westminster Press, 1971), 139n1; C. H. Dodd, *The Interpretation of the Fourth Gospel* (Cambridge: At the University Press, 1970), 3; Ernest DeWitt Burton, *A Critical and Exegetical Commentary on the Epistle to the Galatians* (New York: Scribner's Sons, 1920), 488; Francis Brown, S. R. Driver and C. A. Briggs, *A Hebrew and English Lexicon of the Old Testament* (Oxford: Clarendon Press, 1972), 924; *Gesenius' Hebrew and Chaldee Lexicon*, ed. and trans. by S. P. Tregelles (Grand Rapids: Eerdmans, 1949), 760; Wilf Hildebrandt, *An Old Testament Theology of the Spirit of God* (Peabody: Hendrickson Press, 1995), 3ff.

6. Donald L. Gelpi, *The Spirit in the World* (Wilmington: Michael Glazier, 1988), uses feminine pronouns in conjunction with "Holy Breath."

Isaiah 30:27–30 can speak of the lips, tongues, and *rûaḥ* of Yahweh.⁷

רוח *in humans*

rûaḥ is used in relation to people as the principle of life, seat of emotions, intellect and volition. Once *rûaḥ* was determined to signify life, the next development was a naturalization process which resulted in what moderns call psychology. It later was used for courage (Jos 5:11), anger (Jd 8:3) and patience (Ex 6:9) in humans.⁸

רוח *as an aspect of God*

Walter Knight, Jr., with some support from Alasdair I. C. Heron, has offered the following plausible thesis about the evolution of the term *rûaḥ* to referring to an aspect of God.

> From the idea of moving air, exemplified by the mysterious, vital breath and the powerful elusive wind, the Hebrews expanded the concept of *ruach* to include anything super-human, any power not explainable from simple human cause, from this it was an easy step to the spirit of Yahweh.⁹

George Montague notes the ethical overtones of *rûaḥ* in Micah.¹⁰ William Dyrness rightly points out that *rûaḥ* became increasingly identified with God's self as an expression of moral majesty (Isa 30:1, 32:15, 28:5f., 11:2, 63:10f.).¹¹

---

7. Wright, "Pneuma in the Pauline Corpus," 12f. Also see Schweizer, "πνεῦμα," 360f.; Dunn, "Role of the Spirit;" George Johnston, *The Spirit-Paraclete in the Gospel of John* (Cambridge: University Press, 1970), 3; Eichrodt, *Old Testament* 2:46; Dodd, *Fourth Gospel*, 214; Brown, Driver, and Briggs, *Lexicon*, 924f.; Wood, *Holy Spirit*, 17; *Gesenius' Hebrew and Chaldee Lexicon*, 760.

8. Wright, "Pneuma in the Pauline Corpus," 20ff. Also see F. Baumgärtel, "Spirit in the OT," *TDNT* 6:360ff.; Schweizer, "πνεῦμα," 360f.; Dunn, "Role of the Spirit;" Burton, *Galatians*, 488; Brown, Driver and Briggs, *Lexicon*, 924f.; Wood, *Holy Spirit*, 17; *Gesenius' Hebrew and Chaldee Lexicon*, 925; E. Kamlah, "Holy Spirit," *NIDNTT* 3:690ff.

9. Wright, "Pneuma in the Pauline Corpus," 17; Alasdair I. C. Heron, *The Holy Spirit* (Philadelphia: Westminster, 1983), ch 1. Cf. James D. G. Dunn, *Christology in the Making* (Philadelphia: Westminster Press, 1980), 133.

10. Montague, *Holy Spirit*, 35. See Davies, *Paul*, 217ff.; Leon Morris, *Spirit of the Living God* (Downer's Grove: Inter-Varsity Press, 1960), 28; A. M. Hunter, *Paul and His Precedessors*, (London: SCM Press, 1961), 146; Dunn, "Role of the Spirit."

11. William A. Dyrness, *Themes in OT Theology* (Downer's Grove: Inter-Varsity Press, 1979), 206. See Burton, *Galatians*, 488.

Although purity and power can both be related to *rûaḥ* they can be separated from one another. Consider Psalm 51 which begins with a scribe's claim that the occasion for this psalm was David's confession of his adultery with Bathsheba (2 Sam 11–12). Whether David or another is in view the despair is graphic:

> Create in me a clean heart, O God,
> And renew a steadfast spirit within me
> Do not cast me away from Thy presence,
> And do not take Thy Holy Spirit from me.
> Psalm 51:10f.

This psalm is especially interesting when compared with the behavior of various prominent "charismatics" in ancient Israel. John Koenig provides an excellent summary for us.

> Gideon was moved by God's Spirit to become a mighty warrior, but he remained a vain and half-believing man who kept many wives and eventually combined his devotion to God with worship of a golden vestment (Judg 6:11 to 8:32). Immediately after receiving the Spirit, the Judge Jepthah foolishly vowed that if he emerged victorious over the Ammonites, he would sacrifice up to the Lord as a burnt offering the first person who came out of his house to meet him. The victim was none other than his daughter (Judg 11: 29–40). Samson the strong man came out weak on maturity. Though the Spirit of the Lord had stirred him since his childhood (Judg 13:25), he remained a lifelong adolescent. He married a pagan wife, taunted people with lies and riddles that caused great loss of innocent life, visited prostitutes, and generally multiplied hatred between Israel and the Philistines (Judg chs. 14–16).
> Saul, who had been 'turned into another man' through his ecstatic experience of the Spirit (1 Sam ch. 10), nevertheless disobeyed a clear command of the Lord (1 Sam ch. 15) and lost God's favor. David, who apparently enjoyed an event greater measure of the Spirit, descended to adultery and murder. Elisha the prophet received a double measure of Elijah's spirit, but he was hardly an amiable fellow . . .[12]

---

12. John Koenig, *Charismata: God's Gifts for God's People* (Philadelphia: Westminster Press, 1978), 36. George E. Ladd, *A Theology of the New Testament* (Grand Rapids: Eerdmans, 1974), 295, says: "This official empowering of the Spirit is not associated with moral and ethical qualifications, for sometimes the Spirit endowed a man with supernatural gifts who was not a good man." Cf. Montague, *Holy Spirit*, 18, 36, 40.

Unfortunately the list can be extended, but the point (i.e., that one can be inspired but not purified) has been established. Greatest attention must be given to subdivisions (1) *rûah* as Spirit empowerment.[13] After spending time with the Hebrew canon, one discovers that the various impulses of *rûah* involve more than the political feats of the "judges" and prophetic utterances. Gerhard von Rad concludes:

> It is therefore evident that the charismatic was an absolutely constitutive factor in Yahwism. It appeared in many forms, in the guise of an inspiration for war and in the word of the prophets, in the praises of the Levitical singers and in the counsel and teaching of the wise men.[14]

Additions to this list include hymnology and wisdom. David says of his inspiration, "The Spirit of the LORD spoke by me, and His word was on my tongue" (2 Sam 23:2). Joshua is described as "filled with the spirit of wisdom" (Deut 34:8, Num 27:18). In Proverbs 1:23, "wisdom" exclaims: "Behold I will pour out my spirit on you; I will make my words known to you." Especially to be noted is that wisdom was to be a mark of the future messiah (Isa 11:2). See also Daniel 4:8ff., 18. Space is available only for typical passages dealing with prophecy, politics and acts of craft.

First let us turn our attention to prophecy. Azariah prophesied during the reign of Asa, king of Judah. "The Spirit of God came (*hayah*) upon Azariah . . ." (2 Chr 15:1) and Azariah gave a message that included both encouragement and advice. Jahaziel prophesied to Jehosphaphat, son of

---

13. The structure is an adaptation of that given by James D. G. Dunn, "Role of the Spirit." The examples used are a result of my own research in addition to those accounts listed in the works of Leon Wood, George Johnston, John Koenig, and E. Schweizer. Cf. Walther Eichrodt, *Theology of the Old Testament* (Philadelphia: Westminster Press, 1967), 2:63.

14. Gerhard Von Rad, *Old Testament Theology* (New York: Harper and Row, 1962), 1:102. Professor von Rad argues, 93ff., that JED and even P maintain the legitimacy of charismatic activity. Von Rad also argues (p. 101) that charismatic phenomena were known in post-exilic Israel. See Montague, *Holy Spirit*, 45ff. Montague points out (p. 61) that Ezekiel was a prophet and a priest. Montague argues that the charismatic activity of the Spirit is evidenced in all strata of the Hebrew canon. See Roger Stronstad, *The Charismatic Theology of Saint Luke* (Peabody: Hendrickson, 1984), 15ff.; Heron, *Holy Spirit*, 12ff.; Congar, *Holy Spirit* 1:5ff.; John Rea, "OT Antecedents of Baptism in the Holy Spirit," *Toward A Pentecostal/Charismatic Theology*, ed. by J. Rodman Williams (South Hamilton: Society For Pentecostal Studies, November 15–17, 1984); Dyrness, *OT Themes*, 203ff.; Harold Lindsell, *The Holy Spirit in The Latter Days* (Nashville: Thomas Nelson, 1983), chs. 2–4.

Asa. The "Spirit of the LORD came (*hayah*) upon Jahaziel" and, among other things, he said "... the battle is not yours but God's" (2 Chr 20:14f.). The prophet Zechariah, not to be confused with the later literary prophet, was stoned for the message he gave to Joash. Zechariah had given a message of rebuke after "the Spirit of God took possession (*labash*) of" him (2 Chr 24:20). Balaam, the non-Israelite prophet from Mesopotamia (Deut 23:4), was summoned by the Moabite king, Balak, to curse the tribes of Israel that were in the process of their conquest of Canaan. Balaam came prepared to deliver a curse but when "the Spirit of God came (*hayah*) upon him" (Num 24:2) he pronounced a blessing. Similar examples can be found in the following passages: 1 Chronicles 12:18; Numbers 11:25; 1 Samuel 19:20.

The data relating to certain so called 'judges' are well summarized by Walter Wright, Jr.

> The ruach hovers and lights on Jepthan (Judges 11:29), it leaps or pounces on Samson (Judges 14:6); it hits or stirs Samson (Judges 14:6, 19); 15:14); it takes possession of Gideon, or puts on Gideon like a garment (Judges 6:34).[15]

The Hebrew words used in order of appearance are: Jepthan—*hayah*; Samson—*tsalah, pa'am*; Gideon—*labash*. For similar accounts see the following: Judges 13:25, 3:10.

Finally, a summary look will be made of works of craft carried out under the unction of the *rûaḥ*. When, in the early history of Israel, God wanted a dwelling place, his tent of reunion, he specially equipped Bezaleel to work on it. In fact, the Lord told Moses about Bezaleel: "I have filled (*male*) him with the Spirit of God, with ability and intelligence, with knowledge and all craftsmanship" (Exod 31:3). Many years later King David was given the plans for the building of the Temple. The chronicler tells how David gave to Solomon "... the pattern of all that he had (*hayah*) by the Spirit" (1 Chr 28:12).[16] (For a similar incident see 1 Kings 7:13f.)

---

15. Wright, "Pneuma in the Pauline Corpus," 19. See David Ewert, *The Holy Spirit in the New Testament* (Scottdale: Herald Press, 1983), 23ff.; Hill, *Greek Words*, 207; McNamee, "Role of the Spirit," 228f.; Williams, *The Gift of the Holy Spirit Today*, 16; Stronstad, *Charismatic Theology*, 17–20.

16. Most major translations do not reflect ברוח, which is part of the Masoretic text. So *Biblia Hebraica*, ed. by Rudolf Kittel (Stüttgart: Wurttembergische Bibelanstalt, 1971) 1374. RSV says "all that he had in mind"; NEB has "all he had in mind"; the Jerusalem Bible give "all he had in mind." The KJV is the only one to reflect the actual text as it has "all he had by the Spirit."

Similarly, tailors who made the garments for the priests are said to have been "filled with the spirit of wisdom" (Ex 28:3).

The complexities which resulted from the religious development of Israel are reflected in the continued modification of the definition of *rûaḥ*. It seems to be a sudden change when the prophets of the ninth and eighth centuries are silent (with the possible exception of Micah 3:8) about *rûaḥ* as inspirer of their work. The same concept is in mind as the phrases used (examples: hand of the Lord, word of the Lord) are seemingly interchangeable with '*rûaḥ Yahweh*.' It is possible that this is a reaction to false prophets who claimed inspiration from the *rûaḥ yahweh*.[17]

An interesting development is the institutionalization of the concept of *rûaḥ*.[18] The political arena offers the most explicit example as one can see that an Israelite is Spirit endowed *because* he is king. The concept is found in embryo with Moses (Num 11:17) and then Joshua (Num 27:18) (also Elijah and Elisha in 2 Kgs 2:9, 15; 1 Kgs 18:12). With the advent of the monarchy, the development is quite advanced. Samuel anointed Saul as King of Israel (1 Sam 10:1; cf. 12:3–5) and the Spirit was with him until his second disobedience, at which time the Spirit departed (1 Sam 16:14). When David was anointed by Samuel "the Spirit of the Lord came mightily (*tsalah*) upon David from that day forward" (1 Sam 16:13), which is the juncture at which it is reported that "the Spirit of the Lord departed from Saul" (1 Sam 16:14). Yet, the Spirit is still represented as coming in power for special occasions. During Saul's career the Spirit "came mightily (*tsalah*) upon him" (1 Sam 11:6). The sporadic work of the Spirit is also attested in prophetic writings: Ezekiel 11:5, 3:14, 8:3, 43:5, Zechariah 4:6.

The literature of this time introduce yet another phase of the work of the *rûaḥ*. When looking ahead to the Messiah/Servant of the Lord, one sees a permanence being attached to the possession of the *rûaḥ yahweh*. This is the exception in the Hebrew canon. One example is Elijah:

---

17. The usual explanation is that the prophets wanted to dissociate themselves from the ecstatic prophecy of their predecessors. See Hill, *Greek Words*, 208; Dunn, "Role of the Spirit;" Wright, "Pneuma in the Pauline Corpus," 30; Gerhard Krodel, "The Functions of the Spirit in the Old Testament, the Synoptic Tradition, and the Book of Acts," *The Holy Spirit in the Life of the Church*, Opsahl, 14; Heron, *Holy Spirit*, 14.

18. Eichrodt, *Old Testament* 2:54, notes this tendency and concludes that the account of Moses was influenced by E. Cf. Krodel, "Functions of the Spirit," 13f.; Dyrness, *OT Themes*, 204; McNamee, "Role of the Spirit," 232; Stronstad, *Charismatic Theology*, 20f.

> It was reported of Elijah that the Spirit of the Lord carried him about (1 Kings 18:12). Presumably, the Spirit stayed with him more or less continuously, for his disciple Elisha noticed an extraordinary quality about him and therefore asked for a "double portion" of his spirit (2 Kings 2:9ff.). Elisha's request was granted....[19]

One could also describe Jacob, Moses, Joshua and Daniel as "long term charismatics." Returning to the messianic figure, we turn to the graphic depiction of the anticipated Spirit endowment as recorded in the book of Isaiah:

> And the Spirit of the Lord shall rest upon him,
> the spirit of wisdom and understanding,
> the spirit of counsel and might,
> the spirit of knowledge and the fear of the LORD.
> Isaiah 11:2

> I have put my Spirit upon him,
> he will bring forth justice to the nations,
> He will not cry or lift up his voice,
> or make it heard in the street;
> a bruised reed he will not break,
> and a dimly burning wick he will not quench;
> he will faithfully bring forth justice.
> He will not fail or be discouraged
> till he has established justice in the earth;
> and the coastlands wait for his law.
> Isaiah 42:1–4

> The Spirit of the LORD God is upon me,
> because the LORD has anointed me
> to bring good tidings to the afflicted;
> he has sent me to bind up the brokenhearted,
> to proclaim liberty to the captives....
> Isaiah 61:1

Also, certain Psalms, which may be called Royal Psalms, seem to share the vision of a future Spirit empowerment as evidenced by the use of the word anointed.

---

19. Koenig, *Charismata*, 33. See Ewert, *Holy Spirit*, 27f.; Stronstad, *Charismatic Theology*, 17.

> You love righteousness and hate wickedness
> Therefore God, your God, has anointed you
> With the oil of gladness above your fellows.
> Psalm 45:7

> Now I know that the LORD will help his anointed
> He will answer him from his Holy heaven
> With mighty victories by his right hand.
> Psalm 20:6

This brings me to a conclusion similar to that arrived at by Walter Wright, Jr., who says:

> The same power that produced the ecstatic state effects supernatural feats, especially in the political realm. The same power that provided the constant source of prophetic inspiration and vision equipped the skilled draftsman and directed the kings of the Israelite monarch. Ultimately this same force—*ruach yahweh*—was to empower and guide the Messianic king and servant of Yahweh. Clearly, then, the *ruach yahweh* is the power of God active among his people.[20]

These findings regarding the use of *rûaḥ* in the Hebrew canon will be fundamental to the exegesis of passages selected from writings attributed to Paul, Luke, and John. As a matter of convenience, and reflecting a theological persuasion, reference to Spirit-empowerment will be labeled as "the charismatic work of the Spirit" or simply "the charismatic Spirit."[21] The charismatic work of the Spirit includes the broadest spectrum imaginable.[22] To anticipate further findings, note that Luke (Acts 2:4, 10:46,

---

20. Wright, "Pneuma in the Pauline Corpus," 43. Cf. Paul K. Jewett, "Holy Spirit," unpublished course syllabus (Pasadena: Fuller Theological Seminary, n.d.), 4; Morris, *Living God*, 27f.; H. Berkhof, *The Doctrine of the Holy Spirit* (Richmond: John Knox Press, 1964), 15; Stronstad, *Charismatic Theology*, 24f.; Brown, Driver and Briggs, *Lexicon*, 925f.; D. E. H. Whiteley, *The Theology of St. Paul* (Philadelphia: Fortress Press, 1972), 124; Dodd, *Fourth Gospel*, 214; Johnston, *Spirit-Paraclete*, 54; Johnston, "Holy Spirit," 236f.; Eichrodt, *Old Testament* 2:59.

21. See Von Rad, *Old Testament* 1:93ff; Schweizer, "πνεῦμα," 415, 425; Hill, *Greek Words*; A.L. Humphries, *Holy Spirit in Faith and Experience* (London: SCM, 1917), 244–46; Tappeiner, "Holy Spirit," 65.

22. See James D. G. Dunn, "πνεῦμα," *NIDNTT* 3:703; Koenig, *Charismata*, 28, 94f, 102, 124, 126f; Sullivan, *Charisms*, 17ff; Michael Griffiths, *Grace-Gifts* (Grand Rapids: Eerdmans, 1980), 14; Dunn, *Jesus and the Spirit*, 205f; D. G. Burke, "Gift," *ISBE* 2:466; Rudolph Bultmann, *Theology of the New Testament* (New York: Scribner, 1951), 1:154f,

19:6) would appear to include tongues, prophecy and inspired missionary work in this category. Paul likewise acknowledges tongues and prophecy (1 Cor 12:8ff.), yet he further notes one's ability to bear weakness (2 Cor 12:9) and "institutional gifts" (2 Tim 1:6f.). Additionally, Paul's list of charisms (1 Cor 7:7, 12:19ff., 28, 13:13, Rom 12:6ff., Eph 4:11) are not to be considered exhaustive for God makes his work relevant to the particular people in need.

EXEGESIS

Attention can now be given to selected Pauline texts. Those texts chosen either suggest themselves as relevant to the issue at hand or have been used by those involved in the contemporary debate. The texts quoted will be taken from the RSV unless otherwise indicated and will reflect the Greek text found in Eberhard Nestle's *Novum Testamentum Graece*.

1 Thessalonians 1:5

> For our gospel came to you not only in word, but also in power (δυνάμει) and in the Holy Spirit (πνεύματι ἁγίῳ) and with full conviction.

The first problem is to ascertain the meaning of δυνάμει. There are two frequent usages of δύναμις: (1) the power which is equated to the gospel because God is in it (Rom 1:16, 1 Cor 1:18) and (2) the miraculous power effected by the charismatic Spirit as an evidence of the gospel (1 Cor 12:10, 28, Gal 3:5; cf. 1 Cor 4:19f., 5:4). It is no surprise that commentators representing traditional Protestantism understand δυνάμει in 1 Thessalonians 1:5 as the power inherent in the gospel. In fact, many hasten to add that the sense here completely excludes any possible reference to the miraculous words of the Spirit.[23] Some contend that while the plural might be used elsewhere as the miraculous works of the Spirit, the singular form here sets it apart. As it is argued in the older, yet usable work of James E. Frame:

---

325. The label "supernatural gifts" for a select number of charisms is to be rejected since all of these phenomena are supernatural endowments of χάρις. Cf. Fiddes, "The Theology of the Charismatic Movement," 33f.

23. Leon Morris, *First and Second Thessalonians*, NIC, 57; D. Edmond Hiebert, *A Commentary on the Thessalonian Epistles* (Chicago Moody Press, 1971), 54.

Δύναμις refers not to the results of power, the charismata in general, or those specifically associated with σημεῖα καὶ τέρατα (2 Cor 12:12)—in which case we could expect δυνάμεις (but cf. 2 Thess 2:9) or an added phrase (Rom 15:19) δυνάμει σημείων—but to the power itself, as the contrast with λόγῳ and the explanatory πνεύματι.[24]

But this argument admits too much, for 2 Thessalonians 2:9 is joined by Romans 15:19 and 1 Corinthians 2:4 to demonstrate that the singular can be used with the same meaning as the plural. Additionally, the qualification of πνεύματι is evidence of the charismatic Spirit. E. Earle Ellis rightly says:

> Pneuma and dunamis sometimes appear together as parallel terms . . . (1 Corinthians 15:43-45; Romans 1:3f.). In some passages, however, Paul draws a distinction between "Spirit" and "power" in which pneuma appears to be connected especially with "inspired speech" and dunamis with (other) miraculous acts (Romans 15:18ff.; 1 Corinthians 2:4; 1 Thessalonians 1:5; Galatians 3:5; 1 Corinthians 2:6-16).[25]

G. W. H. Lampe, George T. Montague, Edmond J. Dobbin and Dan Tappeiner add that this is the same concept one associates with Luke-Acts. In an early writing Professor Lampe said:

> As in Luke's writings, the Spirit is the dynamic force and the guide inspiring the apostolic mission, attesting the gospel and commending it with power (Romans 15:19; 1 Corinthians 2:4; 1 Thessalonians 1:5), inspiring Paul himself (1 Corinthians 2:10) and enabling him to convey the gospel to those whom the same Spirit disposes to receive it (1 Corinthians 2:13f.). The Spirit remains the Spirit of prophecy, manifested in prophesying, tongues, and ecstatic utterance (1 Thessalonians 5:19; cf. Ephesians 5:18).[26]

---

24. James Everett Frame, *Epistles of St. Paul to the Thessalonians*, ICC, 81. See also: Ernest Best, *First and Second Epistles to the Thessalonians*, HNTC, 744; William Neil, *The Epistles of Paul to the Thessalonians* (London: Hodder and Stoughton, 1950), 17.

25. E. Earle Ellis, "Christ and Spirit in 1 Corinthians," *Christ and Spirit in the New Testament*, ed. by B. Lindars and S. S. Smalley (Cambridge: University Press, 1973), 270ff. See Montague, *Spirit*, 127, 132f. Cf. J. Terence Forestell, *The Letters to the Thessalonians*, JBC, 229; Hunter, *Paul*, 93.

26. G. W. H. Lampe, "The Holy Spirit in the Writings of St. Luke," *Studies in the Gospels*, ed. by D. E. Nineham (Oxford: Basil Blackwell, 1955), 2:638. Montague, *Spirit*, 127 says: At this point the Holy Spirit seems to be the charismatic spirit promised to accompany

Michael Giffiths notes a similar correlation of some passages that include the word χάρις and in light of its connection with the word χαρίσματα seem to imply charismatic phenomenon. The passages he lists can now be read somewhat differently:

> 1 Corinthians 15:10, "I labored more than them all, yet not I, but the χάρις of God which was with me."
>
> Acts 4:33, ". . . with great power the apostles were giving witness of the resurrection of the Lord Jesus and abundant χάρις was upon them all."
>
> Acts 6:8, Stephen ". . . full of χάρις and power was performing great wonders and signs among the people."[27]

It has been judged that a charismatic work of the Spirit is in view, but can anything be said about its temporal relation to other parts of the ordo salutis? George T. Montague, who agrees that the reference is to the charismatic Spirit, argues that 1 Thessalonians 1:6 and 2 Thessalonians 2:13 deny a "second moment" in the Christian life.[28] However, these Scriptures do not appear to give any insight with regard to the temporal sequence of the elements of the ordo salutis.[29]

1 Thessalonians 4:8

> Therefore whoever rejects this rejects not human authority but God, who also gives (διδόντα) his Holy Spirit (τὸ πνεῦμα αὐτοῦ τὸ ἅγιον) to you. (NRSV)

It is important to note that διδόντα, which describes God's giving of the Spirit, is a present participle. The prevailing opinion of biblical commen-

---

the apostolic preaching (Acts 1:8) by signs of healing, deliverance and miracles but also by utter conviction in the apostle's manner of preaching. Edmond J. Dobbin, "Towards a Theology of the Holy Spirit"-1, *Heythrop Journal* 17:1 (June, 1976): 14; Tappeiner, "Holy Spirit," 40.

27. Griffiths, *Grace-Gifts*, 15. See the treatment of 2 Corinthians 12:9 in Harold D. Hunter, *Spirit Baptism: A Pentecostal Alternative* (Lanham: University Press of America, 1983), 43f.

28. Montague, *Spirit*, 132. But see Howard M. Ervin, *Conversion-Initiation and the Baptism in the Holy Spirit*, (Peabody: Hendrickson, 1984), 83.

29. Similarly Gordon Fee, *God's Empowering Presence: The Holy Spirit in the Letters of Paul* (Peabody: Hendrickson Press, 1994), 43–45.

tators is that there is a no linear motion implied in 1 Thessalonians 4:8. Dunn argues that this is true because,

> Paul elsewhere thinks of the giving of the Spirit as a once-for-all action at conversion (Romans 5:5; 2 Corinthians 1:22, 5:5; 2 Timothy 1:7), and since it is almost certainly a reference to Ezekiel 37:14....[30]

An important hermeneutical issue has been raised. Dunn earlier insisted that a passage which was difficult to understand was not to be interpreted by comparing it to a less obscure passage of similar meaning.[31] It would appear, however, that Dunn has not remained true to this rule. This is not the only time that he steps outside this boundary. When discussing Acts 19:2 (and later Eph 1:13), Dunn argues that the aorist participle πιστεύσαντες is not to be taken in the more natural manner of denoting action antecedent to the main verb, but as action coincidental to the main verb. Dunn's expressed reason for doing so concerns his understanding of Paul's overall pneumatology.[32] Both of these problems recur in Dunn's treatment of 1 Thessalonians 4:8. First, he accepts the unusual howbeit possible alternative that a present participle can be substantival. Secondly, the expressed reason for doing so involves reading this passage in light of other passages. In other words, Dunn has again violated his own rule. This is quite unfortunate, not only because of the inconsistency, but additionally because of the failure to recognize other passages that have a durative force (e.g., Rom 5:5, Jn 3:34, 4:14, 7:37ff.). However, half of Dunn's argument is the primary reason for taking the participle in its more natural sense. That is, it does appear that there is a connection between God giving (διδόντα) (1 Thess 4:8) the Spirit here, and the Ezekiel prophecy that God will give (δώσω, 36:26f., 37:14, LXX) the Spirit. The

---

30. Dunn, *Baptism in Holy Spirit*, 105n2. Cf. page 171. This rationale is shared by the following: Morris, *First Thessalonians*, 128; Neil, *Thessalonians*, 84; Best, *Thessalonians*, 169. Cf. James Moffatt, *First and Second Thessalonians*, EGT 4:35; D. Edmond Hiebert, *A Commentary on the Thessalonian Epistles* (Chicago: Moody Press, 1971), 176.

31. Dunn, *Baptism in the Holy Spirit*, 103f. This means, of course, that he cannot accept the principle of the analogy of faith. This becomes more apparent in Dunn's *Unity and Diversity in the New Testament* and his *Christology in the Making*. cf. Anthony C. Thiselton, *New Horizons in Hermeneutics* (Grand Rapids: Zondervan, 1992) 241.

32. Ibid., 87. Dunn then complains that the Pentecostal translation exhibits an ignorance of Greek! A complaint, which by extension, must then apply to the massive *God's Empowering Presence* by Gordon Fee.

earlier treatment of these particular passages in Ezekiel concluded that they were concerned with ethics. If the Christian's struggle with sin is a continual one, it seems natural to understand διδόντα as suggesting that there is a continual appropriation of the Spirit to cope with this life-long confrontation with satanic influences. In other words, there is no simple once and for all bestowal of the Spirit.[33]

Galatians 3:2, 3, 5, 14

> Did you receive (ἐλάβετε) the Spirit by works of law, or by hearing with faith? Are you so foolish? Having begun (ἐναρξάμενοι) with the Spirit, are you now ending with the flesh? Does he who supplies (ἐπιχορηγῶν) the Spirit (πνεῦμα) to you and works (ἐνεργῶν) miracles (δυνάμεις) among you (ὑμῖν) do so by works of the law, or by hearing with faith?
> ...that we might receive the promise of the Spirit (ἐπαγγελίαν τοῦ πνεύματος) through faith.

It would appear that verses 2 and 3 offer an explanation of when and how the Spirit reception of verse 5 is effected. Verse 2 makes it rather clear that the Spirit is received by faith not works. The matter of when is considerably more complicated. Although verses 2 and 3 report that the receiving was in the past (ἐλάβετε and ἐναρξάμενοι), no particular moment is specified. Therefore, despite the assumption of many commentators that the reference is to initial salvation,[34] the data seem too ambiguous to determine what experience is in view.

Verse 5 suggests that the charismatic work of the Spirit is the object of discussion.[35] The main indicators to that effect are the Greek words

---

33. Also Fee, *God's Empowering Presence*, 50–53. I think Charles Holman and I agree on what this text means even though he misappropriates some of my terms in his "Reception of the Holy Spirit in The Pauline Letters," *Toward A Pentecostal/Charismatic Theology*, ed. by J. Rodman Williams (South Hamilton: Society for Pentecostal Studies, November 15–17, 1984), 5–7. To anticipate later findings, note that it is not the linear dimension of διδόντα which designates this function of the Spirit as sanctification rather than Spirit baptism. Both are appropriations of the indwelling Spirit. The difference is the concern of purity rather than power. See Montague, *Spirit*, 128f.; Ervin, *Conversion-Initiation*, 84.

34. For example see Joseph A. Fitzmyer, "The Letter to the Galatians," *JBC*, 241; Frederic Rendall, *Galatians*, EGT 3:167. Holman, "Reception of the Holy Spirit," says this then adds the charismatic dimension to it. See also Fee, *God's Empowering Presence*, 383f.

35. Bruner's concern is different, but his remarks (*Theology of the Holy Spirit*, 239) are relevant nonetheless:

ἐπιχορηγῶν, ἐνεργῶν, and δυνάμεις. Ἐπιχορηγῶν is present active participle which is much stronger than is apparent in the English translation. The noun form of this verb is found in Philippians 1:19 and, as Raymond Stamm notes, it " . . . indicates a supply of the Spirit so rich that no exigency of life or death can exhaust it (cf. 2 Corinthians 9:10)."[36] Also, the present participle should be given its full durative force and some connection, then, can be seen with Ephesians 5:18.

Further, most English translations slight the word ἐνεργημά. It would appear that there is some parallel too when this same word appears as part of the description of the charismata which Paul outlines in 1 Corinthians 12. First Paul says "there are varieties of works (ἐνεργημάτων)" (v. 6) and later in the list itself he speaks of "the working (ἐνεργήματα) of miracles (δυνάμεων)" (v.10; see Phil 3:21, Eph 3:7, Col. 1:29).[37] This is twice supportive as one can see that the third key word, δυνάμεις, appears in one of the undisputed texts of the charismatic Spirit. Also, the particular use of this word in the Gospel of Luke (1:17, 5:17, 6:19, 8:46, 10:13, 19, 19:37, 24:49) and in Acts (1:8, 2:22, 4:33, 6:8, 8:13, 10:38, 19:11) minimizes the possibility that anything else is in view.

Ὑμῖν is often translated 'in you' rather than 'among you' by those commentators wishing to turn attention away from external miracles to a supernatural work done inwardly. The basis for this move is weakened somewhat by William Hendriksen:

> There is no other means for the full gift of the Holy Spirit than the message of faith in Christ's finished work, either initially (Gal 3:2) or continually (Gal 3:5).
>
> Paul makes clear that God's constant and full supply of the Spirit, and of the miracles which are the Christian life, are *gifts* given as in the very beginning through the unconditioned message of faith in Christ (Gal 3:2&5).

See Montague, *Spirit*, 194; F. F. Bruce, New International Greek Testament Commentary, *The Epistle to the Galatians* (Grand Rapids: Eerdmans, 1982) 151; F. F. Bruce, "The Spirit in the Letter to the Galatians," *Essays on Apostolic Themes*, ed. by Paul Elbert (Peabody: Hendrickson, 1985) 36–39; Ellis, "Christ and Spirit," 270; Tappeiner, "Holy Spirit," 45f; Ervin, *Conversion-Initiation*, 85; Rea, *Holy Spirit*, 177; Herman N. Ridderbos, *The Epistle of Paul to the Galatians*, NICNT, 116. Cf. H. B. Lightfoot, *The Epistle of St. Paul to the Galatians* (Grand Rapids: Zondervan, 1975) 136; Burton, *Galatians*, 151; Donald Guthrie, *Galatians* (Grand Rapids: Eerdmans, 1973) 97; Fee, *God's Empowering Presence*, 388f.

36. Raymond Stamm, *The Epistle to the Galatians*, 1B 10:500f. cf. Stanley Horton, *What the Bible Says About the Holy Spirit* (Springfield: Gospel Publishing House, 1976) 17; Schweizer, "πνεῦμα," 428.

37. See Ladd's explanation, *Theology of the New Testament*, 273, of the use of ἔργα in the Gospels.

Instead of "among you" one can also translate "within you." This means that the miracles, forces, or powers of which the apostle makes mention can be viewed either as outward charismata (special gifts), such as healing, prophecy, tongues, interpretation of tongues (1 Corinthians 12:10f., 2 Corinthians 12:12), or as inward moral and spiritual endowments, such as faith, hope and love. there would be good reason to believe that Paul had both of these groups in mind, for when he himself enumerates the various blessings which the Holy Spirit had bestowed on another church, he proceeds by a very easy transition, from the first group (in 1 Corinthians 12) to the second (1 Corinthians 13).[38]

Verse 14 gives the important phrase ἐπαγγελίαν τοῦ πνεύματος. Understanding the two ἵνα clauses of verse 14 to be coordinate rather than dependent, Ridderbos sums up the meaning of this phrase in this context: "The gift of the Spirit is now designated as the content of the promise to Abraham."[39] Beyond this, it appears that the description of the Spirit parallels that given in verse 5 and therefore strengthens the argument that the charismatic Spirit is in view. Ἐπαγγελίαν τοῦ πνεύματος can be translated the 'promised Spirit.'[40] The best outside control for determination of the meaning seems to be Peter's use of this same phrase when describing the events on the day of Pentecost: "Being therefore exalted at the right hand of God, and having received from the Father the promise of the Holy Spirit (ἐπαγγελίαν τοῦ πνεύματος τοῦ ἁγίου) he has poured out this which you see and hear" (Acts 2:33). During this Pentecostal address, Peter linked the phenomena with Joel 2:28f. The prophetic anticipation's of the community reception of the charismatic Spirit has already been noted and also to be acknowledged is the fact that according to Luke (Lk 24:49, Acts 1:4), Jesus spoke in similar terms with reference to the anticipated events of the day of Pentecost. The cumulative effect is support for the understanding that verse 14 is a reinforcement of what was seen in verse 5.

---

38. William Hendricksen, *Exposition of Galatians, Ephesians, Philippians, Colossians, and Philemon*, 115. See Stamm, *Galatians*, 501. Contra Lightfoot, *Galatians*, 136; A. T. Robertson, *Word Pictures of the New Testament: Galatians* (Nashville: Broadman Press, 1960), 292.

39. Ridderbos, *Galatians*, 128. See also Wright, "Pneuma in the Pauline Corpus," 284; Cole, *Galatians*, 100; Robertson, *Galatians*, 294; Fee, *God's Empowering Presence*, 394f.

40. Burton, *Galatians*, 176; Ridderbos, *Galatians*, 128; George S. Duncan, *Epistle of Paul to the Galatians*, MNTC, 103; Stamm, *Galatians*, 511.

Galatians 4:6

And because (Ὅτι) you are children, God has sent (ἐξαπέστειλεν) the Spirit (τὸ πνεῦμα) of his Son into our hearts, crying
(κρᾶζον), "Abba! Father!" (NRSV)

The interpretation of this passage is complicated by the fact that a related Pauline passage, Romans 8:15–17a, appears to give a different interpretation to the issue of a possible time separation between adoption and reception of the Spirit. That is, the majority of those objecting to a sequence of events being taught in Galatians 4:6 do so on the basis of their interpretation of Romans 8:15–17a.[41] Dunn, however, considers Galatians 4:6 to be the most persuasive Pauline text for the Classical Pentecostal argument, and he is quite surprised at the statement of Ralph Riggs that Galatians 4:6 is proof that the Holy Spirit is received at conversion![42]

Be that as it may, the evidence which cannot be explained away is that a sequence *is* intimated in Galatians 4:6.[43] More important here than Romans 8:15-17a is the use of ἐξαπέστειλλω in Galatians 4:6 and Luke 24:49 which reads, "I send (ἐξαπέστειλλω) the promise (ἐπαγγελίαν) of my Father ... until you are clothed (ἐνδύσησθε) with power (δύναμιν) from on high." It would appear that the sentiments in Galatians 3, those expressed in Luke 24:49 and those found in Luke 24:49 and Galatians 4:6 are intertwined. The designation of the Spirit as the πνεῦμα τοῦ υἱοῦ is not a decisive factor for anyone's argument. Likewise not independently decisive, but interesting in light of the argument here are the remarks on κρᾶζον by Ernest Burton:

> The use of κρᾶζον, usually employed of a loud or earnest cry (Matthew 9:27, Acts 14:40, Romans 9: 27) or a public announcement (John 7:28, 37), in the LXX often of prayer addressed to God

---

41. Bruner, *Theology of the Holy Spirit*, 268; Hoekema, *Spirit Baptism*, 81; Guthrie, *Galatians*, 120; Lightfoot, *Galatians*, 169; Cole, *Galatians*, 116; Fee, *God's Empowering Presence*, 405.

42. Dunn, *Baptism in the Holy Spirit*, 113.

43. L. S. Thornton, *Confirmation* (Westminster: Dacre Press, 1954), 11f.; Burton, *Galatians*, 221f.; S. Horton, *Holy Spirit*, 173; Ervin, *Conversion-Initiation*, 86–88. Cf. Ridderbos, *Galatians*, 157. Contra Holman, "Reception of the Holy Spirit," 10–12. Fee, *God's Empowering Presence*, 407, concedes there is a logical sequence (my point) but denies the possibility of any chronological sequence (contra some Pentecostal formulas).

(Psalm 3:5, 107:13), emphasizes the earnestness and intensity of the utterance of the Spirit within us.[44]

This is reminiscent of the groanings of the Spirit (Romans 8:26, 1 Corinthians 14:15).

Finally, note that it is possible to detect a theological schema utilized by Paul in these verses:

"God sent forth (ἐξαπέστειλεν) his Son..." (v. 4)

and

"God has sent (ἐξαπέστειλεν) the Spirit of his Son..." (v. 6)

The theological motifs are those of the Incarnation of the Son and the Effusion of the Holy Spirit, that is, Pentecost.[45] The cumulative effect is to see Galatians 4:6 as supportive of the view that the charismatic work of the Spirit is to be distinguished theologically, and perhaps chronologically, in formulating the ordo salutis.

1 Corinthians 12:13

For by (ἐν) one (ἑνὶ) Spirit (πνεύματι) we were all (πάντες) baptized (ἐβαπτίσθημεν) into one body-Jews or Greek, slaves or free-and (καὶ) all (πάντες) were made to drink (ἐποτίσθημεν) of one (ἓν) Spirit (πνεῦμα).

This is the only epistolary reference that gives wording similar to the Classical Pentecostal's slogan 'baptism in the Holy Spirit.' There are six other biblical references that are quite similar of which the most relevant words will be extracted to facilitate comparison.[46]

Matthew 3:11, Jesus βαπτίσει ἐν πνεύματι ἁγίῳ καὶ πυρί

Mark 1:8, Jesus βαπτίσει ὑμᾶς ἐν πνεύματι ἁγίῳ

---

44. Burton, *Galatians*, 223. See C. K. Barrett, *Epistle to the Romans*, HNTC, 164. Cf. Ridderbos, *Galatians*, 157.

45. This is an adaptation of the suggestion given by A. J. Mason, *The Relation of Confirmation to Baptism* (London: Longmans, Green & Co., 1891) 44–46.

46. I have added ἐν to Mark 1:8 even though it is excluded from Nestle's text. This is a judgment based on the quality of the respective manuscripts. So also Bruce Metzger, *A Textual Commentary on the Greek New Testament* (New York: United Bible Societies, 1971), 74.

Luke 3:16, Jesus βαπτίσει ἐν πνεύματι ἁγίῳ καὶ πυρί

John 1:33, Jesus βαπτίζων ἐν πνεύματι ἁγίῳ

Acts 1:5, You ἐν πνεύματι βαπτισθήσεσθε ἁγίῳ

Acts 11:16, You βαπτισθήσεσθε ἐν πνεύματι ἁγίῳ

1 Cor 12:13a, All ἐν ἑνὶ πνεύματι ἐβαπτίσθημεν εἰς one body

As noted in the Introduction, Protestants evaluating Pentecostal pneumatology most often view 1 Corinthians 12:13a as the first and last word on the issue of Spirit baptism. An example is John R. W. Stott who encountered Pentecostal-Charismatic pneumatology first hand in the person of Michael Harper, one time curate at All Souls Church while Stott was rector. Stott's published reaction became a textbook for non-dispensational Evangelicals. The key to Stott's dependence on 1 Corinthians 12:13a is his assertion that the seven passages in question are interchangeable.[47]

There is due cause to challenge Stott's decision: 1. Stott insists that a phrase which appears in 'precisely the same' form should be considered a priori to have the same meaning each time.[48] However, the phrases are not identical. (a) The first six references always have the complete πνεύματι ἁγίῳ while Paul has simply ἑνὶ πνεύματι. (b) The use of καὶ πυρί which appears in Matthew 3:11 and Luke 3:16 would seem appropriate with any of the first six references, but not the seventh. (c) Jesus is the obvious activator in the first four passages and the implied activator in the next two, but the Pauline passage seems to place the Holy Spirit as the agent.

2. It is certainly laudable to expect unanimity among New Testament writers. A hermeneutical principle integral to this study is the analogia fidei. However, such an approach is not understood to override the semantic idiosyncrasies of any given writer. Paul is known to use a variety of words with varying meaning, as may be seen from the four ways that he uses the word σάρξ. Therefore, the seventh reference cannot be assumed to have the same meaning as the preceding six; because, unlike the others, it alone is Pauline and epistolary.

---

47. Stott, *Baptism and Fullness* (1964), 23. Cf. Packer, *Spirit*, 203; Morris A. Inch, *Saga of the Spirit* (Grand Rapids: Baker, 1985), 87.

48. Ibid. Rea, *Holy Spirit*, 146, turns this around on Mr. Stott. While Stott reads church initiation back into the first six passages, Rea puts the Pentecostal doctrine of Spirit baptism into the Pauline passage. Cf. Williams, *Holy Spirit*, 18–20.

3. The determining factor for a correct conclusion is the evaluation of the respective contexts. The first six passages have implicit, if not explicit, reference to the day of Pentecost. The Pauline passage, on the other hand, is found in a discussion of the body of Christ, and the use of εἰς with 1 Corinthians 12:13a rather clearly indicates that the Pauline reference is to one's entry in to the body of Christ.[49]

4. All do not feel the force of Stott's argument that the Pauline usage is determinative for present day theology because the writing is didactic.[50] This issue will be given a more extensive treatment later, but suffice it to say that the Lucan Gospel and "historical" account, for example, are hardly biographical reporting in the modern sense of the word. Anyway, it is hardly a fair judgment to discard any passage that is "only" descriptive. Further, it is true that the majority of attempts to harmonize Paul and Luke find Luke getting "... painted with Paul's brush."[51] It seems that the person with the greatest problem is one who believes that Paul was familiar with the events recorded in the Gospels and Acts. Would Paul deliberately give a different meaning to a known phrase? Later argument will suggest that it is likely the phrase 'baptism in Spirit' was not a universal expression used by the early Church to refer to one's endowment with charismatic phenomena. Paul's use of a similar phrase could be purely coincidental. It is clear that the modern day argument over Pentecostal pneumatology has focused undue attention on the similarities between the seven passages in question. If a uniform usage of the phrase "baptism in the Spirit" was not known in the early church, Paul would be little encumbered in this matter.

---

49. See Fee, *God's Empowering Presence*, 178; Hummel, *Fire*, 180-182; Ervin, *Not Drunken*, 46; Hoekema, *Spirit Baptism*, 25; Schep, *Baptism in the Spirit*, 16f.; A. Oepke, "ἅπτω," *TDNT* 1:539. Cf. Clark Pinnock, "The New Pentecostalism: Reflections of an Evangelical Observer," *Perspectives on the New Pentecostalism*, Spittler, 186. No attention can be given to whether entry into the body of Christ is effected by water baptism or simply by an act of the Spirit. Cf. Dunn, *Baptism in the Holy Spirit*, 129ff.

50. Stott, *Baptism and Fullness*, 15; Hoekema, *Spirit Baptism*, 23f.; Culpepper, *Charismatic Movement*, 61.

51. Clark Pinnock, *HIS*, (June, 1976): 21. Ervin, *Not Drunken*, 47, calls this a 'faulty methodology.' See Roger Stronstad, *Spirit, Scripture & Theology* (Baguio City, Philippines: Asia Pacific Theological Seminary Press, 1995), 96; Archer, "Pentecostal Hermeneutics," 70, 73. For an example, see Max Turner, *Power from on High: The Spirit in Israel's Restoration and Witness in Luke-Acts* (Sheffield: Sheffield Academic Press, 1996), 445.

5. The translation of RSV, NIV, and KJV of "with" in the first six occurrences and "by" in the last seems justified on both exegetical and theological grounds. This serves to recognize an important element in determining the nature of the theology which Paul has set forth. It can be remembered that one letter (Athanasius, homoousios; Arians, homoiousios) was the focal point of serious debate in the Arian controversy. To designate Paul's use of the preposition as instrumental rather than locative is to stand equally within the bounds of Pauline grammar, especially in the immediate context where Paul has been using ἐν πνεύματι to note the distribution of spiritual gifts by the Spirit.[52]

If 1 Corinthians 12:13a does not refer to the charismatic work of the Spirit, what can be said of 1 Corinthians 12:13b? Is it simply the same thought repeated or is something else in view? A great deal can be gained by turning to Galatians 3:27 rather than the six non-Pauline verses listed above.[53]

1 Corinthians 12:13a   ἐν ἑνὶ πνεύματι ... εἰς ἓν σῶμα ἐβαπτίσθημεν

Galatians 3:27a   εἰς Χριστὸν ἐβαπτίσθητε

1 Corinthians 12:13b   ἓν πνεῦμα ἐποτίσθημεν

Galatians 3:27b   Χριστὸν ἐνεδύσασθε

It was suggested earlier that much the same point is in view when Paul refers to being "in Christ" and to being in the "body of Christ." Therefore, one could say that the first part of both verses in question seems to be headed in the same direction. Such suspicions are confirmed when it is noted that the latter part of these two verses seems to have reference to the charismatic work of the Spirit. The word ἐνεδύσασθε is readily identifiable with the charismatic Spirit. This is the same word used to describe

---

52. See Ervin, *Conversion-Initiation*, 99; Schep, *Baptism in the Spirit*, 18. Cf. Green, *Holy Spirit*, 140; Rodman Williams, *Renewal Theology* 2:199. Contra: Dunn, *Baptism in the Holy Spirit*, 128; Culpepper, *Charismatic Movement*, 61; Merrill F. Unger, *The Baptism and Gifts of the Holy Spirit* (Chicago: Moody Press, 1974), 100.

53. Others suggest a parallel with Galatians 3:27 but none shared my conclusion until Holman came close in his "Reception of the Holy Spirit," 16–20. See C. K. Barrett, *A Commentary on the First Epistles to the Corinthians* (New York: Harper & Row, 1968), 288. Robertson and Plummer, *1 Corinthians, ICC*, 272, admit one interpretation to be that 13a may refer to water baptism, yet they consider 13a=13b and they believe their case is strengthened by Galatians 3:26f. Cf. E. Earle Ellis, *Pauline Theology*, (Grand Rapids: Eerdmans, 1989), 31; Ervin, *Conversion-Initiation*, 100–102.

the Spirit coming upon Gideon (Judg. 6:34) and the same word which is found in Luke 24:29. As for ἐποτίσθημεν, it leads one to think of John 4:14, 7:37–39. The Johannine usage of this word in these verses is with reference to the charismatic work of the Spirit.[54] All of these data lend support to the conviction that not only is 1 Corinthians 12:13a not the death blow to the Pentecostal position; but, in fact, 1 Corinthians 12:13b seems to support the essence of the pneumatological issue. Interestingly, Bruner speaks in a manner that appears to be supportive of this possibility: "... by the graphic picture of 'drinking in' Paul wishes to emphasize that Christians are not only baptized *by* the Spirit (v. 13a), but they are at the same time filled with him."[55] Further, the repeated use of πάντες is indicative of the universality of such an experience for the audience which Paul addressed.

2 Corinthians 1:21

But it is God who establishes (βεβαιῶν) us with you in Christ (Χριστὸν) and has commissioned (χρίσας) us.

---

54. See Chapter IV. Several commentators point to John 7:37–39 as an appropriate parallel, but none share my conclusion. See F. F. Bruce, *1 and 2 Corinthians* (Grand Rapids: Eerdmans, 1971), 121; Fred Fischer, *Commentary on First and Second Corinthians* (Waco: Word, 1975), 210; William F. Orr and J. A. Walther, *1 Corinthians: A New Translation* (New York: Doubleday, 1976), 884; C. Hodge, *Commentary on the First Epistle to the Corinthians*, (Grand Rapids: Eerdmans, [1972]), 255. The issue of importance to most commentators is whether 13b has reference to the Eucharist. Because it is not related to the issue at hand, it will not be dealt with, but those interested in the subject should consult the following works. Yes: L. Goppelt, "πίνω," *TDNT* 6:160; Hans Conzelmann, *A Commentary on the First Epistle to the Corinthians* (Philadelphia: Fortress Press, 1975), 212; R. P. Martin, *1 Corinthians–Galatians* (Grand Rapids: Eerdmans, 1968), 33. This affirmation was made famous by Augustine, Luther and Calvin. No: Jean Héring, *The First Epistle of Saint Paul to the Corinthians* (London: Epworth Press, 1962), 130; Barrett, *1 Corinthians*, 289; Beasley-Murray, *Baptism*, 170; Findlay, *1 Corinthians*, 890; Fischer, *Commentary on First and Second Corinthians*, 201; John Ruef, *Paul's First Letter to Corinth* (Penguin Books, 1971), 132; Robertson and Plummer, *1 Corinthians*, 272; Bruner, *Theology of the Holy Spirit*, 294; Jewett, "Holy Spirit," 27; Ladd, *Theology of the New Testament*, 54.

55. Bruner, *Theology of the Holy Spirit*, 294. See J. Ysebaert, *Greek Baptismal Terminology* (Nijmegen: Dekker & Vandeveght, 1962), 61; Ervin, *Not Drunken*, 46f.; Unger, *Holy Spirit*, 101; Holman, "Reception of the Holy Spirit," 19f. Contra Ralph P. Martin, *The Spirit and the Congregation* (Grand Rapids: Eerdmans, 1984), 24. Fee, *God's Empowering Presence*, 180f., wrongly casts my views as congenial to those Pentecostals who speak of a "second experience."

There is obviously a word play with Χριστὸν and χρίσας. In light of the earlier analysis of the Hebrew canon, it would seem also that the imagery implies a wealthy experience of those who are the object of the anointing. Remember that Saul and David were, in turn, referred to as an "anointed one" (משיה) (see 1 Sam 2:10, 12:3, 5, 16:6, 26:9, 11, 23; 2 Sam 1:14, 16, 23:1; Ps 2:2, 28:2). Leviticus 4:3, 5, 16 tells of the anointing of priests. Also, Elijah was told to "anoint" Elisha to take his place as a prophet (1 Kgs 19:16).[56] Isaiah (11:2, et. al.) told of a coming deliverer who would be anointed by the rûaḥ *yahweh*. Luke identifies this experience with the special coming of the Spirit upon Jesus at the river Jordan (see Lk 4:18ff., 4:1). In a sermon by Peter we are told

> How God anointed (ἔχρισεν) Jesus of Nazareth with the Holy Spirit (πνεύματι ἁγίῳ) and with power (δυνάμει); how he went about doing good and healing all that were oppressed by the devil, for God was with him (Acts 10:38). (See Acts 4:27, Lk 24:19)

Again the Hebrew canon presents a connection as Israelites are described as "anointed ones" (χριστῶν, Ps 105:15 LXX). In a similar way, the title "Christian" intimates that one shares the empowering of the Spirit which was known by Christ. An evident conclusion, then, is that the "anointing" is a continuation of that imagery, and all ultimately have reference to the charismatic Spirit.[57] It is interesting to note a similar line of thought expressed by a seventh century Spanish bishop, Isidore of Seville:

> The anointing Chrism was first composed and also made by Moses in the Exodus, at the command of the Lord, and with it Aaron and

---

56. Roland DeVaux, *Ancient Israel* (New York: MacGraw-Hill, 1965), 1:104; G. W. H. Lampe, *Seal of the Spirit* (London: SPCK, 1967), 30; William G. MacDonald, "Problems of Pneumatology in Christology," unpublished Th.D. dissertation (Louisville: Southern Baptist Theological Seminary, 1970), 132, 141; D. Müller, "χρίω," *NIDNTT* 1:121f.

57. See Héring, *The First Epistle of St. Paul to the Corinthians*, 12; Fee, *God's Empowering Presence*, 291f.; Lampe, *Seal*, 30; Mason, *Confirmation*, 51; Ervin, *Conversion-Initiation*, 103; Schep, *Baptism in the Spirit*, 49; Ralph Riggs, *The Spirit Himself* (Springfield: Gospel Publishing House, 1949), 71f.; Smail, *Reflected Glory*, 77; Williams, *Holy Spirit*, 44n6; Holman, "Reception of the Holy Spirit," 21f.; Andrew Murray, *The Spirit of Christ* (Fort Washington: Christian Literature Crusade, 1963), 128. Cf. Philip Hughes, *Second Corinthians*, NIC, 39; Fischer, *Commentary on First and Second Corinthians*, 294; C. K. Barrett, *Second Epistle to the Corinthians*, *IB* 10:290. Contra those who limit the reference to a special appointment of Silas, Timothy and Paul: A. Plummer, *Second Corinthians*, ICC, 40; David J. A. Clines, *Second Corinthians, A New Testament Commentary*, 420.

his sons were first anointed for a testimony of priesthood and holiness. Afterwards kings also were consecrated with the same oil; from which they were called "Anointed"; and at that time only kings and priests received the mystical unction, by which the Christ was foreshadowed; whose name itself is derived from the chrism. But ever since our Lord, the true King and eternal Priest, was anointed by God the Father with the mystical heavenly ointment, not only pontiffs and kings, but all the Church is consecrated with the anointing Chrism, inasmuch as each person is a member of the eternal King and Priest. Therefore, because we are a priestly and royal race, after the laver we are anointed, in order to bear the name of Christ. But that after Baptism the Holy Ghost is given by means of the bishops together with the laying on of Hands, we remember that the Apostles did so in the Acts of the Apostles.[58]

Romans 15:18f.

I will not venture to speak of anything except what Christ has accomplished (κατειργάσατο) through me in leading the Gentiles to obey God by what I had said and done (ἔργῳ)—by the power (δυνάμει) of signs (σημείων) and miracles (τεράτων) through the power (δυνάμει) of the Spirit (πνεύματος). (NIV)

The NIV has been used because it, unlike the RSV, NEB, JB, and others, reflects clearly the textual exclusion of ἅγιος.[59]

Earlier, it was argued that there is a conjoining of the work of the Spirit and Christ in the life of the believer. That same thought appears here with the explanation that external manifestations, σημείων and τεράτων, are included among the works (ἔργῳ) produced. Tappeiner says of this verse: "In the Pauline understanding we find the now familiar motif of the Spirit as the source of signs and wonders in mission activity as the source of signs and wonders in mission activity as exhibited in the Luke-Acts materials."[60] The inclusion of words like δυνάμει and which are used in 1 Thessalonians 1:5, 1 Corinthians 2:4 and like

---

58. Isidore quoted in Mason, *Confirmation*, 209f. Note also Ildefonsis quoted in Mason, 211. Later chapters here will bring out many other similar sayings.

59. Nestle, *Graece*, 422; Metzger, *Greek*, 537.

60. Tappeiner, "Holy Spirit," 40. See Fee, *God's Empowering Presence*, 630f.; Dobbin, "Holy Spirit," 14; Ellis, "Christ and Spirit," 270.

passages, strengthens the view that the thought is the charismatic work of the (Christocentric) Spirit (cf. Romans 15:13).

Ephesians 1:13

> In him you also, who have heard the word of truth, the gospel of our salvation and have believed (πιστεύσαντες) in him, were sealed (ἐσφραγίσθητε) with the promised (ἐπαγγελίας) Holy Spirit (τῷ πνεύματι τῷ ἁγίῳ).

The inclusion of πιστεύσαντες presents us with a word, however uncertain, about the temporal relationship of the reception of the charismatic Spirit to one's commitment to Christian belief. Classical Pentecostals and proponents of confirmation have needed only to argue that the aorist participle takes its usual force as an antecedent to the action of the main verb to solidify their position.[61] Those attempting to avoid any idea of temporal separation essentially agree with Dunn, who admits that the antecedent action is the usual force of the aorist participle, but argues that the determining factor is the immediate context.[62] After looking at the context, it would appear that what Dunn really means is his theology of 'conversion-initiation.' It seems preferable to take the aorist participle in the usual sense of being antecedent to the action of the main verb. However, this is not to admit the standard separation which confirmation supporters make between being baptized as an infant and then confirmed at a later age, or the similar argument of some Pentecostals that one's Spirit baptism will quite often occur only after some years of seeking. While it does seem that the thrust of Ephesians 1:13 and Galatians 4:6 is to emphasize that the charismatic work of the Spirit is a distinct work of the Holy Spirit, one cannot claim with any certainty that the same data indicate that this charismatic work is begun after the initial salvation experience.

The determination of the meaning of ἐσφραγίσθητε is a different matter. Some commentators insist that the reference is to water bap-

---

61. For a good summary of the confirmation argument see S. S. Smalley, "Seal," *NBD*, 1156. For the Classical Pentecostal position, shared by some Charismatics, see Horton, *Holy Spirit*, 239; Rea, *Holy Spirit*, 183.

62. Dunn, *Baptism in the Holy Spirit*, 159. Cf. F. F. Bruce, *Commentary on the Epistle to the Ephesians* (Old Tappan: Fleming H. Revell Co., 1961), 36. As noted earlier, Ephesians 1:13 is a passage for which Dunn contends that Pentecostal exegesis is based upon a lack of knowledge of the Greek text.

tism.⁶³ Others say that the reference is to the gift of the Holy Spirit.⁶⁴ The same word is used in connection with 2 Corinthians 1:21f which has been earlier analyzed. David J. A. Clines says that σφραγισάμενος in 2 Corinthians 1:22 may mean "endued with power from heaven."⁶⁵ Others see both 2 Corinthians 1:22 and Ephesians 1:13 as using the word "seal" in the commercial sense of a guarantee.⁶⁶ This judgment is usually based, in part at least, on an alleged equation of water baptism and the concept of sealing by the Fathers. This is true in a general sense, but it must be considerably modified. A later investigation here includes materials which demonstrate that the concept of sealing was most often (but not always) associated with the anointing of oil and/or laying on of hands. Also, some "Enthusiastics" plus "Reformed Sealers" use "seal" as related to "baptism of the Holy Spirit."⁶⁷ Either way, a special bestowal of the Spirit is usually in view. Some Fathers even specified it as invoking the "Sevenfold Spirit." The maxim that sealing means ownership has often been based on passages that speak of water baptism in a general way. This is easily understood, since anointing and/or episcopal consignation were usually considered part of the one baptismal rite. As A. J. Mason says: "Baptism as a whole may be the seal, but usually, at least, it is in virtue of its concluding ceremony [anointing/imposition of hands] that it bears that name."⁶⁸ Thus 2 Corinthians 1:21 shows that the charismatic endowing—anointing- of the Spirit can be called a sealing of the Holy Spirit, just as the Fathers spoke of a sealing of the Spirit which consisted of a bestowal of the charismatic

63. Markus Barth, *Ephesians*, AB (Garden City: Doubleday, 1974), 95; E. F. Scott, *Epistle to the Ephesians*, MNTC, 148; R. W. Beare, *Epistle to the Ephesians*, 1B 10:623.

64. For example Lampe, *Seal*, 6f.

65. Clines, *2 Corinthians*, 420. See Jean Héring, *Commentary on the Second Epistle of St. Paul to the Corinthians* (London: Epworthy, 1967), 12; J. Oliver Buswell, *A Systematic Theology of the Christian Religion*, (Grand Rapids: Zondervan, 1962), 213, 211. The following argue that the reference is to Spirit baptism: Horton, *Holy Spirit*, 283; Rea, *Holy Spirit*, 12. Cf. Hoekema, *Spirit Baptism*, 87.

66. Hughes, *Second Corinthians*, 43f.; G. Fitzger, "σφραγιζῶ," *TDNT* 7:949f.; Fischer, *Commentary on First and Second Corinthians*, 294; E. K. Simpson, *Epistle to the Ephesians*, NIC, 36; Hendriksen, *Ephesians*, 91.

67. Herbert Mühlen, *A Charismatic Theology* (New York: Paulist Press, 1978), 140, brings us up to date noting that in 1971 "Pope Paul VI adapted the formula of administration of confirmation to that of the Orthodox Church. It now runs, 'Be sealed with the gift of the Holy Spirit.'" Mühlen adds, "... this formula is meant to 'recall' more clearly 'the outpouring of the Spirit which took place on the day of Pentecost.'"

68. Mason, *Confirmation*, 256. See later here the 'enthusiasts' and 'Reformed Sealers.'

Spirit. Notice also that Ephesians 1:13 qualifies ἐσφραγίσθητε with τῷ πνεύματι, a possible indicator of the charismatic Spirit (cf. Gal 3:14).[69]

Ephesians 5:18

> And do not get drunk with wine, for that is debauchery; but be filled (πληροῦσθε) with (ἐν) the Spirit (πνεύματι).

The overwhelming consensus among commentators is that this passage is paralleled in the Lucan writings. Many point straight away to the Pentecostal event itself.[70] While employing terms somewhat differently, it would appear that the two major scholarly works which deny some traditional Pentecostal pneumatologies, that is those by Dunn and Bruner, include comments about this passage that are supportive of the findings here. Bruner says:

> The subsequent or later fillings of Christians with the Holy Spirit are due *not* to the fact ... that Christians by their incorporation into Christ into Christ did not receive spiritual fullness (cf. Gal 3:5 with 3:2 and Acts 4:29-31 with Acts 2); Christians can be filled with the Holy Spirit now precisely because when they were incorporated into Christ they were given every spiritual blessing, including the privilege of the continual filling of the Spirit as at the beginning (cf. e.g., Eph 1:3 and 5:18).[71]

Dunn commenting on Ephesians 5:18 says:

> For this is the same distinction as appears in Acts: repeated experiences of being filled (i.e., taken over or controlled) by the Spirit

---

69. Cf. Williams, *Pentecostal Reality*, 23; Holman, "Reception of the Holy Spirit," 25; Horton, *Holy Spirit*, 239; Rea, *Holy Spirit*, 183; Mason, *Confirmation*, 51; Ervin, *Conversion-Initiation*, 123f.; Hunter, *Paul*, 93. Contra S. D. F. Salmond, *The Epistle to the Ephesians*, EGT (Grand Rapids: Eerdmans, 1956), 268.

70. Simpson, *Ephesians*, 129; Lampe, "Holy Spirit," 638; G. E. Harpur, *Ephesians*, A New Testament Commentary (Grand Rapids: Zondervan, 1969), 463; C. C. Ryrie, *The Holy Spirit* (Chicago: Moody Press, 1965), 93; Hendriksen, *Ephesians*, 239; Chafer, *Spiritual*, 44; J. Elder Cumming, *Through the Eternal Spirit* (New York: Fleming H. Revell, 1896), 231ff.; Ervin, *Not Drunken*, 76; George Jeffreys, *Pentecostal Rays* (London: Henry E. Walker, 1954), 234; Montague, *Spirit*, 226; Harold Sala, "An Investigation of the Baptizing and Filling Work of the Spirit in the New Testament Related to the Pentecostal Doctrine of 'Initial Evidence,'" unpublished Th.D. dissertation (Greenville: Bob Jones University, June, 1966), 62.

71. Bruner, *Theology of the Holy Spirit*, 241. See also pages 313 and 239.

on the part of an individual or individuals who had already been once-and-for-all baptized in the Spirit. Of a special once-and-for-all *second* giving of or filling with the Spirit Paul knows nothing.⁷²

It would seem difficult to interpret this passage in a way other than to acknowledge some congruency with Lucan theology. In the best known passages of Luke-Acts which deal with this phenomena, the word πλή- θω (from πίμπλημι) is used (see Lk 1:41, 67, Acts 2:4, 4:31, 9:17, 13:9). The word used in Ephesians 5:18 is πληρόω. Yet there can be little doubt that only a different emphasis is in view for Luke nearly uses these two words interchangeably (Lk 13:9f.), and in fact uses πληρόω in key passages (Lk 4:1, Acts 6:8, 13:52) in the same way passages call for recitation: "And Stephen, full (πλήρης) of grace (χάριτος) and power (δυνάμεως) did great wonders (τέρατα) and signs (σημεῖα) among the people" (Acts 6:8); "And the disciples were filled (επληροῦντο) with joy and with the Holy Spirit (πνεύματος ἁγίου)" (Acts 13:52). All the terms used in connection with πλήρης in Acts 6:8, namely χάριτος, δυνάμεως, τέρατα, σημεῖα, have been designated in this investigation as evidencing the charismatic work of the Spirit and as reinforced in Ephesians 5:18 by the

---

72. Dunn, *Baptism in the Holy Spirit*, 171. Emphasis his. See Dunn, "πνεῦμα," *NIDNTT* 3:701ff. Dunn, "Spirit-Baptism and Pentecostalism," 406, further says:

> Of course, the New Testament also shows that there were various authentic post-conversion experiences of the Spirit—of assurance, of empowering, of inspiration, of exultation, etc.—but if we desire a single name to describe them all we must speak of being 'filled' with the Spirit. Pentecostals may reply that it is simply a matter of names ad titles, but they should not forget that in the New Testament these titles express an understanding of the Spirit in his work which does not square with the distinctive Pentecostal pneumatology. R. A. Torrey and Andrew Murray were more logical on this point than present Pentecostals. Having equated baptism in the Spirit with empowering they felt able to speak of repeated baptisms. Yet for Pentecostals there is only one baptism. Those who have been baptized in the Spirit and have fallen back into the spiritual doldrums need a fresh *filling*. The baptism is only the first filling. But this sort of theological juggling with terms cannot be accepted, for the New Testament confines talk of Spirit-baptism to the experience of the Spirit at conversion-initiation, and speaks of *all* later experiences of empowering as being filled with the Spirit. The powerless non-Pentecostal Christian has a need no different from that of the powerless Pentecostal Christian. (Emphasis his.)

See also: Hoekema, *Spirit Baptism*, 81; Ewert, *Holy Spirit*, 232ff.; Green, *Holy Spirit*, 149, 152; Stott, *Baptism and Fullness*, 50 et passim; Wright, "Pneuma in the Pauline Corpus," 342; O. J. Smith, *The Spirit-Filled Life* (New York: Christian Alliance Publishing Co., 1926), 21.

qualification of ἐν πνεύματι.⁷³ Additionally the linear force of (imperfect passive) ἐπληροῦντο (Acts 13:52) fits in well with other findings, as well as with Ephesians 5:18, for πληροῦσθε is a present passive imperative. The antithesis of drunkenness, which reminiscent of the charges given on the day of Pentecost (Acts 2:13, 15), and fullness leads to the judgment with qualifications that the antithesis is between two levels of existence. The qualification is that repeated experiences of the charismatic Spirit constitute fullness of the Spirit. One does not stay drunk all the time, but rather repeatedly gets drunk thus warranting the categorizing as drunkenness.⁷⁴ Finally, not to be overlooked is that πληροῦσθε is passive. Therefore, it would appear that one who experiences the charismatic Spirit must reckon with the sovereignty of God.⁷⁵

2 Timothy 1:6f.

> Hence I remind you to rekindle (ἀναζωπυρεῖν) the gift (χάρισμα) of God that is within you through the laying on of my hands; for God did not give us (ἡμῖν) a spirit (πνεῦμα) of timidity but a spirit of power (δυνάμεως) and love (ἀγάπης) and self-control (σωφρονισμοῦ).

There is every good reason to understand this passage as being the basis of Timothy's charge to ministry, reminiscent of Acts 13:2, that was to be known as ordination in ecclesiastical history.⁷⁶ At the same time this is presented as a charismatic work of the Spirit.

---

73. James B. Shelton "'Filled with the Holy Spirit' and 'Full of the Holy Spirit': Lucan Redactional Phrases," *Faces of Renewal*, ed. by Paul Elbert (Peabody: Hendrickson, 1988), 80–107. The arguments for pneuma as the human spirit carry little conviction. Cf. J. A. Robinson, *St. Paul's Epistle to the Ephesians* (London: MacMillan & Co. Ltd., 1903), 203; Salmond, *Ephesians*, 362; Beare, *Ephesians*, 714. Incidentally, I agree with Salmond, 363, that the determination of the instrumentality or objectivity of pneuma is a "needless refinement."

74. See Larry Hurtado, "On Being Filled with the Spirit," *Paraclete* 4:1, 32; Horton, *Holy Spirit*, 244. Cf. Salmond, *Ephesians*, 363; Beare, *Ephesians*, 714; T. L. Abott, *Epistle to the Ephesians*, ICC, 161. Contra Ervin, *Not Drunken*, 74ff., who argues that although this interpretation is grammatically possible, it does violence to the context.

75. Cumming, *Eternal Spirit*, 235; Rea, *Holy Spirit*, 193. Abott, *Ephesians*, 161, argues that it is really middle since humans co-operate.

76. 151 See Sullivan, *Charisms*, 102; C. K. Barrett, The *Pastoral Epistles* (Oxford: Clarendon Press, 1983), 93; J. N. D. Kelly, *The Pastoral Epistles*, Black's NT Commentary (London: Adam & Charles Black, 1963), 159; Walter Lock, *The Pastoral Epistles*, ICC, 85; E.

The most obvious indicator of the charismatic dimension is the use of the word χάρισμα. Further we recall the association of the charismatic Spirit with the laying on of hands in Acts 19:6, 8:17. Ἀναζωπυρεῖν is the exhortation given to Timothy with regard to his χάρισμα. The use of "fire" imagery is met in other references to the charismatic work of the spirit (1 Thess 5:19, Matt 3:11, Acts 2:3, Rom 12:11). It is of interest to note that the force of the verb probably indicates that while there is an expected longevity to this experience, it is not an automatic result. George T. Montague rightly comments:

> We are probably justified in extending the principle given here to all the gifts of the Spirit and of concluding that they are capable of waning or waxing in fervor, and that one who is gifted has the responsibility of keeping the gift alive, using it making it fruitful (compare the talents, Matt 25:14–30; Luke 19:12–27). It also means that periodically a gift that has remained largely latent may be re-awakened, as embers may be fanned to flame.[77]

There is a further matter regarding the charismatic work of the Spirit that this passage and the similar one in 1 Timothy 4:14 brings to our attention. The earlier analysis of *rûah* in the Hebrew canon suggested a certain "institutionalizing" of the Spirit's work. In the main it would appear that a similar process has been observed by the writer of the Pastorals. The atmosphere which pervades the Pastorals is reflected in the use of the charismata enumerated in Ephesians 4:11. For one thing, it must be remembered that the Pastorals address a different set of problems. Whereas the earliest epistles dealt with the problem of persecution, the current crisis would appear to be false teaching, perhaps incipient Gnosticism. Nor should it be forgotten that the earliest charismata lists gave recognition to "office" gifts.

F. Scott, *Pastoral Epistles*, MNTC, 91; William Hendriksen, *Exposition of Pastoral Epistles* (Grand Rapids: Baker, 1957), 229. Lindsay Dewar, *The Holy Spirit and Modern Thought* (New York: Harper & Brothers, 1959), 61, argues that this is Timothy's confirmation.

77. Montague, *Spirit*, 235. Barrett, *Pastorals*, 93, says:

> It is implied that the gift is not one that works simply *ex opere operato*; it is received, as it were, potentially, and needs to be put into operation by the faithful and believing service of him to whom it is entrusted.

Cf. Simpson, *Holy Spirit*, 2:91; Fred D. Gealey, *Second Timothy*, IB 11:463; Scott, *Pastoral Epistles*, 125f.; Lock, *Pastoral Epistles*, 85; Fee, *God's Empowering Presence*, 787.

The difference, then, is not a change of theology but a legitimate exercise of particular gifts in different situations. The situation of the Pastorals exhibits a decided preference for the "stabilizing" influence of proper church administration. Although 1 Timothy 4:14 recalls the prophecy which was involved in the bestowal of a charism, the preference of the author is for the past teaching of the church. Dunn argues that the evolution is so marked that we are actually seeing early Catholicism.[78] This may be true in a sense. In the third century, the isolation of "supernatural gifts" from those considered part of the ordinary, permanent endowment of the Church led to the demise of the operation of the spectacular gifts of the Spirit. It would not seem that any of the gifts are to be eliminated prior to the return of our Lord, and hence "The greatest and most important gift is always that which is necessary at that time."[79] The author of the Pastorals does not appear to contradict this.

Titus 3:5f.

He saved (ἔσωσεν) us, not because of deeds done by us in righteousness, but in virtue of his own mercy, by (διὰ) the washing (λουτροῦ) of regeneration (παλιγγενεσίας) and renewal (ἀνακαινώσεως) in the Holy Spirit (πνεύματος ἁγίου) which he poured out (ἐξέχεεν).

There are perhaps two arguments for believing that this passage refers to the Classical Pentecostal doctrine of Spirit baptism: (1) the use of ἐξέχεεν reflects the day of Pentecost as it is the same word used about the Spirit in Joel 2:28 (LXX) and Acts 2:17f., 33, 10:45 [80]; (2) Dunn shows how the passage can be schematized in a manner which is conducive to the Classical Pentecostal argument.

---

78. 153 Dunn, *Jesus and the Spirit*, 349. Cf. Montague, *Spirit*, 236; G. Walter, "Holy Spirit," *NBD*, 5533; Dunn, *Baptism in the Holy Spirit*, 167.

79. 154 Arnold Bittlinger quoted in Hollenweger, *Pentecostals*, 246.

80. 155 This would hold true regardless of how individualized the application of the imagery might be. Cf. Barrett, *Pastorals*, 147; Donald Guthrie, *The Pastoral Epistles*, NCB (Greenwood: Attic Press, Inc., 1969), 206; Lock, *Pastorals*, 156; Kelly, *Pastorals*, 157; William Hendricksen, *Exposition of Thessalonians, the Pastorals and Hebrews*, 391; F. D. Gealy, "2 Timothy," *IB* (New York: Abingdon Press, 1955), 546; Charles L. Holman, "Titus 3:5-6: A Window on Worldwide Pentecost," *Journal of Pentecostal Theology* 8 (1996): 53–62.

Conversion	Baptism in the Spirit
he saved us through the washing of regeneration	and renewal of the Spirit which he poured out upon us richly through Jesus Christ our Savior in order
that having been justified	we might become heirs in hope of eternal life.[81]

Yet neither of these arguments is convincing, and I note here my judgment submitted elsewhere[82] that this passage refers to the purifying not the empowering work of the Spirit. The mixture of Pentecostal language with the purifying work of the Spirit is seen also in Luke himself. At the Jerusalem Council, Peter said of the group gathered in Cornelius' house that "God who knows the heart bore witness to them, giving them the Holy Spirit just as he did to us; and he made no distinction between us and them but cleansed their hearts by faith" (Acts 15:18f.).

CONCLUSIONS

The foregoing investigation has demonstrated the pervasiveness of charismatic theology in the Pauline literature. All the epistles from the Pauline corpus have been examined with the exception of 2 Thessalonians, Philippians, Philemon, Colossians (cf. 1:8f., 2:10) and 1 Timothy. Lack of space accounts for the omission of examining pertinent passages—Philippians 4:13; 1 Corinthians 2:4; 2 Corinthians 12:9; Romans 5:5; Romans 12:11; Ephesians 1:19; Ephesians 3:16, 19.

The major problem in attempting a formulation of this part of Pauline pneumatology is that the material would appear to defy standardization. Any doctrinal investigation made in the Pauline writings is confronted by the lack of uniform terminology. None of the writings is structured like

---

81. Dunn, *Baptism in the Holy Spirit*, 166. Of course he does not consider this to be a viable option. Barrett, *Pastorals*, 142, points out that this passage has been used as support for the doctrine of confirmation. Cf. Lock, *Pastorals*, 155; Holman, "Reception of the Holy Spirit," 29f.; Ervin, *Conversion-Initiation*, 130.

82. Harold D. Hunter, *Spirit Baptism* (1983), 255f. Also Fee, *God's Empowering Presence*, 781f.

European dogmatic works (e.g., Brunner, Barth, Berkouwer, Thielicke). There would appear to be no Pauline passages which outline neatly the mutual relationship between the elements of the dogmatician's ordo salutis. A classic example of this difficulty is how the issue of election affects the manner in which one perceives the relation of regeneration to calling. The complexity of this problem is exhibited in the various solutions. This is not an isolated case, and sanctification as well as the matter of the ontological relation of the risen Christ to the Spirit. Yet truths which appear to be fundamental and this may likely explain the working relation however minimal between groups of varying sectarian interests.

With the reality of these Pauline idiosyncrasies in mind, the following suggestions are made:

1. It seems that Paul identifies a distinct work of the Spirit which is charismatic in nature.

2. Can this charismatic work of the Spirit be separated in time from the initial salvation event? It appears that while Paul would conceive of the norm as a unified experience, he would also allow the possibility of a temporal separation (Gal 4:6; Eph 1:13). However, a divided experience must have been quite a rarity, for Paul could speak freely about the universality of the reception of the charismatic Spirit (1 Cor 12:13b).[83]

3. There is a linear dimension to the charismatic work of the Spirit as it is both "repeated" and "continuous" (Eph 1:19, 5:18; Phil 4:13), but not automatic (2 Tim 1:5f.).

4. Not to be forgotten are implications of the sovereignty of God (Eph 5:18, 3:19).

5. The charismatic Spirit is received by faith and is not contingent upon a list of works (Gal 3:2, 5).

6. The charismatic works of the Spirit make up the broadest spectrum imaginable. Not only to be included are the familiar "spectacular gifts" (1 Cor 12:8ff.), but also the ability to bear witness

---

83. J. Rodman Williams argues (*Pentecostal Reality*, 23) that Paul's circumstances are the basis for his particular explanation. For some thoughts which parallel my original proposal, see the following: Bultmann, *Theology* 1:162, 158f.; H. Berkhof, *Holy Spirit*, 87, 89; Holman, "Reception of the Holy Spirit," 31f.; Steven Barabas, *So Great Salvation* (Westwood: Fleming H. Revell, n.d.), 134.

(2 Cor 12:9), contribute money (Rom 12:8), sacrifice one's life (1 Cor 13:3), celibacy (1 Cor 7:7), and various institutional gifts (2 Tim 1:6f.). No differentiation can be made between some gifts as supernatural and some ordinary, for all these are supernatural empowerments of χάρις.

7. Purity and power are both related to the Holy Spirit but not directly tied to one another. As with Paul's explanation of many doctrines, however, no fine distinction is made between the two (Gal 3:5, 5:22ff.; 1 Cor 12, 13; Rom 5:5; Eph 5:18, 6:10).

3

Luke-Acts

INTRODUCTION

THE CONSIDERABLE DEBATE SURROUNDING the essence of Classical Pentecostal pneumatology might be most affected by an investigation into those New Testament writings which traditionally have been attributed to Luke, namely the Gospel of Luke and the Book of Acts. Some preliminary matters of importance must be dealt with before proceeding to the exegesis of selected texts.

THE UNITY OF LUKE-ACTS

It would appear that the unity of the Gospel of Luke and the Book of Acts is an axiom in modern day theology. C. H. Talbert, in his *Luke and the Gnostics*, puts off a defense of this proposition because of the unanimity among New Testament scholars. In view of the limitations of this investigation and the fact that Talbert represents an influential posture,[1] only a brief pause will be devoted to this concern.

In evaluating the possible unity of Luke-Acts one must grapple with the significance of the prologue to the Third Gospel. Professor Ralph P. Martin presents a convincing case in defense of the thesis that the prologue is related both to the Gospel of Luke and to the Book of Acts: (1) It was a common practice in antiquity to divide lengthy works into volumes and to provide a preface for the entire work at the beginning and secondary prefaces to later volumes. (2) πρῶτον λόγον of Acts 1:1 probably refers to the Third Gospel. (3) Both books are dedicated to the same person. (4) The gospel assertion about "the things accomplished among us"

---

1. For example, see T. W. Manson, *Studies in the Gospels*, ed. by M. Grant (Manchester: Manchester University Press, 1962), 47.

(Lk 1:1) more appropriately describes the events related in Acts.[2] Further, Bo Reicke insists that the literary analysis by Adolf Harnack which demonstrated the unity of the two works has yet to be overthrown.[3] (5) And finally, as pointed out by E. Earle Ellis, common authorship is attested by church traditions from the latter part of the second century.[4]

REDAKTIONSGESCHICHTE

Formgeschichte was the first major science introduced to biblical studies for the purpose of rediscovering the traditions which stood behind the biblical text. This method has served a very useful purpose, but preoccupation with isolating pericopae has often resulted in a distortion of the role of the biblical authors. Redaktionsgeschichte has played a significant role in correcting this misplaced emphasis. The 1954 German edition of Hans Conzelmann's *The Theology of St. Luke* introduced this science to Lucan studies. Norman Perrin, who ranks Conzelmann's work with Bultmann's *History of the Synoptic Tradition* and Jeremias's *The Parables of Jesus*, says of Conzelmann that he "... almost single handedly changed the whole tenor of Lucan studies."[5] Traditionally, attention has centered on Luke as a historian and the issue of his reliability.[6] In contrast, the redactional analysis of Luke done by those in the Hans Conzelmann-Ernst Haenchen line has not only questioned the historical intent of the work, but has

---

2. Ralph P. Martin, *New Testament Foundations* (Grand Rapids: Eerdmans, 1975), 1:244.

3. Bo Reicke, *The Gospel of Luke*, trans. by R. McKenzie (Richmond: John Knox Press, 1964), 11. Cf. Stephen Neill, *The Interpretation of the New Testament: 1861-1961* (New York: Oxford University Press, 1964), 58. A careful reading of the two works almost seems to make this self-evident. See also: G. B. Caird, *The Gospel of St. Luke* (London: Gerald Duckworth & Co. Ltd., 1955), 14; F. F. Bruce, *The Acts of the Apostles: The Greek Text with Introduction and Commentary* (Grand Rapids: Eerdmans, 1952), 3.

4. E. Earle Ellis, *The Gospel of Luke*, NCB, 2. See also: H. J. Cadbury, *The Making of Luke-Acts* (New York: The Macmillan Co., 1927), 8-12; Donald Guthrie, *New Testament Introduction*, (London: Tyndale Press, 1970), 102.

5. Norman Perrin, *What is Redaction Criticism?* (Philadelphia: Fortress Press, 1969), 29f.

6. Cf. George E. Ladd, *The Young Church* (New York: Abingdon Press, 1964), 14ff. See also Bruce M. Metzger, *The New Testament: Its background and Growth and Content* (Nashville: Abingdon Press, 1965), 176. Hence this title: C. K. Barrett, *Luke the Historian in Recent Research* (London: The Epworth Press, 1961).

almost assumed its unreliability.[7] Fortunately this is not a necessary conclusion to Redaktionsgeschichte. More discussion concerning historical reliability is needed, so we will embark on a summary discussion of the salient issues regarding authorship.

Haenchen's massive commentary on Acts (which follows in the German tradition of Tendenzkritik analysis, the older German critical orthodoxy, and the work of Dibelius) seems to represent still much present day German thought on Acts and shall be considered as a representative work. This discussion will anticipate problems which could be raised on each Acts passage analyzed later.

Reviewing Haenchen's treatment of Acts, one discerns that the ultimate issue is methodology. There can be no question of the competence of his work and the meticulousness with which he carries his approach through each passage of Acts. The published monograph of W. Ward Gasque, *A History of the Criticism of the Acts of the Apostles*, is very helpful here. If one may put Gasque's understanding in a word, it would be to say that the greatest problem with Haenchen's work is that it grants sovereignty to the German tradition of criticism, while completely ignoring the work of British and American scholars. The German critical method is embodied in an almost exclusively literary approach which is usually based on the assumption of the unreliability of Luke. The major defect here is the sola norma which ignores British work in history, archaeology and geography. One wonders if other skeptics, like Sir William Ramsay, would not change having once approached the subject with a less subjective methodology. Ramsay's work, *St. Paul the Traveller and Roman Citizen*, which strongly espouses Lucan reliability, contains an interesting testimony:

> I may fairly claim to have entered on this investigation without any prejudice in favor of the conclusion which I shall now attempt to justify to the reader. On the contrary, I began with a mind un-

---

7. Ernst Haenchen, *The Acts of the Apostles: A Commentary* (Philadelphia: Westminster Press, 1971). Haenchen says:

> Upon occasion Luke has been praised for presenting so faithful a picture of the primitive theology of early Christian times. But it is his own simple theology which he everywhere presupposes and which should be understood behind the sermons, prayers, liturgical expressions and occasional pertinent remarks on Acts. (91)

See Guthrie, *New Testament*, 353.

favorable to it, for the ingenuity and apparent completeness of the Tübingen theory had at one time quite convinced me.[8]

Now to the matter of Lucan reliability. (1) External evidence, as seen in the words of the Anti-Marcionite Prologue to Luke, the Muratorian Fragments, Irenaeus, and others, indicates that from at least circa 170, Luke, a companion of Paul was considered to be the author of Luke-Acts.[9] (2) That the author of Luke-Acts was a companion of Paul is suggested by: (a) the "we" passages in Acts[10] and (b) the fact that the Luke referred to in various Pauline epistles (Rom 16:21, Col 4:14, Phlm 24, 2 Tim 4:10) is quite likely the same person.[11] (3) Notice the similarities between the accounts given by Paul himself and those given in Acts: (a) Acts and the Pauline epistles both represent Paul with the same attitude towards Jews, that is, to the Jews first and then the Greeks; (b) both the Pauline epistles and Acts present Paul as having had to support himself at times; (c) both present Paul as being able to adapt to a wide range of audiences; (d) in both works Paul is the specially chosen instrument of God; (e) Paul reproduces in his own experience the marks of the Spirit (tongues-speech, miracles, healings, revelations, etc.) found in the Book of Acts.[12] (4) Luke's meticulous accuracy is abundantly clear in his correct use of titles of various officials and the correct names of provinces.[13] (5) To those concerned with "internal doctrinal inconsistencies" in Luke-Acts, it should be pointed out that an author accurately representing the changes of a young movement is more likely to reproduce a variety of opinions, than a redactor who tried

---

8. W. W. Ramsey, *St. Paul the Traveller and Roman Citizen* (Grand Rapids: Eerdmans, 1967), 7f. See also W. Ward Gasque, "Recent Commentaries on the Acts of the Apostles," *Themelius* 14:1 (Oct/Nov, 1988): 21–23.

9. F. F. Bruce, *Commentary on the Book of Acts*, NIC, 1; E. Earle Ellis, *The Gospel of Luke*, NCB, 41f.; Reiche, *Luke*, 12ff.; Neill, *New Testament*, 124.

10. Bruce, Book of Acts, 2f. Cf. Guthrie, *New Testament*, 116; R. J. Knowling, *The Acts of the Apostles*, EGT 2:5ff.; R. P. C. Hanson, *The Acts, The Clarendon Bible* (Oxford: At the Clarendon Press, 1967), 21ff.

11. Ellis, *Luke*, 41; Reiche, *Luke*, 16f.

12. W. Ward Gasque, *A History of the Criticism of the Acts of the Apostles* (Grand Rapids: Eerdmans, 1975), 136ff.; Hunter, *Paul*, 93; John A. T. Robinson, *Redating the New Testament* (Philadelphia: Westminster, 1976), 86f. Cf. E. F. Harrison, "Acts 22:—A Test Case for Luke's Reliability," *New Dimensions in New Testament Study*, Longenecker and Tenney, 251–60.

13. Bruce, *Book of Acts*, 17; Hanson, *Acts*, 7. Cf. Ladd, *Theology of the Testament*, 314; Neill, *New Testament*, 142.

to manipulate his sources.¹⁴ (6) There are no traces of Käsemann's "early catholicism" in Acts. It can rightly be said that in the Lucan account "... the church as an institution dispensing salvation is completely lacking."¹⁵

RELATION OF LUCAN WRITINGS TO PAULINE LITERATURE

Having said something about the probable historical relationship of the apostle Paul and the New Testament author Luke, a word needs to be said about the use of their writings in formulating present day theology. There are many problems which result from such an attempt. On the one hand one cannot impose the proposed theology of one biblical writer on another and yet it is appropriate to consider a difficult passage in light of (1) other passages by the same author which are not encumbered with controversial decisions and (2) other biblical writers.

Some see a tension here. Dunn would say that biblical theology has been left behind and led to a somewhat irrational jump to the questionable hermeneutics associated with dogmatic theology.¹⁶ This may not be the case. It is true that one should never impose anything upon a given passage. However, it hardly seems to be an imposition when difficult passages which can be interpreted in a variety of ways are interpreted with the aid of word studies, incorporating the use of the word in other texts

---

14. Cf. Ellis, *Luke*, 51; Lampe, *Seal*, 79.

15. W. G. Kümmel, *Introduction to the New Testament* (Nashville: Abingdon Press, 1965), 127. Not putting as much emphasis on the fact that Luke did not create his material ex nihilo, I. H. Marshall offers a fine treatment of the issue in his article, "Early Catholicism in the New Testament," *New Dimensions in New Testament Study*, Longenecker and Tenney, 217–31. Cf. Caird, *Apostolic Age*, 66.

16. Dunn, *Baptism in the Holy Spirit*, 39. The point being made here is well argued by Roger Stronstad in his *Charismatic Theology of St. Luke*, 9ff. It was through my contact with Clark Pinnock that Roger and I became aware of our related work. I had finished a graduate seminar on Luke (the basis of this chapter) and he had completed a master's thesis (the basis for his book). We arrived at our judgments independent of each other and some particulars are different but the general direction is the same. Interestingly, much the same can be said of James B. Shelton and his doctoral dissertation "'Filled With the Holy Spirit': A Redactional Motif in Luke's Gospel" (University of Stirling, May, 1982). Fortunately, this fine work has been released by Hendrickson Publishers. A good introduction to his work may be found in his "'Filled with the Holy Spirit' and 'Full of the Holy Spirit': Lucan Redactional Phrases," *Faces of Renewal*, Elbert, ed., 80–107. Further, Larry Hart completed his doctoral dissertation in 1978 at the Southern Baptist Theological Seminary on Spirit baptism and used the title "A Critique of American Pentecostal Theology." Larry Hart at that time was in line with Dunn, but came to be more aligned with Stronstad.

by the same author and other authors as well as extra-biblical sources, and theological affirmations elsewhere in Scripture which are not easily contested. The biblical hermeneutic known as the analogia fidei is used here in part because apparently the biblical writers achieved unanimity in at least the theological intent of their writings.

The current discussion includes a concern for relating the "didactic" parts of Scripture to those parts categorized as "historical." There is certainly merit in pointing out the dangers of articulating a norm on the basis of historical precedent alone,[17] but for one thing, Luke is hardly historical in the modern sense of the word. In the analysis which follows it will be argued that Luke sees the charismatic Spirit as unpredictable. One may argue that the unity formula of Acts 2:38 should prevail over the subsequence teaching of Acts 8:14-18, 9:17-19, but such an argument wrongly presupposes that the Pauline pattern is always uniform.

It does not appear satisfactory to dismiss Luke as theologically inferior to the apostle Paul. The dual interest of historical fidelity and accomplishing the purposes of his pastoral goals led him to include many elements which may be labeled 'primitive', but surely that does not mean that they are to be erased from the continuing ministry of the church. Further, in view of the probability that the Pauline writings were completed before the Lucan writings, it would be a denial of the intelligence exhibited in Luke's work to say that he was incapable of integrating the "developed" theology of Paul. Rather the problem may well lie with the traditional Protestant understanding of Paul which is likely inadequate at points. Paul certainly amplifies areas left untouched by Luke, but he also reinforces much of what has often been associated with Luke alone.

When Luke uses terms like "baptized into" (Acts 1:5, 11:16), "come upon" (Acts 1:8, 19:6), "poured out" (Acts 2:17f., 23, 10:45), "fell upon" (Acts 8:16, 10:44, 11:15) to describe the work of the Spirit, he can hardly be accused of being crude.[18] Luke is simply driving home his view of the necessity of the charismatic work of the Spirit. Luke is hardly a Eurocentric dogmatic theologian! No nice outline of the elements of the ordo salutis can be discerned in his work. However, his work is not unlike some contemporary historical theologians when using relevant historical

---

17. Gordon D. Fee, "Hermeneutics and Historical Precedent—A Major Problem in Pentecostal Hermeneutics," *Perspectives on the New Pentecostalism*, Spittler, ed., 128.

18. Contra Dunn, *Jesus and the Spirit*, 190. Dunn adds that Luke's presentation is "lopsided" (191).

data to stress the importance of the confession of Jesus as Lord and the sense of urgency to communicate the latter not evidencing an immature theology is the reason for Luke's repeated mention of prophecy, tongues, and evangelism.[19]

So the issue, then, is not whether one can funnel Luke through Paul, but whether an inquirer can afford the luxury of turning to either writer with the presuppositions of one's own theological heritage. This study is committed to the proposition that only as each passage has been studied in its own right can it be used in relation to any other text. This, after all, is foundational for good dogmatic theology. Dogmaticians build on sound biblical theology in formulating theology relevant to the given church generation. The latter involves the previously discussed principle of the analogy of faith.

LUKE THE 'PASTOR'

It is an intriguing and useful venture to attempt to work through the current suggestions about the theological purpose(s) of Luke-Acts. The most urgent concern here, however, is to review the prospects that Luke's work evidences the perspective of a pastor. Ralph P. Martin notes four points in support: (1) the manner in which Luke assembles the traditions; (2) the use of liturgical and catechetical elements; (3) the prominence ascribed to the character of the earthly Jesus as a human among humans; (4) emphasis in the Jesus tradition on those elements which figured so prominently in Paul's kerygmatic message.[20]

There are other marks of Luke-Acts that evidence a pastoral concern. Among them are the following: (1) the early days were days of Spirit and power; (2) the Christian faith is not a threat to good government; (3) an unequivocal emphasis on prayer; (4) a concern for the dignity of women and the welfare of social outcasts; (5) the Christian faith came to being out of the matrices of Judaism; (6) the delay of the parousia should be set aside while the future of the church is considered; (7) the church leaders are called to steadfastness in the face of persecution; (8) in the face of the various heresies, they are reminded that it is the church who is the rightful

---

19. Contra Lampe, *Seal*, 50; Dunn, *Jesus and the Spirit*, 190f. See Montague, *Spirit*, 368.

20. Martin, *Foundations* 1:250. This is the end of the matter for Martin who provides an excellent summary (246–49) of the current opinions about Luke's theological purpose(s).

interpreter of Scriptures; (9) the work itself is a direct confrontation of the dehistoricizing of the gospel by gnosticizing Christians; (10) the work provided an answer to the origins of the movement to a generation that saw new converts who did not have personal contact with eye-witnesses.

It is the first of these 10 marks that requires further consideration here. It is evident to even the cursory reader of Luke that he has a persistent interest in the extraordinary work of the Holy Spirit, or, as labeled here the charismatic work of the Spirit. If the Sitz im Leben for the publication of this work is the latter part of the first century then it is no surprise that a concern of the book is missionary enthusiasm. The martyrdom of the apostles, persecution of the church at large and delay of the parousia would quite likely dampen the spirits of many.[21]

Not a few noted the multiplicity of references to prayer in Luke (Lk. 3:21, Acts 1:14, 4:31, 8:15).[22] One gets the impression that Luke is attempting to remind his audience of elements which were important to the earliest communities. Luke makes a tight connection between the charismatic work of the Spirit and prayer.[23] It appears also that Luke (11:13) has apparently substituted πνεῦμα ἅγιον for the original reading ἀγαθά found in Matthew 7:11. Beasley-Murray comments:

> . . . thus in instruction intended for the church even more than to them that are without, Luke will especially have had in mind the desirability of Christians praying for the charismata of the Spirit . . .[24]

The first two chapters of the Third Gospel are saturated with motifs from the Hebrew canon and the operation of the charismatic Spirit. Although this is not the sole purpose of this section, it is certainly a matter

---

21. Neill, *New Testament*, 264f.
22. See Lampe, *Seal*, 44; Schweizer, "πνεῦμα," 6:214.
23. Lampe, "The Holy Spirit in the Writings of St. Luke," 169f.
24. G. R. Beasley-Murray, *Baptism in the New Testament* (London: Macmillan, 1962), 119. See C. K. Barrett, *The Holy Spirit and the Gospel Tradition* (London: SPCK, 1947), 127; Lampe, "The Holy Spirit in the Writings of St. Luke," 169f.; J. H. E. Hull, *The Holy Spirit in the Acts of the Apostles* (London: Lutterworth Press, 1967), 152; Turner, *Power From On High*; Green, *Holy Spirit*, 38. There is evidence that Luke may have written "Thy Holy Spirit come upon us and cleanse us" rather than "thy kingdom come." See Lampe, "Thy Holy Spirit in the Writings of St. Luke," 170; E. J. Tinsley, *The Gospel According to Luke*, Cambridge Bible Commentary (Cambridge: University Press, 1963), 125; Barrett, *Holy Spirit*, 127; Krodel, "Functions of the Spirit," *Holy Spirit*, ed. by Opsahl, 42n43.

of major concern for Luke. Notice the sporadic outpouring of the charismatic Spirit: Luke tells of the prophetic Spirit upon Mary (Lk 1:40ff.), the same concerning Zechariah (Lk 1:62ff.), similarly Simon (Lk 2:27) and Anna (Lk 2:36–38) and especially John the Baptist of whom it is said (Lk 1:45) that he was filled with the Spirit even from his mother's womb. The continuity of Lucan pneumatology with the dominant ancient Israelite view of *rûaḥ* is so evident that J. H. E. Hull could say:

> Just as the Old Testament can speak of the Spirit as coming upon a man on rare occasions and for short intervals to enable him to perform some specific and urgent task (e.g., Judges 6:34; 1 Sam 11:6; 19:23), so Luke thinks, or appears to think of the Spirit in these very terms.[25]

The power which results from the work of the Spirit is brought to the forefront by Luke. Consider two well known Lucan passages: "I am going to send you what my Father has promised (ἐπαγγελίαν τοῦ πατρός), but stay in the city until you have been clothed (ἐνδύσησθε) with power (δύναμιν) from on high" (Lk 24:49); "But you will receive power (δύναμιν) when the Holy Spirit comes upon you; and you will be my witnesses..." (Acts 1:8).[26] The key words are familiar from the Pauline investigation. Δύναμιν and ἐπαγγελίαν τοῦ πατρός have been used by Paul to refer to the charismatic work of the Spirit and ἐνδύσησθε has been used by ancient Israelite writers as well as Paul in this way.

Luke placed unequivocal emphasis on the visibility of the work of the Spirit. No other New Testament writer so often repeats the working of visible miracles, prophesying, tongues, visible signs, and so on. Hendrikus Berkhof rightly points out that "Wherever Luke ... speaks of being filled with the Spirit, he lays full emphasis ... on external consequences."[27]

---

25. Hull, *Holy Spirit*, 120. Hunter, *Paul*, 91, says that Luke is Hebraic not Gentilic in his pneumatology. See Schweizer, "πνεῦμα," 406; Flender, *Luke*, 40; Barrett, *Holy Spirit*, 122ff.; Lampe, "The Holy Spirit in the writings of St. Luke," 160; Green, *Holy Spirit*, 134; Roger G. Stronstad, "The Holy Spirit in Luke-Acts," unpublished master's thesis (Vancouver: Regent College, April, 1975), 28.

26. See Hull, *Holy Spirit*, 109, 120, 125; Lampe, "The Holy Spirit in the Writings of St. Luke" 52, 74; Caird, *Luke*, 57; Bultmann, *Theology* 1:157ff.; Green, *Holy Spirit*, 134; Adolf von Harnack, *The Acts of the Apostles* (New York: Putnam, 1909), 133; Joseph A. Fitzmyer and Dillon, *The Acts of the Apostles*, 171; Hunter, *Paul*, 92.

27. H. Berkhof, *Holy Spirit*, 89. Cf. Bruce, *Book of Acts*, 230; Stronstad, "The Holy Spirit in Luke-Acts;" Roger Stronstad, *Spirit, Scripture & Theology* (Baguio City, Philippines: Asia Pacific Theological Seminary, 1995), 79ff.

EXEGESIS

It is time to turn to those passages which are germane to the discussion of Spirit baptism. It is true that distinctives of Lucan theology are more easily detected by investigating the Third Gospel, but Acts is the Pentecostal "epicenter" and therefore all passages, with one exception, will be taken from the Book of Acts.[28]

Luke 3:16

> John answered them all, "I baptize you with water. But one more powerful than I will come, the thongs of those sandals I am not worthy to untie. He will baptize (βαπτίσει) you with (ἐν) the Holy Spirit (πνεύματι ἁγίῳ) and fire (πυρί)."

All the Gospel accounts (see Matthew 3:11, Mark 1:8, John 1:33) agree in designating Jesus as the baptizer in the Spirit. Much controversy has centered on the additional word πυρί which is found in Matthew (3:11) and Luke (3:16) alone. The meaning of πυρί probably has little effect on the present inquiry and so no attempt will be made to determine whether the phrase is a hendiadys (which still leaves undecided the nature of the baptism) or refers to two different baptisms.[29] The contexts in Luke and Matthew seem to offer a suitable setting for the inclusion of the word πυρί, but the word itself would not stand in all six related passages (Mark 1:8, John 1:33, Acts 1:5, 11:16). This would be true only of πνεῦμα ἅγιον probably cannot be viewed as a piece of Christian redaction. Further, whatever John the Baptist had in mind when using the phrase, Jesus turned the phrase toward Pentecost and it is there that our interest lies. The ministry of the baptizer in the Spirit seems to be predicated upon Jesus' own experience with the Spirit, as it is said in the Fourth Gospel: "The man

---

28. The translation used, unless otherwise designated, will be the New International Version.

29. I am inclined to believe that it is not a redaction reflecting the "fiery tongues" of Pentecost. B. H. Irwin taught that Spirit baptized (i.e., sanctified) people should seek the further spiritual experience "baptism of fire." Pentecostals generally have often thought of the "fire" reference here as relating to the enthusiasm associated with Spirit baptism and/or the cleansing dimension of the Spirit's work. For the present day opinions on the full phrase see the following: James D. G. Dunn, "Spirit-and-Fire Baptism," *Nov* 14 (1972): 81–92; Barrett, *Holy Spirit*, 125f.; Ysebaert, *Greek*, 61f.; Ellis, *Luke*, 90; Krodel, "The functions of the Spirit," 26; Caird, *Luke*, 74; Plummer, *Luke*, 94; Ladd, *Theology of the New Testament*, 36ff.; I. H. Marshall, *The Gospel of Luke* (Grand Rapids: Eerdmans, 1978), 146–48; Ervin, *Conversion-Initiation*, ch. 1; Heron, *Holy Spirit*, 41.

on whom you see the Spirit (πνεῦμα) come down (καταβαῖνον) and remain (μένον) is he who will baptize (βαπτίζων) with (ἐν) the Holy Spirit (πνεύματι ἁγίῳ)" (John 1:33). It would appear that part of the reason for the Lucan phrase "Spirit of Jesus" (Acts 16:7) is that the Spirit poured out upon believers is the selfsame Spirit that anointed Jesus. The chief exegetical task is to understand better the anointing of Jesus.

When one affirms two natures of Jesus (e.g., God and human), one is hard pressed to understand why he received an anointing of the Spirit. Part of the answer must lie in the fact that God the Son became *incarnate*. As George E. Ladd has said: "Why should the incarnate Son of God need the Spirit to fulfill his messianic mission? The answer must lie in John's conviction of the full humanity of Jesus."[30] One must proceed with a great deal of caution and not make deductions which, although they may be logical, are not biblical. William B. MacDonald lists some theological deductions which are not acceptable.

> The anointing of Jesus was for him neither regeneration nor sanctification; he came to the experience as the holy Son of God. Nor was it the deification of the man as the adopted Son of God; no change in the filial relationship to God is enacted but the existing relationship is confirmed at the threshold of *ebed Yahweh*'s ministry in the Spirit.[31]

What then does the Bible say about this pneumatic experience of Jesus? This is where the messianic title, Χριστός, of Jesus was vindicated.

The words 'Anointed' and 'Messiah' are synonyms, being respectively the translation and transliteration of the same Hebrew word משיה which is rendered χριστός in the Septuagint. Although משיה is rarely used metaphorically in the Hebrew canon, the earlier investigation in to the usage of *rûaḥ* in ancient Israel shows that is can be used in such a manner. Most important is the Isaiah passage in which we are told of a charismatic

---

30. Ladd, *Theology of the New Testament*, 288. Commenting on these verses, William G. MacDonald, "Problems of Pneumatology in Christology," 142, suggests "only at the peril of jeopardizing his likeness to mankind could one posit a spiritual state beyond which nothing could be given beginning with his earliest moment of consciousness."

31. MacDonald, "Problems of Pneumatology in Christology," 144. See Shelton, *Filled with the Holy Spirit*, 135–40, 145; Heron, *Holy Spirit*, 40f.; Jungkuntz, *Confirmation*, 4; Turner, *Power from on High*, ch. 7; Ladd, *Theology of the New Testament*, 164, 184, 421; Ervin, *Conversion-Initiation*, 11–14. Stronstad's language here, *Charismatic Theology*, 39, is somewhat dangerous.

reception of the Spirit by the Messiah (Isaiah 61:1).³² The Lucan account leaves little doubt that at least the enthusiasts in the early church made such a connection. Luke (4:18f.) tells that as a result of the Jordan experience Jesus is able to use Isaiah 61:1 when addressing an audience.

Later a sermon by Peter included these words: "God anointed (ἔχρισεν) Jesus of Nazareth with the Holy Spirit (πνεύματι ἁγίῳ) and power (δυνάμει) . . ." (Acts 10:38. Cf. Acts 4:26f., Luke 24:19). There is further evidence of the charismatic nature of the Spirit-empowerment bestowed on Jesus noted in the Synoptic Gospels but it is not mentioned (for that reason?) in John. When the Gospels present the voice from heaven as saying, "You are my Son, whom I love; with you I am well pleased" (Luke 3:22, Matthew 3:17, Mark 1:11) they are reflecting a saying from a "charismatic" Royal Psalm. In Psalm 2 it is the Anointed (Psalm 2:2) who quotes the LORD as saying "'You are my son, today I have begotten you'" (Psalm 2:7, RSV). Isaiah 11:2 and John 1:33 both point out that the Spirit will rest/remain upon the Messiah. Luke may have had something of the same in mind when he described Jesus as being 'full' (πλήρης) of the Spirit (Luke 4:1). Only Jesus is so designated prior to the day of Pentecost. Selected individuals experience fillings of the Spirit prior to this time (πίμπλημι used in Luke 1:15, 41, 67) but Luke reserves the adjective πλήρης for people who have experienced the permanent indwelling of the charismatic Spirit after the day of Pentecost (Acts 6:3, 5, 7:55, 11:29).

Luke offers a developed theological scheme in which the empowerment and conception do Spiritu sancto of Jesus find a parallel in the experience of the believer. The theological implication for the Christian is that one's charismatic experience of the Spirit can be distinguished from regeneration and may be temporally subsequent to it. However, caution should again be exercised lest improper deductions result in a faulty Christology. The use of such an analogy does mean that there is a certain parallel to Christ's birth and the believer's experience of regeneration. Thomas Smail rebuffed F. Dale Bruner for belittling the Pentecostal use of this analogy. As Smail points out this model has been used by Reformed

---

32. Although Professor Barrett would not accept the terminology used here, it is of some worth to note that he lists, (*Holy Spirit*, 42ff.), various sources from Jewish literature in which this same basic concept is given expression. Cf. Schweizer, "πνεῦμα," 400; Ewert, *Holy Spirit*, 50ff. I think Stronstad is too specific when he uses these data to argue (*Charismatic Theology*, 40–43) that this makes Jesus a prophet.

thinkers, including Barth, Hoskyns, and Davey.[33] Yet we are not to understand that Luke suggests that Jesus requires redemption from sin like any other human. For that matter, neither does the fact that Jesus submitted to water baptism imply that Jesus had sinned. As G. R. Beasley-Murray pointed out: "Jesus came to the baptism of John, among the penitents of Israel responsive to John's proclamation to begin the messianic task in its fullness as He interpreted it from the writings of the Old Testament."[34] Luke's scheme is a theological one with implications for the believer's experience of the Spirit, not for understanding the ontology of Jesus Christ. Many will find this paradoxical if not contradictory. However, in light of the statement by Paul that although Jesus took on the flesh of humans (Philippians 2:6–11) he did not sin (2 Corinthians 5:21; see 1 Peter 2:22, Hebrew 7:26), it would seem unwarranted to read a conclusion into Luke which is at odds with Luke's affirmation of the special conception of Jesus by the Holy Spirit (Luke 1:35) and is flatly denied by Paul.[35]

The connection of the charismatic work of the Spirit effected in Jesus which he in turn effected in his followers leads us to say that "Christian existence is a continuation of the work and mission of Jesus in the world and basis for this is the charismatic presence of the Spirit of Jesus in the early church."[36] It is Professor Lampe who best specifies some of the

---

33. Smail, *Reflected Glory*, 82, 89. Ernest Williams, *Systematic Theology* (Springfield: Gospel Publishing House, 1953), 3:39–61, quotes well known evangelicals who are said to support this interpretation. Cf. Stronstad, *Charismatic Theology*, 45; Ervin, *Conversion-Initiation*, 68. Tom Smail sounded a quite different note in his *The Giving Gift* (London: Hodder and Stoughton, 1988).

34. Beasley-Murray, *Baptism*, 55. See Barrett, *Holy Spirit*, 34f. George T. Montague, *Spirit*, 341, argues that John's baptism of Jesus was omitted by John because the later church was embarrassed by the possible implication that Jesus had sinned. But see A. Alan Richardson, *An Introduction to the Theology of the New Testament* (London: SCM, 1961), 180, who argues that the accounts given in Matthew and John should dismiss any thought of Jesus having sinned.

35. I cannot say, as does Smail (83) following Irving, that Jesus was regenerated. It was this kind of language that got Irving into trouble with his presbytery. A. J. Mason, *Confirmation*, 457, notes that some of the Fathers referred to the baptism of Jesus as his regeneration, to which Mason responds: "It was assuredly no 'regeneration' to Him in that sense in which regeneration has reference to a change from the death of sin to a life of righteousness." Cf. page 461. Paul K. Jewett, "Holy Spirit," 7, 5, rightly argues that the special conception of Jesus by the Spirit is the basis of his sinlessness.

36. Herbert Schneider, "Baptism in the Holy Spirit in the New Testament," *The Holy Spirit and Power*, ed. by Kilian McDonnell (Garden City: Doubleday, 1975), 49. I do not accept, contra a thinker like Dewar, *Holy Spirit*, 56, a meticulous parallel of Jesus to the

actions of the Spirit which Luke sees as having been operative in Jesus, then having become operative in the Church.

> The ministry of the apostles and of other disciples resembles that of Jesus at many points. They perform numerous signs and wonders; Jesus, too, was attested by signs and wonders (Acts 2:22, 43). As Jesus fulfilled the prophecy of Isaiah 35:6 by making the lame to walk, so Peter and John fulfill it even more literally by causing a lame man to "leap" and walk (Luke 7:22; Acts 3:8). This miracle, the first recorded in Acts and the incident which gives rise to the first clash between the apostles and the Jewish authorities, resembles the healing by Jesus of the paralytic, the first miracle which brought him into a similar conflict. Among the points of similarity we notice the command, "arise and walk," the reaction of the healed man, the ἔκστασις of the spectators, and the glorifying of God. The general healings of Jerusalem, when the shadow of St. Peter is said, like the Spirit itself, to "overshadow" the sick (Acts 15:12–16), are somewhat similar to the general healings by Jesus at Capernaum (Luke 4:40f.). St. Peter's cure of Aeneas recalls, once again, the healing of the paralytic by Jesus, and the raising of Dorcas very clearly resembles that of Jairus' daughter, both in it s circumstances and in the method of its accomplishment. Both these raisings of the dead have some affinities with Elisha's miracle at Shunem (2 Kings 4:32–37). It is remarkable that the raising of Jairus' daughter immediately precedes the sending out of the Twelve with power to preach and to heal, and that the similar episode of Dorcas is the immediate prelude to the first preaching of nethe gospel to the Gentiles. The latter event is marked by a 'Gentile Pentecost', an unmediated bestowal of the Spirit on Cornelius and his household. Thereafter a second series of mighty works begins, in many respects parallel to the former.[37]

---

believer where it is suggested that since the descent of the Spirit was after his water baptism, the believer is likely not to expect the two to be together. Cf. Lampe, "The Holy Spirit in the Writings of St. Luke," 168; Dunn, *Jesus and the Spirit*, 195; Ysebaert, *Greek*, 61; Barnabas Lindars, *The Gospel of John*, NCB, 110; Riggs, *Spirit Himself*, 48ff.

37. Lampe, "The Holy Spirit in Writings of St. Luke," 194f. This is one of his earlier works on the subject. His later changes are well known. They were acknowledged following: Scheider, "Baptism in the Spirit," 49; F. F. Bruce, "Christ and Spirit in Paul," *BJRL* 59:2 (Spring, 1977): 275; Dunn, *Jesus and the Spirit*, 321; Green, *Holy Spirit*, 53; George G. Hendry, *The Holy Spirit in Christian Theology* (Philadelphia: Westminster Press, 1965), 26; Wolfhart Pannenberg, *Jesus, God and Man* (Philadelphia: Westminster Press, 1968), 171; Smail, *Reflected Glory*, 12, 14; F. Dale Bruner, "The Holy Spirit: Conceiver of Jesus," *Theology, News and Notes* (Pasadena: Fuller Theological Seminary, March, 1974): 9; J. Rodman Williams, "The Coming of the Holy Spirit," 15; Neil Q. Hamilton, *The Holy Spirit*

One important implication of the foregoing judgment is that there are six uses of the term "baptism in the Spirit" where the charismatic work of the Spirit is in view. How does this relate to the use of this term by Classical Pentecostals and Charismatics? The historical development of the post-Reformation use of the term "baptism in the Spirit" will be dealt with later on, but suffice it here to note that foremost in the minds of many lay Pentecostals and Charismatics seems to be that the term "baptism" adequately represents the overwhelming presence of the Spirit which they feel. Church history teaches that those who articulate theology often have had to make vocabulary accommodations to the masses. It often seems better to use the lay person's terms and offer an orthodox explanation than to try to erase their terminology. At any rate, even church officials have given us "parascriptural" words (e.g., confirmation, incarnation, rapture, trinity) which have proven to be adequate vehicles for theology.

To suggest that the term Spirit baptism is an acceptable vehicle for describing the charismatic work of the Spirit does not imply an approval of the multiplied nuances of the Classical Pentecostal doctrine of Spirit baptism. Many aspects of their doctrine have not been addressed, perhaps most notably the issue of tongues-speech as the initial evidence. The burden of this research is to evaluate the legitimacy of speaking of a distinct work of the Spirit which concerns charisma and may occur "subsequent" to the initial term of salvation. There is no known record of the use of the phrase "baptism in the Spirit" which was understood to be evidenced by tongues until such a formulation was made by Edward Irving. And yet it remained for a small Bible school run by Charles Fox Parham in Topeka, Kansas to codify tongues as *the* initial evidence. The most notable literature excluded then, is patristic literature and Scripture itself. With the possible exception of Luke (Luke 3:16, Acts 1:5, 11:6), the New Testament writers probably did not use *the term* Spirit baptism in the sense suggested here, much less in the manner it is used by Classical Pentecostals.[38] The consternation caused by this evidence, however, is not

---

and Eschatology in Paul (Edinburgh: Oliver and Boyd, Ltd., 1957), 9; Mikaloski, "The Triune God," 75f. Stronstad, *Charismatic Theology*, 43, says that Jesus "deliberately models" his ministry after Isaiah, Elijah, Elisha, and Moses. To whatever extent these parallels exist, it should be Luke who is credited with drawing such to our attention. Shelton's argument in "Filled with the Holy Spirit" is similar to mine.

38. The emphasis is on the lack of usage of the term Spirit baptism, not the basic pneumatological issue that it represents. My patristic and biblical analysis suggests an acceptance of the pneumatological essence of the Pentecostal doctrine of Spirit baptism.

reason enough to abandon this battered term. At various points in the history of Christianity particular biblical and parabiblical words/phrases have served the need of a given generation. A great many phrases used by present day Evangelicals have not been so used previously. Such a phenomenon is at time justifiable. When one takes the Fall of humankind seriously, it becomes evident that no given generation can produce an unimprovable system of doctrine. Although church history verifies the verdict of the limited importance of certain theological nuances and the verbal vehicles which are employed, it is clear also that many of these systems were important to their own time nonetheless. No sound hermeneutic has been violated when one employs a parascriptural word that can convey a biblical truth to a given generation. In fact, the emphasis on using terms found in Scripture alone is apparently not part of the biblical mandate. Therefore, having admitted these limitations and qualifications the term Spirit baptism will be retained here.

It can be an enlightening experience to observe the manner in which some non-Pentecostals develop a definition of the term "baptism in the Spirit." There are a variety of writers who believe that the Spirit, apart from the work of regeneration, works a continual filling in the believer. That is, these writers are in agreement with the essential pneumatological issue at stake they join Pentecostals in saying that an empowering work of the Spirit must be recognized when enumerating the parts of the ordo salutis. However, these same writers deny the Classical Pentecostal use of the term "baptism in the Spirit." While there are seven passages in Scripture which could be translated "baptism in the Spirit," these "Spirit-fullness" theologians look to 1 Corinthians 12:13 as the definitive passage. They argue that the Pauline passage has reference to ecclesiastical admission and it is reasoned that the other six passages are to be understood accordingly. However, the foregoing analysis of the passages in question has suggested that 1 Corinthians 12:13a has reference to one's incorporation into the Church, while the remaining six passages (Matthew 3:11, Mark 1:8, Luke 3:16, John 1:33, Acts 1:5, 11:16) refer to the charismatic work of the Spirit. Here then would be a violation of the biblical writers individuality. In view of the unanimity among other canonical writers, it would not appear equitable to chose the Pauline text as the final wood for determining the manner in which the phrase is used in modern theology. It is likely that the early church did not use the term "baptism in the Spirit" as a popular cliché to refer to one's experience of the charismatic Spirit. It may be that alternatives noted by Luke were more prominent, namely "received the Spirit," "gift of the Spirit," and "Spirit came down" (Acts 2:38, 8:15, 10:45, 11:15).

For reasons unknown to us, Luke chose to limit the phrase "baptized in the Spirit" to the Acts 2 and 10 "Pentecosts." However, in so doing he also used other phrases in parallel. On the day of Pentecost, those promised a baptism in the Spirit were said to have been "filled with the Spirit" (Acts 2:4). When recounting his experience at the house of Cornelius, Peter exchanged the phrase "baptized with the Spirit" (Acts 11:16) for "gift of the Spirit" (Acts 11:17) and the "Spirit came on us" (Acts 11:15). Therefore it is probable that these phrases used elsewhere particularly the primary Spirit-fullness (Acts 6:3, 5, 8, 7:55, 11:24) and Spirit-fillings passages (Acts 4:8, 31, 13:9, 9:17) are relevant to formulating the present day doctrine of Spirit baptism. This judgment is strengthened by the fact that most of the passages in question make explicit reference to the charismatic work of the Spirit.

Non-Pentecostal "Spirit-fullness" theologians who depend on Ephesians 5:18 have often accepted the "fullness" references of Luke as pertinent to their cause, but will not take the next step and accept the fact that Luke used the phrase interchangeably with "baptism in the Spirit." This is inconsistent. The biblical data are supportive of the use of the term "baptism in the Spirit" as having reference to the charismatic work of the Spirit. The fact that this may not have been a catch phrase differently does not seem to be very weighty, especially when a very important theological affirmation is being observed.[39]

It does not seem that the "one baptism" of Ephesians 4:5 can be cited as evidence contrary to the position taken here.[40] Most of those who sug-

---

39. See Gelpi, *Charism and Sacrament*, 150f.; Shelton, "Lucan Redactional Phrases," 82, 85, 87; Hummel, *Fire*, 188; Ysebaert, *Greek*, 58, 60; Pinnock, "Evangelical," 186. Contra Donald Macleod, *The Spirit of Promise* (Houston: Christian Focus Publications, 1986), 2f. Note later here the patristic use of the term in question. I also dissent form the argument of Roger Stronstad, "'Filled With The Spirit': Terminology in Luke-Acts," *Towards A Pentecostal/Charismatic Theology*, ed. by J. Rodman Williams (South Hamilton: Society For Pentecostal Studies, November 15–17, 1984) that "full" of the Holy Spirit refers to enabling, "filling" relates to prophecy, while "baptism" is the consecration. For support of this refection, see Shelton's dissertation "Filled With The Holy Spirit," ch. 9.

40. See Green, *Holy Spirit*, 143. Cf. Bennett, *Holy Spirit and You*, 34; Riggs, *Spirit Himself*, 59. Contra William Fitch, *The Ministry of the Spirit* (Grand Rapids: Zondervan, 1974), 45.

gest that this position is in tension with the Pauline dictum are themselves most likely believers in more than one baptism, sometimes including Spirit baptism as a name for initiation into the Church. Paul's thought concerns water baptism and its unrepeatability, not the world of semantics that has claimed so much attention today. Anyway, a more serious problem is for the "one baptism" people to make sense of the baptisms of Hebrews 6:2, an issue which will not be addressed because of its lack of relevance to the major task at hand. There is the related objection that the term "water baptism" will be confused because of the use of the term "baptism in the Spirit." Those involved in this debate are to be granted a greater amount of ability in being able to discern such basic semantics.

Some have objected to the use of the term "baptism in the Spirit" because it does not occur as such in the New Testament. This objection is somewhat mysterious. It is true that in the six occurrences of interest the various forms of βαπτιζω are always verbal, yet a theologian is well within the boundaries of reasonable theological method to change a verb to a noun. Also this involves putting unwarranted pressure on attempting to reduplicate suspected slogans of the early church.

Finally, note that Protestant and Catholic Charismatic theologians most often prefer to use terms other than Spirit baptism when referring to special pneumatic experiences. This is more for "theological" reasons that "biblical" reasons. That is, the majority of these writers share a similar exegesis of the six passages in question. The rejection of the term "baptism in the Spirit" most often, and perhaps ultimately in all cases, reflects a concern over the theological "baggage" inherent in the Classical Pentecostal doctrine of Spirit baptism. Protestant and Catholic Charismatics agree that there is a distinct work of the Spirit which initiates the believer into the arena of spiritual gifts, but their theologians do not accept many other affirmations made by some Pentecostals including the following: (1) that tongues-speech is *the* initial, physical evidence of Spirit baptism; (2) that Spirit baptism is a second (Keswick Pentecostalism) or third (Holiness Pentecostalism) "work of grace"; (3) that the pneumatic experience reflects a superior righteousness of the recipient.

The result has been that Charismatics have multiplied euphemisms: effusion of the Spirit, actualization, release of the Spirit, among others. Yet even this group is under heavy influence from the mass of lay involvement and it would appear that the term "baptism in the Spirit" will remain with them as a suitable alternative: suitable, because while not accepting much of the Classical Pentecostal baggage. There is essential agreement that there is a distinct, and possibly subsequent, work of the Spirit which empowers one and this work of the Spirit is identifiable in an ordo salutis scheme.

Acts 2:1-4

When the day of Pentecost came, they were all together in one place. Suddenly a sound like blowing of a violent wind came from heaven and filled the whole house where they were sitting. They saw what seemed to be tongues (γλῶσσαι) of (ὡσεὶ) fire (πυρός) that separated and came to rest on each of them. All of them were filled (ἐπλήσθησαν) with the Holy Spirit (πνεύματος ἁγίου)and began to speak in other (ἑτέραις) tongues (γλώσσαις) as the Spirit (πνεῦμα) enabled them.

Two questions regarding this passage must be answered quickly: where? who? There is a good reason to believe that the Temple was the scene of this activity despite the use of οἶκον by Luke.[41] To determine whether this passage refers to the 12 alone, or to the entire 120 has no theological consequence for this investigation, but it seems likely that the entire (approximate, ὡσεὶ Acts 1:15) 120 were involved.[42]

There can be little question about the nature of the Spirit's work in this account. The event is a direct fulfillment of the promise of a spiritual baptism. A series of Bible studies released to prepare participants in the Seventh Assembly of the World Council of Churches sees this as axiomatic and feels constrained to point out that the Spirit must not be limited to the unusual and the extraordinary. This is followed by a series of reports from people in various oppressed nations who testify to the holistic liberation of the Spirit. Perhaps all Pentecostal scholars involved in the 1991 meeting in Austria were able to concur with this line of thinking.[43]

---

41. Dunn, *Jesus and the Spirit*, 147. Luke often uses οἶκος for house/home (example: Acts 16:15, 34) and does on occasion use οἶκος in an almost antithetical manner to the Temple (Acts 2:46, 5:42), but he just as often uses οἶκος as a euphemism for the Temple (Acts 7:47, 49, Lk 6:4, 19:46).

42. Dunn, *Baptism in the Holy Spirit*, 40; Montague, *Spirit*, 276f.; Dunn, *Jesus and the Spirit*, 146; S. Horton, *Holy Spirit*, 142; McNamee, "The Role of the Spirit," 164.

43. See *Come, Holy Spirit—Renew The Whole Creation* (New York: Friendship Press, 1989), 18ff.

The results of the Spirit's coming are readily identifiable as charismatic: (1) The group is enabled to speak in tongues and (2) Peter preaches a missionary sermon which has outstanding results. If there would be any lingering doubts, such should be removed by the Petrine sermon. Peter explicitly relates the phenomena to Joel's prophecy (Joel 2:28f.) and says of Jesus: "Exalted to the right hand of God, he has received from the Father, the promised (ἐπαγγελίαν) Holy Spirit (τοῦ πνεύματος τοῦ ἁγίου),[44] and has poured out (ἐξέχεεν) what you now see and hear" (Acts 2:33). The phrase ἐπαγγελίαν τοῦ πνεύματος τοῦ ἁγίου has been encountered in Galatians 3:14, and ἐκχέω was noted in the previous investigation of *rûaḥ*. Despite one Pauline non-charismatic connotation of ἐκχέω (Titus 3:6), the charismatic connotation of this word was carried over into the Fathers. Notice comments first by Ambrose and then Hilary:

> There follows a spiritual gift which you heard read today, because after the font there remains the effecting of perfecting, when at the invocation of the priest the Holy Spirit is poured forth (*infunditur*), "the Spirit of wisdom, and of understanding, the Spirit of counsel, and of virtue, the Spirit of knowledge, and of godliness, the Spirit of holy fear," as it were seven virtues of the Spirit.[45]

> ... after the washing of water the Holy Spirit comes upon us from the gates of heaven and the unction of celestial glory is poured upon us.[46]

---

44. It is possible that Luke uses the anarthrous and articular construction of πνεῦμα ἅγιον to reflect theological nuances. The argument of Montague, *Spirit*, should be noted. Montague looks to Blass-DeBrunner for the practice of Greek grammar in which a person or thing not yet known or experienced is first introduced without the article, and then concludes, 279:

Thus, since the apostles have not previously experienced the Holy Spirit but now experience the mysterious power for the first time, the article is not used, but when 'the Spirit' is mentioned the second time in the verse the article is used.

The data are too incomplete to justify any definite conclusions, but notice the discussion of the issue (with varying conclusions) in the following works: Dunn, *Baptism in the Holy Spirit*, 68f.; Otto Procksch, "ἅγιος," *TDNT* 1:104; Schoonenberg, "Le Bapteme d'Esprit-Saint," 73; Ewert, *Holy Spirit*, 306nl; H. B. Swete, *The Holy Spirit in the New Testament* (London: Macmillan Co., 1910), 395ff. Also see Stronstad, *Charismatic Theology*, 49ff.

45. Ambrose, "The Sacraments" 3:2:8, *Fathers of the Church* 10:293. Latin from Ambrose, *DES SACREMENTS*, ed. by Don Bernard Botte (Paris: Cerf, 1962), 96. Ἐκχέω is also used in Romans 5:5. See Ewert, *Holy Spirit*, 106.

46. Hilary, "Commentary on Matthew 2:6" *PCC*, Latin, 9:927.

Now a word about the day of Pentecost itself. Modern scholarship has made it very difficult to determine the nature of the Pentecost and the liturgical celebration of Sinai. Evidence of this innovation is based primarily on Second Century AD documentation. Considering the uncertainty, it would seem more likely for there to have been continuity in the Pentecostal celebration up until AD 70 and the innovations to occur afterwards. The practices of fringe sects hardly seem relevant. Nevertheless, the theological implications for either decision seem hardly incompatible. If the feast centered on firstfruits, then the imagery of the 120 being the first to experience the corporate bestowal of the charismatic Spirit is considerably enriched. However, if the connection is with Sinai, the essential point is new people of God with the distinctive mark of the corporate bestowal of the charismatic Spirit.[47]

What, if any, is the significance of γλῶσσαι ὡσεὶ πυρός? The description of tongues as being of "fire" is a matter too controversial for discussion in the limited space here. However, there is a message in that tongues, regardless of their nature, were a part of the Pentecostal phenomena:

> The theological meaning of the Pentecostal miracle is agreed upon: it was the divine antidote to Babel, a display of the grace that heals the broken fellowship of mankind cursed for his arrogance...[48]

The main issue for discussion is how this passage speaks to the Classical Pentecostal doctrine of Spirit baptism. The first decision con-

---

47. For a discussion of the issues raised above, see the following: George Montague, *The Spirit and His Gifts* (New York: Paulist Press, 1974), 24f.; Ewert, *Holy Spirit*, 104; Schweizer, "πνεῦμα," 411; Dunn, *Baptism in the Holy Spirit*, 48f.; F. F. Bruce, *New Testament History* (Garden City: Doubleday, 1972), 208f.; L. Goppelf, *Apostolic and Post-Apostolic Times*, trans, by R. A. Guelich (New York: Harper and Row, 1970), 21; J. C. Rylaards, "Feast of Weeks," *IDB* 4:828; Hull, *Holy Spirit*, 531f.; McNamee, "Role of the Spirit," 163; Stronstad, *Charismatic Theology*, 58f. Montague, *Spirit*, 280f., suggests that one of the parallels made by this connection is the use of various languages at both events. See also pages 282, 275, 283, 287. Cf. Kordel, "Functions of the Spirit," 45n66.

48. Jewett, "Holy Spirit," 32. Of course the parallel is theological, not literal, especially in view of the fact that the day of Pentecost seems to have involved several languages and not just one. See Ladd, *Theology of the New Testament*, 348; Montague, *Spirit*, 277; French L. Arrington, *The Acts of the Apostles* (Peabody: Hendrickson, 1988), 20. An ancient challenge was given to xenolalia to which Gregory of Nyssa responded that the argument failed because akolalia in this instance would mean attributing the miracle to non-believers. This discussion reappears periodically.

cerns whether or not the participants should be referred to as Christians prior to the events of this day.

To understand the position of the Pentecostal participants, one must first understand the basic outline of Heilsgeschichte. Oscar Cullmann, prominent exponent of the modern day theological schema which places emphasis on the role of history in God's plan of redemption, notes that Judaism and Christianity join in the breakdown of salvation-history in to a threefold division, namely, before creation, creation to the parousia, time after the parousia. Christianity distinguishes itself, says Cullman, by its division of the second time period. Although Judaism still considers this period to be futuristic, Christians look back to the ministry of Jesus.[49] Jesus is pivotal in the work of God's redemption. In fulfillment of prophecy Jesus becomes the unique bearer of a permanent possession of the charismatic Spirit and then passes on this same presence to his followers after his ascension.[50]

Prior to the day of Pentecost the core of Jesus' followers were believers in a very real sense of the (Lk 9:20) should not be underplayed. Also important is the truth that Jesus tells his disciples (Lk 10:20) that their names are written in heaven. However, "Christian" in the theological sense of the word involves a confession of Jesus as Lord, trust in him as Savior and evidence of the presence of his Spirit.[51] Further, Acts 11:18 could use the salvation motif as an umbrella that covers events on the day of Pentecost.[52]

Dunn rightly judges that the participants on the day of Pentecost were not 'Christians' in the full sense of the word.[53] Although they had made a commitment to Jesus as the Christ they had not experienced the charismatic Spirit in the corporate, permanent way that was to characterize the

---

49. Oscar Cullmann, *Salvation in History* (London: SCM Press, 1965), 81f.; George E. Ladd, *The Gospel of the Kingdom* (Grand Rapids: Eerdmans, 1959), 24; George E. Ladd, *The Presence of the Future* (Grand Rapids: Eerdmans, 1974), 20.

50. I essentially agree with Dunn, *Baptism in the Holy Spirit*, 41ff., and Green, *Holy Spirit*, 38.

51. Jewett, "Church," unpublished course syllabus (Pasadena: Fuller Theological Seminary, n.d.), 900. Cf. Buswell, *Systematic Theology* 3:210.

52. Larry Christenson, *Welcome Holy Spirit* (Minneapolis: Augsburg Publishing House, 1987), 82.

53. Dunn, *Baptism in the Holy Spirit*, 51, 53. See Packer, *Spirit*, 91. Ervin, *Conversion-Initiation*, 15-19, builds on a different view of covenant and the noted lack of water baptism in the episode to rebuff Dunn at this point.

new covenant. This is because of their unique position in Heilsgeschichte. Immediately after the consummation of their salvation experience, some 3,000 experienced all the elements at one time, but as shall be seen, Luke records other variation (Acts 8, 9) later on.

These followers are in a unique position, and the question must be asked about the relevance of their experience to that of believers today. Can it be said, with the Pentecostals and many Charismatics, that the experience of the 120 is normative, or does one accept the position of most non-Pentecostals that it is Acts 2:38 and the experience of the 3,000 that one should expect to emulate? The position taken here is somewhat mediating. In view of the fact that no other group will be a part of the unique historical events related to Christ's birth and resurrection there is a sense in which the experience of the 120 is not relevant for generations which follow. However, there are two reasons for not pushing this point too far. First, although the historical factors are unique, it is possible that the theological factors are not unique. That is, for whatever else the narrative says, it does made clear that the charismatic work of the Spirit can be isolated as a specific work of the Spirit. Therefore, it is that the specificity of Spirit baptism is supported but not a doctrine of subsequence. Secondly, in view of the fact that Acts 2 is not the only chronological account where the elements of salvation are not in a uniform order, it seems justified to conclude that the theological implications made here are not without foundation.[54]

Acts 8:14–17

> When the apostles in Jerusalem heard that Samaria had accepted the word of God, they sent Peter and John to them. When they arrived, they prayed for them that they might receive (λάβωσιν) the Holy Spirit (πνεῦμα ἅγιον) because the Holy Spirit had not yet come upon (ἐπιπεπτωκός) any of them; they had simply been baptized into the name of the Lord Jesus. Then Peter and John placed their hands on them, and they received (ἐλάμβανον) the Holy Spirit (πνεῦμα ἅγιον).

This passage has long been the center of attention for the Roman Catholic doctrine of Confirmation and the Classical Pentecostal doctrine of the Spirit baptism. Notwithstanding shades of differences, it may be said that

---

54. Turner, *Power from on High*, 777n99, misconstrues my position here.

most interpretations of this text fall within one of three major categories: (1) the case was an obvious exception used by Luke to indicate the correct form of Christian initiation; (2) it was a providential abnormality used to attest the worthiness of the Samaritan church; (3) it confirms the Pentecostal and Catholic doctrine that there is an empowering work of the Spirit, and that it can be experienced subsequent to one' initial salvific experience.

Reasoning that reception of the Spirit is necessary for salvation, Dunn concludes that the Samaritans' confession was deficient and that ἐπίστευσαν here (Acts 8:12f.) refers to mere intellectual consent.[55] Bruner, on the other hand, accepts the initial confession as credible but believes the necessary Spirit reception was providentially withheld until such a time as the Samaritan work could be authenticated by the mother church in Jerusalem. This action, presumably, was to guard against a possible Samaritan sect running independently of the other churches.[56] Contending that water baptism and the gift of the Spirit are inextricably intertwined, John J. McNamee argues that Luke reworked history for the sake of tying the Samaritans to Jerusalem.[57]

The amount of material produced by the Pentecostal-Charismatic Movement concerning the confirmation of the doctrine of subsequence based on this passage is too voluminous to list.[58] Despite the weakness of many of their arguments, it would appear that the weight of evidence supports the teaching that charismatic work of the Spirit can be subsequent to the initial saving act of the Spirit.[59] Support for this is seen in the

---

55. Dunn, *Baptism in the Holy Spirit*, 65. When reviewing Acts 11:17, Dunn insists that πιστεύσασιν ἐπί refers to Christian commitment (52). Cf. Lowell J. Sarte, *All Christians Are Charismatic* (Philadelphia: Fortress, 1988), 25.

56. Bruner, *Theology of the Holy Spirit*, 175. Bruner does not use my terms, but he means the saving Spirit not the charismatic Spirit. See Green, *Holy Spirit*, 137; Stott, *Baptism and Fullness*, 32f.; Ryrie, *Holy Spirit*, 71; Chafer, *Systematic Theology* 6:132; Packer, *Spirit*, 117ff., parallels my own work here.

57. McNamee, "The Role of the Spirit," 188.

58. A sampling of the traditional opinions may be found in the following works: Williams, *Systematic Theology* 3:43; Harper, *Beginning*, 92; Ervin, *Not Drunken*, 94. Interesting enough, there is some parallel thought in A. C. Winn, *Acts of the Apostles* (Atlanta: John Knox Press, 1974), 63f. Winn sees a distinction between the indwelling Spirit and the Charismatic manifestation of the Spirit. Note John Calvin's treatment, *Institutes* (Grand Rapids: Associated Publishers and Authors, Inc., n.d.), 4:19:8, of this passage.

59. Cf. A. M. Stibbs and J. I. Packer, *The Spirit Within You* (London: Hodder and Stoughton, 1967), 35; R. B. Ricklam, *Acts of the Apostles: An Exposition* (Grand Rapids:

following: (1) If the Spirit was withheld in order for a new phase in the missionary movement to receive Jerusalem authentication, one must ask why the same was not done with the Ethiopian eunuch (Acts 8:26-39). (2) Contra Dunn, the fact that the people had been previously deluded by Simon is not sufficient evidence to conclude that ἐπίστευσαν, used almost exclusively in Luke to refer to saving faith, refers only to intellectual commitment. (3) Dunn's charge of the inadequacy of Philip's preaching is not upheld by the text. The crux of Philip's message is quite orthodox. Peter and John did not come to Samaria to preach fundamental issues, but came *because* Samaria had "received the word of God" (Acts 8:14). (4) Luke indicates that after Philip's preaching many experienced χαρά. Luke (and Paul) uses this term to express, among other things, the feeling of a Christian: ". . . the Eunuch . . . went on his way rejoicing (χαίρων)" (Acts 8:39); "And the disciples were filled with joy (χαρᾶς) and with the Holy Spirit" (Acts 13:52. See Lk 8:13, Romans 14:17, 15:13, Gal 5:22, 1 Thess 1:6; cf. Acts 16:34). (5) That this isolated work of the Spirit is the charismatic work of the Spirit is indicated by the lack of elements important to Christian initiation, such as water baptism, and because of the use of ἰδών (v. 18) and secondarily ἐλάυβανον (v. 17). The group had been baptized by water prior to the arrival of the apostles and it is unlikely that they would have received such a rite had they not been considered to be Christians. Λαμβάνω has been shown (Gal 3:2) to have been used often in connection with the charismatic Spirit, and ἰδών demonstrates that there were some external phenomena listed, whatever their specific nature may have been.

Acts 9:17-18

Then Ananias went to the house and entered it. Placing his hand on Saul, he said, 'Brother Saul, the Lord—Jesus, who appeared to you on the road as you were coming here—has sent me so that you may see again and be filled (πλησθῇς) with the Holy Spirit (πνεύματος ἁγίου). Immediately, something like scales fell from Saul's eyes, and he could see again. He got up and was baptized.

The major issue is whether one can discern a separation of the saving grace of the Spirit and the charismatic work of the Spirit in this three day

---

Baker, 1978), 116f.; Ervin, *Conversion-Initiation*, ch. 4; J. Rodman Williams, *Renewal Theology* (Grand Rapids: Zondervan, 1990), 2:187; Arrington, *Acts*, 55. The Church of England uses this passage as support for its doctrine of confirmation.

experience of Saul. Denials of the possibility of subsequence have taken two main courses: (1) Paul was not actually converted on the Damascus road;[60] (2) the three days are to be understood as one event. A published support of this last view is given by Michael Green. Green offers twofold support: (1) Paul decidedly favors one stage in his epistles; (2) Luke demonstrates the unity of the experience by the manner in which the event is retold in Acts 22:10f and Acts 26:12ff.[61]

It seems, however, that this passage teaches that the charismatic work of the Spirit can be subsequent to initiatory salvation. This conclusion reflects the following points: (1) It is inappropriate to impose the non-Pentecostal view of Paul on a Lucan text. The investigation into the Pauline literature indicated that Paul did identity the charismatic work of the Spirit. And even though he seemed to think of the usual experience as being unified, it appeared that Paul left open the possibility that a discernible time sequence could be involved. Thus a look to the Pauline literature does not deny a priori the possibility of subsequence taught in this passage. (2) Only those who teach the inseparable relation of water baptism to salvation can see the belated water baptism as proof that Paul was not regenerated three days prior. It seems such theologians should review the data again, and see this passage as evidence that no strict connection can be made between baptism and salvation, primarily because baptism may not be a sacramental conferral of the Spirit but may be given in response to the bestowal of the Spirit. Similarly in light of Paul's reputation, something substantive must account for Ananias' greeting Paul as ἀδελφέ. The term would appear to be more than a fraternal greeting and perhaps suggests that the Damascus Road experience was a turning point in Paul's pilgrimage. However, no support of this understanding is seen in Paul's use of the vocative κύριε when addressing Jesus. The term as used here most likely means simply "Sir." (3) Ananias' time with Paul appears to have been for the purpose of Paul's restoration of sight, commissioning, reception of water baptism, and Spirit baptism. The second Lucan account (Acts 22:10ff.), like the first, emphasizes that the experience with Ananias was for the purpose of restoration of sight and missionary commissioning. The third account (Acts 26:12ff.), which is only a summary,

---

60. Charles R. Erdman, *The Acts: An Exposition* (Philadelphia: Westminster Press, 1929), 80.

61. Green, *Holy Spirit*, 134. Similarly Dunn, *Baptism in the Holy Spirit*, 74f. and McNamee, "Role of the Spirit," 210f.

simply emphasizes Paul's commissioning. Paul's own account is as follows: "I became a servant of this gospel by the gift (δωρεὰν) of God's grace (χάριτος) given me through the working (ἐνέργειαν) of his power (δυνάμεως)" (Eph 3:7). Notice Bruner's assessment of Acts 8:

> No mention is made in the text of the occurrence of the promised filling of the Holy Spirit. Is this because the promised filling did not occur? Such an assumption is foreign to the intention of the text.
>
> ... the Spirit was given with this event, or, summarily, that to "be baptized" = to "be filled with the Spirit."[62]

Indeed, and the most prominent evidence of the charismatic Spirit in the life of Paul according to the remaining chapters in the Book of Acts may be his missionary activity. It is not to be forgotten, however, that Paul tells us in his writings about his personal involvement with charismatic phenomena including tongues-speech.

Acts 10:44–47

> While Peter was still speaking these words, the Holy Spirit (τὸ πνεῦμα τὸ ἅγιον) came on (ἐπέπεσεν) all (πάντας) who heard the message. The circumcised believers who had come with Peter were astonished that the gift (δωρεὰ) of the Holy Spirit (τοῦ ἁγίου πνεύματος) had been poured out (ἐκκέχυτα) even on the Gentiles. For (γὰρ) they heard them speaking (λαλούντων) in tongues (γλώσσαις) and praising God. Then Peter said, "Can anyone keep these people from being baptized with water? They have received (ἔλαβον) the Holy Spirit (τὸ πνεῦμα τὸ ἅγιον) just as (ὡς καὶ) we have."

The Classical Pentecostal argument for subsequence from this passage has traditionally pivoted on the claim that Cornelius was saved prior to his encounter with Peter.[63] Dennis Bennett, however, speaks on behalf of those who have modified the scheme by admitting that Cornelius and the others were not saved before hearing Peter preach, but that a time

---

62. Bruner, *Theology of the Holy Spirit*, 190. Cf. Ervin, *Conversion-Initiation*, ch. 5; Stronstad, *Charismatic Theology*, 66; Arrington, *Acts*, 99f.; Shelton, "Lucan Redactional Phrases," 87–89.

63. Myer Pearlman, *Knowing the Doctrines of the Bible* (Springfield: Gospel Publishing House, 1937), 317f. Cf. Arrington, *Acts*, 112f.

lapse can be discerned in the course of events which followed the homily, namely saving faith and then (later) reception of the Spirit.[64]

However, the weight of appropriate evidence supports the view of Bruner and Dunn that the group had a unified experience.[65] There does not appear to be any evidence that Cornelius was a Christian prior to this encounter. Luke's description of him is hardly equivalent to the description of a Christian: no confession of Jesus as Lord, lack of awareness of the Holy Spirit, and so on. If Cornelius and his group had already accumulated this knowledge, Peter's sermon was a surprise since Peter covered the basic elements of a Christian confession. Also, the group was shortly to be baptized in water.

The evidence of the group's experience including the charismatic Spirit seems rather straightforward: (1) they spoke in tongues, λαλούντων γλώσσαις; (2) the words ἐκκέχυται (v.45) and ἔλαβον (v.47) are used to describe their reception of the Spirit; (3) the imagery projected by the word ἐπέπεσεν is congenial to other biblical descriptions of the charismatic work of the Spirit. It is not surprising to find the word used in the following passages: "And he said to me . . . (v.2) . . . prophesy against them, son of man, prophesy (v.4). Then the Spirit of the Lord fell upon (ἔπεσεν ἐπ') me . . ." (v.5) Ezekiel 11; ". . . the Holy Spirit had not yet come upon (ἐπιπεπτωκός) any of them" Acts 8:16; "Just as I was starting to speak, the Holy Spirit came on (ἐπέπεσεν) them as he had come on us at the beginning" Acts 11:15; (4) Peter identified their experience with that of the Jewish believers in Jerusalem.

This last point calls for elaboration, especially in light of two other recorded occasions where Peter retold this story: "Just as I was starting to speak, the Holy Spirit (τὸ πνεῦμα τὸ ἅγιον) came on (ἐπέπεσεν) them as he had come on us at the beginning. Then I remembered what the Lord had said, 'John Baptized with water, but you will be baptized (βαπτισθήσεσθε) with (ἐν) the Holy Spirit (πνεύματι ἁγίῳ).' So if God gave (δωρεὰν) them the same gift he gave us, who believed (πιστεύσασιν) in the Lord Jesus Christ, who was I to think that I could oppose God!" (Acts 11:15-17); "God, who knows the heart, showed that he accepted them by giving (δοὺς) the Holy Spirit (τὸ πνεῦμα τὸ ἅγιον) to them, just as he did to us" (Acts 15:8). Both Dunn and Bruner use these remarks of Peter

---

64. Bennett, *Holy Spirit and You*, 33. Cf. Riggs, *Spirit Himself*, 111.

65. Dunn, *Baptism in the Holy Spirit*, 79; Bruner, *Theology of the Holy Spirit*, 192. See Ewert, *Holy Spirit*, 123; McNamee, "Role of the Spirit," 198.

to conclude that the disciples were not true believers before the day of Pentecost.[66] There would be many others who would have to wrestle with the implications of their position if it could be substantiated, because the position of most Protestant theologians is that the Pentecostal experience is unrepeatable, but most of them concede that the disciples experienced more than one stage in the working of the Spirit in their lives. It does not seem appropriate to deny the stages which the disciples experienced. Their experience on the day of Pentecost is nothing like those which follow all the other cases involve a confrontation with the message of Jesus as Christ. The disciples had already accepted this and because of their commitment had gone to Jerusalem to wait for the promise of the Lord. In fact, the group is even described as "brothers" (ἀδελφῶν) (Acts 1:15).

There are two other matters that deserve brief attention. notice that all (πάντας) in Cornelius' house experienced the charismatic work of the Spirit. Also, note that they had experienced the completeness of God's work in their lives before they were baptized in water.

Acts 19:1–6

> While Appollos was at Corinth, Paul took the road through the interior and arrived at Ephesus. There he found some disciples (μαθητάς) and ask them, "Did you receive (ἐλάβετε) the Holy Spirit (πνεῦμα ἅγιον) when you believed (πιστεύσαντες)?" They answered, "No, we have not even heard that there is a Holy Spirit" (πνεῦμα ἅγιον). So Paul asked, "Then what baptism did you receive?" "John's baptism," they replied. Paul said, "John's baptism was a baptism of repentance. He told the people to believe in the one coming after him, that is, in Jesus." On hearing this, they were baptized into the name of the Lord Jesus. When Paul placed his hands on them, the Holy Spirit (τὸ πνεῦμα τὸ ἅγιον) came on (ἦλθε) them, and they spoke (ἐλάλουν) in tongues (γλώσσαις) and prophesied (ἐπροφήτευον).

Acts 19:1–6 is the final Lucan passage chosen for exegesis. There is a textual variant in verse 2 which is worthy of attention. The variant issue here exemplifies the distinction between the thought of the Alexandrian text and the Western text of Acts. The received reading has been ἔστιν, which is from the Alexandrian text, while λαμβάνουσίν τινες, which is from the Western text, has been designated as the variant. The Alexandrian reading

---

66. Bruner, *Theology of the Holy Spirit*, 196; Dunn, *Baptism in the Holy Spirit*, 52.

is to be preferred because it has more and better support and because it is the more difficult reading. The Western reading seems to have been an attempt to smooth over the literal text, since it could be used to raise many theological questions. It would appear that the intent of the Western text is to confirm beyond all reasonable doubt the understanding that these men were not ignorant of the person and work of the Holy Spirit but were only uninformed concerning the Christian pneumatic phenomena. This conciliatory spirit is not uncharacteristic of the Western text.[67]

Advocates of Classical Pentecostal pnuematology have not been hard pressed to find supportive material from writers outside their tradition. F. F. Bruce is one among many who has argued that the use of μαθητάς and πιστεύσαντες and the lack of explicit reference to John the Baptist is evidence that these men were Christians, albeit incomplete Christians.[68]

Non-Pentecostal writers have meant to say that they were "incomplete Christians" until the rite of water baptism resulted in reception of the indwelling Holy Spirit. Pentecostals, however, have gone in a different direction from the same starting point. Classical Pentecostals have said the group was "saved" and knew the "indwelling of the Holy Spirit" but had not yet come to know the power of the (possibly) subsequent experience of Spirit baptism. This position is modified somewhat by Protestant Charismatics, including Howard Ervin, who accepts the understanding that they were not previously Christians but that a time lapse is apparent between the time of conversion at water baptism (which is not to be understood as a sacramental effection) and the later Spirit baptism.[69]

Ervin and others have overstated their case. The account seems to teach clearly a unified experience of the Ephesians. The position taken here, then, is a modification of the argument given by J. D. G. Dunn and followers.[70]

---

67. Metzger, *Commentary on the Greek NT*, 259–72. Cf. Haenchen, *Acts*, 51; Dillion and Fitzmyer, *Acts, JBC*, 167

68. Bruce, *Book of Acts*, 385; Johannes Munck, *Acts of the Apostles*, AB, 187; Dillion and Fitzmyer, *Acts*, 201; Hull, *Acts of the Apostles*, 112; William Barclay, *Acts of the Apostles* (Philadelphia: Westminster Press, 1955), 154; Haenchen, *Acts*, 556; Knowling, *Acts*, 402. Cf. Arrington, *Acts*, 191f.

69. Ervin, *Not Drunken*, 102, 104. Ervin elaborates on this in ch. 7 of his heated rebuttal in *Conversion-Initiation*, in which he, unfortunately, repeatedly identifies his view as "the pentecostal position." He maintains the same posture in his *Spirit Baptism* (Peabody: Hendrickson, 1987), 80.

70. Dunn, *Baptism in the Holy Spirit*, 85–89; R. B. Rackham, *The Acts of the Apostles: An Exposition* (Grand Rapids: Baker, 1978), 346; Stott, *Baptism and Fullness*, 35; Green, *Holy*

(1) Μαθητάς in this passage is anarthrous. Although every other plural use of this term in Acts refers to Christian congregations, all of those constructions are articular. (2) Their rebaptism, which is the only event of its kind in Acts, indicates that their previous baptism was not Christian. (3) After some discussion with the group, Paul discovered that he had mistakenly applied πίστις to them and he began to instruct them about repentance. (4) Could a Christian group be ignorant of the work of the Holy Spirit in the new age? By current definitions, this seems improbable.

CONCLUSIONS

Few can be surprised to see overwhelming emphasis on the charismatic work of the Spirit in Luke. Certain specific observations must be made from the findings in the texts analyzed.

1. No comprehensive list of charismatic works is to be found in Luke, for preferential treatment is reserved for the spectacular. Luke centers his attention on tongues-speech (Acts 2:4, 10:46, 19:6), prophecy (Acts 19:7), missionary work (Acts 2:14) and numerous related workings found throughout Luke-Acts.

2. The most important contribution of Luke to this investigation is that he recounts cases where the charismatic work of the Spirit is separated from the initial salvific event. Acts 8:14–18, 9:17–19, extenuating circumstances notwithstanding, appear supportive of ecclesiastical subsequence formulas that intend to acknowledge the "pattern" in Acts is the absence of uniformity in sequence.[71]

If additional texts could have been consulted it would have been shown that Luke also notes the linear dimension of the charismatic work of the Spirit (see his use of πλήρης) and that the purifying work of the Spirit is not equivalent to his empowering work (note Paul's behavior).[72]

Spirit, 134; Bruner, *Theology of the Holy Spirit*, 209; Ewert, *Holy Spirit*, 124ff.; McNamee, "Role of the Spirit," 206f. Contra Ervin, *Conversion-Initiation*, ch. 7. The KJV "since you believed" should give way to the more accurate reading "when you believed." Riggs, *Spirit Himself*, 53, notes this and still considers the passage supportive of subsequence.

71. Cf. William Atkinson, "Pentecostal Responses to Dunn's *Baptism in the Holy Spirit*: Luke-Acts," *Journal of Pentecostal Theology* 6 (1995): 129.

72. Cf. Turner, *Power from on High*, 445–49.

4

The Johannine Literature

INTRODUCTION

ALL OF THE JOHANNINE Literature will be analyzed with the exception of the Book of Revelation. A separate investigation into the Paraclete-sayings has led to the conclusion that they are not critical to this study.

The publication of Gary M. Burge's *The Anointed Community* demonstrates a more substantial shortfall. Burge's biblical theological treatment of the Johannine tradition raised Pentecostal-Charismatic scholarship to a higher notch. After demonstrating a command of the literature that accounts for the scholarly endorsement of James D. G. Dunn and Ralph P. Martin, Burge can make the following judgments:

> Finally, this dual message of John—that the Spirit is released through the cross and that Christ and Spirit must never be separated—has an important contemporary relevance. Any theology which separates salvation from the life-creating Spirit is inadequate (contra many "second-blessing" theologies.) But at the same time the reception of grace and the birth of a Christian cannot be devoid of pneumatic experience (contra many non-Pentecostal theologies.)[1]

Limitations of space account for the elimination of some tasks normally associated with biblical exegesis. A determination of authorship(s), for instance, will not be attempted. This section will assume the conve-

---

1. Gary M. Burge, *The Anointed Community: The Holy Spirit in the Johannine Tradition* (Grand Rapids: Eerdmans, 1987), 149. See the review of Burge by Charles S. Gaede in *CT* (2-3-89): 59f. Dr. Burge, who now serves on the faculty of Wheaton College, no longer identifies with the Charismatic Movement.

nience of designating "John" the author of the Fourth Gospel and the Johannine Epistles. This does not imply a preference for any particular historical personage; and, consequently, no attempt will be made to buttress any argument by connecting the material with a known person of history.

The composition date of the epistles in relationship to the Gospel is a matter of dispute. However, because the Gospel is the substantive precedent of the epistles, it will be treated first.

No detailed account of the Johannine theological frame of reference will be given. We need only to defend the use of the earlier analysis of *rûaḥ* as a determining factor in the exegesis which follows. Although John's Gospel was once thought of totally in terms of Hellenistic influence, it would now appear preferable to assert the essential Jewishness of the work, perhaps one could say a Hellenistic Jewishness. A rather lengthy quotation from I. Howard Marshall serves to qualify this assertion.

> Much evidence has been found of Aramaic traditions behind the synoptic Gospels and John. The thought in John is often expressed with the parataxis and parallelism....
>
> Although there are comparatively few quotations, most of key ideas in John are taken from the Old Testament (e.g., word, life, light, shepherd, Spirit, bread, vine, love, witness) and Jesus is portrayed as the fulfillment of the Old Testament.
>
> Parallels with contemporary Jewish thought, especially with orthodox rabbinic Judaism, may also be found.... Since Palestinian Judaism had been subject to Hellenistic influences for about two centuries, there is no need to look wider for Hellenistic influence upon John. The degree of resemblance between ideas found in John and in Philo of Alexandria is variously estimated.
>
> The Jewish sectarian texts from Qumran also help to fill in the background of John ... it is doubtful whether a direct influence from Qumran upon John requires to be postulated.
>
> C. H. Dodd ... rightly rejected Mandaism.... But he devotes considerable attention to Hellenistic mystery religion, especially as depicted in the Corpus Hermeticum.... But, while there are interesting parallels of thought which demonstrates that John would be intelligible to pagans and not merely to Jews, a close affiliation of thought is unlikely.[2]

---

2. I. Howard Marshall, "Gospel of John," *NBD*, 648f. See Martin, *Foundations* 1:274ff.; Neill, *New Testament*, 315f.

EXEGESIS

We are now prepared to turn to the texts which will always be taken from the NIV (unless otherwise indicated) and will reflect the Greek text of Nestle's *Novum Testamentum Graece*.

John 3:34

> For the one whom God has sent (ἀπέστειλεν) speaks the words of God; to him God gives (δίδωσιν) the Spirit (τὸ πνεῦμα) without measure (οὐ ἐκ μέτρου).

A Protestant Charismatic may be inclined to see here a description of believer Spirit-fullness similar to that given in Ephesians 5:18. She/he can hardly be blamed for such a decision because the interpretation of this text is considerably hampered by the fact that "God," as read in the third clause is excluded in the most reliable manuscripts.[3] This means that Messiah, or for that matter some manuscripts supply πνεῦμα, could be the subject and the believer the recipient. This suggestion is rejected by most commentators on the ground that only Jesus has the Spirit οὐ ἐκ μέτρου. Typical here is the argument given by Leon Morris:

> But it is not true that the New Testament regards believers as receiving the Spirit without measure. In the first place no one else has the Spirit in any way comparable to Jesus ... second ... "unto each one of us was the grace given according to the measure of the gift of Christ."[4]

---

3. C. H. Dodd, *The Interpretation of the Fourth Gospel*, (Cambridge: At the University Press, 1953), 311; B. F. Westcott, *The Gospel According to St. John* (Grand Rapids: Eerdmans, 1975 [1881]), 61; C. K. Barrett, *The Gospel According to St. John*, (London: SPCK, 1955), 189; J. N. Sanders and B. A. Mastin, *A Commentary on the Gospel According to St. John* (New York: Harper and Row, 1968), 136; Edwyn Hoskyns, *The Fourth Gospel* (London: Latimer Trend & Co. Ltd. Plymouth, 1947), 231; Nestle's text, page 238.

4. Leon Morris, *The Gospel According to John* (Grand Rapids: Eerdmans, 1971), 247. Demonstrating part of the problem with this kind of argument, George T. Montague, *Spirit*, 344, points out, "in the Pauline letters, charismatic grace is said to be measured out (Eph 4:7. Cf. 1 Cor 12), whereas the grace that saves 'abounds beyond measure' (2 Cor 9:14, Eph 2:7, Rom 5:17)." Some have used Jn 3:34 (Christ as the recipient) as the argument against Pentecostals. See J. Dwight Pentecost, *The Divine Comforter* (Chicago: Moody Press, 1963), 247; Fitch, *Spirit*, 188.

Schnackenburg sees this position strengthened by the rabbinic saying that the prophets received the Spirit in different measures.[5] However, C. K. Barrett rightly judges this particular piece of extra-biblical material is of dubious help here.[6] Be that as it may, considering the context and particularly the verse which follows (v. 35 which seems to be a Hebrew parallelism), it is possible that God is the subject and Jesus the recipient of the Spirit 'without measure' here.

This is done with qualification, however. The logic of the commentators seems elusive. In what sense can it be said that the believer's reception of the Spirit is measured? Surely there can not be a quantitative improvement on the reception of the Spirit which is procured by the believer at the moment of his or her conversion. This opinion is strengthened by a Johannine affirmation found in the prologue: "And from his fullness (πληρώματος) have we all (πάντες) received (ἐλάβομεν), grace (χάριν) upon grace (χάριτος)" (John 1:16, RSV). When the phrase Spirit-fullness is used here, it is only an attempt to reflect the words of Scripture itself. This phrase is not understood to be explanatory of human ontology. It is quite true that none of us share the ontology of Jesus, but that does not appear to be the point of the verse. As Professor Barrett says, the sense is that it is "because God gives (the Spirit) to Jesus in no measured degree but completely that Jesus speaks the words of God."[7]

It seems that there is some connection between John 3:34 and John 1:33 in that both passages point to Jesus as recipient of the Spirit. This in turn means that this endowment with the charismatic Spirit is the basis for the later dispersion of the Spirit by Jesus to his people. Considering this parallel between Christ and the believer, it is of importance to note also that δίδωσιν is present indicative. That is, there is a linear dimension to the charismatic experience of Christ and the believer (see Ephesians 5:18; cf. 1 Thessalonians 4:8, Ezekiel 36:26f., 37:14, LXX). It was the outpouring of the Spirit which was part of the decisive movement in Heilsgeschichte from the Old Age to the New Age, and reception of the Spirit in the Christian era accordingly had new trademarks permanence

---

5. Rudolf Schnackenburg, *The Gospel According to St. John* (Freiburg: Herder, 1968), 1:386. Schnackenburg does not specify the reference but notes that it can be found in Billerbeck 2:431. See J. H. Bernard, *A Critical and Exegetical Commentary on the Gospel According to John* (Edinburgh: T & T Clark, 1928), 125; Hoskyns, *Fourth Gospel*, 230.

6. Barrett, *Gospel According to St. John*, 189.

7. Ibid. See Burge, *Anointed Community*, 61f., 84.

and completeness. Again, therefore, the theological deduction with regard to the charismatic Spirit is not that the Spirit is given in limited quantity to the believer at the beginning or that it is metered in parts throughout the life, but that the works of the Spirit may be actualized in a manner which is discernible temporally.

John 4:14

> But those who drink (πίη) the water that I will give them will never be thirsty. The water that I will give (δώσω) will become in them a spring (πηγή) of water gushing up (ἁλλομένου) to eternal life. (NRSV)

The first exegetical task is to determine the meaning of the term "water." John 7:37–39 explicitly identifies the "living water" with the Holy Spirit,[8] and this identity is rooted in one of John's sources, namely, the Hebrew Scriptures.

> Therefore you will joyously draw water from the springs of salvation.
> *Isaiah 12:3*

> For I will pour out water on the thirsty land
> And streams on the dry ground;
> I will pour out my Spirit on your offspring
> And my blessing on your descendants.
> *Isaiah 44:3* (NASB)

There is evidence from the Talmud that Jews considered the libation of water at the Feast of Tabernacles to symbolize the outpouring of the Spirit.[9]

Beyond the possible connection of John 4:14 with John 7:37–39, the strongest indication that it is the charismatic Spirit in view is the saying that this water will "well up." Ἁλλομένου is used of the leaping of

---

8. Dunn, *Baptism in the Holy Spirit*, 187, agrees that water is used in chapters 4 and 7 to refer to the Spirit.

9. See Bernard, *Gospel According to John*, 284. Bultmann, *Gospel of John*, 183, says, "The 'Spirit' is also thought of as water when it is said that God will 'pour it out'; Isaiah 44:3, Joel 3:1, Acts 2:17ff., Titus 3:6 and in the Rabbinic exegesis the 'water' of the Old Testament is frequently interpreted as the Spirit." Cf. Morris, *Gospel According to St. John*, 123. The pouring imagery is perhaps often associated with the charismatic work (Joel 2:28, Acts 2:17, 10:45), but not always (Ezek 38:29, Titus 3:6).

the man formerly lame (Acts 3:8), but the most important use is pointed out by Professor Schnackenburg: "The metaphor is used in another way, Judges 14:6, 19; 5:14; 1 Samuel 10:10 (LXX), of the Spirit of God who 'leapt' upon the men of God..."[10] As seen in the earlier analysis of *rûaḥ*, these Scriptures refer to the charismatic work of the Spirit.

It is important to note that John indicates that Jesus bestows this Spirit upon the believer and that the welling up occurs within the believer himself. As J. H. Bernard says:

> In verse 10 the thought is of God as the Eternal Fountain, but it was also a Hebrew thought that the man who assimilated the Divine Wisdom becomes himself, as it were, a fountain from which streams of water of life proceed. Thus the promise of Isaiah 58:11 is, 'Thou shalt be like a spring of water, whose waters fail not.'[11]

The final exegetical task is to determine the best translation of πίῃ. Professor Barrett comments:

> The aorist subjunctive must be translated, "Whosoever shall drink," not "whosoever drinks..." A single draught of the water of life is contrasted with the necessarily frequent drinking of ordinary water. The variant ὁ δέ πίνων... which misses this point, is perhaps due to the influence of Sirach 24:21.[12]

Barrett's judgment is to be preferred despite the contrary translation given by NIV, RSV, NEB, NASB, and the Jerusalem Bible. If John had desired to emphasize the durative force of the drinking, the present subjunctive would have served his purpose better than the aorist subjunctive which he used. This is not to deny the linear dimension of Spirit reception, for such is expressed in the present particle ἁλλομένου (δώσω—progressive future?), but it is to admit the force of the context where the natural water is set in antithesis to spiritual water.

A word needs to be said about the implications of ἁλλομένου being a present participle. When those of the "traditional" Protestant persuasion attempt to distinguish their position from the Pentecostal by talk-

---

10. Schnackenburg, *Gospel According to John*, 431. See Burge, *Anointed Community*, 97; Bernard, *Gospel According to John*, 141; Montague, *Spirit*, 347. Cf. Dunn, *Baptism in the Holy Spirit*, 187.

11. Bernard, *Gospel According to John*, 140. See Schnackenburg, *Gospel According to John*, 430f.; Barrett, *Gospel According to St. John*, 196.

12. Barrett, *Gospel According to St. John*, 196.

ing of a "one-stage" theology, the layperson's version seems to be that this means there are no future pneumatic experiences. However, as Robert Culpepper points out, this is hardly the case. Perhaps most adherents to Evangelicalism would agree with Culpepper's comments on Dunn's conversion-initiation scheme: "The appropriation of all that is latent in this relationship, however, is the process of a lifetime. . . ."[13] Culpepper, however, stretches the good wishes of evangelical theologians when he thus summarizes Spirit reception as it is seen in Acts:

> Sometimes the Spirit is given after baptism. Sometimes before it. Sometimes his coming is connected with the laying on of hands; sometimes it is not. Sometimes it is a two-stage experience, more often not.[14]

Yet, perhaps the distance from Pentecostals is not so great if the remarks of Clark Pinnock, although a charismatic, represent a present day expression of the Evangelical position.

> Now it could be argued that conversion ought to be the occasion when we enter into a fully conscious experience of the Spirit. But it can hardly be denied that this is not always the case. It often happens that people live the Christian faith for a time before actualizing the encounter with the Spirit in their conscious experience. In charismatic terminology, "baptism in the Spirit," refers to that moment when the resources of the Spirit, given to the believer at conversion, but up till then untasted, becomes a matter of personal experience.[15]

It appears that these basic thoughts are present in John 4:14.

John 7:37–39

One the last and greatest day of the Feast, Jesus stood and said in a loud voice, "If any man is thirsty, let him come (ἐρχέσθω) to me and drink (πινέτω). Whoever believes in me, as the Scripture

---

13. Culpepper, *Charismatic Movement*, 67.

14. Ibid.

15. Clark Pinnock, "An Evangelical Theology of the Charismatic Renewal," *Theological Renewal* 7 (October/November 1977): 29. See Michael Harper, *Three Sisters* (Wheaton: Tyndale, 1979); Kilian McDonnell, *Presence, Power, Praise*, 3 volumes; Arnold Bittlinger, *The Church is Charismatic* (Geneva: World Council of Churches, 1981); Packer, *Spirit*, ch. 5; Lindsell, *Holy Spirit*, 93; *Theological Renewal* occasional paper #1 published with *Renewal* 68 (April/May 1977).

(ἡ γραφή) has said, streams of living water will flow (ῥεύσουσιν) from within him (ἐκ τῆς κοιλίας)." By this he meant the Spirit (πνεύματος), whom those who believed in him were later to receive (λαμβάνειν). Up to that time the Spirit (πνεῦμα) had not been given (οὔπω ἦν), since Jesus had not been glorified (ἐδοξάσθη). (NIV)

On the last and greatest day of the festival, Jesus stood and cried aloud, "If anyone is thirsty let him come to me; whoever believes in me, let him drink." As Scripture says, "Streams of living water shall flow out from without him." He was speaking of the Spirit which believers in him would receive later, for the Spirit had not been given, because Jesus had not yet been glorified. (NEB)

These verses are complex and therefore regularly debated. Fortunately, some matters that concern the commentators are not directly relevant here. The matter of determining whether the "last day" was the seventh or eight day is not a concern.[16]

Bultmann charges that the term "living water" reflects gnostic dualism.[17] However, Schnackenburg, Barrett and others rightly argue that Bultmann has not given sufficient credit to the influence of the writings of the Hebrew Bible and rabbis.[18] This point was made earlier when analyzing John 4:14.

The similarity between John 4:14 and John 7:37-39 in addition to various passages where this imagery projects the charismatic Spirit (including 1 Corinthians 12:13b) seem particularly supported in this passage by the reference to the water as the Spirit not yet given. Notice ἐδοξάσθη whose importance will loom larger later on. Westcott gives a helpful analysis:

---

16. For comments on this debated issue, see Barrett, *Gospel According to St. John*, 269; Montague, *Spirit*, 347f.; Hoskyns, *Fourth Gospel*, 320f.; Sanders and Mastin, *John*, 212; Bernard, *Gospel According to John*, 280; Westcott, *Gospel According to John*, 123; John Marsh, *The Gospel of St. John* (London: Cox & Wyman Ltd., 1968), 340, 343; William Barclay, *Promise of the Holy Spirit* (Philadelphia: Westminster Press, 1960), 31; Swete, *New Testament*, 143; Stott, *Baptism and Fullness*, 52f.; Ervin, *Not Drunken*, 215.

17. Bultmann, *Gospel of John*, 185, 182.

18. Schnackenburg, *Gospel According to John*, 430f.; Barrett, *Gospel According to St. John*, 195f.; J. N. Sanders and B. A. Mastin, *The Gospel According to St. John* (London: Adam & Charles Black, 1968), 143; Marsh, *Gospel of John*, 213; Hoskyns, *Fourth Gospel*, 241.

> St. John regards Christ's death as a Victory (cf. 12:32f., 11:4, 40), following the words of the Lord who identified the hour of His death with the hour of His glorification (12:32f.) ... Christ spoke of Himself as "glorified" when Judas had gone forth to his work (13:31); and so He had already received His glory by the faith of His disciples before He suffered (17:10). In another aspect His glory followed after His withdrawal from earth (17:5, 16:14). By the use of the phrase the Evangelist brings out clearly the absolute divine unity of the word of Christ in His whole "manifestation" (1 John 3:5, 8; 1:2), which he does not (as St. Paul) regard indistinct stages as humiliation and exaltation.[19]

The issue that will soon loom large is whether this specifically includes the ascension of Christ. It seems that it does, primarily because of the comprehensive sense in which John uses the term "glorification" and because of the Paraclete sayings, John 14–16, where Jesus must go away so the ἄλλον παράκλητον (John 14:16; cf. 16:7) can come. This is the same basic idea which is expressed in the phrase οὔπω ἦν πνεῦμα. This is not a denial of the existence of the Holy Spirit, but an awareness that the Spirit-fullness which is essential to the New Age, has yet to be initiated. Hence it is quite proper for the exegetes to translate "The Spirit has not yet given' rather than the literal 'the Spirit was not yet.'"[20]

Another matter of concern is the problem of punctuation. The diversity of opinion is indicated by offering the NEB's version along with the NIV. Professor Barrett explains these two important options.

> The punctuation of the words ascribed to Jesus is uncertain. (1) We may place a stop after πινέτω, with a comma after εἰς ἐμέ. The phrase ὁ πιστεύων εἰς ἐμέ is then a *nominatius pendens*, resumed in αὐτό. The rivers of living water flow out of the belly of the believer, and to this the "Scripture" refers. (2) We may (as e.g., Bultmann, 228, on account of the difficulty of finding an Old Testament text to satisfy #1, and the rhythm of the clause) place a comma after πρός με and a stop after εἰς ἐμέ.

---

19. Westcott, *Gospel According to John*, 124. See Barrett, *Gospel According to St. John*, 272; Bultmann, *Gospel of John*, 304; Tappeiner, "Holy Spirit," 54; Ladd, *Theology of the New Testament*, 275.

20. Barclay, *Spirit*, 31f.; Morris, *Gospel According to St. John*, 427; R. E. Brown, *The Gospel According to St. John* (Garden City: Doubleday, 1970), 324; Sanders and Mastin, *John*, 215; Marsh, *Gospel of John*, 342. Agnes Ozman (Sarah Parham, *Parham*, 66) made reference to John 7:37–39 when first explaining her Spirit baptism.

This gives a couplet in parallelism: If any man thirst let him come to me/He that believes on me, let me drink. The reference to Scripture, καθὼ εἶπεν ἡ γραφή, may now be applied either to what precedes or to what follows and in ἐκ τῆς κοιλίας αὐτοῦ the pronoun may refer to Christ or to the believer.[21]

Barrett's analysis was chosen because he is one of the few who perceives that the second option does not automatically present Christ as the source. Since this is true, it means that the importance of the punctuation issue has been greatly exaggerated. Nonetheless, Barrett's reasoning for favoring the first option remains the most convincing.

> The ancient authority for #2 consists of some Western Fathers, the colometry of the old Latin MSS, d and e, and a possible allusion in the Epistle of the Martyrs of Vienne. This does not weigh heavily against the majority of Greek Fathers, who take the alternative view. Certainty is not attainable, but #1 may be preferred because (1) the parallelism produced by #2 is at best imperfect, and there is therefore no compelling reason for thinking that it was intended; (b) the invitation πινέτω is better connected with Ἐάν τις διψᾷ than with ὁ πιστεύων; as thirsty, a man is properly summoned to come and drink; as a believer, who has come and drunk, he can be the subject of a statement.[22]

With this consideration and especially John 4:14, it seems possible that the believer and not Christ is the fountain of living waters referred to here. This is, of course, not to deny that John may have intended somewhat of a double meaning.

This book is known to be full of much imagery and we know Christ to be the ultimate source of any spiritual reality in the believer.[23] Paul speaks of Christ as the dispenser of the Spirit and Luke speaks of the risen Jesus, "Being therefore exalted at the right hand of God, and having

---

21. Barrett, *Gospel According to St. John*, 270. Lindsay Dewar, *Holy Spirit*, 31f., relates a novel but unacceptable approach to the problem.

22. Ibid. Gordon Fee, "Once More—John 7:37-39," *ExpTim* 89:4 (January 1978): 116f., argues that the believer theory is proven by verse 39. Contra Sanders and Mastin, *John*, 213. Brown, *Gospel According to St. John*, 329, suggests the Eastern preference for the believer theory was a result of their denial of the procession of the Holy Spirit from the Son.

23. See Morris, *Gospel According to St. John*, 243; Bernard, *Gospel According to John*, 281; Montague, *Spirit*, 348; Hoskyns, *Fourth Gospel*, 321.

received from the Father the promise of the Holy Spirit, he has poured out this which you see and hear" (Acts 2:33, RSV).

The determination of ἡ γραφή also seems to favor the believer theory. Advocates of Christ as the source insist that ἡ γραφή when used by John always refers to a particular Scripture and no such Scripture can be shown which has the believer as the source.[24] The exact wording apparently cannot be correlated in the writings of ancient Israel for the defense of either position. It seems, rather, that one has to depend on the general sense of the Hebrew canon. This would mean that data could be provided for either argument, which is acceptable, because while this particular passage may single out the believer, Christ is obviously the ultimate source.[25] Nevertheless, Isaiah 58:11 is an excellent example of the Hebrew canon conceiving of the believer as a source.

> And the LORD will continually guide you,
> And satisfy your desire in scorched places,
> And give strength to your bones;
> And you will be like a watered garden,
> And like a spring of water whose waters do not fail.
> (NASB)

What do these data mean? It would appear that one can draw the same deduction from John 7:37–39 that was taken from John 4:14. The appropriation of the indwelling of the Spirit in charismatic works may be indicated by ῥεύσουσιν which is probably progressive future. The closeness of the Pentecostal and Reformed position is demonstrated when Bruner says,

> The John 7 passage teaches also that the Spirit given to *sola fidei* is not anemic. The Spirit shall "*flow* with *rivers* of *living* water." It is not flattering to faith in Christ when it is identified only with a semi-initiation and is allowed only a trickle of nearly powerless

---

24. See Hoskyns, *Fourth Gospel*, 322f.; Sanders and Mastin, *John*, 213; Brown, *Gospel According to St. John*, 328f.; W. F. Howard, *Gospel According to St. John*, 1B 8:588; Dunn, *Baptism in the Holy Spirit*, 179f.

25. See Burge, *Anointed Community*, 88–93. Cf. Morris, *Gospel According to St. John*, 424; Barrett, *Gospel According to St. John*, 271; Swete, *New Testament*, 144. I find Barrett's treatment, 271, of the rabbinic use of Jerusalem as the heart more satisfying than that suggested by Bultmann in *The Gospel of John*, 303. Interestingly, the original edition of the KJV tied Joel 2:28, John 7:38 and Acts 2:18 to Isaiah 44:3.

life. . . . faith in Christ . . . receives from Christ not only spiritual existence and revivification, but spiritual power as well.[26]

John 20:22

And with that he breathed (ἐνεφύσησεν) on them and said, "Receive (Λάβετε) the Holy Spirit (πνεῦμα ἅγιον)."

Pentecostalists who address the issue of Spirit baptism are likely to show only casual interest in the writings of John. Having turned to John, however, they will perhaps pause briefly at John 7:37:39, and quickly make their way to John 20:22. Unfortunately, so much uncertainly prevails about the correct interpretation of this passage that exegetes of all generations and varying persuasions fail to reach any significant agreement. In our day, three positions command attention.

The first position has been taken from the early days of the Reformation and has come to be known as the proleptic view. That is, the actions recorded in John 20:22 are seen to be part of an acted out parable in anticipation of the fulfillment which occurred on the day of Pentecost.[27]

The second argument has come into prominence in the past century. Often influenced by form criticism, proponents of this view argue that it is an exercise in the Spirit reception events as recorded in John 20 and Acts 2. In fact, some argue that John's story is "more accurate" than Luke's.[28]

The third option is to suggest that John 20:22 and Acts 2:4 speak of two impartations of the Spirit. This seems to be the most plausible explanation especially in view of the distinct place of the disciples in Heilsgeschichte. This uniqueness enhances their correlation with the fundamental movement of God's revelation:

---

26. Bruner, *Theology of the Holy Spirit*, 254. See also Congar, *Holy Spirit* 1:50; Burge, *Anointed Community*, 97. No tension is seen here with my judgment that should be given a puncticular sense rather than a continuous one. The difference can be explained in that the concern of the former passage (i.e., antithesis to natural water) is not shared in Jn 7:37–39.

27. See Ladd, *Theology of the New Testament*, 292; Packer, *Spirit*, 88f.

28. See Barrett, *Gospel According to St. John*, 478; Lindars, *Gospel of John*, 612; R. E. Brown, *Gospel The According to St. John* (Garden City: Doubleday, 1970), 2:1038f.; Bernard, *Gospel According to John* 2:677; Sanders and Mastin, *John*, 433; Bultmann, *Gospel of John*, 693; McNamee, "Role of the Spirit," 170f.; Green, *Holy Spirit*, 41f.

CREATION	REDEMPTION	EFFUSION
Luke 9:20	John 20:22	Acts 2:4
Confession	Indwelling	Charismatic

The Pauline affirmation that post-Pentecostal believers experience the indwelling of the Holy Spirit from the beginning of their Christian pilgrimage accounts for referring to these impartations of the Spirit as works of the Spirit.[29]

It is clear that the disciples prior to this event were in a right relationship with God: they had confessed their sins and received forgiveness; the Holy Spirit was the source of the fruit they bore; they were empowered by the Spirit for various tasks; Jesus told them that they were children of God and that their names were written in heaven; the disciples are told that they know the Spirit in contrast to the world. We cannot know for certain the actual meaning of each of these points, but there should be no quarrel about the thrust of these data.[30]

The scene in John 20:22 is significant because it seems to be the first time that the Spirit of God began to continuously indwell believers. This reality could be accomplished only by the special series of events related to the new covenant that were actualized in the life and death of Jesus Christ. This does not deny the work of the Holy Spirit in the lives of believers prior to this time, but it does suggest that from a New Testament point of

---

29. See Morris, *Gospel According to St. John*, 847; Westcott, *Gospel According to John*, 295; Hoskyns, *Fourth Gospel*, 547; Tappeiner, "Holy Spirit," 55; Congar, *Holy Spirit* 1:53; Harold Horton, *Baptism in the Holy Spirit*, 128; Chafer, *Spiritual*, 25. John Calvin, *Commentary on the Gospel According to John* (Grand Rapids: Eerdmans, 1949), 2:268f says:

> I reply, the Spirit was given to the Apostles on this
> occasion in such a manner, that they were only sprinkled
> by his grace, but were not filled with holy power; for,
> when the Spirit appeared to them in *tongues of fire*,
> (Acts 2:3) they were entirely renewed.

30. John Christopher Thomas, "The Spiritual Situation of the Disciples Before Pentecost," *Toward A Pentecostal-Charismatic Theology*, ed. by J. Rodman Williams (South Hamilton: Society for Pentecostal Studies, November 15–17, 1984). This compares favorably to Harold D. Hunter, *Spirit Baptism* (1983), 92. See also John Rea, "The Personal Relationship of Old Testament Believers to the Holy Spirit," *Essays on Apostolic Themes*, ed. by Paul Elbert (Peabody: Hendrickson, 1985), 101; Packer, *Spirit*, 87.

view that those labeled Christians must confess Jesus as savior and from John 20:22 onwards they know the indwelling of the Holy Spirit.[31]

Ἐνεφύσησεν does not occur elsewhere in the New Testament, but it is in Genesis 2:7 (LXX) and Ezekiel 37:9 (LXX). These are uses of *rûaḥ* in the sense of the coming of the Spirit which are not charismatic.[32] As it is said in Ezekiel 37:14, "I will put my Spirit within you, and you will come to life" (NASB).

James D. G. Dunn wavers when dealing with John 20:22. After giving space to the second position which has been considered, Dunn says:

> It may well be best, therefore, to interpret the Paraclete promise... not of John 20:22... but of a later bestowal of the Spirit, following Jesus' final return to the Father after his various appearances to the disciples. John's account could then dovetail chronologically into the Acts narrative: John would then know of two bestowals of the Spirit, though recording only one, and the promised baptism in the Spirit (1:33) could easily be referred to the unrecorded Pentecost.[33]

Dunn's refuge, after admitting "the Pentecostal thesis at this point cannot entirely be rejected," is to say that because of the unique position of the disciples in the scheme of Heilsgeschichte, their experience cannot be considered normative.[34] But as was argued when reviewing the Lucan material, it is because the Acts accounts show other examples where the charismatic is manifested subsequent to initiatory salvation that a valid implication from the disciples' experience where it is made clear that there is a charismatic work of the Spirit is that the charismatic Spirit may be so manifested in the lives of other believers.

The distinctiveness of the Pentecostal bestowal of the Spirit seems supported by the observation of John 7:37–39 that the charismatic work

---

31. Burge, *Anointed Community*, 149.

32. John Rea, "Old Testament Believers," 101–3, sees this strengthened by John 14:16f. Rea concludes the future tense is in view rather than the present tense. Contra Thomas, "Disciples Before Pentecost," 17f. Cf. Bernard, *Gospel According to John*, 677; Marsh, *Gospel of John*, 693; Ervin, *Not Drunken*, 29. Contra Bultmann, *Gospel of John*, 693. Dunn, *Baptism in the Holy Spirit*, 180, allows John 20:22 to be described as regeneration. See Hummel, *Fire*, 240f.; MacDonald, "Pentecostal Theology," 70; Rea, *Holy Spirit*, 47.

33. Dunn, *Baptism in the Holy Spirit*, 177. Being aware of the implications for his overall scheme of conversion-initiation, Dunn adds (178): "I must confess that I am torn between these two interpretations."

34. Ibid., 178, 181f.

of the Spirit would not be known in its fullness until after the glorification of Jesus. The term glorification and the qualification given in John 16:7 both seem to imply that the concept of glorification involves the ascension. Advocates of the second position noted above agree that the bestowal of the Spirit would be after the ascension of Jesus.

> When therefore the disciples have received the Spirit through his "insufflation" (20:22), we may know that Christ has finally ascended. And this seems implied when Thomas is invited to touch His hands and side, in contrast to Mary Magdalene, who was not permitted to touch Him, because He was not yet ascended.[35]

These writers therefore postulate that Jesus ascended between the events recorded in John 20:17 and John 20:22.

Such reasons seem circular. It seems better to suggest that because no ascension account can be reasonably understood to have occurred before John 20:22, and since such is obviously the case before the Lucan Pentecost, and seeing that Acts 2 is much more in keeping with what one would expect from John 7:37–39 than John 20:22, it can be concluded that the role of the ascension is detrimental to the second argument and supportive of the third. The fact that Thomas was invited to touch Jesus (John 20:27) is not proof of a prior ascension. The prohibition which Jesus extended to Mary (John 20:17), had to do with Mary staying when she should have been going; it was not a denial of her right to touch Jesus. As Harold Horton points out, ". . . the word *touch* in 20:17 means grasp, take hold of, and the form of the Greek word indicates a command to stop doing something one is already doing."[36]

1 John 2:20, 27

> But you have (ἔχετε) an anointing (χρῖσμα) from the Holy One (τοῦ ἁγίου), and all of you (πάντες) know the truth. As for you, the anointing (χρῖσμα) you received (ἐλάβετε) from him (αὐτοῦ) remains (μένει) in you and you do not need anyone to teach you. But as his (αὐτοῦ) anointing (χρῖσμα) teaches you about all

---

35. Dodd, *Fourth Gospel*, 443. See R. H. Lightfoot, *St. John's Gospel* (New York: Oxford University Press, 1956), 231.

36. Harold Horton, *Baptism in the Holy Spirit*, 130. See Congar, *Holy Spirit* 1:51; Heron, *Holy Spirit*, 52. An excellent treatment of this passage may be found in Gary M. Burge, *The Anointed Community*, 114–49.

things and as that anointing is real, not counterfeit—just as it has taught you, remain in him.

The main question of interest is the identification of χρῖσμα. The prior analyses of 2 Corinthians 1:21f and John 1:33 led to the conclusion that the phrase "anointing of the Spirit" was a reference to the charismatic work of the Spirit. In evaluating 1 John 2:20, 27, A. E. Brooks makes these pertinent observations.

> Anointing was the characteristic ceremony of consecrating for an office, and of furnishing the candidate with the power necessary for its administration. It is used of *priests*, Exodus 29:7, 40:13, Leviticus 6:22, Numbers 35:25; of *kings*, 1 Samuel 9:16, 10:1, 15:1, 16:3, 12; 1 Kings 19:15f; of *prophets*, 1 Kings 19:16, Isaiah 61:1. Those who were so consecrated were regarded as thereby endued with the Holy Spirit, and with divine gifts.[37]

Similarly John R. W. Stott argues that the Messiah was anointed with the Holy Spirit (Isa 61:1, Lk 4:18, Acts 4:27, 10:38).

> It is likely, therefore, that the *unction* or anointing which we have received from God is the same Holy Spirit. If the false teachers were antichrists, there is a sense in which every Christian is a true "Christ," having received the same spiritual "chrism" as He received (cf. 2 Cor 1:21f.).[38]

This was the essence of my argument in John 1:33. Jesus was endowed with the charismatic Spirit and believers can have this same experience. For much the same reason, χρῖσμα seems to be used in the same manner in 1 John 2:20, 27. This would be especially pertinent if Burge can be borne out when he says in reference to the text: "In the Johannine controversy it is this charismatic authority that is being tapped in order to counter the secessionists."[39] The use of μένει may reflect John 1:33, thus teaching the

---

37. A. E. Brooks, *Johannine Epistles*, ICC, 55. I do not, therefore, accept the suggestion by C. H. Dodd, *The Johannine Epistles*, MNTC, 61, that Hellenistic rather than Hebrew thought is the background. In a similar vein, I do not accept the suggestion, also made by Dodd, that χρῖσμα has reference to the Gospel. See Montague, *Spirit*, 334.

38. John R. W. Stott, *The Epistles of John*, TNTC, 106. See F. B. Westcott, *Epistles of St. John*, ed. by F. F. Bruce (Grand Rapids: Eerdmans, 1966), 73; F. F. Bruce, *The Epistles of John* (Old Tappen: Fleming H. Revell, 1970), 82; J. L. Houlden, *A Commentary on the Johannine Epistles* (New York: Harper and Row, 1973), 79; A. B. Simpson, *Holy Spirit* 2:235f.

39. Burge, *Anointed Community*, 175. I accept Lampe's judgment, *Seal* that Gregory Dix (*The Theology of Confirmation in Relation to Baptism*, 7) has erred in saying that 1

linear dimension of the charismatic work of the Spirit (cf. Isa 59:21, 1 Jn 3: 24).[40]

If this argument is correct, there is a parallel to the Pauline assertion of the expected universality of this experience (1 Cor 12:13b). This is based on the reading of πάντες over the well attested πάντα.[41]

The identification of τοῦ ἁγίου cannot be resolved completely. Do we suggest the Father or the Son as the giver of this anointing? In light of the connection of ἁγίου (Christ) with χρῖσμα in verse 27, it is my opinion that Christ is in view. As Bultmann observes:

> The "holy one" is certainly an epithet of God in the Old Testament, but Jesus can be designated as the holy one, John 6:69. Since ἐπ' αὐτοῦ in verse 27a refers to Jesus, and he is mentioned in verse 25 as αὐτός, the latter (e.g., Son not Father) is probable.[42]

1 John 2:20, 27 is treated in Dunn's monograph and this is one of the few occasions where Dunn's argument parallels the negative concerns of Dale Bruner. Pentecostals are accused of paralleling an early form of Gnosticism. Dunn notes the teaching of the embryonic Gnosticism that purported a "superior gnosis" of which the ordinary believer was not a recipient and says:

> With this claim we may compare the Pentecostal teaching on the "baptism in the Spirit" for though they are hardly Gnostics, in that they believe all Christians could and should have this greater and deeper experience of God, yet, *in fact* since *in their eyes* only a minority of Christians have had this experience, the practical outworking of the doctrine is the same: only they have had this "second blessing," and all other Christians are less well equipped for service and much power in spiritual experience. It is precisely against such esoteric and factious teaching that John directs his

---

John 2:20, 27 refers to an actual rite of anointing such as became part of the baptismal rite in the church of the early centuries (61).

40. Burge, *Anointed Community*, 54–56.

41. See Metzger, *Greek*, 710; R. Bultmann, *The Johannine Epistles*, trans. by R. P. O'Hara, L. C. McGaugly, F. W. Funk (Philadelphia: Fortress Press, 1973), 37; Nestle's text, 600; Houlden, *Johannine Epistles*, 53; Bruce, *Epistles of John*, 106; Dunn, *Baptism in the Holy Spirit*, 199; R. Schnackenburg, *Die Johannesbriefe* (Basel: Herder, 1965), 155. Contra: Alexander Ross, *Epistles of James and John*, NIC; W. Grundmann, "χρίω," TDNT 9:572.

42. Bultmann, *Johannine Epistles*, 37. So also: Montague, *Spirit*, 335; Westcott, *Epistles of St. John*, 73; Brooke, *Johannine Epistles*, 55.

polemic. *All* Christians have knowledge, because all have been anointed with the Holy Spirit.[43]

It does appear that John affirms a potential universality of spiritual anointing (Jn 7:37–39, 1:16). However, much the same can be said of Paul (1 Cor 12:13b), while at the same time the ideal is admittedly not achieved. Hence Paul (2 Tim 1:5f.) and especially Luke (Acts 8:17, 9:17) recognize the potential lack of a uniform experience. This does leave open the issue of classifications among Christians, but an assessment of that problem will not be made until the final chapter.

CONCLUSIONS

The investigation into Johannine Literature has evidenced some striking parallels with the charismatic theology found in the writings of Paul and Luke. It remains to enumerate some particulars which have appeared in John.

1. There is a charismatic work of the Spirit (Jn 7:37–39, 4:14, 6:27, 1:16, 1 Jn 2:20, 27) but the specifics are not identified in the selected texts (but see John 4:1–6).

2. Can the charismatic work of the Spirit be separated in time from the initial salvific experience? John's emphasis is on a unified experience. John spoke freely about the universality of the reception of the charismatic Spirit (Jn 7:37–39, 1:16).

3. The charismatic work of the Spirit is dynamic not static (1 Jn 2:27, Jn 1:33, 4:14).

---

43. Dunn, *Baptism in the Holy Spirit*, 199. See Ervin, *Conversion-Initiation*, 148f.

5

Patristic Literature

THIS STUDY HAS SUGGESTED that the essence of Classical Pentecostal Spirit baptism theology is found in Scripture itself. Is the same true in later ecclesiastical history? Are there writers who follow a similar pneumatology? These next two chapters will attempt to answer these questions.

The first chapter deals with possible parallels to the essence of Classical Pentecostal Spirit baptism theology in patristic literature. This study is undertaken with the understanding that there is a peculiar importance to this literature. While it would be presumptuous to assume all patristic doctrines to be biblical, the prestige of the Fathers demands that attention be paid to their assessment of any doctrine which claims to be biblical.

True to the pastoral rather than theological orientation of the Apostolic Fathers, Clement said little about the Spirit's work other than his role as the inspirer of Old Testament Scriptures. Yet he reflects an awareness of the charismatic work of the Spirit. Clement speaks of the Christians in Corinth as having received an "outpouring" (ἔκχυσις) of the Spirit in "fullness" (πλήρης)[1] The possibility exists that ἐκχέω is an allusion to the day of Pentecost since it is the same word used about the working of the Spirit in Joel 2:28 (LXX) and Acts 2:17, 33 (see John 4:14, 7:37–39). Πλήρης was used by both Luke (Luke 4:1) and Paul (Ephesians 5:18) when referring to the charismatic work of the Spirit. This conviction is confirmed somewhat by Clement's allusion to Ephesians 4:6f when he says, "Have we not one God, and one Christ, and one Spirit of grace (χάριτος) poured out (ἐκχυθὲν) upon us?"[2] The Ephesian passage delin-

---

1. Clement, *Ep Cor* 1:2:2, *LCL* 24:10–11. See James E. Davison, "Spiritual Gifts," Ph.D. dissertation (Iowa City: University of Iowa, 1981), ch. 2.

2. Clement, *Ep Cor* 1:46:4, *LCL* 24:89.

eates charismatic works of the Spirit (e.g., apostles, prophets, evangelists, pastors, teachers) used for the unification and maturity of the church a solution which Clement would find quite helpful in attempting to deal with the schismatic nature of the congregation in Corinth. And of particular relevance is Clement's exhortation to "let each be subject to his neighbor as his particular χάρισμα dictates."[3]

Ignatius (35–107), bishop of Antioch, does not offer a theological treatise on any work of the Holy Spirit, since, as H. B. Swete has said ". . . the Spirit is with him a primary fact of Christian experience rather than a subject of investigation and exact definition."[4] Despite the occasional claim that Ignatius' *Epistle to the Smyrneans* 8 has reference to confirmation, J. E. L. Oulton offers the more satisfactory solution, saying that the problem is schismatic baptism.[5]

It seems that Hermas would insist that a Christian have the indwelling Holy Spirit *Man* 3:1, 10:2, *Par* 5:7. Its direct relationship to water baptism or anything like Spirit baptism can not be determined to my satisfaction. What about baptismal regeneration in light of the writer's insistence on water baptism? Wading through the mixture of metaphors in an attempt to resolve this issue leaves the matter begging. A key passage is *Parable* 9:13:

> "And the virgins, who are they?" "They," saith he, "are holy spirits" and no man can otherwise be found in the kingdom of God, unless these shall clothe him with their garment; for if thou receive only the Name, but receive not the garment from them, thou profitest nothing. For these virgins are powers of the Son of God. If (therefore) thou bear the Name and bear not His power, thou shalt bear His name to none effect.[6]

Rather than speaking to the issue of baptism regeneration, Hermas seems to indicate that one's belief, aided by the Spirit, will be validated by

---

3. Clement, *Ep Cor* 1:38:1, *LCL* 24:72. Attention should be given also to *Epistles* 1:2. Cf. L. Goppelt, *Apostolic and Post-Apostolic Times* (New York: Harper & Row, 1970), 193; A. C. Piepkorn, "Charisma in the New Testament and the Apostolic Fathers," *CTM* 42, 372.

4. H. B. Swete, *The Holy Spirit in the Ancient Church* (Grand Rapids: Baker, 1912), 16.

5. J. E. L. Oulton, "Second Century Teaching on Holy Baptism," *Theology* (March, 1947): 87, specifies Dix as an offender here.

6. *AF*, ed. and trans. by J. B. Lightfoot (Grand Rapids: Baker, 1956), 229.

works of faith.⁷ Notice also that these works include the charismatic work of the Spirit. The following answer is given to Hermas' question regarding differentiating the false from the true prophet.

> In the first place, he that hath the (divine) Spirit ... is gentle and tranquil and humbleminded ... When then the man who hath the divine Spirit cometh into an assembly of righteous men ... the angel of the prophetic spirit, who is attached to him, filleth the man, and the man, being filled with the Holy Spirit, speaketh to the multitude, according as the Lord willeth.⁸

In the search for a description of the early practice of baptism, one finds in Justin Martyr a detailed account, which among the Ante-Nicene Fathers is second only to Hippolytus' *Apostolic Tradition*.⁹ Justin is probably the first writer to describe water baptism as illumination and he does so in the often quoted passage from 1 *Apology* 61. It would appear that Justin's remarks concerning Spirit reception show a connection between the Spirit and water baptism:

> "And we, who have approached God through Him (Christ), have received not carnal, but spiritual circumcision ... and we have received it through baptism."¹⁰

> Essentially the same point seems to be in view when Justin says, "What need, then, have I of circumcision, who have been witnessed to by God? What need have I of that other baptism, who have been baptized with the Holy Ghost?"¹¹

Justin has not been so precise in his language that one can deduce a teaching of baptismal generation. Also, despite the way he uses the phrase "baptism in the Spirit" it appears that something similar to Classical Pentecostal pneumatology may be found in his 1 *Apology* 65.

> But we, after we have thus washed him who has been convinced ... bring him to the place where those who are called brethren are

---

7. See *LCL* 25:295, 263. Cf. Dewar, *Spirit*, 90f.; G. F. Snyder, *The Apostolic Fathers* 6 (New York: Nelson, 1968), 6:142. Contra Lampe, *Seal*, 106.

8. Hermas, "Mandate" 11, *AF*, Lightfoot, 195.

9. L. W. Barnard, *Justin Martyr: His Life and Thought* (Cambridge: At the University Press, 1967), 135.

10. Justin Martyr, "Dialogue with Trypho," 43, *ANF* 1:216.

11. Ibid, 20, *ANF* 1:208f.

assembled, in order that we may offer hearty prayers in common for ourselves and for the baptised person . . . now that we have learned the truth, by our works also to be found good citizens and keepers of the commandments, so that we may be saved with an everlasting salvation.[12]

There exists the possibility that this post-baptismal prayer—although still considered to be an indissoluble whole with the believer's initiation—was an occasion for one being introduced to the empowering work of the Spirit, perhaps what was later termed the 'Sevenfold Spirit' (cf. *Dialogue* 87, 39).[13]

Irenaeus speaks in general of a connection between water baptism and reception of the Holy Spirit (*Against the Heresies* 5:11:2; *Demonstration of Apostolic Preaching* 42). However, Irenaeus' pneumatology has yet to be exhausted, for when referring to the powerful work of the Holy Spirit which Simon the Samaritan sought, Irenaeus spoke of the believer's "filling with the Holy Ghost, through the imposition of hands..."[14] While this passage is not relieved of ambiguity, there remains some parallel to the essence of the Pentecostal pneumatology.

The *Apostolic Tradition*, produced by Hippolytus (160–236) a Roman presbyter, is probably the earliest complete liturgical text of a baptismal rite, which reads:

> Then the bishop, laying his hands on them, shall pray, saying: O Lord God, who hast made them worthy to obtain remission of sins through the laver of regeneration of (the) Holy Spirit, send into them thy graces that they may serve thee.
> What is the oil but the power of the Holy Ghost? As after the washing those who believe are anointed with chrism.[15]

---

12. *ANF* 1:185.

13. Contra McDonnell, *Baptism in the Holy Spirit*, 37. Cf. G. T. Purves, *The Testimony of Justin Martyr to Early Christianity* (London: James Nisbet and Co., n.d.), 277; E. G. Goodenough, *The Theology of Justin Martyr* (Amsterdam: Philo Press, 1968), 267f. I do not, however, accept the validity of Dewar's argument (*Spirit*, 95) that Justin used Jesus' water baptism to teach subsequence for believers.

14. Irenaeus, "Against Heresies" 1:23:1. See Bernard Leeming, *Principles of Sacramental Theology* (Westminster: Newman Press 1956), 22. Later on (*Heresies* 4:38:2), Irenaeus seems to isolate a work of the Spirit with regard to believer purification. Cf. R. N. Flew, *The Idea of Perfection in Christian Theology* (London: Oxford University Press, 1934), 37.

15. The first quotation is from *The Apostolic Tradition of Hippolytus* 22:1, trans. by B. S. Easton (Ann Arbor: Anchor Books, 1961), 47 and the second one is found in Leonel

It must be remembered that the ceremony had not undergone the temporal separation which becomes final in the Western Church. Here the rite is considered one unit, but the theological distinction made is not irrelevant to pentecostal pneumatology.[16]

Author of the first treatise on water baptism, Tertullian's position does not appear to have changed in his later years.[17] In reviewing Tertullian, one confronts two views which are prominent today: Does on deny, with Lampe and others,[18] that a special gift of the Spirit is known to Tertullian, or does one deny, with Dix and others,[19] that the indwelling of the Holy Spirit is given in water baptism according to Tertullian?

Fortunately there is a third option. That is, it is possible that Tertullian understands water baptism to be the occasion for the work of regeneration, yet one can know an additional work of the Spirit which was bestowed, perhaps at the imposition of hands.[20]

This conclusion can best be illustrated by using Tertullian's treatise on water baptism as a basic outline while drawing from other passages to

---

L. Mitchell, *Baptismal Anointing* (London: SPCK, 1966), 22. See Lampe, *Seal*, 141; A. P. Milner, *The Theology of Confirmation* (Notre Dame: Fides Publishers, 1971), 17, 26. John E. Estam, "Charismatic Theology in the Apostolic Tradition of Hippolytus," *Current Issues in Biblical and Patristic Interpretation*, ed. by G. F. Hawthorne (Grand Rapids: Eerdmans, 1975), 270, concludes: "Confirmation is viewed here entirely as a charismatic action whose significance is realized in the fullness of the Holy Spirit and his grace, besought from God in prayer." Contra Jean Laporte, "The Holy Spirit, Source of Life and Activity According to the Early Church," *Perspectives on Charismatic Renewal*, ed. by E. D. O'Connor (Notre Dame: University of Notre Dame Press, 1975), 79.

16. Philip Hughes, *Confirmation in the Church Today* (Grand Rapids: Eerdmans, 1973), 10; McDonnell, *Baptism in the Holy Spirit*, 37. Theodore R. Jungkuntz, *Confirmation and the Charismata* (Lanham: UPA, 1983), 22f says there is textual uncertainty at this point.

17. See Dewar, *Spirit*, 144, then Swete, *Ancient Church*, 114.

18. Lampe, *Seal*, labels Tertullian as "confused" and "inconsistent." For support of Lampe's position, see the following: Laporte, "Holy Spirit," 79; Ernest Evans, *Tertullian's Homily on Baptism* (London: SPCK, 1964), XXXIIf.; Cyril E. Pocknee, *Water and Spirit* (London: Darton, Longman & Todd, 1967), 12, 54; Oulton, "Holy Baptism," 90; Simon Tugwell, "Pentecostal Doctrine of 'Baptism in the Holy Spirit,'" Part I, *HeyJ* (1972): 274.

19. Dix, *Confirmation*, 17; Dewar, *Spirit*, 114, 122; L. S. Thornton, *Baptism and Confirmation* (London: Society of SS. Peter & Paul, 1923), 154; E. K. Lee, "The Holy Spirit in Relation to Baptism and Confirmation," *Modern Churchman* 13 (July, 1970): 317.

20. Cf. Leeming, *Principals of Sacramental Theology*, 201, 220; Lorna Brockett, *The Theology of Baptism* (Notre Dame: Fides Publishing Inc., 1971), 62; Milner, *Confirmation*, 17f.; McDonnell, *Baptism in the Holy Spirit*, 37; Harper, *Beginning*, 94.

clarify the issue. First, Lampe is quite right to say that Tertullian espouses baptismal regeneration.

> Therefore, when the soul embraces the faith, being renewed in its second birth by water and the power from above, then the veil of its former corruption being taken away, it beholds the light in all its brightness, it is also taken up (in its second birth) by the Holy Spirit, just as in its first birth it is embraced by the unholy spirit.[21]

> But Tertullian indicates that there is more to the work of the Spirit, saying, "Not that in the waters we obtain the Holy Spirit; but in the water, under (the witness of) the angel, we are cleansed, and prepared for the Holy Spirit."[22]

The occasion for this special reception seems to be the post-baptismal imposition of hands:

> In the next place [following water baptism] the hand is laid on us, invoking and inviting the Holy Spirit through benediction.[23]

At least we know it was at this time that Tertullian expected one to receive the initial outpouring of the charismatic work of the Spirit:

> ...when you ascend from the most sacred font of your new birth, and spread your hands for the first time in the house of your mother, together with your brethren, ask from the Father, ask from the Lord, that His own specialties of grace and distributions of gifts may be supplied you.[24]

Origen exercised a freedom with his vocabulary that it is not without difficulty that one comes to his writings today. Unfortunately, an outstanding example of this complexity concerns the topic before us. The peculiarities of Origen's vocabulary enable most writers to mold Origen into their theological likeness.[25]

---

21. Tertullian, "A Treatise on the Soul," 41, *ANF* 3:221. See "On Baptism," 5, 10, "On Modesty," 10. Cf. "On Prescription Against the Heretics," 36 and Lampe, *Seal*, 158f.

22. Tertullian, "On Baptism," 6, *ANF* 3:672.

23. Ibid, 8, *ANF* 3:672.

24. Ibid, 20, *ANF* 3:679. See "On the Resurrection of the Flesh," 8, 3:551; "Against Marcion" 5:12, 3:465; "On the Soul" 11, 3:191; "On the Exhortation to Chastity" 4, 4:53.

25. See Lampe, *Seal*, 164; Swete, *Ancient Church*, 134; Dewar, *Spirit*, 98; Pocknee, *Water and Spirit*, 27; Dix, *Confirmation*, 17.

The most convincing passage for the argument that the Holy Spirit is experienced at the moment of water baptism is Origen's *Homily on Ezekiel* 6:5 16:4:

> Those of us who have received the grace of baptism in the name of Christ are "washed," but I cannot tell which are washed "unto salvation." Simon was "washed" . . . but because he was not washed unto salvation he was condemned . . . he who is washed but not unto salvation receives the water but not the Holy Spirit. He who is washed unto salvation receives both.[26]

However, a formidable argument can be made for Origen deferring Spirit-reception to the time of the imposition of hands: "Lastly, for this reason was the grace and revelation of the Holy Spirit bestowed by the imposition of the apostles' hands after baptism."[27]

It would appear in fact that Origen makes reference to more than one work of the Spirit in the life of the believer. The following passages from Origen seem to indicate that it is the charismatic work of the Spirit which may be expected to be effected by the episcopal consignation:

> But now, when through faith in Christ it (the soul) has merited the grace of the Holy Spirit, and the "spirit of wisdom . . . and fear of the Lord" has filled it, the "barren" has beyond question "borne seven" . . .[28]

> There is also another grace of the Holy Spirit, which is bestowed upon the deserving . . . in proportion to the merits of those who are rendered capable of receiving it. This is most clearly pointed out by the Apostle Paul . . . "There are diversities of gifts, but the same Spirit" . . .[29]

Another quotation from the same work as the last one will suffice to show that this charismatic bestowal of the Spirit did not break the unity of

---

26. As quoted in Benjamin Drewery, *Origen and the Doctrine of Grace* (London: Epworthy Press, 1960), 174f. Cf. Henry Bettenson, *The Early Christian Fathers* (London: Oxford University Press, 1956), 342, for Origen's commentary on Romans 5:8.

27. Origen, "De Principiis," 1:3:7, *ANF* 4:254.

28. Origen, "Homily on 1 Samuel 18 on 2:5," quoted in Drewery, *Origen*, 174. Cf. Origen, "De Principiis," 2:7:3, *ANF* 4:285.

29. Origen, "De Principiis" 1:3:7, *ANF* 4:255. Cf. "Homily on Leviticus 8:2" in Bettenson, *Early Christian Fathers*, 341.

Christian initiation: "In the Acts of the Apostles, the Holy Spirit was given by the imposition of the apostles' hands in baptism."[30]

Cyprian identifies the water baptismal ceremony as the time when the believer is regenerated.

> But further, one is not born by the imposition of hands when he receives the Holy Ghost, but in baptism, that so, being already born, he may receive the Holy Spirit, even as it happened in the first man Adam. For first God formed him, and then breathed into his nostrils the breath of life. For the Spirit cannot be received, unless he who receives first have an existence.[31]

This passage intimates, and the next one clarifies, that Cyprian saw water baptism as a spiritual birth to be distinguished from the laying on of hands by virtue of which the new Christian receives the Spirit in a manner to supplement the Spirit reception at water baptism. Speaking of the Samaritan converts of Acts 8, Cyprian says:

> ... there was no need that they should be baptized any more, but only that which was needed was performed by Peter and John; viz., that prayer being made for them, and hands being imposed, the Holy Spirit would be invoked and poured out upon them, which now too is done among us, so that they who are baptized in the Church are brought to the prelates of the Church, and by our prayers and by the imposition of hands obtain the Holy Spirit, and are perfected with the Lord's seal.[32]

A work known as simply *A Treatise on Re-Baptism* added fuel to the heated third century debate on the possible re-baptism of heretics who returned to the Church. This work, written by someone unknown to us,

---

30. Origen, "De Principiis" 1:3:2, *ANF* 4:242.

31. Cyprian, "Epistles" 73:7 (Oxford, 74:7), *ANF* 5:388. See also "Epistle" 62:8 (Oxford 63:8), *ANF* 5:360; "Epistle" 1:4 ("Against Donatius" 4), *ANF* 5:276. Cf. Milner, *Confirmation*, 19, 21; G. A. Poole, *The Life and Times of Saint Cyprian* (London: Griffith Farrah Okeden and Welsh, n.d.), 240; Mitchell, *Anointing*, 81; Mason, *Confirmation*, 74; Swete, *Ancient Church*, 117; Dix, *Confirmation*, 20; Pocknee, *Spirit*, 28, 66; Lampe, *Seal*, 172, and Bettenson, *Early Christian Fathers*, 372, claim that Cyprian is inconsistent.

32. Cyprian, "Epistle," 72:9 (Oxford, 73:9), *ANF* 5:381. See also "Epistle," 69:2 (Oxford, 72:2), *ANF* 5:376; "Epistle" 1:4 ("Against Donatus," 5), *ANF* 5:276. Cf. McDonnell, *Baptism in the Holy Spirit*, 39; J. G. Lawson, *Deeper Experiences of Famous Christians* (Chicago: Glad Tidings Pub. Co., 1911), 45.

was at one time attributed to Cyprian, but it was actually written to refute him and the African position which Cyprian represented.

It appears that not only did the author refer to the charismatic work of the Spirit, but he could even feel the freedom to describe this as a baptism in the Spirit:

> "... our salvation is founded in the baptism in the Spirit, which for the most part is associated with the baptism of water."[33]

> ... in the Acts of the Apostles, according to that same promise of our Lord, on the very day of Pentecost, when the Holy Spirit had descended upon the disciples, that they might be baptized in Him, there were seen sitting upon each one tongues as if of fire, that it might be manifest that they were baptized with the Holy Ghost and with fire ...[34]

The author identified the charismatic work of the Spirit as having reached back into the Old Testament.

> For since water is poured forth even as blood, the Spirit also was poured out by the Lord upon all who believed. Assuredly both in water, and none the less in their own blood, and then especially in the Holy Spirit, men may be baptized. For Peter says: 'But this is that which was spoken by the prophet ... which Spirit we discover to have been communicated in the Old Testament, not indeed everywhere nor at large, but with other gifts ... God put upon them (the seventy) ... the Spirit which had been upon Moses, and they prophesied in the camp. Further, also in the book of Judges, and in the books of Kings too, we observe that upon several, there either was the Spirit of the Lord, or that He came upon them, as upon Gothoniel, Gideon, Jephthah, Samson, Saul, David, and many others. ... the same Spirit is, moreover, sometimes found to be upon those who are unworthy of Him ... as He was upon Saul, upon whom came the Spirit of God, and he prophesied.
> Which Spirit also filled John the Baptist even from his mother's womb and it fell upon those who were with Cornelius the centurion before they were baptized with water. Thus, cleaving to the baptism of men, the Holy Spirit either goes before or follows it; or failing the baptism of water, it falls upon those who believe.[35]

33. "Treatise on Re-Baptism," 10, *ANF* 5:673. The phrase appears frequently.
34. "Treatise on Re-Baptism," 17, *ANF* 5:677.
35. "Treatise on Re-Baptism," 15, *ANF* 5:676.

Methodius (d.c. 311), probably at one time bishop of Olympus, authored works attacking Origen and then Gnosticism, and his only complete extant work written prior to his anti-Origen days is *Symposium* or *Banquet of Ten Virgins*. Methodius identifies water baptism as the time of one's regeneration, but he also speaks of another work of the Spirit in the life of the believer which effects power. Calling Christ the "true Adam," Methodius builds on the analogy:

> For he who says that the bones and flesh of Wisdom are understanding and virtue, says most rightly; and that side is the Spirit of truth, the Paraclete of whom the illuminated receiving are fitly born again to incorruption.
>
> For it is impossible for any one to be a partaker of the Holy Spirit, and be chosen a member of Christ, unless the Word first come down that he, being filled with the Spirit, and rising again from sleep with Him who was laid to sleep for his sake, should be able to receive renewal and restoration. For He may fitly be called the side of the Word, even the sevenfold Spirit of truth...[36]

The illustrious bishop Athanasius was primarily occupied with the person of the Holy Spirit and consequently had little to say about the role of the Spirit in Christian initiation. However, Athanasius appears to consider the imposition of hands as that part of the baptismal ceremony with which one was given the gifts of the Holy Spirit.

> What had they received (The Galatians—Gal 3:2), if not the Holy Spirit, which has been given to those who believe, to those who are born again through washing and renewal.
>
> Here then by the laying-on-of-the-hands of the Apostles, the Holy Spirit was given to those who were born again.[37]

---

36. Methodius, "Banquet" 3:8, *ANF* 6:320. In "Banquet" 8:8, *ANF*, 6:337, Methodius says:
> ...each of the saints, by partaking of Christ, has been born a Christ. According to which meaning it is said in a certain Scripture, "Touch not mine anointed, and do my prophets no harm," as though those who were baptized into Christ had been made Christs by communication of the Spirit...

37. Athanasius, "To Serapion" 1:6, Ibid., 114. See Athanasius, "Letters," 3:6, *NPNF* 2:4:515; "Four Discourses Against the Arians," 1:47, *NPNF* 2:4:333. Leeming, *Sacramental Theology*, 223, and Mitchell, *Anointing*, 53, cite two references which they understand as placing Holy Spirit reception as the post-baptismal chrismation. But see J. N. D. Kelly, *Early Christian Doctrines* (New York: Harper & Row, 1960), 432; Pocknee, *Spirit*, 83; Lampe, *Seal*, 197.

SPIRIT BAPTISM

Held in high esteem for his *Catechetical Instructions*, Cyril (310–386), bishop of Jerusalem, has thereby achieved literary fame. Despite some controversy over the authorship of the so called *Mystical Catechetics*, I shall consider them as reflecting the view of Cyril.[38] Those who have analyzed Cyril on matters relevant to the concern of this study have failed to reach a unanimous decision: (1) Tugwell, Laporte and Swete insist that Cyril sees the Holy Spirit as coming at the moment of water baptism;[39] (2) Dewar, Pocknee, Kelly, Bettenson, Neunhesuer and Brockett, while not agreeing on particulars, basically view Cyril as singling out the post-baptismal anointing as the time of the reception of the Spirit;[40] (3) Finally, Lampe and McDonnell believe that Cyril one time says Holy Spirit at water baptism, and at another turns his attention to that ceremony immediately following water baptism.[41]

A good starting point for clarification is Cyril's *Lecture* 20:6 (*On the Mysteries* 2:6).

> Let no one then suppose that Baptism is merely the grace of remission of sin, or further, that of adoption; as John's was a baptism conferring only remission of sins; whereas we know full well that as it purge our sins, and ministers to us the gift of the Holy Ghost, so also it is the counterpart of the sufferings of Christ.[42]

Confusion over Cyril allegedly placing reception of the Holy Spirit at the time of water baptism and then later at a post-baptismal anointing, could

---

38. Some believe that there is too marked a difference in thought to have been produced by one person. Some consider this proven on the basis of meager textual evidence which indicates that Cyril's successor, John, is responsible for the authorship of the remaining lectures. On the basis of all the evidence, it seems that the most one can concede is that Cyril is the original author while John was responsible for transcription and perhaps some minor revision. For a discussion of the matter of genuineness, see the following: J. Quasten, *Patrology* (Westminster: Newman Press, 1953), 3:364ff.; Leeming, *Sacramental Theology*, 198; B. Neunheuser, *Baptism and Confirmation* (Freiburg: Herder, 1964), 139; Milner, *Confirmation*, 35; Mitchell, *Baptismal Anointing*, 43.

39. Tugwell, "Baptism in the Holy Spirit," 52; Laporte, "Holy Spirit," 80; Swete, *Ancient Church*, 200.

40. Dewar, *Spirit*, 105; Kelly, *Early Christian Doctrines*, 433, 428f.; Pocknee, *Spirit*, 59; Henry Bettenson, *The Later Christian Fathers* (London: Oxford University Press, 1975), 22; Mitchell, *Anointing*, 41; Neunheuser, *Confirmation*, 145; Brockett, *Baptism*, 39.

41. Lampe, *Seal*, 216; Kilian McDonnell, "The Holy Spirit and Christian Initiation," *Holy Spirit and Power*, ed. by Kilian McDonnell (New York: Doubleday, 1975), 78.

42. *NPNF* 2:7:148. Cf. Cyril, "Procatechesis" 4, 2 *NPNF* 2:7:3, 2; "Lecture" 3:, 17:36 *NPNV* 2:7:15, 132f.

be averted if it be understood that what Cyril has said is that the regenerating work of the Spirit is known at the time of water baptism, but another work would be initiated at a post-baptismal anointing. *Lecture 21 (On the Mysteries* 3) is helpful in its entirety, but sufficient here will be section #4:

> And ye were first anointed on the forehead ... Then on your ears ... Then on the nostrils ... Afterwards on your breast; that having put on the breast-plate of righteousness, ye may stand against the wiles of the devil.
>
> For as Christ after His Baptism, and the visitation of the Holy Ghost, went forth and vanquished the adversary, so likewise ye, after Holy Baptism and Mystical Chrism, having put on the whole armour of the Holy Ghost, are to stand against the power of the adversary, and vanquish it, saying, I can do all things through Christ which strengtheneth me.[43]

Another helpful passage is *Lecture* 17:37:

> If thou believe, thou shalt not only receive remission of sins, but also do things which pass man's power. And mayest thou be worthy of the gift of prophecy also ... All thy life long will thy guardian the Comforter abide with thee ... He will give thee gifts of grace of every kind, if thou grieve Him not by sin ...[44]

Gregory Nazianzen (330–390), a Cappadocian Father and monk for a period of time, notes the reception of the Holy Spirit at the baptismal ceremony, but when clarifying particulars, points out a time after water baptism, probably the anointing, for the Spirit's gift. First of all, Gregory speaks in general terms:

> John also baptized; but this was not like the baptism of the Jews, for it was not only in water, but also "unto repentance." Still it was not wholly spiritual, for he does not add "and in the Spirit." Jesus also baptized, but in the Spirit. This is the perfect Baptism.[45]

---

43. *NPNF* 2:7:150. See "Lecture," 16:26 *NPNF* 2:7:122.
44. *NPNF* 2:7:133. Cf. "Lecture," 1:5.
45. Gregory of Nazianzus, "Oration," 37:17, *NPNF* 2:7:358. Cf. "Oration," 40:10, *NPNF* 2:7:362.

Expounding the particulars of his understanding, Gregory says that it is the Holy Spirit ". . . that perfecteth so as even to anticipate Baptism, yet after Baptism to be sought as a separate gift. . . ."[46]

St. Ambrose (339–397), a bishop of Milan, an exponent of monasticism and the baptizer of Augustine, notes that the neophytes experience the regenerating work of the Holy Spirit in the act of water baptism and not in any post-baptismal rite.[47] When enlarging on the baptismal ceremony, Ambrose notes a rite which follows the water baptism. This is the occasion for one to experience a work of the Spirit which is distinct from his regenerating work. This additional work of the Spirit enables one to experience the 'Sevenfold Spirit', that is those characteristics listed in Isaiah 11:2f.

> There follows a spiritual sign which you heard read today, because after the font there remains the effecting of perfection, when at the invocation of the priest the Holy Spirit is poured forth, 'the Spirit of wisdom, and of understanding, the Spirit of counsel, and of virtue, the Spirit of knowledge, and of godliness, the Spirit of holy fear', as it were seven virtues of the Spirit.[48]

Chrysostom (347–407) evidences the theological influences of his geographical setting. That is, Chrysostom insists that an anointing must precede the actual water baptism. Chrysostom does not appeal to this pre-baptismal unction as the point of reception of the Spirit but, speaking generally, refers to the whole of the ceremony.

---

46. Gregory of Nazianzus, "Oration," 5:29, *NPNF* 2:7:329. Cf. "Oration," 18:13, *NPNF* 2:7:258. Cf. A. T. Floris, "Two Fourth Century Witnesses on the Charismata," *Paraclete* 4:4 (1970): 15; Leeming, *Sacramental Theology*, 205; Lampe, *Seal*, 235. Contra Simon Tugwell, "Reflections on 'Baptism in the Holy Spirit,'"—Part II, *HeyJ* (1972): 405.

47. See Ambrose, "On the Mysteries," 9:59, *NPNF* 2:10:325; Ambrose, "On the Holy Spirit," 1:6:79, 3:10:64, *NPNF* 2:10:103, 144.

48. Ambrose, "The Sacraments," 3:2:8, *FC* 44:293; see "The Sacraments," 1:2:4, 2:7:24, *FC* 44:270, 287; "Epistle," 41:6, *NPNF* 2:10:445; "On the Mysteries," 7:42, *NPNF* 2:10:322. Cf. F. H. Dudden, *The Life and Times of St. Ambrose* (Oxford: At the Clarendon Press, 1935), 2:643; Kelly, *Early Christian Doctrines*, 435; Bettenson, *Later Christian Fathers*, 22; Milner, *Confirmation*, 26; Lampe, *Seal*, 99. Contra McDonnell, *Baptism in the Holy Spirit*, 40; Mitchell, *Anointing*, 8; T. M. Hesburgh, "The Relation of the Sacramental Character of Baptism and Confirmation in the Lay Apostolate," Catholic University of America, *Studies in Sacred Theology* #97 (Washington, D.C.: Catholic University of America Press, 1946), 165; B. Neunhauser, *Baptism and Confirmation* (London: Burns and Oates, 1964), 115.

> And as the element of fire, when it meets with ore from the mine, straightway of earth makes it gold, even so and much more Baptism makes those who washed to be gold steaded of clay, the Spirit at that time falling like fire into our souls ...[49]

When being more specific, Chrysostom indicates that there is a work of the Spirit effected in the believer immediately following the actual baptism in water. With reference to Paul's "we were all given the one Spirit to drink" (1 Cor 12:13b), Chrysostom has this to say: "... to me he appears now to speak of that visitation of the Spirit which takes place in us after Baptism and before the mysteries."[50]

Apparently with reference to the same phenomenon, Chrysostom clarifies that it is the charismatic work of the Spirit which is to be effected in the believer. Speaking of the Samaritans of Acts 8, Chrysostom says:

> They had received the Spirit, namely of remission of sins, but the Spirit of miracles they had not received. Seest thou that it was not to be done in any ordinary manner. but it needed great power to give the Holy Ghost? For it is not all one, to receive remission of sin, and to receive such a power.[51]

It is well known that Chrysostom discounted "extraordinary signs" for his day,[52] and probably with reference to the same pneumatological issues, he refers to those manifestations of the Spirit considered most accepted to his day.

> Through baptism we received remission of sins, sanctification, participation of the Spirit, adoption, eternal life. What would ye more?

---

49. Chrysostom, "Homilies of St. John," 10:3, *NPNF* 1:14:36.

50. Chrysostom, "Homilies on First Corinthians," 30:2, *NPNF* 1:12:176. See also the following: "Baptismal Instructions," 2:25, 6:21, *ACW* 31:52, 101; "Homilies of St. John," 24:2, *NPNF* 1:14:85; "Instructions to Catechumens," 1:3, *NPNF* 1:9:162. Cf. Thomas M. Finn, *The Liturgy of Baptism in the Baptismal Instructions of St. John Chrysostom*, Catholic University of America, Studies in Christian Antiquity #15, ed. by J. Quasten (Washington, D.C.: Catholic University of America Press, 1967), 143, 178f.; Mitchell, *Anointing*, 39.

51. Chrysostom, "Homily on the Acts of the Apostles," 18, *NPNF* 1:11:114, 116. Cf. "Homily on the Acts of the Apostles," 1, *NPNF* 1:11:7; "Baptismal Instructions," 3:6, *ACW* 31:57. See also Lampe, *Seal*, 201, 225; Leeming, *Sacramental Theology*, 201; A. T. Floris, "Chrysostom and the Charismata," *Paraclete* 5:1 (1971): 17–22.

52. See Harold D. Hunter, "Tongues-Speech: A Patristic Analysis," in *Journal of the Evangelical Theological Society* 23:2 (June 1980): 125–37.

Signs? But they come to an end. Thou has "faith, hope, charity," the abiding things: these seek thou, these are greater than signs.[53]

Augustine does not give a particular exposition of the exact order and significance of baptism. This results in some confusion over specifics. Nevertheless, Augustine seems to adhere to baptismal regeneration (*Letter* 98:2) and then looks to an anointing followed water baptism as the time of a special reception of the Spirit: "

> The spiritual unction is the Holy Spirit Himself, of which the Sacrament is the visible unction."[54]

There is more to the baptismal ceremony for Augustine. He tells of an impartation of the Spirit received at the imposition of hands. In reference to "evidence," Augustine insists that the miraculous phenomena in the early church had given way to the more scrutinizable and less imitable demonstration of Christian love.

The group known as Messalians or Euchites ("Those who pray") apparently existed in Syria and Asia Minor during the fourth to sixth centuries. The primary source of information about them are 50 homilies attributed to the Egyptian saint Macarius, but perhaps are actually the work of one Symeon of Mesopotamia, the outstanding theologian of the Messalian ascetics.[55] Martien Parmentier says that they stressed the following: (1) the vivid experience of the Holy Spirit brought about by constant prayer (1 Thess 5:17), which "draws" the Spirit from heaven and (2) the experience of lasting sinfulness, even after baptism.[56] Simon Tugwell adds that they regarded the most important coming of the Spirit as being the descent of the prophetic Spirit upon people already purified.[57] Both the Synod of Side (388 or 390) and the Council of Ephesus condemned

---

53. Harold D. Hunter, *Spirit Baptism* (1983), 133f.

54. Augustine, "On the Epistle of St. John," 3:5, *NPNF* 1:7:477f. See "On the Epistle of St. John," 3:12, *NPNF* 1:7:480; "Sermon," 227, *FC* 38:196f.; "On the Trinity," 15:26:46, *NPNF* 3:224.

55. Martien Parmentier, "Two Early Charismatic Movements; Montanism and Messalianism," *Theological Review* #3, 19, published with *Renewal* #63 (June/July, 1976).

56. Parmentier, "Montanism and Messalianism," 19.

57. Tugwell, "Reflections on 'Baptism of the Holy Spirit,'" 405. See Louis Bouyer, "Some Charismatic Movements in the History of the Church," *Perspectives on Charismatic Renewal*, ed. by E. O'Connor (Notre Dame: University of Notre Dame Press, 1975), 121. Cf. Burgess, "Medieval Churches," *DPCM*, 442. For Simon Tugwell's later thoughts see *Ways of Imperfection* (London: Darton, Longmann and Todd, 1984), 47.

the Messalians as heretical. Although Gregory of Nyssa reacted favorably to them, other church leaders apparently were confused about some aspects of the charismatic phenomena.[58]

Leo (1) the Great became bishop of Rome in 440. When speaking in general terms about believer initiation, he had this to say: "... remain firm in that Faith, which you have professed before many witnesses, and in which you were reborn through water and the Holy Ghost, and received the anointing of salvation, and the seal of eternal life."[59] When clarifying his understanding of this event as it relates to schismatic baptism, he spoke of more than one work of the Spirit.

> But if it is established that a man has been baptized by heretics, on him the mystery of regeneration must in no wise be repeated, but only that conferred which was wanting before, so that he may obtain the power of the Holy Ghost, by the laying on of the Bishop's hand.[60]

The event is one, but the work of the Spirit is multifold, or as Professor Lampe has summarized the pontiff:

> ... though he distinguishes between regeneration by water and the Spirit, conferred in baptism, and, on the other hand, the *"charisma salutis et signaculum vitae aeternae,"* yet he does not interpose any interval or separation between regeneration effected in Baptism and the gift of the Spirit.[61]

CONCLUSIONS

The foregoing leads to the conclusion that there are certain parallels between the pneumatology enunciated by various Fathers and that advocated by Classical Pentecostalism. The key is the essence: both groups speak of a distinct work of the Spirit which accomplishes acts of service

---

58. Martien Parmentier, "Montanism and Messalianism," 19; Bouyer, "Charismatic Movements," 121; *Westminster Dictionary*, 799. Parmentier says that Gregory of Nyssa wrote a corrected version of a Messlian work, the so called *Great Letter of Macarius*. Knox, *Enthusiasm*, 82, says that these people most deserve the name Enthusiasts.

59. Pope Leo I, "Sermons," 24:6, *NPNF* 2:12:136. See "Sermons," 21:3, *NPNF* 2:12:129; "Letters," 16:6, *NPNF* 2:12:129.

60. Pope Leo I, "Letters," 166:2, *NPNF* 2:12:108. Cf. "Letters," 159:8, *NPNF* 2:12:103.

61. Lampe, *Seal*, 207. Of course the case of baptized heretics would prove the exception when they returned to the church.

for the body of Christ. Although the exposition by the Apostolic Fathers, and some Ante-Nicene Fathers, cannot be said to be articulate, the later Fathers, particularly those in the West, remove most doubts. I have concluded that there are at least three reasons for any discernible ambiguity in the patristic literature relevant to my concern: (1) Most of the earlier writings were primarily concerned with pastoral theology. (2) The various cultures produce multiple terms. (3) Among those Fathers that did share the same terms, one can find a lack of unanimity in the definition.

The confirmation theology of the fifth and sixth centuries seems in pneumatological essence to be that era's manifestation of Spirit baptism theology. It would be ludicrous to expect unanimity from the Fathers in their pneumatology. Nevertheless, there are a prominent number of writers who distinguish this special empowering work of the Spirit. That this is often thought of as the charismatic work of the Spirit, is seen in the frequent use of the phrase Sevenfold Spirit.[62]

A later tendency among the Fathers and Mothers was to separate temporally the charismatic work of the Spirit from Christian initiation. I suggest four reasons for this development.[63] (1) The inability of the bishop to participate in all exercises formed a decisive break with the regular theological formula of Christian initiation. (2) Various exegetes of the Book of Acts postulated a work separate from the initial salvific event. (3) There were cases where baptism did not achieve the anticipated results and some were left wanting a second experience. (4) The baptism of infants created a need for an assertion of belief when the child matured, which often led many to postulate a special working of the Spirit on this occasion.

---

62. George T. Montague, *Spirit*, 41, makes this pertinent note regarding Isa. 11:2f: "In the Greek text and the Vulgate which followed it, the word "piety" was found instead of "the fear of the Lord" in its first occurrence, thus bringing the "gifts" to seven. The Hebrew text, however, lists only six.

63. For similar opinions, see the following: Gelpi, *Charism*, 114; B. Luykx, *Confirmation in Relation to the Eucharist*, 192f.; Hans Küng, "La confirmation comme parachevement du baptême," *L'EXPERIENCE DU L'ESPIRIT* (Paris: Beachesen, 1976), 135; McDonnell, *Baptism in the Holy Spirit*, 52; Maurice Wiles, *The Christian Fathers* (London: SCM, 1977), 116; Jungkuntz, *Confirmation*, 25–27.

6

Selected Literature from 600–1900

THE INVESTIGATION CARRIED OUT in the patristic literature will now be extended to include literature from the beginning of the Medieval period up until the beginning of the Classical Pentecostal Movement.

First for review is the Spanish saint Isidore (560–636). One finds in Isidore a biblical explanation of the post-baptismal anointing which will be repeated elsewhere.

> But according as our Lord was anointed by God the Father being (or, to be) the true king and eternal priest, with a celestial and mystic unguent, so now not only pontiffs and kings, but the whole Church is consecrated with the unction of chrisms, because it is a member of the eternal king and priest because we are a *priestly and royal nation* (1 Peter 2:9), after baptism we anoint that we may be called by the name of Christ (i.e., the anointed one).[1]

Most important is that Isidore does not acknowledge the baptismal rite as the point of reception of the Spirit. Building on the precedents of Acts 8:14–17 and Acts 19:1–17, he says:

> But since after baptism the Holy Spirit is given through the bishops with the laying on of hands, we recall that the apostles did this in the Acts of the Apostles. For thus it is written . . .[2]

Ildefonsus (607–667) entered the monastery at Analia near Toledo and eventually became its abbot. He later (657) became the archbishop

---

1. Isidore, "Concerning the Church's Institutions," 2:26:2, *Documents*, Whitaker, 101. See Mason, *Confirmation*, 209.

2. Isidore, "Concerning the Church's Institutions," 2:27:1, *Documents*, Whitaker, 101. See Pocknee, *Spirit*, 86; Mason, *Confirmation*, 210.

of Toledo.³ Ildefonsus had apparently studied under Isidore. It is at least clear that there is a marked dependence on Isidore's work and Ildefonsus, therefore, rightly disclaims originality.⁴ It occasions no surprise to see repeated the existence of post-baptismal anointing and the laying on hands, which, premised on the accounts in Acts, is understood to be the point at which one receives a gift from the Holy Spirit. Ildefonsus puts it this way:

> As soon as the man ... has been brought again out of the waters ... he is brought forward to be touched with the sacred Chrism, in order that he may be anointed with the Spirit of God, and may be, and be called, a Christ, from the name and unction of Christ.
>
> So with this holy Chrism the man is outwardly anointed, and inwardly the power (*virtus*) of the Holy Spirit falls upon him (*illabitur*), so that as the whole man has been purified by the laver, the whole man may be enriched (*pingvescat*) by the unction of the Spirit....
>
> After Baptism is the fitting time for the Holy Ghost to be given, together with the Laying on of the Hand; for thus the Apostle is proved to have done in the Acts of the Apostles.⁵

Originating in perhaps the seventh century, an evangelical antihierarchal sect on Rome's eastern border in Armenia, Mesopotamia and N. Syria were known as the Paulicians. There are questions about various areas of orthodoxy, specifically: Christology (possibly adoptionistic); rejected mariolatry, images and hagiolatry; authority of Scripture (rejected, like Marcion, the OT); possible dualism, though they rejected Manichaeism.⁶ They later gave birth to groups known to be Spirit-oriented like the Bogomites, Cathari and Albigenses. In the 16th century the Anabaptists apparently met up with a group using the same name and a group in 1828 in Russian Armenia was found with the manual of Paulician doctrine, *The Key of Truth*, which includes the following:

---

3. James DeJong, "Ildefonsus," *NIDCC*, 499. His name is variously spelled Ildefonsus, Hildefonsus and Ildephonius.

4. Mason, *Confirmation*, 210.

5. The quotations are excerpts from sections 122–32 of Ildefonsus' "De Cognitione Baptismi," taken here from Mason, *Confirmation*, 211f., but also found in *Documents*, Whitaker, 105 and Pocknee, *Spirit*, 86.

6. *NIDCC*, "Paulicians," 755.

Then after this prayer do thou give the peace to all the people; and the bishop shall take the newly-elected one to himself and instruct him with great love, and give him to read the holy Evangel ever and always. Yes and also the holy testament of the universal and apostolic church; in order that thereby he may in fullness receive the grace of the Holy Spirit, during a space of 40 days.[7]

There is a record, not satisfactorily substantiated that this included the exercise of the extraordinary gifts of the Spirit.[8]

The Gelasian Sacramentary is a presbyterial liturgy which was composed in Gaul in the eighth century. However, the principal manuscript of the book is much earlier, perhaps the fourth century, and is from Rome.[9] The document testifies to a ceremony of christening and laying on of hands after one has been baptized in water.

> Then when the infant has gone up from the font he is signed on the head with chrism by the presbyter, with these words:
>
> The Almighty God, the Father of our Lord Jesus Christ, who has made thee to be regenerated *of water and the Holy Spirit* (John 3:5), and has given thee remission of all thy sins, himself anoints thee with the chrism of salvation in Christ Jesus unto eternal life.
>
> Then the sevenfold spirit is given to them by the bishop. To seal them (*ad consignandum*), he places his hands upon them with these words:
>
> Almighty God, Father of our Lord Jesus Christ, who has made thy servants to be regenerated of water and the Holy Spirit, and has given them remission of all their sins, do thou, Lord, pour upon them thy Holy Spirit the Paraclete, and give them the spirit of wisdom and understanding, the spirit of counsel and might, the spirit of knowledge and godliness, and fill them with the spirit of fear of God, in the Name of Our Lord Jesus Christ with whom thou

---

7. Fred C. Conybeare, *The Key of Truth: A Manual of the Paulician Church in Armenia* (Oxford: Clarendon Press, 1898), 112.

8. David Benedict, *A General History of the Baptist Denomination* (New York, 1849), 13.

9. See J. D. C. Fisher, *Christian Initiation: Baptism in the Medieval West* (London: SPCK, 1965), 1; Pocknee, *Spirit*, 14; "Gelasian Sacramentary," *Westminster Dictionary*, 354; Mitchell, *Anointing*, 102; *Documents of the baptismal liturgy*, ed. by E. C. Whitaker (London: SPCK, 1970), 156.

liest and reignest ever God with the Holy Spirit, through all ages of ages.[10]

Another document from the eighth century, this one known as the *Sacramentary of Gellone*, has this to say about events immediately following one's water baptism.

> And being robed, they are arranged in order in a circle as their names are written. And the pontiff makes the prayer over them with the chrism, making the sign of the cross on their foreheads, with the invocation of the Holy Trinity, and giving them the sevenfold grace of the Holy Spirit.[11]

For a mixture of political and religious reasons, Charlemagne insisted that his empire unite with regard to church liturgy. In response to his desire to implement the usage of the Roman liturgy, Pope Hadrian sent to the king a document now known as the *Gregorian Sacramentary* (8th century). The name can be attributed to the fact that part of the liturgy is probably from the papacy of Gregory the Great (590–604).[12] Of interest is the prayer for confirmation which has been repeated in several liturgies including those of our own century.

> Almighty and everlasting God, who has given new life through water and the Holy Ghost to these thy servants, and granted them forgiveness of all their sins, send down upon them from heaven thy sevenfold Holy Spirit, the Paraclete, the spirit of wisdom and of understanding, the spirit of counsel and of fortitude, the spirit of knowledge and of piety, fill them with thy goodness sign them with the sign of the cross of Christ. Through the same Jesus Christ, thy Son, our Lord, who lives and reigns with thee for ever and ever.[13]

The title "the Venerable Bede" (673–735) was conferred, posthumously, on the astute monk of Jarrow who gained renown for his scholastic achievements despite the fact that he was moved a few miles to a monastery when he was age nine and remained there until his death. His

---

10. "Gelasian Sacramentary," 1:43:94, 95, *Documents*, Whitaker, 178. See also "Gelasian Sacramentary," 1:75:127, Ibid., 185. Cf. Pocknee, *Spirit*, 119, 75; Dix, *Confirmation*, 32ff.; Milner, *Confirmation*, 32; Congar, *Holy Spirit* 1:105.

11. Quoted in Pocknee, *Spirit*, 119. See Milner, *Confirmation*, 57.

12. "Gregorian Sacramentary," *NIDCC*, 432; Milner, *Confirmation*, 55f.

13. Quoted in Milner, *Confirmation*, 55f. See Pocknee, *Spirit*, 42.

traveling friends sought materials for him and his work on the history of the English people was of such repute that he was called "the Father of English History."[14] Concerning the theology of Christian initiation, it would appear that the English view had come under the influence of the persuasive writings of Augustine. Bede concurred with episcopal confirmation and told of St. Cuthbert making his way through rural areas (while executing other duties) with a view to laying his hands on those who had previously been baptized. Commenting on the eighth chapter of Acts, Bede said:

> Note that Philip, who evangelized Samaria, was one of the seven. If he had been an apostle he would himself have been able to lay his hand that they might receive the Holy Spirit ... presbyters ... are not allowed to seal the forehead with the same oil, for this pertains to the bishop alone when they give the Paraclete Spirit.[15]

An important clarification is undertaken when Bede concludes that an implication of this doctrine of confirmation is that one receives two works of the Spirit.

> But the Holy Spirit rested upon him not only from the time when he was baptized by John in the Jordan but rather from the time when he was conceived in the Virgin's womb. The Spirit was seen to descend at the baptism as a sign that spiritual grace would be conferred on us in baptism, and that, born in the remission of sins by water and the Spirit, a further grace of the same Spirit, would be given from heaven through the imposition of the hand.[16]

A well known theologian of the East, John of Damascus (675–749) was virtually unknown in the West during his lifetime. The situation later changed since Peter Lombard used John's writings as authoritative, and in 1890 Pope Leo XII declared the Damascene to be a "Doctor of the

---

14. R. E. Nixon, "Bede," *NIDCC*, 155f.; Pocknee, *Spirit*, 86; Mason, *Confirmation*, 213.

15. In Act VIII by Bede as quoted in Milner, *Confirmation*, 52f. Pocknee, *Spirit*, 87, says:
> Upon the events recorded in Acts 19:1-6, and St. Paul's question to the disciples of St. John the Baptist, "Did you receive the Holy Spirit?" Bede comments, "that is, did you, after Baptism, receive the imposition of the hand, by which the Holy Spirit is customarily given (*dari solet*)?"

16. Bede's commentary work on Mark 1:1 as taken from Milner, *Confirmation*, 53.

Church."[17] Noting humans consist of soul and body, John explained the pneumatological ramification of his view of baptism.

> For since man's nature is twofold, consisting of soul and body, He bestowed on us a twofold purification, of water and of the Spirit ....
>
> The remission of sins, therefore, is granted alike to all through baptism: but the grace of the Spirit is proportional to the faith and previous purification. Now, indeed, we receive the first-fruits of the Holy Spirit through baptism and the second birth is for us the beginning and seal and security and illumination of another life.
>
> But we, too, are baptised in the perfect baptism of our Lord, the baptism by water and the Spirit.[18]

His views on the baptismal event appear to be traditionally Eastern as he specifies the anointing with oil as the point of reception of the Spirit.

> ... since it is man's custom to wash himself with water and anoint himself with oil, He connected the grace of the Spirit with the oil and the water made it the water of regeneration ...[19]

Alcuin of York (d. 804), a pupil of Bede, was among those scholars called to work in Charlemagne's court (742). With regard to the baptismal ceremony, we will quote Alcuin on the sequence of events which were to follow upon one's water baptism.

> Then he is clad in white robes to signify the joy of regeneration and purity of life and the beauty of splendour. Then his head is anointed with holy chrism and covered with a mystic covering, so that he may understand that he wears the diadem of kingship and the dignity of priesthood in accordance with the words of the Apostles, "Ye are a royal and priestly race, offering yourself to the

---

17. Peter Toon, "John of Damascus," *NIDCC*, 542.

18. John of Damascus, "An Exact Exposition of the Orthodox Faith" 4:9, *NPNF* 2:9:78f. Mason, *Confirmation*, 384f., quotes John's comments on 1 Thess 5:25:

> By the "Spirit" He means the gift (χάρισμα) which each received through Baptism, for in those days each person baptized received a gift, and worked signs.... He prays therefore that this gift, which he calls their "Spirit," may abide in them whole, that they may in no way be deprived of the working of the Holy Ghost.

19. John of Damascus, "An Exact Exposition of the Orthodox Faith," 4:13, *NPNF* 2:9:83. See also *St. John Damascene: Barlaam and Ioasapt* 19:164, LCL, 279; Mason, *Confirmation*, 385; Milner, *Confirmation*, 39.

living God a holy sacrifice and pleasing to God" . . . Last of all through the imposition of hand by the chief priest (i.e., bishop) he receives the Spirit of sevenfold grace, so that he may be strengthened through the Holy Spirit to preach to others, who was in baptism endowed by grace with eternal life.[20]

Alcuin has more to say on the subject:

> In Christ's Baptism is the remission of sin, and sanctification, and the gift of the Holy Ghost, as John testifies, who says "This is He who baptized with the Holy Ghost."[21]
>
> Christ is so called from the chrism,—Anointed from the anointing—because His name is poured out upon all the faithful with the grace of the Holy Ghost in baptism.[22]

These remarks reinforce the initial impression that Alcuin may be espousing the position that there is a twofoldness to the reception of the Spirit.[23]

Rabanus (776–856) studied under Alcuin. The influence of Alcuin on his writings is easily discerned. When he speaks of the work of the Holy Spirit in baptism and confirmation, it is possible that he is making explicit what is implicit in Alcuin. From his *On the Training of the Clerks* 1:30, we have the following discussion:

> Finally the Holy Ghost, the Comforter, is transmitted to him by the chief priest through the laying on of the Hand, that he may be fortified through the Holy Ghost to preach to others the gift which he himself gained in Baptism, having been endowed through grace with eternal life. For the baptized is sealed with Chrism by the priest (*per sacerditem*) on the top of the head, but by the pontiff on the brow, in order that by the former unction may be signified the descent of the Holy Ghost upon him to consecrate him for a habitation of God (*ad habitationem Deo consecrandam*), and in the second the grace of the same sevenfold Spirit may be declared to come into the man (*venite in hominen declaretur*) with all the

---

20. Alcuin's Epistle 134 as quoted in Fisher, *Medieval West*, 60f and verified in Mason, *Confirmation*, 215f and Milner, *Confirmation*, 58. Jungkuntz, *Confirmation*, 30f., says that the concept of confirmation as "strengthening" was made famous by the ninth century "Pseduo-Isidorian Decretals."

21. Alcuin's Exposition on Psalm 131:18 quoted in Mason, *Confirmation*, 215.

22. Alcuin's *Comped in Cant Cant* 1:2 as quoted in Mason, *Confirmation*, 215.

23. Fisher, *Medieval West*, 63. Fisher adds, 75, that the hand laying ceremony was to have followed seven days after the Easter vigil.

> fulness of sanctity and of knowledge and of power. For on the former occasion the Holy Ghost Himself after bodies and souls are cleansed and blessed, willingly descends from the Father to sanctify and enlighten by His visitation His own vessel and on this latter occasion He comes into the man, with this intent, that the seal of the faith, which he has accepted on the brow, may make him replete with heavenly gifts and strengthened by His grace to bear the name of Christ fearlessly and boldly before kings and rulers of this world and to preach it with a free voice. Nor is it strange that the man should be twice anointed with the same chrism for receiving the Holy Ghost, when the same Holy Ghost was given to the Apostles themselves twice over,—that is, once upon earth, when after His resurrection the Lord breathed upon them, and once from heaven, when after the ascension of the Lord, He came upon the Apostles on the day of Pentecost in fiery tongues, and granted them to speak with the tongues of all natures.[24]

The practical problem facing Rabanus was that of precedence for episcopal hand-laying or presbyterial anointing.[25] He gave the most significance to confirmation, noting that the anointing was most useful in the case of a child who would die unconfirmed. The theological explanation which he offers when demonstrating the necessity of the anointing immediately following water baptism reinforces my understanding that Rabanus is advocating a double work in Spirit reception.

> Rightly does this unction with chrism follow at once upon Baptism, because the Holy Ghost who sanctifies the believer by the influx of His power through this chrism, descended forthwith upon Jesus after His baptism ... and so it is necessary that he baptized should at once be strengthened with the unction of chrism, in order that by receiving participation in the Holy Spirit he should not be left unlike to Christ.[26]

---

24. Quoted in Mason, *Confirmation*, 227f., and verified in Milner, *Confirmation*, 60f. See Harris, "The Anglican Understanding of Confirmation," 20; Fisher, *Medieval West*, 64. Aquinas, *Summa* 3:72, 11, quotes this passage from Rabanus.

25. Dix, *Confirmation*, 26, says that Rabanus had to grapple with the implications of the act of the Carolingian bishops putting in confirmation at the end of one's youth. Fisher, *Medieval West*, 66, disputes this.

26. "Clerks," 1:28 as quoted in Dix, *Confirmation*, 26 and verified in Mason, *Confirmation*, 255 and Fisher, *Medieval West*, 63. See Milner, *Confirmation*, 59.

A pupil of Alcuin, by the name of Haymo (ninth century), became the bishop of the extreme eastern German see founded by Charles the Great at Halberstadt. Speaking in general terms, Haymo cites baptism as the occasion for reception of the Spirit. In an exposition of Ephesians 1:13, Haymo says:

> "In Whom"—that is, in Christ—"believing ye were signed"—that is, sealed or marked—"with the Holy Spirit of promise,"—that is through the Holy Ghost, Who was promised by the Lord to the Apostles, and through Whom we have the promise of life in Baptism. We are therefore marked as God's through the Holy Ghost Whom we received in Baptism—because we recover in Baptism in the seal of the likeness of God, which we lost by the sin of our first parent, namely innocence and holiness of soul.[27]

Apparently this manner of speaking was utilized in an effort to accentuate the unity of Christian initiation. However, when being more specific about the baptismal event, Haymo speaks of two works of the Spirit.

> By grace we must understand . . . the remission of sins, which the elect receive at the time of Baptism: the gift also of the Holy Ghost which is given as well in Baptism as through imposition of the Hand of the bishops (*tam in baptismate quam per impositionem manus episcoporum*).[28]

The writings of Symeon (949–1022), surnamed "the New Theologian," are repeatedly referred to by Roman Catholic and Eastern Orthodox church leaders involved in the modern day Charismatic Movement. Athanasios F. S. Emmert notes that Symeon lamented over those who thought they had the Holy Spirit and yet they did not because they did not

> . . . believe that there can be in our generation men who are equal to the Apostles of Christ and to the saints of all ages, and are, like them, moved and influenced by the Divine Spirit, or consciously see and apprehend him.[29]

---

27. Quoted in Mason, *Confirmation*, 229f.

28. *PCC* 117:938 as quoted in Mason, *Confirmation*, 230 and verified in Pocknee, *Spirit*, 86. Pocknee, 85, accuses Professor Lampe of being negligent in the manner in which he used the writings of Haymo.

29. Athanasios F. S. Emmert, "Charismatic Developments in the Eastern Orthodox Church," *Perspectives on the New Pentecostalism*, ed. by Russell P. Spittler (Grand Rapids:

Yves Congar called Symeon a mystic who exalted experiencing the Spirit. Controversial Orthodox Charismatic Eusebius Stephanou uses the name St. Symeon the New Theological Orthodox Renewal Center for his work in Florida, declaring Symeon's *Catechesis* 22 to be about a seeker being "enriched by His (e.g., Holy Spirit) charismata."[30] Simon Tugwell adds that Symeon refers to baptism of tears as 'the second baptism.' This second baptism is the baptism by or in the Holy Spirit which is the reality of which the first baptism, water baptism, is the sign. Yet, noting Acts 2:38, Symeon says that the experience should be united but ". . . if they do get separated, the experience of the Spirit, 'the second baptism', is simply, as it were, the reality catching up with the sign."[31]

A monastic teacher in the Orthodox Church, Theophan the Recluse had this to say about the reception of the Holy Spirit: "All of us who have been baptised and charismated, have received the gift of the Holy Spirit. He is in all of us, but He is not active in all of us."[32] When Theolphan spoke of being 'filled with the Spirit' he said:

> . . . the commandment to "be filled with the Spirit" is simply an injunction to behave and act in such a manner as to cooperate with or allow free scope to the Holy Spirit to make it possible for

---

Baker, 1976), 42. See Cardinal L. J. Suenens, *A New Pentecost?* (New York: Seabury Press, 1975), 29; Louis Bouyer, "Some Charismatic Manifestations in the History of the Church," *Perspectives on Charismatic Renewal*, O'Connor, 123; Parmentier, "Two Charismatic Movements," 20; Congar, *Holy Spirit* 1, Chapter 4.

30. Congar, *Holy Spirit* 1:93ff.; Eusebius Stephanou, *The Charismata in Early Church Fathers* (Brookline: Holy Cross Orthodox Press, 1976). Stephanou says of Symeon that he is "probably the most outstanding representative and exponent of the pentecostal experience and theology among Fathers." See Stanley M. Burgess, "Medieval Churches," *DPCM*, 35f.; Bouyer, "Charismatic Movements," 122f.

31. Tugwell, "Reflections on 'Baptism in the Holy Spirit,'" 404. The references are to things which Symeon said in his *Catechesis*, notably 32, 52; 24, 12; 9, 154; 32, 59ff and *Capital* 3, 89; 1, 36. See Tugwell, *Did You Receive the Spirit?*, 53; Suenens, *A New Pentecost?*, 229; Judith Tydings, *Gathering a People* (Plainfield: Logos, 1977), 103f.; Stanley M. Burgess, *The Holy Spirit: Eastern Christian Traditions* (Peabody: Hendrickson, 1989), 58-61. Andrew Walker, "The Orthodox Church and the Charismatic Movement," *Strange Gifts?*, 166, cites Symeon as repudiating modern pentecostalism. Burgess [pp.60-62] says that Symeon did not advocate a second work of grace Spirit baptism accompanied by initial evidence. However, he claims Symeon exercised a gift of knowledge, prophesied and brought healing to many.

32. As quoted in Emmert, "Charismatic Developments," 38.

the Holy Spirit to manifest Himself by perceptively touching the heart.[33]

Insufficient information is available to review the group known as Bogomites[34] and that which is known about Cathari/Albigenses is complicated by hostile interpretations. No less a phenomenon than the Inquisition itself can be attributed to the hostility which these groups generated. Few are there among modern historians, Protestant or Catholic, who consider this tradition as anything other than abhorrent heresy.

Deviations from scriptural norms are not peculiar to Enthusiastic Pneumatomania, but neither are they foreign to them. To the degree that the Cathari were influenced by extraneous influences, such as Zoroastrianism, is difficult to judge. Varying forms of Platonism and Aristotelianism are stapled into most Christian traditions, and the directness of influence and consequences are not all the same. Equally difficult to judge is Warfield's contention that one local body of Cathari perpetuated a dreaded farce on numerous Christians by getting them to venerate a maligned portrait of Mary, the mother of Jesus.[35]

Whatever the various influences, it is obvious that a dualistic system was integral to the Cathari distinctive identity. In a way familiar to various perfectionistic schemes, this teaching ranked believers as ordinary unless they achieved the high level of "spiritual." It is sometimes alleged that at least part of the constituency carried the dualism towards libertine Gnosticism by ignoring sinful deeds of the flesh since these would not contaminate the soul. However, without sufficient documentation to the contrary, it seems most likely that the spirit-flesh dualism was used to move participants to ascetic ideals. That in fact well known examples of practice to the contrary would exist would not of itself evidence lower standards from the group as a whole.

---

33. Ibid.

34. See Knox, *Enthusiasm*, 80–82; Harold O. J. Brown, *Heresies* (Garden City: Doubleday, 1984), 249ff.; Bresson, *Ecstasy*, 36.

35. See R. G. Clouse, "Albigensians," *NIDCC*, 22; J. G. D. Norman, "Cathari," *NIDCC*, 20; G. Giacomalas, Jr., "Bogomites," *NIDCC*, 139; Knox, *Enthusiasm*, 73; Philip Schaff, *History of the Christian Church* (Associated Published, n.d.), vol. 2, vol. 5, Chp 10, #80, 201; John Clare, "The Cathari" *Eerdmans' Handbook to the History of Christianity* (Grand Rapids: Eerdmans, 1977), 319f.; B. B. Warfield, *Counterfeit Miracles* (New York: Scribners, 1918), 67; Bresson, *Ecstasy*, 34f.; Donald L. Gelpi, *Pentecostalism: A Theological Viewpoint* (New York: Paulist Press, 1971), 12; Brown, *Heresies*, 253f.

Part of the identity of the Perfecti was formed by the rite of consolamentum. Consolamentum was sometimes called the baptism of the Spirit, or as it is worded in the opening lines of the liturgy: "Peter, ye would fain receive the spiritual baptism by which is given the Holy Spirit in the Church of God, with the Holy prayer, with the imposition of hands of the 'good men.'"[36] This rite was thought to provide absolution for sins of the past and insure the lack of the same for the future. This resulted in a high level of austerity and, surely, some occasional flexibility in defining sin.

The idea of no repentance after consolamentum has seemed to lend credibility to the alleged rite of endura. It is claimed, by some modern authors, that for someone who had never had the consolamentum, or who had fallen from it, usually a sick person or a child, the method vindication was endura = starvation. But surely this is questionable. It would have been extremely illogical for the Cathari explicitly to prohibit homicide in the rite of consolamentum, and then to have allowed the alternative to the rite to be suicide.[37]

Accounts of erratic behavior are not uncommon with groups of this kind, but when the story relates an act of this nature it is quite hard to accept. The sources of such accounts are from those outside and these same stories, always from outsiders, are told of the Montanists and most other 'enthusiastic' movements known to church history.

The Cathari/Albigenses appear to have been most active in the eleventh century and finally have succumbed to the Inquisition by the fourteenth century. Some of them are believed to have been involved with spectacular gifts of the Spirit. Although originally from the lower caste, they eventually made inroads into higher levels of society.

Anselm of Laon (c. 1117) is the famous Schoolman known as the "Doctor Scholasticus." He is not to be confused with his teacher, Anselm

---

36. "The Ritual of Consolament" cited in Conybeare, *The Key of Truth*, 165. Cf. H. J. Warner, *The Albigensian Heresy* (New York: n.p., 1928), 55. Schaff, *History*, Vol 2:5, Chp 10, #80, 204, quotes them as saying that Christ made a clear distinction between baptism with water and the baptism of power (Acts 1:5). Bresson, *Ecstasy*, 37, claims that the monk Eckbert said the Albigenses ". . . claimed the baptism of the Holy Ghost and laid hands on people that they might be filled with the Spirit." See Tugwell, "Reflection on 'Baptism in the Holy Spirit,'" 405. Damboriena, *Tongues*, 7, 187n23, says that there is no record of tongues-speech among the above named groups.

37. See Conybeare, *Key of Truth*, 166. Contra: Damboriena, *Tongues*, 7; Schaff, *History*, Vol 2:5, Chp 10, #80, 205; Clouse, "Albigensians," 22; J. L. González, *A History of Christian Thought* (Nashville: Abingdon Press, 1970), 1:191.

of Canterbury. Anselm does not hesitate to portray a twofold Spirit reception.

> Why is confirmation needful after Baptism? I answer that in Baptism what is given is the remission of sins, but afterward the baptized must be confirmed with another gift of the Holy Ghost, as for combat. For example, the sons of Israel after they had crossed the Red Sea, because they had to pass through the desert, needed still the help of God. A twelfth century writer, Geoffrey (d. 1132), was Abbott of Vendrôme. When elucidating the pneumatological implications of his doctrine of confirmation, he seems to espouse a twofold work in Spirit reception.
>
> In Baptism is given remission of sin through the Holy Ghost; in Confirmation the Holy Ghost is invited to enter into the house which he has sanctified, to dwell in it, fortify it, and defend it. The Apostles themselves after Baptism received the Holy Ghost, whom they had received in Baptism for the remission of sins; but they received the Spirit again on Pentecost for the perfection of virtue and knowledge.[38]

Exerting an influence far beyond his own geographical and temporal limitations, Peter Lombard (1095–1169) was given the title "Master of the Sentences." These famous sentences were completed shortly before he was elected bishop of Paris in 1159 and were not replaced until the seventeenth century when finally surpassed in use by the writings of Thomas Aquinas. A thinker of this stature obviously had a great affect on the development of confirmation theology. Lombard emphasized that confirmation was a communication of the Spirit 'who gives force' (*ad robur*) in contrast with the communication of the Spirit at water baptism which is fulfilled ad remissionem.[39] A. P. Milner summarizes Lombard's view about this strengthening effected in confirmation.

1. A strengthening by the Holy Spirit so as to be able to preach to others what is received in baptism. This is taken from Rabanus.
2. The reception of the Holy Spirit so as to become a full Christian—that is supported by a citation of the false decretals of the Urban.

---

38. Geoffrey, *Upusculum* 8, PL 157:226, given in Leeming, *Sacramental Theology*, 624.

39. *PCC*, Latin, 192:855, "Virtus autem sacrament est donatio Spiritus sancti ad robur, qui in Baptismo ditus est ad remissionem." See Hans Küng, *La Confirmation comme parachèvement du baptême* (Paris: 1976), 123; Fisher, *Medieval West*, 128.

3. Reception of the sevenfold grace with all the fullness of holiness and virtue—this again is from Rabanus.[40]

William of Auxerre (1150–1231) served as the archdeacon of Beauvals and then proctor of the University of Paris and later was appointed to a special commission by Pope Gregory IX.[41] His writings evidence the influence of Peter Lombard and when he treats confirmation he makes explicit what is implicit in Lombard.

> The Lord twice gave the Holy Spirit to the disciples: once on earth when he breathed on the disciples saying *Receive the Holy Spirit*, etc; this gift signified the grace which is given in baptism. Once he gave the Holy Spirit from heaven on the day of Pentecost for strength when they were confirmed with power from on high; and this signified confirmation and the strengthening of grace which is given in the sacrament of confirmation.[42]

The theological distinction drawn between baptism and confirmation could hardly have been drawn more distinctly than is done by Bruno of Segni. Bruno claimed that the disciples received the Holy Spirit three times.

> ... the apostles themselves after their baptism received the Holy Spirit, whom they had already received in baptism for the remission of sins ... they received the Holy Spirit a second time, so that by him they could bind and loose from sins ... They received him a third time on the day of Pentecost, for the perfecting of all virtue and all knowledge.[43]

Bruno considered the third impartation of the Spirit to be the equivalent of confirmation. Presumably the affirmation that the disciples received the Holy Spirit at their baptism was considered quite logical to Bruno in light of the theology of baptism which he must have been taught, although there could be no support from explicit biblical data.

The classical structure of the present day Roman Catholic rite of confirmation may be attributed to the long time teacher in Paris, Thomas

---

40. Milner, *Confirmation*, 70. Cf. Jungkuntz, *Confirmation*, 30.

41. C. Gregg Singer, "William of Auxerre," *NIDCC*, 1048f.

42. Quotation found in Fisher, *Medieval West*, 128.

43. *PL* 165:1102 as translated in Fisher, *Medieval West*, 128 and verified in Mason, *Confirmation*, 465.

Aquinas (1224–1274).⁴⁴ The Thomistic designation of confirmation as the sacrament of robur associated with the augmentum gratiae is well known. On the other hand, this meant for Aquinas that spiritual maturity was to be expected with confirmation: "... baptism is a spiritual generation into Christian life, so confirmation is spiritual growth bring man to spiritual maturity."⁴⁵ On the other hand, notice the following remarks by Aquinas:

> ... this sacrament gives the Holy Spirit to the baptized for their strengthening just as he was given to the apostles on the day of Pentecost, and as he was given to the baptized through the imposition of hands by the apostles....⁴⁶

> Those who receive confirmation, the sacrament of the fullness of grace, are conformed to Christ is so far as he himself was from the first moment of his conception full of grace and truth. This fullness was proclaimed at his baptism when the Holy Spirit descended upon him in bodily form. For this reason Luke also states that Jesus, full of the Holy Spirit, returned from the Jordan. But it did not suit the dignity of Christ, the author of the sacraments, that he should receive the fulness of grace of a sacrament....⁴⁷

> Baptism is given simply to attain the life of the Spirit and thus it properly uses simply matter. But this sacrament is given for the purpose of attaining the fullness of the Holy Spirit who works in manifold ways....⁴⁸

---

44. Küng, "La Confirmation," 124.

45. Thomas Aquinas, *Summa Theologiae* 3:72:5, "Baptism and Confirmation," ed. and trans. by J. J. Cummingham (New York: McGraw-Hill, 1975), 57:205. Fisher, *Medieval West*, 130, says that Aquinas took the words *augmentum praestat ad gratiam* from Pseudo-Isidore and interpreted them as meaning spiritual growth when the intended meaning was 'supplied an addition to grace.' See the following explanation of the Thomistic definition of confirmation as the completion of baptism: Harris, "Anglican Understanding of Confirmation," 21; Adolf von Harnack, *History of Dogma* (New York: Dover Publications: [1961]), 6:231; Küng, "La Confirmation," 124; Pocknee, *Spirit*, 98f.

46. Aquinas, *Summa* 3a:72:7, Ibid 57:210.

47. Aquinas, *Summa* 3:72:1, Ibid 57:189. Cf. Fisher, *Medieval West*, 131; Jungkuntz, *Confirmation*, 33f.

48. Aquinas, *Summa* 3:72:2:2, Ibid 57:195. See *Summa* 3:72:5, Ibid 57:205. R. J. Pettey, *In His Footsteps: the priest and the Catholic Charismatic Renewal* (New York: Paulist Press, 1977) says that the passage just cited, answers the question (i.e., in the positive) whether or not Aquinas believed the Spirit could be given more than once. Cf. Milner, *Confirmation*, 72.

In the last year of his life, he was in an ecstatic state for almost three days. When Reginald, his associate, prompted him to speak, he said, "Reginald, my son, I will tell you a secret which you must not repeat while I remain alive. All my writing is now at an end; for such things have been revealed to me that all I have taught and written seem quite trivial to me now."[49] Thomas died less than six months later. This story aside, various contemporary Roman Catholic Charismatics have presented Aquinas—when articulating his doctrine of confirmation—as an adherent to something like their 'actualization' theology. Donald Gelpi says:

> Aquinas correctly distinguished two aspects of the Spirit's ministry: His permanent indwelling and His "surprises" (innovationes). . . . His "surprises are the pneumatic breakthroughs He effects especially by means of the gifts of service. . . . The sacrament of confirmation pledges the believer to stand in lifelong openness to the Spirit's surprises . . ."[50]

Two points of Thomistic theology now emerge. First, Aquinas does not relegate "charismatic" "surprises" of the Spirit to "actualizations" of sacramentally conferred graces, but he most usually would have preferred that they operate in that fashion. Second, it would appear that Aquinas differentiates between "the gift of grace which makes us pleasing to God (gratia gratum faciens) and the charismatic gift (gratia gratis datae)." These two elements run parallel to the basic pneumatological issues of Classical Pentecostalism's doctrine of Spirit baptism: that is, actualization approximates subsequence and the separate grace is that distinct work of the Spirit which initiates charismatic activity in the believer.

Aquinas put it this way:

> . . . there is a special instance of an invisible mission based on an increase in grace when someone advances to a new act or new stage of grace, e.g., to the grace of miracles or prophecy or to delivering himself in the fervour of his charity to martyrdom or to renunciation of all he possesses or to taking up any sort of heroic task.

---

49. Warren Lewis, *Witnesses to the Holy Spirit* (Valley Forge: Judson Press, 1978), 126. See Morton T. Kelsey, *Healing and Christianity* (New York: Harper & Row, 1973), 216–20.

50. Gelpi, *Charism*, 148f. See Laurentin, *Catholic Pentecostalism*, 45; Pettey, *In His Footsteps*, 19f.; Bouyer, "Charismatic Developments," 128; Bruner, *Theology of the Holy Spirit*, 187f.

> ...when the apostles imposed their hands or simply reached, the Holy Spirit descended upon the faithful under visible signs as he first descended on the apostles themselves. So Peter says, As I began to speak, the Holy Spirit fell on them just as on us at the beginning. Thus there was no need to use the sensible matter of a sacrament as long as God himself miraculously manifested sensible signs.[51]

Among the friends and supporters of the Hesychasts, one of the most gifted and attracted is Nicholas Cabasilas (1320–1371), a nephew of Nilus Cabasilas, Archbishop of Thessalonica. Nicolas, so far as is known, never became priest or monk, but was a layperson, serving at the court and in the civil service. Nicolas is known in part because of influencing Luther on the matter of literal exegesis. He dealt with baptism and chrismation in a manner which is reflected even in present day theological manuals of the Greek church.[52]

> We are baptized in order that we may die his death and rise in his resurrection; we are anointed that we may share with him in the anointing of the kingdom of his deification. For baptism is birth; the chrism means for us operation and movement....

---

51. Aquinas, *Summa* 3:72:7, 57:193, 5. See Leming, *Sacramental Theology*, 632f. Williams and Waldvogel write, "Speaking in Tongues," 71, "Thomas suggested that men of his day could gain the same gift of tongues as appeared at Pentecost by assiduous linguistic study." J. S. Kerr, *The Fire Flares Anew: a look at the new Pentecostalism* (Philadelphia: Fortress Press, 1974), 34, casts Aquinas as portraying tongues to be diabolically inspired. See Gelpi, *Pentecostalism*, 143; Pettey, *In His Footsteps*, 34; O'Connor, *Pentecostal Movement*, 273; M. T. Kelsey, *Tongue Speaking* (New York: Doubleday and Co., 1968), 48f.; Tugwell, "Baptism in the Holy Spirit"—1, 274. Contra James G. King, "A Brief Overview of Historic Beliefs in Gifts of the Spirit," address to the Society for Pentecostal Studies (Springfield: December 6, 1977), 7. Worthy of noting in passing is the following statement by Tugwell, "Baptism in the Holy Spirit"—1, 273:

> Incidently, it is on the basis of the Cornelius episode that the only use of the term "Spirit-baptism" in Classical Catholic Theology rests: baptisma flaminiis, as "baptism of desire," in anticipation of (or in the impossibility of) proper sacrament of baptism.

Lewis, *Witnesses to the Holy Spirit*, 125f., acknowledges Thomas's exegetical conclusions about charisms, but then reports that Thomas had an extended ecstatic experience in the last year of his life. Thomas is reported to have dismissed all his writings in light of this experience.

52. Nicholas, *De Vita in Christo* 11, PG 150:521 as quoted in Milner, *Confirmation*, 40.

> Baptism reconciles a man with God; the chrism provides gifts for the one who has just been made worthy....[53]

Lesser known is that Nicholas Cabasillas may have taught that some received gifts of healing, prophecy and tongues like the early Church, but all receive gifts of piety, prayer, love, chastity and the like. The following is said to come from his *De Vita in Christo* 3:2:

> In the early times this mystery [sacrament of chrismation] distributed among the baptized ones charismata such as healing, prophecy, and tongues....
>
> ...Of course, even in our own day and in the recent past, some have possessed such charismata and, as an effect of the Unction, they have predicted the future, expelled demons, healed diseases with prayer alone...[54]

The 1439 Council of Florence canonized much of the work done by the scholastics on the sacraments. This meeting saw the official recognition of the seven sacraments. The council is everywhere in the debt of Thomas Aquinas, particularly when dealing with confirmation.

> The second sacrament is confirmation, of which the matter is chrism, made from oil and balsam signifying the aroma of good reputation and which is blessed by the bishop.
>
> ...while a simple priest is competent to perform other anointings, this must not be performed except by a bishop. For only of the apostles, whose representatives the bishops are, do we read that they gave the Holy Spirit by the imposition of the hand. This is made clear in the Acts of Apostles (Acts 8:14–17 is cited). Confirmation is given in the Church in the place of that imposition of the hand.
>
> The effect of this sacrament is that the Holy Spirit is given in it for strengthening as it was given to the apostles on the day of Pentecost, so that the Christian may boldly confess the same of Christ.[55]

---

53. Nicholas, De Vita in Christo 11, PG 150:521 as quoted in Milner, Confirmation, 40.

54. Cabasillas as found in Eusebius Stephanou "Charismata," 19 and Burgess, *Holy Spirit: Eastern Christian Traditions*, 76. See also De Vita in Christo 11, *PG* 150:521. Cf. Tugwell, *Spirit*, 135; Milner, *Confirmation*, 40.

55. Quoted in Milner, *Confirmation*, 73. See Küng, "La Confirmation," 124.

Martin Luther (1485–1546), the well known reformer, can hardly be expected to have been generous to the Roman church. His writings on confirmation are no exception, for he sometimes uses harsh words to express his disagreement with their "mockery" which he considered to be biblically false. In its place Luther suggested something of a simple blessing, and reoriented it towards admission to the Lord's Supper.[56] More closely related to our concern is Luther's exposition of Titus 3:5:

> You hear: *the water*, that is the bath; you hear: *to be born again*, that is the regeneration and the renewal, and the Spirit, whom here St. Paul interprets as the Holy Spirit. And here it is to be noticed that the apostle knows nothing of the sacrament of confirmation. For he teaches that the Holy Spirit is given in baptism, as Christ also teaches, indeed, in baptism we are reborn by the Holy Spirit. We read in Acts of the Apostles that the apostles laid their hands on the heads of the baptized, so that they might receive the Holy Spirit, which is analogous to confirmation; but there it happens that the Holy Spirit is given with outward signs and causes men to speak in many tongues in order to preach the gospel. But this was a temporary measure and does not continue any more.[57]

Luther appears to speak of a twofold reception of the Spirit but because it is related to a phenomenon now ceased (e.g., tongues), there is an implied confusion as to its relevance for any later generation. Unfortunately, Luther does not clarify his meaning in that regard.

The great French reformer who continues to be at the center of Evangelical theology, John Calvin (1509–1564), had little use for Roman Catholic confirmation or Greek Orthodox chrismation. He called them "sacrilegious" and "madness" (*Institutes* 4:19:10) and invited anyone to "spit" on him if he were wrong (*Institutes* 4:19:12). Yet Calvin did support a form of confirmation, but it was essentially catechetical with a blessing added. Calvin mistakenly claimed that this was the primitive practice of the church.[58] It happens that the most pertinent material from Calvin

---

56. Fisher, *Medieval West*, 173; Robert H. Fischer, "Confirmation Outside the Anglican Tradition," *Confirmation: History, Doctrine and Practice*, Cully, 37; Jungkuntz, *Confirmation*, 45f.

57. Translated in J. D. C. Fisher, *Christian Initiation: The Reformation Period* (London: SPCK, 1970), 172. Verified in Martin Luther, *Werke* 10:1:1 (Weimar: Hermann Bohlaus Nachfolger), 117.

58. Pocknee, *Spirit*, 94f.; Fisher, *Reformation*, 260. Jungkuntz claims, *Confirmation*, 55, that Calvin tied visible miraculous gifts to "apostolic confirmation."

is his own confusing decisions on the meaning of baptism in the Holy Spirit. He seems to have used the phrase in two different ways. On the other hand, he identifies it with regeneration:

> ...as we have said that salvation is perfect in the person of Christ, so, in order to make us partakers of it, he baptizes us "with the Holy Spirit and with fire" (Lk 3:16), enlightening us into the faith of his Gospel, and so regenerating us to be new creatures. Thus cleansed from all pollution, he dedicated us as holy temples to the Lord.[59]

On the other hand, Calvin almost seems to be speaking the language of a modern day Pentecostal. Commenting on the disciples of Ephesus of Acts 19, Calvin says:

> Their answer, therefore, that they knew not whether there was a Spirit, must be understood as if they had said, that they had not yet heard whether or not the gifts of the Spirit, as to which Paul questioned them, were given to the disciples of Christ.
> ... the baptism of the Holy Spirit, in order words, the visible gifts of the Holy Spirit, were given by the laying on of hands. These are sometimes designated under the name of baptism. Thus on the day of Pentecost, the apostles are said to have remembered the words of the Lord concerning the baptism of the Spirit and of fire. And Peter relates that the same word occurred to him when he saw these gifts poured out on Cornelius and his family and kindred.[60]

Calvin elsewhere commented on Acts 8:16:

> And certainly Luke is not speaking here about the general grace of the Spirit, by which God regenerates us to be His own sons, but about those special gifts, with which the Lord wished some to be endowed in the first days of the Gospel, for the bestowing of honor on the kingdom of Christ. It is in this sense that John's words (7:30) ought to be understood, that the Spirit was not yet given to the disciples, since Christ was still active in the world. Not that they were completely without the Spirit for of course they had received from Him both faith and a devout desire to follow Christ; but that they were not yet rich in the extraordinary gifts in which the glory of the Kingdom of Christ later shone more completely. To sum up, since the Samaritans had the Spirit of adoption conferred on them already, the extraordinary graces of the Spirit are added as a culmi-

---

59. Calvin, *Institutes* 3:1:4. See *Institutes* 4:16:25.
60. Calvin, *Institutes* 4:15:18.

nation. In these God for a time showed to His Church something like the visible presence of His Spirit...[61]

The assessment of J. Rodman Williams is, then, an accurate one:

> Calvin's position is a peculiar one. Exegetically, it seems that he favors the latter position, viz., baptism in the Spirit as not identical with regeneration but with the "visible" gifts of the Spirit. Yet since he views those gifts as having been *withdrawn*, baptism in the Spirit from this perspective can hardly have relevancy for the church today. Here, Calvin's first position (Spirit baptism = regeneration)—even though less satisfactory—is seemingly the only one that relates to a continuing possibility.[62]

The *1549 Book of Common Prayer* is largely the work of Thomas Cranmer (1489–1556), archbishop of Canterbury.[63] The prayer book suggested that the greeting at the water baptism should include these words:

> Dear beloved ... I beseech you to call upon God ... that of his bountiful mercy he will grant to these children that thing, which by nature they cannot have, that is to say, that they may be baptized with the holy ghost, and received into Christ's holy Church, and he made lively members of the same.[64]

Included in the prayers of the priest were these words:

> We beseech thee that thou wilt mercifully look upon these children, and sanctify them with thy holy ghost, that by this wholesome laver of regeneration, whatsoever sin is in them, may be washed clean away....
>
> Give thy holy spirit to these infants, that they may be born again, and be made heirs of everlasting salvation....[65]

---

61. John Calvin, *Acts of the Apostles*, trans. by J. W. Fraser and W. J. G. McDonald (Grand Rapids: Eerdmans, 1965), 236.

62. J. Rodman Williams, "The Charismatic Movement and Reformed Theology," 17. See Mühlen, *Charismatic Theology*, 205; Paul Elbert, "Calvin and the Spiritual Gifts," *JETS* 22:3 (Sept 1979): 235–56.

63. So: Harris, "Anglican Understanding of Confirmation," 22; Pocknee, *Spirit*, 98; Fisher, *Reformation*, 236; Dix, *Confirmation*, 34; John Tiller, "Book of Common Prayer," *NIDCC*, 243; Noel Pollard, "Thomas Cranmer," *NIDCC*, 269.

64. *The First Prayer-Book of King Edward VI* (London: Griffith Farrah Okeden and Welsh, n.d.), 217f.

65. Ibid., 21, 220 respectively. Cf. Harris, "Anglican Understanding of Confirmation," 21.

For the rite of confirmation a prayer of the bishop is:

> Almighty and everlasting God, who has vouchsafed to regenerate these thy servants with water and the holy ghost: And has given unto them forgiveness of all their sins: Send down from heaven we beseech thee, upon them thy holy ghost the comforter, with the manifold gifts of grace, the spirit of wisdom and understanding; the spirit of counsel and ghostly strength; the spirit of knowledge and true godliness, and fulfill them, with the spirit of thy holy fear.[66]

The second edition of the prayer book, which was published in 1552, has the same words about water baptism as those previously noted. The parallel prayer in the rite of confirmation, however, has undergone change. We now read the following:

> Almighty and everlasting God, who has vouchsafed to regenerate these thy servants by water and the holy ghost, and hast given unto them forgiveness of all their sins; *strengthen them, we beseech thee,* with the holy ghost the comforter, *and daily increase in them thy manifold gifts of grace,* the spirit of wisdom and understanding, the spirit of counsel of ghostly strength, the spirit of knowledge and true godliness: and fill them, with the spirit of thy holy fear.[67]

I have italicized those words which were introduced into the second edition in order that one may readily see the changes incorporated into the 1552 text. Modern opinion varies on the intended theological implications of these changes. C. U. Harris and C. E. Pocknee[68] say that the change is from a patristic viewpoint to a medieval one, while J. D. C. Fisher and Gregory Dix[69] argue that the second rite is less identifiable as a sacrament. Most important, however, is the fact that it would appear that both editions refer to a twofold reception of the Spirit. Both rites accept some kind of identification of regeneration and a giving of the Holy Spirit and both refer to an additional work or coming of the Spirit into the one baptized

---

66. Ibid., 231. Cf. Pocknee, *Spirit*, 100; Fisher, *Reformation*, 241.

67. *The Second Prayer-Book of King Edward VI* (London: Griffith Farrah Okeden and Welsh, n.d.), 187. Cf. Pocknee, *Spirit*, 97f.

68. Harris, "Anglican Understanding of Confirmation," 22; Pocknee, *Spirit*, 98.

69. Fisher, *Reformation*, 253; Dix, *Confirmation*, 34.

(1549—"Send down"; 1552—"strengthen thee"). The same seems to be true of the 1662 Prayer Book.[70]

The Council of Trent (1545-1563) was at least a reaction to the Reformation, and work on confirmation was little more than a ratification of the 1439 Council of Florence's version of Thomistic confirmation. Hans Küng has said about this borrowing that:

> Against Luther, the Council of Trent (1547) resumes this doctrine (Aquinas and Florence on confirmation) without adding anything to the theological reflection, since it is still the distinction of two habitual ministries (the priest for baptism and the bishop for confirmation) which furnish the major argument.[71]

It was earlier explained how the Scholastic argument, embodied in the person of Thomas Aquinas, saw confirmation as a distinct sacramental act associated with an augmentum gratiae. It is also of importance to note that the council abolished infant confirmation.[72] thus insuring, for Catholic history, a distinction of the sacraments of baptism and confirmation.

The Anabaptist movement of the 16th century has been described by the alleged center as the "left wing" of the Reformation. R. A. Knox in *Enthusiasm* defined an Anabaptist as one who denies the efficacy of infant baptism, and therefore receives or administers the sacrament afresh when years of discretion have been reached. Roman Catholics and Reformers regarded the Anabaptists as enemies of God and emissaries of Satan.

Müntzer and Karlstadt have sometimes been labeled Anabaptists. The answer to this proposal is complicated by the varying groups which adhered to some common beliefs. Fr. Donald Gelpi uses four primary categories: (1) pacifists, (2) revolutionaries, (3) rationalists, (4) spiritualists.[73] Like Luther, Thomas Müntzer was an educated monk and an inspiring preacher. He had read Joachim of Fiore. Luther himself had recommended him for the post of vicar in 1520, where Muntzer would end aligning with the Zwickau prophets. He came to emphasize a "gift of the living Spirit" over against "dead letters of Scripture" and "priests and monkeys" over against a church "of the elect friends of God." In his opposition Luther, he

---

70. *The Book of Common Prayer* (Cambridge: Pitt Press, 1833), 127.

71. Küng, "La confirmation," 124. Cf. Milner, *Confirmation*, 74.

72. Fisher, *Medieval West*, 127; Pocknee, *Spirit*, 99. Cf. Karl Rahner, *Meditations on the Sacraments* (New York: Seabury Press, 1977), 21f.

73. Gelpi, *Pentecostalism*, 13.

repudiated an external baptism and advocated an inner baptism "in water and the Holy Spirit." He also spoke of an age of the Holy Spirit, imminent, that would establish a theocracy in this world. The implementation of these ideas led to bloody deaths and his own execution.[74]

Andreas Karlstadt had been Luther's friend and had even awarded him his doctor's degree in 1512. He held the same doctrine as Luther on justification by faith alone, but when Luther was hiding, Karlstadt came under the influence of the Zwickau prophets. This contributed to his campaign against images, transubstantiation and paedobaptism. Apparently, the writings of Joachim of Fiore helped ferment Kalstadt's specific involvement in the peasants' revolt. He was saved during this time by Luther. He then spent time in Zürich and ended his days as a theology teacher at the University in Basel.[75]

The main stream of Anabaptists most nearly related to the present day Mennonite church, goes back to Menno Simmons.[76] Obviously Simons was completely committed to pacifism. Lesser known is that Simmons himself may have experienced tongues-speech. Simmons' group had a teaching called "inward baptism." This inward baptism was perhaps equivalent to regeneration. It was sometimes called baptism of the Holy Spirit, and it was considered a prerequisite for water baptism. John J. Yoder has compared, favorably, the original evangelical Anabaptists to classical Pentecostalism and Lindberg classes some of the Anabaptists as Charismatics.[77]

The term Huguenots was used as a nickname for French Calvinists. A group of Huguenot extremists were known as Camisards. The Camisards were often militant and they believed their actions to be in response to the beckoning of the Spirit: ". . . they obeyed the Spirit, which they said filled them, without reservation, hesitation, or delay, although they were

---

74. Küng, *Church*, 194; Schaff, *History* 3:2:170, 195; Lindberg, *Third Reformation?*, 75ff., 112; Knox, *Enthusiasm*, 126ff.; Edgar, *Gifts*, 243f.

75. Congar, *Holy Spirit* 1:138ff.; Schaff, *History* 3:2:270f.; Lindberg, *Third Reformation?*, 57ff.

76. *Eerdmans' Handbook to the History of Christianity*, 402.

77. Lindberg, *Third Reformation?*, 13f., 122; Williams and Waldvogel, "Tongues," 73f.; Damboriena, *Tongues*, 11; Schaff, *History* 1:2:190; George H. Williams, *The Radical Reformation* (Philadelphia: Westminster Press, 1975), 133; J. C. Wenger, *Our Christ-Centered Faith* (Scottsdale: Herald Press, 1973), 51; Bresson, *Ecstasy*, 46f.; Donald D. Smeeton, "William Tyndale: A Theological Renewal," *Faces of Renewal*, ed. by Paul Elbert (Peabody: Hendrickson, 1988), 164.

led to certain death."[78] No material is available regarding the particulars of their pneumatology but it does appear that their pneumatic experiences included tongues-speech.[79]

The origins of the present day churches commonly called "Baptists" are not without their complexities, and the multiplied branches hinder the understanding of an onlooker. Of some relevance to modern day Baptist churches is the 1742 Baptist Association meeting in Philadelphia which adopted the following statement:We believe that (Heb 6:2, Acts 6:1f., 8:17f., 19:6) laying on

> of hands (with prayer) upon baptized believers, as such, is an ordinance of Christ, and ought to be submitted unto by all such persons that are admitted to partake of the Lord's Supper; and that the end of this ordinance is not for the extraordinary gifts of the Spirit, but for (Eph 1:13f.) a further reception of the Holy Spirit of promise, or for the addition of the graces of the Spirit, and the influences thereof: to confirm, strengthen, and comfort them in Christ Jesus, it being ratified and established by the (Acts 8 and 19) extraordinary gifts of the Spirit in the primitive times....[80]

---

78. G. B. Cutten, *Speaking with Tongues* (New Haven: Yale University Press, 1927), 60. Cutten, 65f., adds, "The Camisard chiefs were designated by the Spirit. They believed themselves to be filled with it...." See Gelpi, *Pentecostalism*, 22; Knox, *Enthusiasm*, 601; Dirk Jellema, "Huguenots," *NIDCC*, 489; J. G. G. Norman "Camisards," *NIDCC*, 184; Damboriena, *Tongues*, 12.

79. Williams and Waldvogel, "Tongues," 75, "The Camisards maintained that 'God has no where in Scripture concluded himself from dispensing again the extraordinary Gifts of His Spirit unto Man.'" Williams and Waldvogel, 76, claim that some of the accounts refer to xenolalia. See Damboriena, *Tongues*, 12; Bresson, *Ecstasy*, 42.

80. As quoted in R. C. Dalton, *Tongues Like As of Fire* (Springfield: Gospel Publishing House, 1945), 113. Dalton was originally a Baptist minister. Bernard Bresson, *Ecstasy*, 87, claims the following is true of the seventeenth century General (or Arminian) Baptists:

> Their confession of faith published in Amsterdam in 1612, says in Article 53, "That although there be diverse gifts of the Spirit, yet there is but one spirit, which distributeth to everyone as he will 2 Corinthians 12:4, Ephesians 4:4 that the outward gifts of the Spirit which the holy ghost poureth forth upon the day of Pentecost upon the disciples, in tongues of prophecy, and gifts, and healings, and miracles, which is called the baptism of the holy ghost and fire (Acts 1:5)...."

Michael A. G. Haykin, "Hanserd Knollys (ca. 1599–1691) On the Gifts of the Spirit," *Westminster Theological Journal* 54 (1992): 103 says the General Baptists thought prophecy fulfilled in "extemporaneous messages after, or even in the place of, the sermon." In contrast, Haykin interprets the reference to "prophesie" in article 45 of the *First London Confession* as teachers appointed by the congregation. Cf. Knox, *Enthusiasm*, 174.

Although the so called "extraordinary" gifts are viewed as extinct, there remains the teaching of a special reception of the Spirit which is not identified with regeneration. A forerunner of this platform can be seen in the response of Hanserd Knollys to the Seekers. Although both the First and Second London Confessions of the 17th century espoused "gifts" given to believers, Knollys would distance this position from the Seekers by suggesting miraculous gifts were not vital beyond their origination. After all, he reasoned, regeneration and preaching empowered by the Spirit is miraculous. This position was maintained while Knollys practiced a belief in physical healings.[81] Present day Baptist churches apparently have continued both doctrines. That is, while they continue to endorse a liturgy which essentially espouses a special work of the Spirit,[82] they steadfastly refuse to recognize the legitimacy of those who claim to have experienced a variety of "primitive" charismatic phenomena. Garrett gives this account:

> The situation of prominent Baptists like Meacham when confronted with convulsions, visions, or entranced prophecy in the revivals of the New Light Stir—and later with the ecstatic worship of the Shakers—resembled that of John Wesley, faced with the outbreaks of possession in Bristol in 1741, or of Jonathan Edwards when he attempted in *The Distinguishing Marks of a Work of the Spirit of God* to fit the revivals of the Connecticut Valley into the divine scheme.[83]

John Goodwin (1594–1665), a Puritan divine, was educated at Queen's College, Cambridge, where he later became a fellow.[84] He was

---

81. Haykin, "Knollys On the Gifts of the Spirit," 108.

82. See Peter J. Jagger, *Christian Initiation: 1552–1969* (London: SPCK, 1970). Jagger, 209, includes their ceremony of "laying on of hands with prayer upon those who have been baptized." In this ceremony the minister greets the congregation with these words:

> Beloved brethren: we are now to pray for and lay our hands upon those who have been baptized, and receive them into church membership. This rite practiced by apostles is an act of acceptance and commissioning. Let us pray therefore that they, being blessed and strengthened by the Holy Spirit, may be fully equipped. . . . In his prayer, the minister says: Almighty and everlasting God strengthen, we beseech thee, these thy servants with the Holy Spirit the Paraclete: the Spirit of wisdom and understanding, the Spirit counsel and might, the Spirit of knowledge, piety and godly fear. This is the language of the rite of confirmation!

83. Garrett, *Spirit Possession*, 166. See also pages 134 and 164f.

84. Peter Toon, "John Goodwin," *NIDCC*, 422.

author of a book entitled Τό Πνευματικόν or *A Being Filled With the Spirit*. In this book Goodwin argues that Jude 19 shows there can be a sensual Christian, that is, one without the Spirit. Commenting on Romans 12:10f, Goodwin says:

> So, then, if it be a duty lying upon all Christians to be fervent in spirit, serving the Lord, then is it a duty that beareth with the same weight upon them to be filled with the Spirit inasmuch as the performance of the latter, so that from here it is evident that it is a duty incumbent upon all Christians to be filled with the Spirit.[85]

Thomas Goodwin (1600-1685) was educated at Cambridge and in 1634 became a Congregationalist. He was appointed to the Westminster Assembly, was of high repute among the assemblymen and led the "Dissenting Brethren" in the assembly. John Schep mixes comments with quotations when he says:

> According to Goodwin, in Ephesians 1:13b, the apostles speaks of "a work of the Holy Spirit distinct from faith: after ye believed ye were sealed."
>
> The seal is not water baptism but the "fruit of baptism ... You shall therefore find in the Acts that upon baptising men that were of age the Holy Spirit fell upon them."
>
> Goodwin goes on to show that this being sealed with the Spirit gives the extraordinary, unspeakable joy which the readers of Peter's epistles had (1 Pt 1:8) and show it causes rivers of living water to flow from the heart that it is so blessed, according to Jesus' word in John 7:38.
>
> "That is," he writes, "the great fruit of your baptism ... You have not that great fruit of your baptism till you have this ... Therefore you shall find it called: baptized with the Holy Ghost. ... Therefore Peter bids them to be baptized and they should received this promise, Acts 2:38."[86]

---

85. John Goodwin, Τό Πνευματικόν *or A Being Filled with the Spirit* (Edinburgh: James Nichol, 1867), 21. See page 17 for Jude 19.

86. John A. Schep, *Baptism in the Spirit* (Plainfield: Logos, 1972), 52-54. Dunn, *Baptism in the Holy Spirit*, 1, referring to Goodwin's *Works* 1, Sermon XV, XVI, says: "Thomas Goodwin equated the experience of assurance with the 'seal of the Spirit' in Ephesians 1:13f and with the baptism with the Holy Ghost; he even called it 'a new conversion.'" Cf. Williams, *Gift*, 137n36; Pocknee, *Spirit*, 197.

Educated at Emmanuel College, Cambridge, and for a time a fellow there, William Law (1686–1761) was author of the influential work *A Serious Call to a Devout and Holy Life* (1728). With regard to the topic of our interest, Law had this to say:

> "As truly as John baptized with water," said Christ to His disciples after His resurrection, "you shall in a few days be baptized in the Holy Spirit."
>
> This power they then received when the Holy Ghost with His cloven tongues of fire came down upon them, filling them with all the fullness of God....
>
> When, however, that baptism in the Spirit was no longer preached or believed, the heavenly fire being extinguished in the Church, Christianity lost its first glory ... Instead of the gifts and grace of Christ by the manifestation and power of the Holy Spirit, heathenistic learning and temporal power and carnal strife after earthly honor became the sad mark of an apostate body of water-baptized religionists. Only when men are called again to that same manifest presence of the risen Christ that was "seen and heard" in the first disciples; only then can there be a revival of that first life and light, and love. Once again multitudes will be baptized in the Holy Ghost ...
>
> Then His divine love, as a heavenly fire, will burn up the dross, purify every motive ...[87]

As indicated by the last sentence, Law conceived of this spiritual baptism as involving power and purification. This view of Spirit baptism will be repeated often in the nineteenth century.

A colleague of John Wesley, and the man Wesley wanted to become his successor, John Fletcher (1729–1785), served as vicar of Madeley in Shropshire.[88] Fletcher described his difference from Wesley in the following terms:

> I would distinguish more exactly between the believers baptized with the Pentecostal power of the Holy Ghost, and the believer who, like the Apostles after our Lord's ascension, is not yet filled with that power.[89]

---

87. William Law, *Power of the Spirit*, ed. by Dave Hunt (Fort Washington: Christian Literature Crusade, 1971), 126, 128f. See page 123.

88. A. Skevington Wood, "John William Fletcher," *NIDCC*, 380; Williams and Waldvogel, "Tongues," 21.

89. This is from a letter of March 7, 1778, from Fletcher to Mary Bosanquet, reprinted in Luke Tyerman, *Wesley's Designated Successor* (London: Hodder and Stoughton, 1882), 411.

The difference is one of nuance and not of theology. Dividing holy history into three dispensations, each identified with a person of the Trinity, Fletcher was led to impose Pentecostal language on Wesley's doctrine of sanctification. Fletcher's intentions and jargon can be seen clearly in the following remarks:

> Should you ask, how many baptisms, or effusions of the *sanctifying* Spirit are necessary to *cleanse* a believer from all sin, and to kindle his soul into perfect love; I reply... if one powerful baptism of the Spirit "seal you unto the day of redemption, and cleanse you from all (moral) filthiness," so much the better. If two or more be necessary, the Lord can repeat them...[90]

Nonetheless, the confusion which ensued led Wesley to persuade Fletcher to rescind the practice. This retraction by Fletcher signaled the same for Methodism until such language was revived a century later in America.[91]

A straight line can be drawn from the French Prophets in Europe and the Great Awakening in America to the sect known as Shakers. The group's founders, James and Jane Wardley, may have experienced some Quaker influence but undoubtedly came out of the matrix of the French Prophets. Pockets of receptive Baptists, Freewill Baptists and separatists would await the 1774 arrival of the Shakers when they crossed the Atlantic in obedience to Mother Ann's divine revelation. The Great Awakening had left behind believers given to frenzied worship. Although Jonathan Edwards repeatedly exhorted to "test the spirits" as did Wesley across the ocean, this was not taken as a direct assault on all enthusiastic manifestations. Consequently, scattered instances of preaching with a "holy whine," burning books, claims to immortality and attacks on "unconverted" min-

---

90. John Fletcher, "To imperfect believers, who embrace the doctrine of Christian perfection," *Checks to Antinomianism* 7:19 (New York: Carlton and Porter, n.d.), 2:632 (emphasis mine). Similarly, "Directions on how to secure the blessings of peace and brotherly love," Ibid, 356. Cf. Williams and Waldvogel, "Tongues," 81; Synan, *Holiness-Pentecostal*, 62.

91. Donald Dayton, "Theological Roots of Pentecostalism," AAR Annual Meeting (Washington, D.C.: October 26, 1974), 4; Timothy Smith, "Finney and the Baptism with the Holy Spirit," (Pasadena: Fuller Theological Seminary, February 4, 1977). Synan, *Old-Time Power*, 83, says that B. H. Irwin's three stage salvation scheme was probably a result of his understanding of Fletcher. Perhaps the same is true of R. C. Horner. See Donald Dayton, "The Doctrine of the Baptism of the Holy Spirit: Its Emergence and Significance," 121.

isters who had blocked the erection of a purified church preceded the missionary efforts of Mother Ann Lee and her followers in the colonies.

Perhaps the mystic Jacob Boehme, who decided his relationship with the Holy Spirit allowed him to dismiss reading more books, was a factor in the forbidding of printing doctrine and history by the Shakers. This ellipsis easily accommodated later interpolations like the Nineteenth Century Shaker declaration that Mother Ann Lee had in fact been the second appearing of Jesus Christ. Lee's own claim was that she was the lady clothed with the sun made famous by the Apocalypse.

The 1848 *Summary View of the Millennial Church* puts tongues-speech, dancing and various ecstatic states as the highest expressions of Shaker worship. This reflects a long tradition of sacred theater that incorporated shaking, shouting, leaping and "wordless" songs along with healing and prophesying. Some among the group practiced glossographia and mythical proportions were evident in Shaker claims that Mother Ann Lee experienced a range of 70 languages as part of her xenolalic vocabulary. Similarly distancing reality was the search for missionaries endowed with permanent xenolalia and the use of unknown tongues to preach to the dead, some of whom were said to have been converted by this means.

Whereas the Wardleys had recommended celibacy and confession to "Mother," Mother Ann Lee made these cardinal tenets of faith for those seeking perfection. This contributed to the troublesome demoralizing of family relationships. Advocating pacifism in face of the Revolutionary War proved costly especially because the leaders were from England. One convert described an experience that was a "seal" to his faith and a baptism of the Holy Spirit. The extent of opposition to education can be measured somewhat by a son of Samuel Johnson. Yale trained and licensed by a Presbyterian church notwithstanding, Samuel Johnson became an ardent advocate of Shakerism after his "baptism in the Spirit." One of Johnson's sons left behind a diary that reveals semi-literate skills at best. Early attempts at communism were fraught with the perils of divesting possessions, howbeit for the sake of building a pure community, helping the poor and financing missionary efforts. Perhaps this was the context for their shunning of jewelry and fine clothing even though a few converts from the very beginning were of considerable means financially. In time the Shakers established communities renowned for their accomplishments.

The Shakers did not lack for critics. Perhaps, however, the most damaging reports that persist concern bizarre episodes in the last part of Ann

Lee's life. Rumors and reasonable evidence seem to charge Ann Lee and some of her closest associates for drunkenness. To what extent this would have contributed to elevating the hysteria of worship times is difficult to judge. Another ugly experiment was naked dancing. Arguably, this was intended to show that the innocence of the Garden of Eden had been regained. However, their extreme attacks on human sexuality failed on this point as the practice was limited to Niskeyuna and of short duration. Both examples add weight to the complaint that Shakers could supersede Scripture. Although the Bible was a fixture in the movement and they might have denied having knowingly contradicted Scripture, their pneumatic impulses were of such strength that biblical teachings were easily suspended. Remarkably, however, the first five years in America brought thousands of converts to the 'true church' even if only temporarily.[92]

John Morgan was a member of the original faculty of Oberlin College. In an article entitled "The Gift of the Holy Ghost" published in the first volume (1845) of the *Oberlin Quarterly Review*, Morgan had this to say:

> In an experience subsequent to conversion, the Holy Spirit, who is with the Christian prior to this event, comes to him in a more intimate relationship. He enters his being.
>
> The baptism in the Spirit was given to prepare the saints to convert sinners.
>
> The baptism in the Spirit did not communicate power to perform miracles. The disciples had such power even prior to Pentecost. Nor did it consist in the gift of tongues, though such activity could be an evidence of the Spirit.
>
> Though it is true that the Spirit is received in a new way, (i.e., from 'with you' to 'in you') is the baptism in the Spirit, it is an error to conclude that therefore the blessing of the Spirit may not

---

92. See Garrett, *Spirit Possession*, chs. 5–10; Williams and Waldvogel, "Tongues," 82; E. D. Andrews, *People Called Shakers* (New York: Dover, 1963), 27–30; Hugh Wamble, "Glossolalia in Christian History," *Tongues*, ed. by L. B. Dyer (Jefferson City: LeBoi, 1971), 37; Robert C. Lindar, "Shakers," *NIDCC*, 900f.; Knox, *Enthusiasm*, 558ff.; Anderson, *Disinherited*, 26; C. W. Ferguson, *The Confusion of Tongues*, (Garden City: Doubleday, 1928), Chapter 15; Damboriena, *Tongues*, 12; Bresson, *Ecstasy*, 71ff.; Kelsey, *Tongue Speaking*, 57; Kerr, *Fire*, 42; Lewis, *Witnesses*, 230; E. Glenn Hinson, "A Brief History of Glossolalia," *Glossolalia* (Nashville: Abingdom Press, 1967), 66; Samarian, *Tongues*, 185; Edgar, *Gifts*, 246. See also *The Shakers: Two Centuries of Spiritual Reflection*, edited with an introduction by R. E. Whitson (Ramsey: Paulist Press, 1983).

thereafter be increased. There is one baptism, but there may be many further infillings of the Spirit.[93]

The language of Pentecost has appeared in various places up until this time, but he can draw an unbroken line of persistent usage of this language from the 1850s up to our own day. One of the pivotal works seems to have been William Arthur's *Tongue of Fire*. Arthur, a British Methodist, first published his work in 1856 and seems to be the source from which many American evangelicals took their cue. Arthur sent out a call for a Pentecostal effusion, an effusion which, he believed, would include a "baptism with purifying flames of fire."[94]

It is no small chore to determine whether Asa Mahan should be categorized as Holiness or Keswick. Writers on both sides of the issue have claimed him in their respective camps.[95] Mahan's theology underwent various modifications as his Christian pilgrimage took him from the Presbyterian church to the faculty of Oberlin College, serving as its first president. Two factors lead me to believe that he is most properly termed Keswickian: (1) His earliest commitment to traditional perfectionism was changed by the recognition of the empowering work of the Spirit as well as the purifying work. An obvious indicator of this is his work originally entitled *Christian Perfection*, later reissued, with some revision,[96] under

---

93. As given in Wessels, "The Doctrine of the Baptism in the Holy Spirit Among the Assemblies of God," 29–31. Cf. Timothy Smith, *Revivalism and Social Reform* (Glouchester: Peter Smith, 1976), 110. Donald Dayton, "Emergence," 116, points out that at this stage Morgan was still steeped in holiness theology. The same issue carried an article by Morgan entitled "The Holiness Acceptable to God," which Finney incorporated into the first edition (1847) of his systematic theology.

94. Synan, *Holiness-Pentecostal*, 142; Dayton, "Emergence," 118; Smith, *Revivalism*, 122. Chapter three of Donald Dayton's doctoral dissertation, "Theological Roots of Pentecostalism," (University of Chicago, December, 1983) details many of the other sources related to this. W. Arthur, *The Tongue of Fire* (London: Kelly, 1901), 100f., claimed tongues-speech could not be counted as a permanent gift to the church. He did add, however, that it was possible that the gift could be restored, and that it would be xenolalic not glossolalic.

95. Holiness: Donald Dayton, *The American Holiness Movement: A Bibliographic Introduction* (Wilmore: Asbury Seminary, 1971), 19f. Keswick: David D. Bundy, *Keswick: A Bibliographic Introduction to the Higher Life Movement* (Wilmore: Asbury Seminary, 1975), 13.

96. Roland Wessels, "Baptism in the Holy Spirit," 48, says that one move was from Christocentrism to Pneumocentrism. Dayton, "Theological Roots," 104, says that sanctification is still the main issue. It is not a matter of concern for this inquiry, but it should be noted that there is controversy as to whether Mahan or Finney was the first to associ-

the title *Baptism of the Holy Ghost*. (2) He stood by the side of Pearsall Smith at the Oxford Convention of 1874 and thus became with him a factor in the initiation of the Keswick conventions.[97] That is, although Oberlin Theology is not the exact equivalent of Keswick theology, it is less like Holiness theology.[98]

Mahan recognized two views regarding reception of the Spirit.

> According to one, "the promise of the Spirit" is always fulfilled at the moment of conversion. What is subsequently to be expected is merely a continuation and gradual increase of what was then conferred.
>
> According to the other view, "the Spirit falls upon," "comes upon," believers, and the "sealing and earnest" of the Spirit are given, not in conversion, but "*after* we have believed." The Spirit, first of all, induces in the sinner "repentance toward God, and faith toward our Lord Jesus Christ." "After he believed," that is, after conversion, "the Holy Ghost comes upon," "falls upon," and is "poured out upon him," and thus "endues him with power from on high," and thus "endues him with power from on high" for his life mission and work. In his baptism of power, this "sealing and earnest of the Spirit" which is always given, not in conversion, but "*after* ye believed," "the promise of the Spirit" is fulfilled.[99]

Mahan's investigation led him to conclude that the second option was biblical. From this he was able to enumerate seven consequences of this baptism of the Spirit, of which the leading characteristics are permanence and power.[100]

---

ate empowering with Spirit baptism. Donald Dayton, "From Christian Perfection to the 'Baptism of the Holy Ghost,'" *Aspects of Pentecostal-Charismatic Origins*, Synan, argues that Mahan influenced Finney. Timothy Smith, "Finney," believes the reverse to be true. Wessels claims that Mahan was influenced by John Morgan of Oberlin ("Baptism in the Holy Spirit," 37). Dayton's contribution to the discussion, "Emergence," 117f., reiterates the priority of Mahan over Finney but also acknowledges that both were preceded by Henry Cowles and John Morgan at Oberlin.

97. B. B. Warfield, *Perfectionism* (New York: Oxford University Press, 1931), 213.

98. Bundy, *Keswick*, 43, gives an undocumented story that Mahan later abstained from Keswick involvement because "it did not go deep enough."

99. Asa Mahan, *Baptism of the Holy Ghost* (New York: Palmer and Hughes, 1870), 16.

100. Ibid., 52ff. See Dayton, "Theological Roots," 105, 111 et al.; Paul G. Chappell, "The Divine Healing Movement in America," Ph.D. dissertation (Drew University Graduate School, 1983), 77; R. F. Martin, "The Early Years of American Pentecostalism,

Mahan said that various people had this experience including, among others, Thomas A. Kempis, Martin Luther, Scotch Worthies, John Wesley, Willian Tennant, and Mere D' Aubigné. Of course his colleague Charles G. Finney was noted.

> ... the special power which attended the preaching of President Finney, during the early years of his ministry, was chiefly owing to a special baptism of the Spirit, a personal manifestation of Christ to his mind, a baptism which he received not long *after his conversion.*
>
> The reason, also, why he is bringing forth such wondrous "fruit in his old age," is, that while his whole ministry has been under the power of the Spirit, his former baptisms have been renewed with increasing power and frequency during a few years past.[101]

In many present day conservative churches, Charles G. Finney (1792–1875) is revered for his famous 'revival' campaigns. Finney had practiced law before his conversion, but thereafter he received ordination with the Presbyterian church. In fact, in 1832 he became pastor of the Second Presbyterian Church in New York City. However, he withdrew from the presbytery and in 1832 became professor of theology at Oberlin College and during the years 1851 to 1866 served as its president.[102] Apparently, it was not until age 80 in 1871 when he addressed the National Council of Congregational Church meeting at Oberlin that Finney publicly used the formula of a Spirit baptism consisting of purity and power.[103] Since my

---

1900–1940: Survey of A Social Movement," Ph.D. dissertation (University of North Carolina, 1975), 48.

101. Ibid., 88. Emphasis mine.

102. Bruce L. Shelly, "Charles Grandison Finney," *NIDCC* 377; Wessels, "Baptism in the Holy Spirit," 41ff.; Leslie Davison, *Pathway to Power* (Watchung: Charisma Books, 1971), 82.

103. Dayton, "Emergence," 117, discovered that although Finney used some Pentecostal language in 1839 and 1840, this language is absent from his *Views of Sanctification* and his published work on systematic theology. The first clear public pronouncement by Finney falls to the year 1871. See Wessels, "Baptism in the Holy Spirit," 42; Dayton, "Christian Perfection," 43. Wessels, 41, 54, and now Dayton, "Theological Roots," 125, claim that Finney's Spirit baptism theology was concerned only with power. Timothy Smith, "Finney," could not agree with this. Smith, seeking material relevant to his fellow Nazarenes, argues convincingly that Finney never gave up the thought of purification. My position is somewhat mediating. The concern of my investigation has led to emphasis on what Finney said about Spirit empowerment, yet I acknowledge that Finney's view of Spirit baptism incorporated a mixture of purification and empowerment. Cf. Davison, *Power*, 82.

concern is with his final formulation, I will quote from his autobiography, which was published in 1876. Reading this, one must remember that he has imposed his theology of later years on events of earlier years.

> I received a mighty baptism of the Holy Ghost. Without any expectation of it, without ever having the thought in my mind that there was any such thing for me, without any recollection that I had ever heard the thing mentioned by any person in the world, the Holy Spirit descended upon me in a manner that seemed to go through me body and soul.
>
> No words can express the wonderful love that was shed abroad in my heart. I wept aloud with joy and love; and I do not know, but I should say, I literally bellowed out the unutterable gushings of my heart. These waves came over me, and over me, and over me, one after the other, until I recollect I cried out, "I shall die if these waves continue to pass over me: I said, 'Lord, I cannot bear any more....'"[104]

Also important for determining Finney's Spirit baptism theology is his reaction to his earliest mentor, Mr. Gale.

> But there was another defect in brother Gale's education, which I regarded as fundamental. If he had ever been converted to Christ, he had failed to receive the divine anointing of the Holy Spirit that would make him a power in the pulpit and society, for the conversion of souls. He had fallen short of receiving the baptism in the Holy Spirit, which is indispensable to ministerial success.
>
> When Christ commissioned his apostles to go and preach, he told them to abide at Jerusalem till they were endued with power from on high. This power, as every one knows, was the baptism of the Holy Ghost poured out upon them on the day of Pentecost. This was an indispensable qualification for success in their ministry. I did not suppose then, nor do I now, that this baptism was simply the power to work miracles. The power to work miracles and the gift of tongues were given as signs to attest the reality of

---

104. Charles G. Finney, *Charles G. Finney: An Autobiography* (Old Tappan: Fleming H. Revell Co., 1908), 20. See page 22. Harold Sala, "An Investigation of the Baptizing and Filling Work of the Holy Spirit in the New Testament Related to the Pentecostal Doctrine of 'Initial Evidence,'" Th.D. dissertation (Greenville: Bob Jones University, June, 1966), 169, has found some Pentecostals that take Finney's "I literally bellowed out the unutterable gushings of my heart" as being tongues-speech. This opinion was cautiously hinted at during the 1918 Assemblies of God discussion on initial evidence. I am not inclined to believe that it has reference to tongues-speech. Cf. Synan, *Holiness-Pentecostal*, 218.

their divine commission. But the baptism itself was a divine purifying, an anointing bestowing on them a divine illumination, filling them with faith and love, with peace and power; so that their words were made sharp in the hearts of God's enemies, quick and powerful, like a two-edged sword.[105]

Therefore, I understand Finney to view Spirit baptism as a distinct work of the Spirit which includes both elements of purifying and empowering. The doctrine of subsequence can be seen in the constant reminder given to his audiences: "All beings have a right to complain of Christians who are not filled with the Spirit."[106]

During it's opening decades, Classical Pentecostals in North America at large did not evidence awareness of a gifted thinker who parallels their own theology in many respects. This despite a 1909 tract entitled "History of Tongues" by V. P. Simmons that clearly put Irving on the landscape.[107] Largely through the writings of Thomas Smail, Gordon Strachan and Larry Christenson,[108] Pentecostals and Charismatics first came to realize the

---

105. Ibid., 55. A lot of what Finney says has reference to pulpit manner. Although many other ministers led people to the Lord and carefully shepherded them during their lifetime, Finney thought a minister full of the Holy Ghost could be extemporaneous (95) and could speak in very direct terms to his audience (53).

106. Charles G. Finney, *Lectures on Revivals of Religion* (Oberlin: E. J. Goodrich, 1868), 116. Elsewhere, 111, he said, "Often the elders, and even the minister, will oppose you, if you are filled with the Spirit of God." Wessels, "Baptism in the Holy Spirit," 50, says Finney's view can be distinguished from Mahan's and Morgan's position because he does not say that the Spirit, who was with the Christian, now enters and indwells the Spirit baptized Christian. Cf. Bruner, *Theology of the Holy Spirit*, 41.

107. This tract originally appeared in *Bridegroom's Messenger* 1:3 (December 1907): 2. The Church of God of Prophecy continues to print a tract by V. P. Simmons entitled "History of Tongues." There is only slight variation in wording from this tract as published by White Wing Press and the article in *Bridegroom's Messenger*. The Pentecostal ignorance of Irving persisted despite the fact that R. C. Dalton, *Tongues*, 22–30, devoted several pages to Irving in 1945.

108. Smail, *Reflected Glory*; Gordon Strachan, *The Pentecostal Theology of Edward Irving* (London: Darton, Longman and Todd, 1973); Larry Christenson, "Pentecostalism's Forgotten Forerunner," *Aspects of Pentecostal-Charismatic Origins*, Synan. The account which follows is reconstructed from material in these works as well as the following: P. E. Shaw, *The Catholic Apostolic Church: Sometimes Called Irvingite* (New York: King's Crown Press, 1946); A. L. Drummond, *Edward Irving and His Circle* (London: James Clark and Co. Ltd., 1871); Mrs. Oliphant, *The Life of Edward Irving*, 2 volumes (London: Hurst and Blackett Publishers, 1862); Edward Miller, *The History and Doctrine of Irvingism*, 2 volumes (London: Kegan Paul & Co., 1878); Cutten, *Tongues*; B. B. Warfield, *Counterfeit Miracles* (London: Banner of Truth Trust, 1972); Williams and Waldvogel, "Tongues;" Bresson, *Ecstasy*; J. D. Douglas, "Edward Irving," *NIDCC*, 517.

importance of the thought of Edward Irving (1793–1834). Irving's fame centers on the series of events which occurred at his Presbyterian church in London. He had been trained at Edinburgh and had taught at Haddington and Kirkcaldy. An assistant to Thomas Chalmers in Glasgow for a period, he finally became senior pastor at the Caledonian Chapel, London. The people he attracted included the educated and the important, and their numbers were so large that in 1827 Regent Square had to be built to accommodate the congregation. During this time Irving held to the traditional Presbyterian position that the spectacular gifts of the Spirit had ceased long ago. However, events transpiring in Scotland and the opinion of his associate, A. J. Scott, conspired to further modify Irving.[109]

Mary Campbell of Fernicary, Scotland lay in bed sick apparently soon to die. A visit by A. J. Scott led Mary to reread the Acts of the Apostles and John's Gospel. After having done so, she came to accept Scott's view that Spirit baptism was not the same as regeneration and that it was to be accompanied by extraordinary phenomena.[110] She began to pray for the experience and yet it seemed quite unexpected when, on March 28, 1830, she began to speak in tongues and prophesy for a quarter of an hour, but returned to her bed in weakness. A few miles away, in Port Glasgow, the MacDonald family had a daughter, Margaret, who was dying. Then the unexpected thing happened (April, 1830).

> She (Margaret) had scarcely been able to have her bed made for a week, but on a sudden one morning she broke forth, saying that "there will be a mighty baptism of the spirit this day," into almost

109. Not to be overlooked is his 1820's conversion to imminence millenniarian thought which permitted him to announce the wait for the seventh and final sign of the Second Coming. This according to W. H. Oliver, *Prophets and Millennialists: The Uses of Biblical Prophecy in England from the 1790s to the 1840s* (Auckland: Auckland University Press, 1978), 103. Cf. Timothy M. Powell, "Edward Irving and the Catholic Apostolic Church," *Paraclete* (Spring 1978): 24.

110. Mrs. Oliphant, *Irving*, 105, quotes Irving's response to Mary Campbell's initial encounter with A. J. Scott:

> Being a woman of very fixed and constant spirit, he was not able, with all his power of statement and argument... to convince her of the distinction between regeneration and baptism with the Holy Ghost; and when he could not prevail he left her with a solemn charge to read over the Acts of the Apostles with that distinction in her mind, and to beware how she rashly rejected what he believed to be the truth of God. By this young woman it was that God, not many months later, did restore the gift of speaking with tongues and prophesying to the church.

> marvelous setting forth of the wonderful works of God, and, as if her own weakness had been altogether lost in the strength of the Holy Ghost, continued with little or no intermission for two or three hours, in mingled praise, prayer and exhortation.
>
> At dinner-time James and George came home as usual, whom she then addressed at length, concluding with a solemn prayer for James, that he might at that time be endowed with the power of the Holy Ghost. Almost instantly James calmly said, "I have got it." He walked to the window "and stood silent for a minute or two.
>
> I looked at him and almost trembled, there was such a change in his whole countenance. He then, with a step and man of almost indescribable majesty, walked up to Margaret's bedside, and addressed her in the words of the twentieth Psalm, "Arise, and stand upright." He repeated the words, took her by the hand, and she arose . . .[111]

Miller says that Mary Campbell, who had studied languages in preparation for mission work, initially thought that she miraculously spoke in a language of one of the southern Pacific Islands. After being healed, she concluded that her base broadened to include a Turkish dialect and the language of the Pellen Islands. Predictably, Oxford and Cambridge professors were also not able to identify the languages as written by Mary. Irving would later deny the possibility of permanent xenolalia.[112] A pamphlet entitled *The Unknown Tongues Discovered to Be English, Spanish and French* was written by former enthusiast George Pilkington. The author

---

111. As quoted in Miller, *Irvingism*, 55. See Gordon, *Healing*, 109f.

112. Miller, *Irvingism*, 52f., 58, 60, 73; Edward Irving, "The Church with Her Endowment of Holiness Power," *The Collected Writings of Edward Irving*, ed. by G. Caryle (London: Alexander Strahan Publisher, 1866), 5:489; Shumway, "Glossolalia," 7. Cf. Dorries, "Irving," 50. Miller (147) adds this cursory note:

> An article in the *Baptist Argus* (Louisville, Kentucky, 23 January, 1908) cites eighteen different instances of men and women gifted with "tongues," who had gone to India, China and Japan in the past few years trusting to these gifts instead of the knowledge of the languages necessary, and how several of these deluded people were saved from starvation by the missionaries.

Cf. William S. Merricks, *Edward Irving: The Forgotten Giant* (East Peoria: Scribe's Chamber Publications, 1983), 160f., 165; Arnold Dillimore, *Forerunner of the Charismatic Movement: The Life of Edward Irving* (Chicago: Moody Press, 1983), 134, 138f.; Edgar, *Gifts*, 244f. Dillimore and Edgar give similar condemnations of Irving.

credits Robert Baxter, a person who later became attached to Irving, with "automatic writing" in French, Italian, and Spanish "while in ecstasy."[113]

The complete healing of Margaret led James to write Mary Campbell, telling her that if she would arise from her bed she would be healed. Upon receiving the letter, she did arise and was healed. News of these events in Scotland which involved people who were influenced by Irving's christology, dismissed the remaining doubts which he had about Scott's teaching that God was restoring charismatic gifts in their own age. J. Philip Newell documents well how Scott anticipated Irving. It is also interesting that Newell says Mary had tuberculosis while Shumway says she was an epileptic. Merrick claims that various ministers thought her gifts were genuinely of God. Drummond seems to suggest Irving got his Spirit Christology from Mary, but Smail and Dorries argue realistically that the reverse was true. Gordon Strachan shows that Mary's implementation of his christology was instrumental in his volte face on gifts.[114]

On April 30, 1831, Mrs. Cardale, from Irving's parish, spoke three sentences in tongues and three in English interpretation.[115] While Irving encouraged these developments in prayer meetings, he prohibited their exercise in public worship. Concerning the phenomena, Irving wrote to a friend: "Every Wednesday night I am preaching to thousands 'the Baptism with the Holy Ghost,' and the Lord is mightily with us."[116]

The main body of the congregation did not seem concerned while the matter was well disciplined, and perhaps not all were well informed of the events. But finally, October 16, 1831, the inevitable happened. A vivid account is given by Edward Miller.

> At length, on Sunday, October 16th, 1831, when the chapter was just finished at the forenoon service, Miss Hall left her seat in great

---

113. Shumway, "Glossolalia," 105f. Robert Baxter wrote *Narrative of Facts* which is listed in Shumway's bibliography as reprinted in 1902 by The Prophetic News Office in London.

114. J. Philip Newell, "Scottish Intimations of Modern Pentecostalism: A. J. Scott and the 1830 Clydesided Charismatics," *Pneuma* 4:2 (Fall, 1982); Shumway, "Glossolalia," (Boston University, 1919), 46; Merrick, *Irving*, 160f.; Drummond, *Irving*, 159; Smail, *Reflected Glory*, 74; Dorries, "Irving," 43; Gordon Strachan, "Theological and Cultural Origins of the Nineteenth Century Protestant Movement," *Essays on Apostolic Themes*, ed. by Paul Elbert (Peabody: Hendrickson, 1985), 147–49.

115. Drummond, *Irving*, 153; Miller, *Irvingism* 1:66. The sentences were: "the Lord will speak to His people—the Lord hasteneth His coming—the Lord cometh."

116. Drummond, *Irving*, 159.

agitation, and went hastily into the vestry, and shutting the door, spoke by herself, first in an "unknown tongues," and ending with the words in English, "How dare ye to suppress the Voice of the Lord?" The confusion in the congregation of some 1,500 or 2,000 persons, as they listened to the "sudden, doleful, and unintelligible sounds," may be imagined. Mr. Irving begged for attention, and when order was restored, he explained the occurrence, which he said was not new, except in the congregation, where he had for some time considering the propriety for introducing the habit; but, though satisfied of the correctness of such a measure, he was afraid of dispersing the flock; nevertheless, as it as now brought forward by God's will, he felt it his duty to submit. He then said he would change the discourage intended for the day, and expound the fourteenth chapter of Corinthians, in order to elucidate what had just happened. The sister was now returning to her seat, and Mr. Irving, observing her from the pulpit, said, in an affectionate tone, "Console yourself, sister! console yourself!" He then proceeded with the discourse. The prophetess did not let him off so easily. In an interview which he had with her immediately after service, accompanied by his elders and deacons, he was reminded in prophetic language, that "Jesus hid not His face from shame and stirring; and that His servants must be content to follow Him without the camp, bearing His reproach." Poor Irving sunk on a chair, and groaned aloud in distress of spirit. Thenceforward the prophets had their way with him.[117]

Miss Hill had initially gone to the vestry because of Irving's ban on any such activity in the main auditorium, although many of the tongues speakers had previously confronted him regarding the prohibition. After this Sunday, the prophets were more open about their activity and finally caved Irving under with their condemnatory 'Spirit-sayings.' The body of the congregation became quite concerned and eventually, on the basis that Irving had allowed unauthorized personnel to speak in public service, he was dismissed by his presbytery.[118] Central to developments was Irving's Spirit christology, an issue too complicated to consider here.[119]

117. Miller, *Irvingism* 1:68f. See Shaw, *Irvingite*, 34; Cutten, *Tongues*, 93. Miller [75] says that Miss Hill later recanted her commitment.

118. Christenson, "Forerunner," 20; John Roxborough, "As At the Beginning in Britain: Michael Harper, Edward Irving and the Catholic Apostolic Church," *Theological Renewal* 11 (February 1979), 19f.; Drummond, *Irving*, 153; Christenson, *Message*, 36; Strachan, *Irving*, 16.

119. Strachan, *Irving*, 132, emphasizes that earlier the board stood with Irving on the initial charge against his christology, but after the gifts appeared they let the presbyters'

Irving led—or should one say was led—the group to other facilities and there they continued their style of worship. Despite the limitations which Irving tried to impose, the group was carried on its way and outstripped the guidelines (e.g., prophecy judged by moral conduct of person, relation to "sound doctrine" and the time in a church service) of his theology. The group which came to be known as the Catholic Apostolic Church appointed apostles based on various "Spirit-sayings." Irving was accorded the lower status of "angel" or pastor. A somewhat broken man, Irving died at the early age of 42 while on a trip to Scotland in 1834. This trip was undertaken because of a prophetic command to which was added a promise that Irving would have a major ministry in that area. Irving went despite warnings from his physicians that the area would be hazardous to his health.[120]

Williams and Waldvogel report the following:

> All the more grievous to him they claimed the authority to direct all aspects of church life and they silenced their leader in the name of the Holy Spirit. He died in 1834, a still young, much worn, and lonely proclaimer of the place of tongues in the context of a pre-millennial eschatology. His work continued, without due recognition, in the hands of "prophets" and "apostles" under the banner of sacramental Apostolic Church, which was Catholic in its use of incense, vestments, and creeds based on Roman Catholic, Orthodox, and Anglican rites, and Apostolic in its endorsement of tongues and in the active roles assigned to deacons, elders, prophets, and apostles in its ministries and polity.[121]

---

judgment be sustained. This would be especially obvious given the direct line Irving ran from the Spirit empowerment of Christ to that bestowed upon apostles and later believer as noted by Garry Dale Nation, "The Hermeneutics of Pentecostal-Charismatic Restoration Theology: A Critical Analysis," unpublished Ph.D. dissertation, Southwestern Baptist Theological Seminary, December, 1990, 45. Strachan [21] points out Karl Barth's acknowledgment of the usefulness of Irving's christology. See Shaw, *Irvingite*, 23; Smail, *Reflected Glory*, 77; Dorries, "Irving," 45; Dave MacPherson, *The Incredible Cover-Up* (Plainfield: Logos, 1975), 29; H. D. Whitley, *Blinded Eagle* (London: SCM Press, 1955).

120. See Miller, *Irving*, 127, 144; Christenson, "Forerunner," 20; Strachan, *Irving*, 14; Warfield, *Perfectionism*, 134.

121. Williams and Waldvogel, "Tongues," 86. See David Bundy, "Edward Irving," *DPCM*, 370f.

I have given a brief historical context to Irving's "charismatic" theology and now will look at the theology that resulted from these pneumatic experiences and his christology.

> Therefore it is that in our baptism, we have promised to us, not only the cleansing away of sin,—the remission, the dismissal or divorcement of it; which being put away, what is there left but holiness?—but we have also the promise of the Holy Ghost, as given by the prophet Joel, for the purpose of demonstrating that we are children of the risen Christ, members of the glorified and omnipotent Head.
>
> Therefore also the apostles and disciples were not permitted to go and preach until they had received that heavenly baptism. Their word must first be instinct and heavenly power, before it can convert men unto God. So also it was with Christ himself. He undertook not His public ministry till He had received the baptism of the Holy Ghost, and to that baptism Peter expressly referreth His miraculous power and doings: Acts 10:37f...[122]

> So also Christ by regeneration, becomes in His own personality the upholder of our person—we have the Spirit of Christ—but it is the Holy Ghost which brings us the spirit of Christ, the super human is of the Father; both inwrought by the Holy Ghost, acting in the former work as the regenerating Spirit of Christ, in the latter as the baptizing Spirit of the Father...[123]

Modern writers form the Charismatic Movement make the claim that Irving believed tongues to be the special evidence of Spirit baptism. Irving is quoted as saying of the doctrine of the baptism with the Holy Spirit that its "... standing sign, if we err not, is the speaking with tongues."[124]

---

122. Edward Irving, "On the Gifts of the Holy Ghost," *The Collected Writings of Edward Irving* 5:524. Strachan, *Irving*, 130, quotes Irving's *Day of Pentecost or the Baptism with the Holy Ghost*: "My idea, therefore, concerning the baptism of the Holy Ghost, or the promise of the Father, is simply this, that it is superhuman, super-natural power, or set of powers, which God did from the beginning purpose to place in man, but which he accomplished not to do until his own Son had become man, and kept man's original trust."

123. Ibid., 529. See Strachan, *Irving*, 95, 18, 125; Hopwood, *Spirit*, 159; Nichol, *Pentecostals*, 24; Christenson, *Message*, 62. Notice that Irving's christology allows him to say that Christ was regenerated.

124. Strachan, *Irving*, 19, 127. See also Dorries, "Irving," 48–50. Bresson, *Ecstasy*, 96, says that Irving made the statement in 1930. Bresson adds, "Reverend R. H. Everly quotes Edward Irving in his magazine *Pentecost*, as saying that a person does not have the Holy Ghost at all unless he speaks with tongues." Cf. Merricks, *Irving*, 174; A. A. Dallimore,

It is true that tongues were an important part of Spirit baptism according to Irving.

> ...we find it (tongues) always to have been the gift first bestowed upon the baptized (Acts 2, 10:46, 19:1) and in the instances now appearing in the Church, this is the only gift which hath been given....
> ...that the utterance of tongues which no one understandeth ...is the forthcoming of the soul filled with the Holy Ghost....
> ...there is not any believer in the Lord Jesus Christ who ought not to desire and to pray for, and who may not expect, the gift of tongues....[125]

Incidentally, he offered the following reasons for the demise of tongues in the Church: insufficient doctrine, natural methods of teaching about the Holy Spirit; theories which advocated cessation; lack of humility and fasting; contentment to be without them.[126]

My reading was severely restricted due to the lack of available original sources, especially Irving's *Day of Pentecost or the Baptism with the Holy Ghost*, but of those sources available, I saw Irving make a special connection between tongues *and prophecy* as relating to Spirit baptism.

> In one word, therefore, I gather from the study of the prophet [Isa] that the gift of tongues is a chief means of God for training up the children of the Spirit into the capacity of prophesying and speaking in the Church for the edification of all; whether "by revelation, or by knowledge, or by prophesying, or by doctrine."
> It is clear to me, both from what I have witnessed and from what I see written in the word of God concerning this thing that it was only subsidiary to the work of prophesying, of magnifying God, or testifying that Jesus is Lord. The great and chief thing was, the declaration of God's mind in an unintelligible tongue; the un-

---

Forerunner of the Charismatic Movement: The Life of Edward Irving (Chicago: Moody Press, 1983), 131.

125. Irving, "Gifts of the Holy Ghost," 539, 559 respectively. Elsewhere [544] commenting on Acts 2, 10 and 19, he says: "Beyond all question, therefore, speaking with tongues is the sign of the Holy Ghost in the person who so spake." He also listed [p.560] reasons for the demise of tongues in the Church: insufficient doctrine; natural methods of teaching about the Holy Spirit; theories which advocated cessation; lack of humility and fasting; contentment to be without them.

126. Irving, "Gifts of the Holy Ghost," 560.

known tongue was only the sign that it was God's mind which the person was declaring.[127]

Merricks claims that they also sung in tongues while Dallimore claims that they also believed they had the power to handle serpents and consume poisons without harm. Dallimore is probably misapplying Irving's use of Mary's interpretation of Mark 16:17. Since the specification of the relation of tongues to prophecy as evidential of Spirit baptism is not germane to this study, I shall have to leave the matter unresolved. One observation, of some importance, is that Irving himself never spoke in tongues. One could say that if this be true, then Irving would have to believe that he was never Spirit baptized. Also, Gottfried Arnold's (in his *Imperial History of the Church and of Heretics*) chapter on Montanism was printed in John Lacy's *The General Delusion of Christians* (London: 1713). This book puzzled John Wesley, but convinced him that Montanists were "real scriptural Christians." It was reprinted by Edward Irving.[128]

Finally, the Catholic Apostolic Church officially adopted Spirit baptism theology. Larry Christenson says that the church used the term "sealing" but meant what Pentecostals mean when they say Spirit baptism. Merricks cites Irving as using the word seal in this fashion. G. Atter says that Irvingites who came to Canada in the nineteenth century exercised charismatic phenomena but did not teach Spirit baptism as subsequent nor tongues as initial evidence. Schaff says the Irvingites made a distinction between xenolalia of Pentecost and glossolalia at Corinth with the latter common among them. In referring to perhaps the 1870s he says,

---

127. Ibid., 544, 546, respectively. See Edward Irving, "The Sealing Virtue of Baptism," Homilies on Baptism 2, *Writings* 2:277f. A. L. Drummond, *Irving*, 164, quotes Irving from an article he published in *Fraser's Magazine*, April, 1832:

> Again, no one doubteth that Christian baptism doth convey to the believer the gift of repentance towards God, and the remission of sins by the regeneration of the Holy Spirit: and why should they doubt that it doth convey also the baptism with the Holy Spirit for speaking with tongues and prophesying?

See Christenson, *Message*, 56.

128. See Merricks, *Irving*, 165–74; Dallimore, *Forerunner*, 131–38; Strachan, "Nineteenth Century Pentecostal Movement," 148; Parmentier, "Two Early Charismatic Movements," 19n15. Arguing from the premise that Irving defended initial evidence Spirit baptism, Dorries, "Irving," 53, decides that Irving must have spoken in tongues. The following authorities say that Irving did not speak in tongues: Williams and Waldvogel, "Tongues," 86; Cutten, *Tongues*, 100; Shumway, "Glossolalia," 106; Christenson, "Forerunner," 19; Damboriena, *Tongues*, 189n48; MacPherson, *The Incredible Cover-Up*, 29.

Several years ago I witnessed this phenomenon in an Irvingite congregation in New York; the words were broken, ejaculatory and unintelligible, but uttered in abnormal, startling, impressive sounds, in a state of apparent unconsciousness and rapture, and without any control over the tongue, which was seized as it were by a foreign power.

A friend and colleague—Dr. Briggs—who witnessed it in 1879 in the principal Irvingite church at London, received the same impression."[129]

The title of Strachan's article, "Nineteenth Century Pentecostal Movement," clearly shows his belief that this group had much in common with Classical Pentecostalism in the USA. When listing differences between the two movements, Strachan said the following was true of the group in the nineteenth century: they were all formally educated and theologically cultivated; they were not anti-intellectual nor unduly emotional; they were influenced by the Reformed doctrines of sola fide and sola gratia but not by a second blessing theology; they defended a christology that emphasized the humanity of Jesus; they were discriminating but basically world affirming. Finally, W. J. Hollenweger says that the Irvingites directly influenced pentecostal origins in the USA, but I join Strachan, Christenson, and Purves in dissenting from that view. Irvingites did go to Canada, New Zealand, and the eastern U.S. in addition to sundry parts of Europe and Russia.[130]

Mainstream Christianity has viewed the Mormon Movement with great suspicion. The quasi-Christian classification is primarily attributable to the Mormon belief in authoritative revelation which is in addition to the Scriptures.[131] Joseph Smith, Brigham Young and many early adher-

---

129. Schaff, *History* 1:1:115. See Christenson, "Forerunner," 30; Merricks, *Irving*, 172; Atter, *Force*, 35; Nichol, *Pentecostals*, 24; J. E. Worsfold, *A History of the Charismatic Movements in New Zealand* (West Yorkshire: Puritan Press Ltd., 1974); Stephen C. Neal, *Interpretation of the New Testament, 1861–1961*, 123; Abraham Kuyper, *The Worth of the Holy Spirit* (New York: Funk and Wagnells Co., 1900), 85–87. Worsfold, *Charismatic*, 56, 64, and others show that the Catholic Apostolic Church went to various parts of the world.

130. Strachan, "Nineteenth Century Pentecostal Movement," 144n1; Hollenweger, *The Pentecostals*, 4; Christenson, "Forerunner," 20; Jim Purves, "The Interaction of Christology and Pneumatology in the Soteriology of Edward Irving," *Pneuma* 14:1 (Spring 1992): 190.

131. This is a relevant issue since present day Pentecostals and Charismatics often have allowed words of prophecy to be outside the parameter of explicit biblical teaching. Smith's group was perhaps more aligned with Christendom than Brigham Young's followers.

ents exercised various "spectacular" gifts of the Spirit including tongues-speech. With regard to the doctrine of Spirit baptism, it is said that the

> Early Mormons considered the hands the "natural channel through which those who are filled with the Holy Ghost . . . can communicate it to others and practiced the laying on of hands for the Holy Ghost mentioned in Acts 8 and 19.[132]

Born in a Quaker family, Hannah Whitall Smith (1832–1911) is best remembered for her involvement in the "Higher Christian Life" Movement and her book *The Christian's Secret of a Happy Life* (1875). The earliest editions of this book had a chapter on the Holy Spirit; a chapter which is deleted from most editions today. Catherine Marshall summarizes Mrs. Smith's views expressed in this chapter: "We make the mistake of looking upon the baptism of the Spirit as a single experience rather than a life, as an arbitrary bestowment rather than a necessary vitality."[133]

Reportedly, Mrs. Smith did not identify Spirit baptism with either the regenerating work of the Spirit or with sanctification. Rather it is said that Mrs. Smith would equate the filling of the Spirit with Spirit baptism and would add, ". . . we are to receive in a new and far fuller sense that which He has already given at Pentecost."[134] In light of Mrs. Smith's involvement in the 'higher life' theology which developed markedly after the first edition of her book, I was initially inclined to believe that this section on the Holy Spirit had been wrongly placed there by the publisher. However, while her later writings are primarily concerned with sanctification, there would not appear to be cause for her to have recanted anything expressed in this earlier writing. Hannah and her husband Pearsall were the cornerstones for the later Keswick Conventions[135] and while Keswick emphasized sanc-

---

132. Williams and Waldvogel, "Tongues," 87f. See S. A. Manwell, "Speaking With Tongues II," *The Wesleyan Methodist* (February 20, 1907), 8; Kelsey, *Tongue Speaking*, 58; Anderson, *Disinherited*, 26; Lewis, *Witnesses*, 249; Hinson, "History of Glossolalia," 66; Wamble "Glossolalia," 39f.; Cutten, *Tongues*, 70; John DeSoyres, *Montanism and the Primitive Church* (Cambridge: Deighton, Bell and Colk, 1878), 128; Kendrick, *Promise*, 24. It is revealing that G. B. Cutten's opening shot at pentecostalism was an entire chapter devoted to "glossolalia" in his 1908 *The Psychological Phenomena of Christianity* in which he pulls in the Mormon story (53).

133. Catherine Marshall, *Something More* (New York: Avon Books, 1974), 239.

134. Smith quoted in Marshall, *Something More*, 240.

135. Williams and Waldvogel, "Tongues," 94; S. R. Kamm, "Hannah Whitall Smith," *NIDCC*, 910; Warfield, *Perfectionism*, 213. Wessels, "Baptism in the Holy Spirit," 13, says that Hannah was influenced by Asa Mahan.

tification it also insisted on the filling of the Spirit. In a later writing which was published posthumously, she used the same terminology while seeking to limit emotional excitement. Writing of what she now termed religious fanaticism—she was the mother of Logan Pearsall Smith—she told of "... several cases of people desperately seeking a 'conscious' Baptism of the Holy Spirit that would result in 'physical thrills.'"[136]

The nineteenth century English Baptist minister renowed for his pulpit oratory, Charles Spurgeon (1834-1894), seems to have believed in a special work of the Spirit which can be called the fullness of the Spirit. In a published edition of some of his sermons on the Holy Spirit, Spurgeon gave the following exhortation:

> Let us not be satisfied with the sip that saves, but let us go on to the baptism which buries the flesh and raises us in the likeness of the risen Lord: even that baptism into the Holy Ghost and into fire which makes us spiritual and sets us all on flame and zeal for the glory of God.
>
> You know how our Lord puts it, "He dwelleth with you and shall be in you." That indwelling is another thing from being *with* us. The Holy Spirit was with the Apostles in the days when Jesus was with them; but he was not in them in the sense in which he filled them at and after the day of Pentecost.
>
> I pray that some who have never received the Holy Spirit at all may now be led, while I am speaking, to pray, "Blessed Spirit, visit me; lead me to Jesus." But especially those of you that are children of God,—to you is this promise especially made. Ask God to make you all that the Spirit of God can make you, not only a satisfied believer who has drunk for himself, but a useful believer, who overflows the neighborhood with blessing.[137]

136. Dayton, "Christian Perfection," 51. Williams and Waldvogel, "Tongues," 95, say:

> She had observed how the question for certainty had too often resulted in the elevation of particular manifestations over concern for authentic experience. Some claimed that a certain dance or laugh was some evidence of Spirit baptism; others found that undue emphasis of the "holy kiss" led to unfortunate consequences.

See R. A. Knox, *Enthusiasm*, 15, 76f.

137. C. H. Spurgeon, *Twelve Sermons on the Holy Spirit* (Grand Rapids: Baker, 1973), 105f., 107, 114 respectively. Waldvogel, "Origins," explains that Spurgeon contributed to preparing Britain for Hannah and Pearsall Smith. Cf. J. Edwin Orr, *Full Surrender* (London: Marshall, Morgan and Scott, Ltd., 1951), 104; Rice, *Charismatic*, 78, 97. Walter J. Chantry, *Signs of the Apostles* (Edinburgh: Banner of Truth Trust, 1976), 143, quotes Spurgeon against the miraculous in his own day.

As a young layperson in a Presbyterian church, W. E. Boardman (b. 1810) began reading the works of Finney and Mahan for illumination on the doctrine of sanctification. Boardman and his wife soon claimed the experience and while he began studies at a seminary, his wife prepared a manuscript describing their experiences. His efforts of working over the text led him to produce the best seller *The Higher Christian Life*. This book, published in 1858, was essentially Christocentric. Edith Waldvogel summarizes his work:

> ... the ordinary Christian should proceed in his spiritual life from an experience of conversion to a conscious appropriation of "Christ as all."
>
> Only when the Christian consciously surrendered himself fully to the indwelling Christ could he know the twofold power of the Holy Spirit: "power to stand' and 'power to work."[138]

An active man of many capabilities and laudable ambitions, Dwight L. Moody (1838–1899) may be best remembered for his evangelistic ministry. There were a variety of influences that led Moody to a special pneumatic experience which he called Spirit baptism. Not the least of these influences was the method of exegesis which he learned from the Plymouth Brethren, Finney's autobiography and two older women who encouraged the successful pastor to seek the "power." Shortly before his death in December, 1899, Moody reflected over the two major spiritual experiences in his life.

> There are two epochs in my life which stand out clear. One is when I was born of the Spirit. There never can come a greater blessing to a man on this earth than to be born again from above, to have the God nature implanted in him.
>
> God has been good to me. He has showered blessing after blessing upon me; but the greatest blessing next to being born again came sixteen years after, when I was filled with the Spirit, and it has never left me.[139]

---

138. Waldvogel, "Origins," 82f. See T. Smith, *Revivalism*, 145; Synan, *Holiness-Pentecostal*, 30; Bruner, *Theology of the Holy Spirit*, 43.

139. Dwight L. Moody in *Institute Tie*, September, 1900 as quoted in Waldvogel, "Origins," 27. See Harper, *Beginning*, 96; Rice, *Charismatic*, 75. The story of the two women who confronted Moody and his resultant Spirit baptism in 1871 is told in W. R. Moody, *Dwight L. Moody* (New York: Fleming H. Revell Co., 1900), 146–49. See Waldvogel, "Origins," 22, 36; Dayton, "Christian Perfection," 47.

Speaking theologically, it would appear that Moody could not accept the formula "The Spirit is with you and shall be in you." Moody thought that the Spirit already dwelt within a Christian, but not necessarily "in power." He finally used the summary phrase, "He is in you and shall come upon you."[140] If Moody commented on the relation of sanctification, it was that "Spirit-baptism is the short cut to holiness."[141] Moody's Northfield Conferences involved A. J. Gordon and C. I. Scofield and were eventually administered by R. A. Torrey. I shall turn to these men momentarily, but remember that Moody ". . . frequently requested his associate and successor, R. A. Torrey, to preach his sermon on the baptism with the Holy Spirit which claimed that baptism resulted in power for service."[142]

A. J. Gordon (1836–1895), a Baptist minister, graduated from Brown University (1860) and Newton Theological Seminary (1863). During his pastorate at Clarendon St. Baptist Church, Boston, he founded a school from which came Gordon College and its divinity school.[143] In his book *Ministry of the Spirit* (1894), Gordon approvingly quotes Andrew Murray's affirmation of two works of the Spirit and he seems inclined to accept a similar statement by J. Elder Cumming on the Spirit: "It is only when he is consciously accepted in all his power that we can be said to be either 'baptized' or 'filled' with the Holy Ghost."[144] Gordon's own expression is that "The baptism in the Spirit, already bestowed at Pentecost,

---

140. Wessels, "Baptism in the Holy Spirit," 54f.; Waldvogel, "Origins," 59; Dayton "Theological Roots," 127.

141. Waldvogel, "Origins," 39; Wessels, "Baptism in the Holy Spirit," 51, 56; Rice, *Charismatic*, 75.

142. Williams and Waldvogel, "Tongues," 91. The same quotation is given in Rice, *Charismatic*, 76. I am not aware of any of Moody's writings that would advocate tongues-speech as a regular accompaniment of Spirit baptism. However, there is a "tongues" story, frequently repeated, about an 1873 Moody campaign in Sunderland:

> . . . Robert Boy wrote about his visit: "When I got to the rooms of the YMCA I found the meeting on fire. The young men were speaking in tongues and prophesying. What on earth did it mean? Only that Moody had been addressing them that afternoon."

As given in Harper, *Beginning*, 23. See Synan, *Pentecostal*, 99; Brumback, *What Meaneth This?*, 93. I have been unable to verify the original source.

143. C. G. Thorne, Jr., "A. J. Gordon," *NIDCC*, 423; Waldvogel, "Origins," 23.

144. A. J. Gordon, *The Ministry of the Spirit* (Grand Rapids: Zondervan, 1949), 86. Murray is quoted on page 66. Cf. Williams and Waldvogel, "Tongues," 92; Dayton "Theological Roots," 136.

must be appropriated."¹⁴⁵ Gordon says that Acts 2:38 indicates that the gift of the Spirit is received subsequent to repentance. On Galatians 3:2, 14 he says, "These texts seem to imply that just as there is 'faith toward the Holy Ghost for power and consecration."¹⁴⁶ Gordon says that there are three aspects to the enduement of the Spirit: sealing, filling, anointing. With regard to "anointing" he refers to the Old Testament anointings (Lev 8:12, 1 Sam 16:15, 1 Kgs 19:16, Lev 14:17), the anointing of Jesus (Lk 4:18, 27, Acts 10:38), and the anointing of the believer (1 Cor 1:21, 1 Jn 2:20). Gordon notes that the Spirit works our sanctification, but the important thing about Spirit baptism is power: "We conceive that the great end for which the enduement of the Spirit is bestowed is our qualification for the highest and most effective service in the church of Christ."¹⁴⁷

A nineteenth century Congregationalist by the name of Sherlock Bristol (1815–1906), was the author of a work entitled *Paracletos or Baptism of the Holy Ghost*. Bristol argued that this special work of the Spirit in the Old Testament was confined to selected people, but today all were invited to share in it. Among those receiving this experience he suggested Wesley, Whitefield, Spurgeon and Moody. In a seven point summation of the ramifications of the day of Pentecost, Bristol made the following affirmations:

1. It clearly teaches that the baptism of the Holy Spirit is a great spiritual endowment bestowed upon Christians, *subsequent to their conversion*. Perhaps this is not always so, but we believe it is, usually.
2. We must seek the gift.
3. All classes can have it.
4. It changes one from weakness to power.
5. In it we see how Christians are to be sanctified.
6. We see how nations are to be converted.

---

145. Ibid., 74. He was commenting on Acts 8.

146. Ibid., 71. Acts 2:38 is treated on pages 91–95. He points out, 82, that those in Acts 2:4 were already converted. Similarly, 71, Acts 19 shows that one can be a disciple and yet not have the gifts of the Spirit. See William Menzies, "The Non-Wesleyan Origins of the Pentecostal Movement," *Aspects of Pentecostal-Charismatic Origins*, Synan, 88.

147. Ibid., 74. Cf. page 90. Sanctification is mentioned on page 69 and the anointing sequence, which he treats in a different order, is on page 88. Gordon says, 77, that Jesus was sealed at the Jordan (Jn 6:27) and then known to be full of the Spirit (Lk 4:1).

7. We see also that if the Church would see sinners converted, it must first of all be baptized by the Holy Ghost.[148]

Notice the mixture of purity and power when he says, "A revival sought by Christians all over the world much after the Pentecost pattern, and received, first in sanctifying power upon them, and then in an outgoing power upon the nations."[149]

Andrew Murray (1828–1927) was the son of a South African minister in the Dutch Reformed Church. Andrew's father, also named Andrew, often prayed for an outpouring of the Holy Spirit, but it remained for the prayer to be answered during the son's ministry. In 1845 at age 17, Andrew completed M.A. exams at Aberdeen. Later in his ministry, he served as moderator of the Dutch Reformed Church in Cape Colony. In 1895, he addressed the conventions at Keswick and Northfield. In Africa, he was responsible for the initiation of the Bible and Prayer Union, the 'holiness' conventions, and the Student Christian Association.[150] In opening the question of Spirit baptism, Andrew said that there were two diverse views and then a third one, somewhat mediating, the last which he preferred: (1) every believer receives the Holy Spirit in regeneration, there is no Spirit baptism to be sought for (so Ernest Boys); (2) a true believer may be without the promised Spirit (so Asa Mahan); (3) the Holy Spirit dwells in every believer, yet a believer may from time to time receive very special conscious renewals of the Spirit's presence and power from on high; these may be regarded as fresh baptisms of the Spirit. Andre comments:

> Let me say at once, that if it be maintained in connection with this second view that every believer must consciously seek and receive, as a distinct experience, such a Baptism, this does not appear to me what the Word of God teaches. But if it be put in this way, that in answer to believing prayer many believers have received, and those who seek it will often receive, such an inflow of the Spirit of God as will to then indeed be nothing less than a new Baptism of

---

148. Sherlock Bristol, *Paracletos or Baptism of the Holy Ghost* (New York: Fleming H. Revell, 1892), 29. Only numbers 1, 5, 7 are actual quotations.

149. Ibid., 13. Bristol said, 35f., there were certain phenomena relevant for the early days alone. These gifts are: power to work miracles, power to write inspired books, speak in tongues, and the ability to forecast the future. Later, however, Bristol tells, 59, of a friend who received the "Pentecostal baptism" and "God gave him the tongue of fire." Bristol does not explain what constituted the tongue of fire.

150. Hollenweger, *Pentecostals*, 111–13; C. G. L. Cragg, "Andrew Murray," *NIDCC*, 685; Steve Barabas, *So Great Salvation* (Westwood: Fleming H. Revell, n.d.), 175ff.

the Spirit. I cannot but regard it as in harmony with the teaching of Scripture.[151]

Notice how he pulls together the paradoxical received-not received affirmation:

> From God's side the twofold gift is simultaneous. The Spirit is not divided: in giving the Spirit, God gives Himself and all He is.
> And yet we have indications in Scripture that there may be circumstances . . . in which the two halves of the promise are not so closely linked.[152]

Andrew also insists that this pneumatic empowering is predicated on a thorough spiritual cleansing.[153]

J. Elder Cumming (1830–1917), who pastored a Presbyterian church, first spoke at Keswick in 1883 and did so thereafter for 24 years in succession. It is reported that Cumming was converted when, as a theological student at Glasglow University, he prepared a sermon.[154] Speaking of the work of the Spirit, Cumming said:

> It seems . . . that in addition to the gift of the Spirit received at conversion, there is another blessing, corresponding to its signs and effects to the blessing received by the Apostles at Pentecost . . .
> . . . one of their terms by which we may designate it is to 'be filled with the Spirit.'[155]

Cumming said that the initial filling could be called the "baptism of the Holy Ghost." This baptism was accomplished by Christ and was to be distinguished from the Spirit's baptizing one into Christ.[156] Cumming favorably quotes Boardman, Mahan, H. C. G. Moule, Andrew Murray and John Wesley. Like Mahan, he reacted against the Brethren Ernest Boys. Boys argued that the accounts given in Acts 8 and 10 were of such an

---

151. Andrew Murray, *The Spirit of Christ* (Fort Washington: Christian Literature Crusade, 1963), 218. But see pages 220, 23. The introduction to the three views is given on page 213.

152. Ibid., 15. See pages 21, 23. Cf. Hollenweger, *Pentecostals*, 114.

153. Andrew Murray, *The Full Blessings of Pentecost* (Plainfield: Logos, n.d.), 138.

154. Barabas, *So Great Salvation*, 163f. F. B. Meyer in the preface to Cumming's *Through the Eternal Spirit* (New York: Fleming H. Revell, 1896), 7f., notes that Cumming was a friend of A. J. Gordon.

155. Cumming, *Eternal Spirit*, 114. Cf. Ernest Williams, *Systematic Theology* 3:60.

156. Ibid., 115f.

exceptional nature they could not be used as a theological precedent.[157] Cumming suggested that a term other than Spirit baptism should be used in an effort to avoid confusion. He believed that the phrase had fallen into disuse for two reasons: one, because of confusion with water baptism, and the other:

> When the miraculous accompaniments of the Apostolic ministries were disappearing and the providential guidance of the Lord was taking their place, then the thing to be looked for was, not a childhood of Christian life, such as the Apostles had before Pentecost, but a life which had the fullness of blessing from the beginning, and did not need a crisis such as the Apostles subsequently found. And as the Epistles set before us, the high, the ideal standard of life, they do not propose that we should aim at such marked crises of experiences as would be indicated by expecting a subsequent baptism of the Holy Spirit.[158]

Cumming hastened to add that the ideal was often not achieved and that many experienced Spirit baptism subsequent to their conversion. This citation also shows how Cumming, like all of those involved with the Keswick Conventions, included purification with empowerment in the concept of Spirit baptism.

A graduate of Yale College (1875) and Yale Divinity School (1878), R. A. Torrey (1856–1928) was ordained to the Congregational ministry in 1878. It was during this period of time that Torrey read Charles G. Finney's *Autobiography* and his *Lectures on Revivals of Religion*. For four years Torrey was pastor of a Congregational church in Garrettsville, Ohio, at the conclusion of which he spent a year studying at Leipzig and Erlangen. When Torrey returned, he first worked with several midwestern congregations before becoming the first supervisor of Moody's Chicago Training Institute (1889) and soon thereafter pastor (1894) of the Chicago Avenue Church. The years 1902–1921 saw Torrey involved in preaching tours in various countries while from 1912 to 1924 he was dean of the Bible Institute of Los Angeles (BIOLA) and from 1915 to 1924 also pastor of The Church of the Open Door of Los Angeles.[159] Torrey's book entitled *Baptism of the Holy Spirit*, which has been reprinted today

157. Ibid., 111.

158. Ibid., 121. Cf. page 88. Cumming's book has been reprinted under the title *Handbook of the Holy Spirit*.

159. Waldvogel, "Origins," 23, 66; J. G. G. Norman, "R. A. Torrey," *NIDCC*, 981.

by those opposing Classical Pentecostalism, was first published in 1895. He used Scriptures like Acts 1:5, 2:4, 38, 4:8, 10:44–46, 11:15–17, 19:2–6 to say that the following terms are interchangeable: Spirit baptism, filled with the Holy Ghost, gift of the Holy Ghost, Holy Ghost fell, received the Holy Ghost, endued with power from on high, promise of my Father.[160]

Without any hesitation, Torrey says that Spirit baptism is "... an operation of the Holy Spirit distinct from and subsequent and additional to His regenerating work."[161] It was concerned with proper use of biblical phrases that promised Torrey to caution that "baptized with the Holy Spirit" is

> ... nowhere used in the Bible of any experience but the first, and that furthermore the word *baptized* of itself suggests an initial or initiatory experience. Therefore, do not say "fresh baptism with the Spirit" but of being "filled with the Spirit."[162]

Spirit baptism was not the eradication of the carnal nature or a cleansing from an impure heart, for "It has to do with gifts for service rather than with graces of character."[163] Torrey amplifies this understanding:

> It is the impartation of supernatural power or gifts in service, and sometimes one may have rare gifts by the Spirit's power and few graces.
> The gifts vary with the different lives of service which God has called different persons. The church is a body and different parts of the body have different functions ...[164]

The remarks on gifts prompts one to ask how he viewed tongues-speech. When the Pentecostal Movement began at the turn of the century, Torrey

---

160. R. A. Torrey, *The Bible Teaches* (n.p.: Fleming H. Revell, 1898–1933), 269f. Mr. Revell was Moody's brother-in-law. So Waldvogel, "Origins," 68.

161. Ibid., 271. He immediately says, on the basis on Rom 8:9 and 1 Cor 6:19, that every true believer has the Holy Spirit. See Wessels, "Baptism in the Holy Spirit," 10; Sala, "Holy Spirit," 167. Bruner, *Theology of the Holy Spirit*, 45, says that Torrey's world traveling and teaching of this subsequent experience made fertile ground for Pentecostals. See Waldvogel, "Origins," 11.

162. R. A. Torrey, *The Baptism with the Holy Spirit* (Minneapolis: Dimension Books, 1972), 69. Also Torrey, *Bible Teaches*, 278f. Cf. Wessels, "Baptism in the Holy Spirit," 58.

163. Torrey, *Bible Teaches*, 273. See Waldvogel, "Origins," 31f.

164. Ibid., 273f. Also Torrey, *Baptism*, 20. See Wessels, "Baptism in the Holy Spirit," 57. Waldvogel, "Origins," 37, points out that Torrey, like Moody, thought one should not witness until Spirit-baptized.

tried to make sure that his position was understood to be different from that of the "tongues-speakers." Apparently Torrey did not see the implications of his own affirmation that it is acceptable to "covet the best gifts" (1 Cor 12:31), but one cannot ask for a particular gift. His main conclusion was that God

> is absolutely sovereign, and our position is that of unconditional surrender to Him. I am glad that this is so: that He in His infinite wisdom and love, is to select the field, service, and gift and not I, in my shortsightedness and folly.[165]

This logic would also imply the appropriate of tongues, but that was not Torrey's conclusion. Spirit baptism was, first and last, 'power.'

C. I. Scofield (1843–1921), reared in Tennessee, was awarded the Confederate Cross of Honor while serving with Lee's army. He practiced law of some years and after his conversion was ordained to pastor a Congregational church in Dallas. It was in response to Moody's invitation that Scofield took the Moody Church in East Northfield, Massachusetts. In 1902 Scofield returned to the Dallas church. It was his reference Bible, which appeared in 1909, that was to leave a mark beyond his own time. Scofield was joined in the venture by other conservative evangelicals including James J. Gray and Arthur T. Pierson.[166] The Scofield Bible evidences the influence of Plymouth Brethren theology when it includes tongues in the category of temporary gifts. The essentials of Scofield's view on Spirit baptism have been perpetuated in dispensational circles by its repetition in the influential writings of L. S. Chafer, C. C. Ryrie, and John Walvoord. While Scofield saw a time lapse between receiving Christ and Spirit baptism in some earliest accounts, he argued that by the time of Cornelius there was no such separation,

> Henceforth, wherever the gospel is believed among Gentiles, the Holy Spirit in the moment when they believe, regenerates and indwells them, and baptizes them into the Body of Christ. To this the Epistles bear consistent and unvarying testimony.[167]

---

165. Ibid., 275. Williams and Waldvogel, "Tongues," 93, say that 1 Cor 12:30 convinced Torrey that tongues were not necessary. See Bloch-Hoell, *Pentecostals*, 189n91. Torrey has a grandson in Korea who is charismatic and he uses his grandfather's theology to support his own point of view.

166. Earle E. Cairns, "C. I. Scofield," *NIDCC*, 889.

167. C. I. Scofield, *A Mighty Wind* (Grand Rapids: Baker, 1973), 47. Williams and

Scofield used 1 Corinthians 6:19, Romans 8:9, and Galatians 4:6 to argue that all have the Holy Spirit dwelling within and the true meaning of Spirit baptism, namely incorporation into the Church, is explicated in 1 Corinthians 12:13. However, Scofield argued that Acts and the Epistles also make it clear that possession of the Spirit is not the same as being full of the Spirit: "It is when the Christian is filled with the Spirit that all the marvelous results of His indwelling are realized."[168] It is not the exception when one is indwelt, baptized and filled at the moment of conversion. Arguing that the experience of the disciples was a unified one he said, "Doubtless, many believers are filled with the Spirit when (in the moment of conversion) He regenerates, indwells and baptizes them."[169] The filling of the Spirit, said Scofield citing Luke 24:48f., Acts 1:8 and Acts 6:1-3, brings power. To a minister who said "I will check into filling some day," Scofield responded that without the Spirit's filling his service was without power.[170] Scofield gave us the cliché, often wrongly interpreted, that shows the distinctiveness of his Spirit baptism theology: "one baptism, many fillings."[171]

An exhaustive biblical and historical investigation into the doctrine of confirmation was undertaken by the nineteenth century Anglican A. J. Mason. Mason believed that his confirmation theology was essentially a sacramentalization of Keswickian theology. Mason defended the teaching of two works of the Spirit and when he came to 1 Corinthians 12:13 remarked: ". . . the text requires us to think of two distinct moments in our Christian initiation, and of a double work of the Holy Spirit upon the soul."[172]

Along with William Miller, Ellen G. White (1827–1915) was responsible for the organization later known as the Seventh-Day Adventist Church. This inspired lady, considered by her followers to be a prophetess,

---

Waldvogel, "Tongues," 93f., point out that Scofield was pastor of the Moody church when he first published this work, originally titled *Plain Papers on the Doctrine of the Holy Spirit*, in 1899.

168. Ibid., 88.

169. Ibid., 54f.

170. Ibid., 83.

171. Ibid., 56.

172. Mason, *Confirmation*, 44. The first half of this chapter benefited from his historical work.

disclaimed the title of leader.¹⁷³ Mrs. White spoke of the filling of the Spirit that could be obtained by all. She understood it to be a special work of the Spirit that empowered Joshua and Caleb and then later the Waldensians, whom she viewed as forerunners of the Reformation. Commenting on these people she says, "And as they continue to let their light shine, as did those who were baptized with the Spirit on the day of Pentecost, they receive more and still more of the Spirit's power."¹⁷⁴ Speaking to people of her own generation she said:

> Since this the means by which we are to receive power, why do we not hunger and thirst for the gift of the Spirit?
> For the daily baptism of the Spirit, every work should offer his petition to God.
> Especially should they pray that God will baptize His chosen ambassadors in mission fields with a rich measure of His Spirit.¹⁷⁵

F. B. Meyer (b. 1847) first spoke at the Keswick Convention in 1887 and later became one of its most influential participants. Twice he was President of the National Free Church Council, and once, President of The Baptism Union.¹⁷⁶ Meyer wrote the forewords to the books on the Holy Spirit by A. J. Gordon and J. Elder Cumming. Meyer was an open advocate of a special Christocentric work of the Spirit.

> You have known the Holy Ghost regenerating and quickening and blessing you. But have you known Him infilling you with His mighty presence and power?
> The blessing of the day of Pentecost is always described as being 'filled' with the Holy Spirit. God's will for believers is that they should be filled, women as well as men.
> There are thousands of Christians living on this side of Pentecost, as if that great event had never occurred. They are living on the same plan as the early disciples before they were filled with the Holy Spirit. Historically and chronologically they are on this side, experimentally they are on the other side of Pentecost.
> There are just five tests by which you may know that you have received this infilling...(1) is the Lord Jesus a living reality to you?

---

173. Robert C. Newman, "Ellen G. White," *NIDCC*, 1043.

174. Ellen G. White, *The Acts of the Apostles* (Portland: Pacific Press Publication Assoc., 1911), 54.

175. Ibid., 50.

176. Barabas, *Salvation*, 182ff.

(2) Have you assurance that you are a child of God? (3) Have you victory over known sin? (4) Have you power to witness-bearing? (5) Have you the spirit of holy love?[177]

The founder of the Christian and Missionary Alliance, A. B. Simpson (b. 1843), was a graduate of Knox College and originally a Presbyterian minister.[178] Although he worked in relative independence of direct influence, Simpson developed views similar to Torrey, Scofield and Gordon.[179] Considering the explosion of this kind of theologizing since the beginning of the nineteenth century, it does not seem proper to designate any of these writers as having arrived at their conclusions completely "independently." Simpson used Ephesians 5:18 to illustrate a difference between "having the Spirit" and being "filled with the Spirit." A similar exhortation, according to Simpson, was that Timothy was told to "rekindle the gift" within him (2 Timothy 1:6f.). The filling of the Spirit excluded self and sin, while bringing joy and the fruit of the Spirit.[180] While Simpson connected the "anointing" of 2 Corinthians 1:21f with Spirit baptism, his primary emphasis seems to be on purification. He comments on "walk in the Spirit" (Galatians 5:16): "Here is God's great secret of holiness; not fighting sin, but being filled with God."[181] Simpson's view on tongues-speech came of final form after the advent of Pentecostalism which took so many from Alliance ranks. Simpson allowed some connection between tongues and Spirit baptism, but only as an evidence, not the evidence. In the formula-

---

177. F. B. Meyer, *Back to Bethel* (Chicago: Moody Press, 1901), 95, 94, 90, 97-101 respectively. See Meyer's *A Castaway and Other Addresses*, 92ff., quoted in Bruner, *Theology of the Holy Spirit*, 340f. Frodsham, *Signs*, 201, claims that Meyer wrote a favorable account of the operation of tongues-speech in Russia.

178. Williams and Waldvogel, "Tongues," 90; Donald Tinder, "Christian and Missionary Alliance," *NIDCC*, 220; Waldvogel, "Origins," 24. Waldvogel says the organization was cemented in 1897, Tinder says 1887.

179. When Simpson began a training school in 1882, the faculty included some who regularly assisted Moody, e.g., Arthur Pierson, A. J. Gordon, George Pentecost. So Waldvogel, "Origins," 74f. Menzies, "Origins," 88, says Simpson was Keswickian.

180. A. B. Simpson, *The Holy Spirit or Power From on High* (Harrisburgh: Christian Publications, Inc., 1896), 2:95. Eph 5:18 is dealt with on page 90 and 2 Tim 1:6f on pages 91 and 182. Williams and Waldvogel, "Tongues," 93, bring to our attention the fact that Simpson's work was published about the same time as Torrey's *Baptism with the Holy Spirit*. See also Dayton, "Theological Roots," 138.

181. Ibid., 139. 2 Cor 1:21 is on page 127. See Waldvogel, "Origins," 26; Williams and Waldvogel, "Tongues," 93; Charles Nienkirchen, "Albert B. Simpson: Forerunner of the Modern Pentecostal Movement," *Azusa Street Revisited*, ed. by Edith Waldvogel (Costa Mesa: SPS, November 13-15, 1986).

tion of his view he coined the phrase still used today by the Christian and Missionary Alliance: "Seek not, forbid not."[182]

A final moment will be taken to mention briefly a few other persons of interest. J. Edwin Orr identifies William Booth (1829–1912) with Finney, Moody, Simpson and Torrey for using the term baptism for enduement of power.[183] S. H. Froadsham also tells of W. Jethro Walthell who, in 1879, was filled with the Spirit' and spoke in tongues.[184] Anglican F. W. Puller, in his 1880 book *What is the Distinctive Grace of Confirmation?*, reportedly distinguished between the operation of the Spirit in baptism, which consists of 'His purifying, consecrating, regenerating influence,' and the post-baptismal gift of the Spirit which effects an 'indwelling presence' of the Holy Spirit.[185]

Timothy Smith relates Henry Clay Fish's view that Spirit baptism was "the secret of pulpit power and the foundation of that energy which alone could accomplish the evangelization of the world."[186] Smith also quotes an anonymous Unitarian editor who said that

182. Widely distributed is the following account related by Brumback, *Suddenly*, 95:

Nyack students who managed to see Dr. Simpson alone in his later years declare that he manifested a deep interest in the Pentecostal revival which he had reluctantly rejected. David McDowell reports that Simpson made this sad remark in a conversation with him in 1912: "David, I did what I thought was best, but I am afraid that I missed it."

Charles W. Nienkirchen, *A. B. Simpson and the Pentecostal Movement* (Peabody: Hendrickson Press, 1922), 106, convincingly argues for the authenticity of this recollection. Cf. Williams and Waldvogel, "Tongues," 101; John Sawin, "The Response/Attitude of A. B. Simpson and the Christian and Missionary Alliance to the Initial Pentecostal Movement," *Azusa Street Revisited*, ed. by Edith Waldvogel (Costa Mesa: SPS, November 13-15, 1986).

183. Orr, *Full Surrender*, 104. Bresson, *Ecstasy*, 109, claims that the "glory fits" of the early days of the Salvation Army included speaking in tongues.

184. Frodsham, *Signs*, 10-12. Walthell moved from the Baptist church to the Holiness Baptists to the Assemblies of God.

185. Ysebaert, *Greek Baptismal Terminology*, 56. Ysebaert indicates that the author was consciously opposing the concept that the post-baptismal rite effected an increase of a gift already imparted in baptism.

186. Congar, *Holy Spirit* 1:108-55. Joachim has received a lot of attention including Laurentin, *Pentecostalism*, 139f and M. Reeves and B. Hirsch-Reich, *The Figurae of Joachim of Fiore* (Oxford: At the Clarendon Press, 1969). Basil Pennington, "The Baptism in the Holy Spirit and Christian Tradition," *The Spirit and the Church*, ed. by Ralph Martin (New York: Paulist, 1976), 193-96, would add the twelfth-century English saint Aelred of Rievaulx to the list. Judith Tydings, *Gathering a People* (Plainfield: Logos, 1977) unearths much relevant material from the saints and the mystics.

> ... the "perilous experiment of liberty" in America, accompanied as it was by the passing away of old creeds and usages, could only succeed if the ministry were baptized with the Holy Spirit and each disciple clothed anew with the "tongues of fire."[187]

William Menzies indicates that Asbury Lowrey, co-editor with Asa Mahan of *Divine Life*, gave the following answer to the question, Is the baptism of the Holy Ghost a third blessing?

> But if the question be asked, "May we have a dispensation of the Holy Ghost after sanctification and supplementary to that grace, a dispensation greater and more powerful that necessarily belongs to a state of a pure heart?" I unhesitatingly answer, *Yes*. The Gospel evidently promises such accessions.[188]

Menzies also says that Ralph C. Horner, a minister of the Methodist church in Canada, published *From the Altar to the Upper Room* in 1891 in which he distinguished baptism of the Spirit from sanctification.[189] Morton Kelsey says that James J. McConkey's *The Three-Fold Secret of the Holy Spirit*, written in 1897, supported a third experience (i.e., one beyond sanctification) called a "baptism of burning love, the baptism of fire, of the Holy Spirit, in which one was filled with more than human spiritual life valuable in itself."[190] Phoebe Palmer received national attention for her "Tuesday Meeting(s) for the Promotion of Holiness" in her home(s) in New York. Addressing a Canadian Methodist camp meeting during the later 1850s Mrs. Palmer said: "The question now before us is . . . May we ask in faith . . . that we may be endued with power from on high, baptized with the Holy Ghost and fire?"[191] The result was that various people testified to having received the "baptism of fire."[192]

---

187. Smith, *Revivalism*, 145. Dayton, "Theological Roots," 88f., says Fish used the language of Pentecost in his 1855 *Primitive Piety Reviewed*.

188. Ibid.

189. Menzies, "Origins," 71f. See Dayton, "Theological Roots," 117.

190. Ibid., 72. Dayton, "Theological Roots," 123, says that Horner's third blessing teaching was accompanied by "demonstrations of the Spirit."

191. Kelsey, *Tongue Speaking*, 73.

192. M. E. Deiter, "Wesleyan-Holiness Aspects of Pentecostal Origins," *Aspects of Pentecostal-Charismatic Origins*, Synan, 65. See Smith, *Revivalism*, 105 et passim; Dayton, "Christian Perfection," 46. Deiter and Dayton both believe that Mrs. Palmer was influenced by William Arthur's *The Tongues of Fire*.

CONCLUSIONS

This inquiry has progressed to the beginning of the Pentecostal movement and has shown that pneumatologies similar in essence to Pentecostal Spirit baptism are to be found in several places. In the writers reviewed, there was both a sacramental and an existential version of this theology.

In the category of the sacramental version of Spirit baptism theology, the most prominent member is the Roman Catholic doctrine of confirmation. When J. D. G. Dunn published his book on the Pentecostal question, he asserted that the disarming of Pentecostal theology was also the death of Catholic confirmation theology.[193] F. Dale Bruner notes the Catholic and Pentecostal development "from Acts 9 of a second experiential (Pentecostal) or sacramental (Catholic) blessing."[194] Then editor of the *Catholic Biblical Quarterly*, George T. Montague, said:

> In the Catholic tradition, though the Holy Spirit has been understood to be given in baptism, the sacrament of confirmation has always been explained in terms of a distinct gift of the Spirit, and the effort to establish the distinctiveness of the sacrament has led for a long time at least to a use of many of the biblical texts used by the Pentecostals to support 'Baptism in the Spirit' as the second and distinctive moment of the full Christian Initiation. Though some contemporary Catholic sacramental theologians are less eager than formerly to separate the two aspects of initiation, the biblical basis for confirmation still remains a problem.[195]

The parallel is to be considered intact regardless of the stage, namely patristic, medieval, post-Reformation. Concerning the Catholic confirmation theology, it is not of great concern here to draw attention to shifts from associating confirmation as the reception of the Spirit to understanding it as giving an increase of grace conferred in baptism. The point is essentially the same. That is, this theology recognizes a special work of

---

193. Dunn, *Baptism in the Holy Spirit*, 3f. See G. W. Bromiley, "Holy Spirit," *CT* (August 30, 1968); Dunn, "Spirit-Baptism and Pentecostalism," *SJT* 23 (1970): 405.

194. Bruner, *Theology of the Holy Spirit*, 187. It is interesting to note that both Dennis Bennett and Stephen Clark initially thought of their charismatic experiences in relation to confirmation.

195. George T. Montague, "Baptism in the Spirit," *TD* 21, 342f. See Tugwell, "Reflections on 'Baptism in the Holy Spirit,'" 407; McDonnell, *Holy Spirit*, 35.

the Spirit which cannot be identified with regeneration and this work is believed especially to be associated with the Spirit's empowerment.[196]

It is interesting to see that notwithstanding the move of Vatican II to emphasize the unity of Christian initiation,[197] many prominent theologians admit the force of their tradition. Karl Rahner refers to confirmation as the sacrament of the "charismatic Spirit."[198] Hans Küng emphasizes the unity of grace bestowed in water baptism and yet explains at length the distinguishing marks of confirmation.[199] Theodore Jungkuntz wrote an entire book entitled *Confirmation and Charismata*. The sacramental category also includes the Eastern Orthodox use of chrismation. J. Rodman Williams speaks similarly when he says,

> . . . the long history of ecclesiastical recognition (especially in Eastern Orthodoxy and Roman Catholicism) of two sacramental moments in Christian initiation cannot be disregarded. Whether the second moment follows directly upon the first (as in Eastern baptism-chrismation) or many years thereafter (as in Roman baptism-confirmation) in both cases there is recognition of a distinction between the two.[200]

---

196. After referring to confirmation as a "sacramental baptism in the Spirit," Herbert Mühlen, *Charismatic*, 141, says:

> The New Testament as a whole therefore distinguishes very clearly between the birth effected by one and the same Spirit and the power he gives to exercise the charisms. From this there emerges a *theological* distinction between baptism and confirmation. . . .

Lutheran Charismatic Jungkuntz has many other pertinent observations and examples in his *Confirmation and Charismata*. See Williams, *Reality*, 25.

197. Milner, *Confirmation*, 76. Cf. James Egan, "A Contemporary Approach to Sacramental Grace," *Readings in Sacramental Theology*, ed. by C. S. Sullivan (Englewood Cliffs: Prentice Hall, 1964), 136.

198. Karl Rahner, *The Church and Sacraments* (New York: Herder and Herder, 1963), 91. Rahner, *Meditations on the Sacraments*, 27, says, "Therefore confirmation is also the sacramental sign of a beginning for life, in whose length and breadth the real baptism in the Spirit, all-saving and sheltering within the mystery of God, must occur." See Egan, *Athanasius*, 137.

199. Küng, "La confirmation." See also Yves Congar, *I Believe in the Holy Spirit* (New York: Seabury Press, 1983), 3:217–27.

200. J. Rodman Williams, "Pentecostal Theology: A Neo-Pentecostal Viewpoint," *Perspectives on the New Pentecostalism*, Spittler, 81. See Milner, *Confirmation*, 40.

And finally, as noted when reviewing the *1549 Book of Common Prayer* (and its late editions) and then A. J. Mason, the Anglican view of confirmation reflects the same pneumatological issue.

To those who may be categorized as existentialists, it should be noticed that there were groups of this kind before the Reformation, but the turning point for the articulation of the doctrine in a manner more familiar to present day Pentecostal theology would be the Reformation itself. Specifically, it was after the Second Great Awakening of 1792 that the terminology "baptism in the Spirit" became prominent in expressing this theology.[201] Before the Reformation, most of those in this category disappeared during their third phase. The same is true for many groups after the Reformation, yet there remain some organizations that contain the essence of this theology in their creeds. R. A. Knox's massive *Enthusiasm* includes many fascinating if not always accurate observations. He says that eighteenth century Convulsionaries used "seal of the Spirit" in a charismatic context. The Shakers are quoted as equating seal of the Spirit with baptism of the Holy Spirit.[202] Henry Lederle refers to "Reformed Sealers" and early Primitive Baptists who describe a "second experience" somewhat related to "baptism with the Holy Spirit." His list includes not only Thomas Goodwin but also Richard Sibbes, John Owen, Charles Hodge, Charles Simeon and J. K. Parratt.[203]

The line of demarcation drawn here is not intended to obscure the fact that many sacramentalists were also existentialists. The main point is that the essence of Spirit baptism is known in every century and perhaps most every location of Christians. The spectrum has been broad theologically. It has included "liberals," "fundamentalists," "sects," and "historic denominations." One possible reason is there may be something in Scripture itself which led people of many different times and places to have propagated a theology that included the particular nuance of the pneumatology in question.

---

201. J. Edwin Orr, interview at Fuller Theological Seminary on November 7, 1977. Related here is Jungkuntz's observation, *Confirmation*, 29, that medieval theologians did not "break through" to the "experiential definition" of confirmation as "expressed in the NT."

202. Knox, *Enthusiasm*, 380, 561f.

203. Henry Lederle, "An Appraisal of Some Aspects of the Theology of the Charismatic Movement" (Pretoria: University of South Africa, 1985), 11–15. Those so named did not tie this to extraordinary gifts but there often was an experiential dimension to the experience.

7

The Doctrine of Salvation

INTRODUCTION

THE CHRISTIAN CANON AND ecclesiastical history testify to works of the Spirit which are charismatic in nature and unpredictable in action during the Christian pilgrimage. It is then appropriate to see how these data relate to a systematic evaluation of the biblical doctrine of salvation. Since it is the raison d'etre of dogmatic theology to formulate doctrines from the biblical study, this study will incorporate much of the language of dogmatics and many of its classical concepts.[1] However, due to the limitations of space, it will not be possible to expound all the regula fidei of the traditional dogmatic formulation of soteriology. The translation used in this chapter will be the RSV unless otherwise indicated.

UNION WITH CHRIST/INDWELLING HOLY SPIRIT

The particulars of the ordo salutis will soon be enumerated, but traditional dogmatics expound the believer's union with Christ as the overarching theological concept for salvation applied. However, the biblical picture of a dynamic interwovenness between Christ and the Spirit led to the title "Union with Spirit/Indwelling Holy Spirit." In treating this subject, the discussion will build on a lengthy study on the ontological relation of Jesus to the Spirit. This is a result of a twofold circumstance: (1) the goal of treating pneumatological issues raised by the Pentecostal-

---

1. This contrasts to the emerging group of Pentecostal scholars who imagine their biblical theological treatments superior to constructive theologies. Among other things, this is a naïve appropriation of the hermeneutic that exegesis which conforms to certain criteria is void of extraneous influences. See Stronstad, *Spirit, Scripture and Theology*. Notice also that this same group invariably engages J. D. G. Dunn while ignoring F. Dale Bruner's work on Pentecostal pneumatology.

Charismatic Movement and (2) the contemporary debate regarding the relation of the exalted Jesus to the Spirit. The original aim was to analyze the legitimacy of the affirmation made by many in the North American Classical Pentecostal Movement that "Christ" is received at "conversion" and that the "full personality of the Spirit" is known at the baptism of the Holy Spirit.[2] The investigation led to the heated debate over whether Scripture moves toward a functional, if not ontological, merging of the exalted Christ and the Spirit. My first contribution to this discussion was published in the *Heythrop Journal*.[3]

This analysis gives another dimension to the overarching theological concept which describes salvation: union with Christ/indwelling Holy Spirit. Scripture has this to say about this fundamental aspect of soteriology: Christ in us—"... it is no longer I who live, but Christ who lives in me ..." (Gal 2:20); the Spirit in us—"Now we have received not the spirit of the world, but the Spirit which is from God ..." (1 Cor 2:12), "... the Holy Spirit who dwells within us" (2 Tim 1:14); that there is a conjoining of the union with Christ and the indwelling of the Holy Spirit—"But you are not in the flesh, you are in the Spirit, if the Spirit of God really dwells in you. Anyone who does not have the Spirit of Christ does not belong to him. But if Christ is in you, although your bodies are dead because of sin, your spirits are alive because of righteousness. If the Spirit of Him who raised Jesus from the dead dwells in you, he who raised Jesus from the dead will give life to your mortal bodies also through his Spirit which dwells in you" (Rom 8:9–11).

These Scriptures (also: Jn 14:16, 1 Jn 4:13, Rom 8:23, 2 Cor 5:5, Gal 3:2) reaffirm the findings of the related investigation.

> The Spirit, as it were, actualizes in the hearts of believers and in the fellowship of the Christian society the presence of Christ, who, except in so far as He is thus operative in the Church through the Spirit, is regarded as being "seated on the right hand of God."[4]

2. Hughes, *What Is Pentecost?*, 25; T. W. Walker, "Baptism in the Holy Spirit," *Pentecostal Doctrine*, ed. by P. W. Brewster (Grenehurst Press, 1976); Williams, *Systematic Theology* 2:233, 3:47; Bruner, *Theology of the Holy Spirit*, 60; Dunn, *Baptism in the Holy Spirit*, 107.

3. Harold D. Hunter, "Spirit-Christology: Dilemma and Promise." *Heythrop Journal* 24:2 & 24:3 (1983).

4. A. E. J. Rawlinson, *The New Testament Doctrine of Christ*, (London: Longmans, Green & Co., 1926), 159. See also McDonnell, "Holy Spirit and Christian Initiation," 63; C. F. D. Moule, "The Christology of Acts," *Studies in Luke Acts*, ed. by L. E. Kecker and J. L. Martyn (London: SPCK, 1968), 180; Rudolf Schnackenburg, *Baptism in the Thought of St.*

One important implication from this study is that the occasional Pentecostal formula of "Christ" at "conversion" and the Spirit at Spirit baptism has been shown to be foreign to Scripture. However, the essential pneumatological issue raised by Spirit baptism has not been called into question and must now be scrutinized in light of the traditional dogmatic formulation of the ordo salutis.

THE ORDO SALUTIS

The term ordo salutis is a product of dogmaticians working with the issue of salvation applied. It is an acceptable facet of biblical investigation to determine the logical and temporal relation of the components of salvation applied. It will be the primary concern of this review to establish the nature of the components of the ordo salutis.[5]

The aim is to identify the parts of salvation applied. The Arminian arrangement here of the ordo salutis does not materially affect the limited goals of the identification process, and it indicates that while many Calvinists may find Romans 8:29f as the appropriate order, they do this without reckoning with the word foreknowledge and the varying sequences given in 2 Thessalonians 2:13, 1 Corinthians 6:11, 2 Timothy 1:19 and Titus 3:4–7. Further, since the concern is ordo salutis and not Christian initiation, the subject of water baptism will not be given consideration. Perhaps it should be added that any use of male-oriented terminology is a reflection only of the terms which are embedded in biblical revelation and their usage is not intended to imply sexual discrimination.

Calling

To engage in a discussion about the doctrine of calling is to encounter the focal point of the Calvinistic-Arminian argument. While it has been

---

Paul (New York: Herder & Herder, 1964), 138; Morris, *Living God*, 43; Arminius, *Writings*, 112; E. F. Kevan, *Salvation* (Grand Rapids: Baker, 1983), 46; Humphries, *Holy Spirit*, 231; Stibbs and Packer, *Spirit Within*, 37f.

5. G. C. Berkouwer rightly argues in his *Faith and Justification* (Grand Rapids: Eerdmans, 1954), 25ff., that it would be wrong for the order to become more important than the salvation. Thus the order is relevant "only in that it aids us to appreciate the fullness of divine salvation" (27). On the other hand, it is imperative to articulate a way of salvation "to cut off every way in which Christ is not confessed exclusive as *the Way*" (36). If this treatment of ordo salutis could be extended, it would seek to be in conformity with these guidelines.

deemed inappropriate to analyze the election issue to the extent of making a decision, it will, nonetheless, be considered imperative to acknowledge the various viewpoints. The present discourse, therefore, will be somewhat meager as words of Scripture are sought regarding the essence of calling without the aid of a particular view of election.

The investigation has been considerably hampered by the lack of standardization of terminology. While one writer calls the external call the general call,[6] others equate the external call with common grace.[7] One writer identifies regeneration with the inner call[8] while another refers to it as a special call.[9] One writer creates chaos by using the label indirect and general to refer to a call which cannot be identified with the traditional meaning of external or internal calling.[10]

These various terms are attempts to deal with three calls: (1) vocatio realis—that appeal to all people made through their conscience and their surroundings, Romans 1:19f., 2:15; (2) vocatio verbalis externa—the proclamation of God's saving Word, Romans 10:14, Acts 13:38 (cf. 2 Tim 4:2); (3) vocatio verbalis interna—the convicting work of the Spirit, John 16:8, Revelation 22:17. The vocatio realis is a complicated subject not relevant to our narrow interest here and will therefore not be treated.

All sides acknowledge the vocatio verbalis externa and vocatio verbali interna, but the issue in the Calvinistic-Arminian debate is (1) whether the calls are conjoined and the role of the Spirit viewed as limited, or (2) whether they are to be considered as distinct calls and the role of the Holy Spirit viewed as a dominating factor. Neither side denies that the work of grace effected is an act of the Triune God that is especially associated with the Holy Spirit.[11] Furthermore, both sides are agreed that the Word

---

6. A. H. Strong, *Systematic Theology* (Philadelphia: The Judson Press, 1960 [1907]), 3:791.

7. Harold Ockenga, *The Spirit of the Living God* (New York: Fleming H. Revell Co., 1947), 36; A. A. Hodge, *Outlines of Theology Theology*, (Grand Rapids: Zondervan, 1972), 450.

8. H. Bavinck, *Our Reasonable Faith* (Grand Rapids: Baker, 1977 [1956]), 432; L. Berkhof, *Systematic Theology* (Grand Rapids: Eerdmans, 1941), 457.

9. Heinrich Heppe, *Reformed Dogmatics*, ed. by Ernst Bizer (Grand Rapids: Baker, 1950), 518.

10. Henrich Schmid, *The Doctrinal Theology of the Evangelical Lutheran Church* (Philadelphia: Lutheran Publication Society, 1899), 442. See also the 'universal call' of H. Orton Wiley, *Christian Theology* (Kansas City: Beacon Hill, 1945), 2:334.

11. Calvinistic—L. Berkhof, *Systematic Theology*, 452. Arminian—Wiley, *Christian Theology*, 340, 342.

of God involved in the externa can have a rather broad definition in light of the existence of the Christian church prior to written and canonized Scripture, we believe that the concept includes at least oral tradition.[12]

In acknowledgment of the issue of election, I will quote representatives of those involved in the conflict. Methodist Richard Watson deals with the parable of Jesus in Matthew 22:1–4, and after noting that all three classes of people represented were called he says, "... it depended upon their choice and conduct whether they embraced the invitation, and were admitted as guests."[13] On the other end of the spectrum, Presbyterian A. A. Hodge says: "Common grace is only mediate ... But efficacious grace is immediate and supernatural ... since it implants a new spiritual life ..."[14] It is of interest to note that most Calvinists are not logically consistent with their monergism since they do not use the label irresistible grace, saying the term efficacious is more suitable since, in fact, God's grace can be resisted.[15] This is an interesting development in light of the fact that many of these scholars rebuke Lutheran theologians for not accepting reprobation as a withholding of divine grace rather than a resistance of the will. The Arminian is wont to label the qualifications given by the Calvinists as being synergistic.

---

12. E. A. Litton, *Introduction to Dogmatic Theology* (London: Clarke, 1960), 243; Bavinck, *Reasonable Faith*, 418.

13. Richard Watson, *Theological Institutes* (New York: Carlton & Phillips, 1856), 2:353.

14. A. A. Hodge, *Outline of Theology*, 450.

15. Litton, *Dogmatic Theology*, 250f.; Strong, *Systematic Theology*, 792; A. A. Hodge, *Outline of Theology*, 542. Finding implications of a "life insurance policy" in the phrase "eternal security," Paul K. Jewett, "Salvation," unpublished course syllabus (Pasadena: Fuller Theological Seminary, n.d.), 767, says:

> ... the traditional doctrine of perseverance of the saints carries with it the implication that we have to make some effort if we are to be saved at last ... Eternal security ... in its most popular statement, is "once saved, always saved" ... I cannot ... feel that the animus ... of such an expression, "once saved, always saved," is consonant with the Scriptures, with the constant admonition that we should give diligence to make our calling and election sure, that we should reckon with the fact that we wrestle against principalities and powers, that we should put on the whole armor of God and fight the good fight of faith, run the race with patience.

It is interesting to note that most Classical Pentecostals speak of a person being converted only after having been "convicted by the Holy Spirit."

The Doctrine of Salvation 207

I need do no more than recognize calling as a part of the ordo salutis. Leon Morris rightly observes:

> The very preaching of the gospel is done by or in the Holy Spirit (1 Pet 1:12), and its content is something that is revealed by the same Spirit (Eph 3:5). When men are convicted of their sin, that is a work of the Spirit (Jn 16:8f.). Preaching may be the means the Spirit uses, but it is always the work of the Spirit to convict men.[16]

Conversion

The next aspect of the ordo salutis to be noted is conversion. Conversion is the act of a person in which one turns.[17] Of course Calvinists hasten to add that humans have been enabled to accomplish this because of having been previously regenerated.[18]

Despite a few dissenting writers, I view repentance and saving faith as constituting conversion. W. G. T. Shedd has said about conversion: "As the etymology implies, it is turning towards (con-verto) a certain point, and away from a certain point. Conversion consists of two acts: 1. Faith; 2. Repentance."[19]

I understand saving faith to incorporate the total person, that is, one's intellect, emotions and volition. Similarly, the elements of repentance involve the intellectual, emotional and volitional parts of people. R. A. Torrey offers a workable definition: "Repentance of sin is such a sorrow for sin or abhorrence of sin, such a change of mind about it, as leads the sinner to turn away from it with all his heart."[20]

---

16. Morris, *Living God*, 72. See also John Macquarrie, *Principles of Christian Theology* (New York: Charles Scribners Sons, 1966), 300f.; Ryrie, *The Holy Spirit*, 65.

17. Abraham Kuyper, *Work of the Holy Spirit* (Grand Rapids: Christian Classics, n.d.), 180; Shedd, *Dogmatic Theology* (Grand Rapids: Zondervan, n.d.), 2:529; L. Berkhof, *Systematic Theology*, 490; Henry C. Thiessen, *Lectures in Systematic Theology* (Grand Rapids: Eerdmans, 1976 [1949]), 179; Wiley, *Christian Theology*, 362.

18. Bavinck, *Reasonable Faith*, 433; C. Hodge, *Systematic Theology*, 41; Shedd, *Dogmatic Theology* 2:529.

19. William G. T. Shedd, *Dogmatic Theology*, 29. Cf. Thiessen, *systematic Theology*, 179; Strong, *Systematic Theology*, 829.

20. R. A. Torrey, *What the Bible Teaches* (London: James Nisbet & Co., Ltd., n.d.), 3-5. Cf. L. Berkhof, *Systematic Theology*, 486; C. Hodge, *Outline of Theology*, 91; Bavinck, *Reasonable Faith*, 437; Shedd, *Dogmatic Theology*, 529.

The immediate problem arises about the temporal/logical/theological sequence of repentance and faith. W. B. Pope speaks for those who place repentance before faith:

> They cannot be separated, as repentance implies pre-existing faith, and faith implies pre-existing repentance. But they differ in this, that faith is the instrument as well as a condition of individual acceptance, and, as such, springs out of and follows repentance.[21]

Despite those thinkers that Pope represents and the use of "Repent and Believe" (cf. Mk 1:15), it seems that what I have said constitutes saving faith must precede repentance. Many of the writers reviewed attributed a saving acknowledgment of Christ's demands to repentance, while attributing the grace of vindicating one's trust in God to saving faith.[22] I would, however, understand saving faith to involve knowledge, notitia; assent, assensus; and trust, fiducia. I understand these to have a logical order and to be the basis for repentance. It is only after the demands of the Gospel are admitted that one can cry out for forgiveness. Emil Brunner offers a satisfactory explanation of the biblical command "repent and believe." Brunner judges "repent and believe" to be the missionary order while the reverse order is of a theological nature.

> In Paul, in the Epistle to the Romans, we find both orders of sequence. For even his Epistle to the Romans is both missionary gospel and theological word, whose purpose is to make intelligible the missionary event in all its depth. Romans 1–3 follows the order "repentance and faith," Romans 3–7 follows the order "faith and repentance."[23]

Regeneration

Without attempting to establish a particular position on the issue of election, it is in order to summarize the three major views of election as they relate to the doctrine of regeneration. Semi-Pelagians teach that fallen

---

21. W. B. Pope, *A Compendium of Christian Theology* (London: Wesleyan Conference Office, 1875), 371. Here, as in other places, Wiley (358) follows Pope.

22. For an example see L. Berkhof, *Systematic Theology*, 486.

23. Emil Brunner, *Dogmatics* (Philadelphia: Westminster, 1960), 3:283. Bavinck, *Reasonable Faith*, 437, says: "We should not dare to turn around towards God if we did not trust inwardly in our souls through the Holy Spirit that as a Father He will accept our confession of sins and forgive us."

humans have been graciously restored by the redemptive work of Christ to the extent that the will is given its freedom and power. Hence, regeneration is regarded as the divine blessing upon human volition. Calvinists place regeneration before conversion. This monergism views humans as passive since it is understood that this work is effected by the Holy Spirit without preparatory steps. Arminians claim that prevenient grace is effected and one repents, believes, and calls on God which becomes the basis for regeneration.[24] A. A. Hodge offers a helpful summary of the major nuances of the basic issue.

> A and B are alike sinners. A believes and B remains a reprobate. The Pelagian says because A wills to believe and B to reject. The Semi-Pelagian says because A commenced to strive and was helped, and B made no effort. The Arminian says, because A co-operated with common grace, and B did not. The Lutheran says both were utterly unable to co-operate, but B persistently resisted grace, and A ultimately yielded. The Calvinist says, because A was regenerated by the new creative power of God, and B was not.[25]

I would now like to call attention to two basic characteristics associated with the doctrine of regeneration. Note that when speaking of regeneration, the Bible places major emphasis on the role of God, for regeneration is "from above" (John 3:3). We are further told that we are "born ... of God" (John 1:13), and even when we were dead that God "made us alive" (Ephesians 2:5), or as it is exclaimed in the doxology, "Blessed be the God and Father of our Lord Jesus Christ! By his great mercy he has given us a new birth" (1 Peter 1:3). I am unwilling to lay this point aside even

---

24. See Wiley, *Christian Theology*, 415ff.; L. Berkhof, *Systematic Theology*, 465f.; A. A. Hodge, *Outline of Theology*, 456ff.; Francis Pieper, *Christian Dogmatics* (Saint Louis: Concordia Publishing House, 1951), 2:455; Otto Michel, "Regeneration," *Basic Christian Doctrines*, ed. by Carl F. H. Henry (Grand Rapids: Baker, 1962), 187ff. Incidentally, the word synergism ("co-operation") which is often used to describe Arminians, was coined to categorize Melanchton's followers. This latter group took the position that regeneration was a combination of the Word of God, the Holy Spirit, and the human will consenting to, not resisting, the Word of God.

25. A. A. Hodge, *Outline of Theology*, 448. For monergism see H. Berkhof, *Holy Spirit*, 70; L. S. Chafer, *Systematic Theology* (Dallas: Dallas Theological Seminary, 1934), 3:334; Shedd, *Dogmatic Theology* 3:509; James I. Packer, "Regeneration," *Baker's Dictionary of Theology*, Harrison, 440; Bavinck, *Reasonable Faith*, 433; G. W. Bromiley, "The Holy Spirit," *Fundamentals of the Faith*, ed. by Carl F. H. Henry (Grand Rapids: Zondervan, 1969), 162. For synergism see Ockenga, *Living God*, 73f.; E. A. Litton, *Dogmatic Theology*, 326; Pope, *Christian Theology*, 5; Wiley, *Christian Theology*, 412; Watson, *Theological Institutes*, 268.

though it is most often used as self-evidencing monergism.[26] Contrary to the claims of many Reformed theologians, Arminians do not quarrel with the teaching that regeneration is God's work alone. The Reformed retort that since Arminians say regeneration follows conversion that it is not actually God's work.

Scripture tells us that while regeneration is a work of the Godhead, this work is to be particularly associated with the Holy Spirit.[27] We know that we must be born of the Spirit (Jn 3:5f., 8) for we are saved "... through the water of rebirth and renewal by the Holy Spirit" (Titus 3:5). To reiterate an earlier point, note the conjoining of the work of Jesus and the Spirit. The Spirit ἐστιν τὸ ζωοποιοῦν (Jn 6:63) while the resurrected Jesus is described as πνεῦμα ζωοποιοῦν (1 Cor 15:45).[28] These and related definitions stress the two biblical components of regeneration:[29] (1) impartation of a new life into the person dead in sins. (2) which ushers in a new moral disposition.

A number of writers in the contemporary debate on the pneumatological issues raised by the Pentecostal-Charismatic Movement are biblical theologians and their biblical language has needlessly confounded the theological issue with a semantic one. When using regeneration, others the indwelling of the Holy Spirit, and still others the whole event

---

26. Karl Barth, *Church Dogmatics*, ed. by G. W. Bromiley and T. F. Torrance (Edinburgh: T&T Clark, 1956), 4:1:9; Kevan, *Salvation*, 63; John Owen, *The Holy Spirit* (Grand Rapids: Kregel Publications, 1954), 120; E. H. Palmer, "Adoption," *NBD*, 82; Paché, *Holy Spirit*, 69; M. R. Bordon, "Regeneration," *NBD*, 1081; L. Berkof, *Systematic Theology*, 473.

27. Ockenga, *Living God*, 77; Pope, *Christian Theology*, 5; D. A. Tappeiner, "Holy Spirit," 44f.; Strong, *Systematic Theology*, 811; Herman Hoeksema, *Reformed Dogmatics* (Grand Rapids: Reformed Free Publishing Association, 1966), 454; Watson, *Theological Institutes*, 267; Packer, "Regeneration," *NBD*, 440; Ryrie, *Holy Spirit*, 64.

28. H. D. McDonald, *Living Doctrines of the New Testament* (Grand Rapids: Zondervan, 1972), 163, says: "It is within the sphere of salvation that Christ's work overlaps with that of the Spirit, so that the regenerative activities of divine grace are attributed to both the Son and the Spirit."

29. See Hoeksema, *Reformed Dogmatics*, 460; Heppe, *Reformed Dogmatics*, 518f.; Thiessen, *Systematic Theology*, 189; C. Hodge, *Systematic Theology*, 33, 35; Chafer, *Systematic Theology* 6:35; Shedd, *Dogmatic Theology*, 491; Brunner, *Dogmatics*, 269; Bavinck, *Reasonable Faith*, 424; Arminius, "Certain Articles" 20:1, *Writings* 2:501–7; F. Büchsel, "παλιγγενεσία," *TDNT* 1:699; Pope, *Christian Theology*, 7; Strong, *Systematic Theology*, 810; Owen, *Holy Spirit*, 189; Kevan, *Salvation* 2:238ff. Cf. H. Kuiper, *By Grace Alone: A Study in Soteriology*, (Grand Rapids: Eerdmans, 1955), 151; Litton, *Dogmatic Theology*, 320.

of Christian initiation.[30] Some needless obstruction to the fundamental theological issues would be removed if these writers made some point of contact with the language of dogmatic language. The phrase gift of the Spirit may be a biblical expression, but without sufficient qualification, its elasticity proves to be most awkward.

Justification

That aspect of the ordo salutis known as justification may be most familiar to those counted as Protestants. It is the doctrine of justification sola fide, as enunciated by Martin Luther, which is credited with being the basis for the Reformation. After having propelled the historical movement, Luther is reported to have described justification as the "articulus stantis aut cadentis ecclesiae."[31] Calvin talked about justification involving forgiveness of sins, the imputation of the righteousness of Christ, its being obtained by faith, not by the works of the law.[32] Helpful summaries are provided also by James Arminius[33] and the Westminster Confession of Faith.[34]

The use of the word "justify" is a deliberate choice reflecting a commitment that this has reference to a judicial act of God. It is Paul who articulates this facet of redemption by the use of legal language.[35] Humans have transgressed the law and are therefore under condemnation: "Therefore,

---

30. See Dunn, *Baptism in the Holy Spirit*; Ryrie, *Holy Spirit*; Stott, *Baptism and Fullness*.

31. Wiley, *Christian Theology*, 379.

32. Calvin, *Institutes* 3:11:2. Cf. Dabney, *Systematic Theology*, 619; Strong, *Systematic Theology*, 819; Hoeksema, *Reformed Dogmatics*, 493.

33. Arminius, "Private Disputations" 48:2, *Writings* 2:116. Cf. Pope, *Christian Theology*, 407. Some later "Arminians" have talked about the imputation of faith rather than the content of faith. Cf. Wiley, *Christian Theology*, 400, 380.

34. *Westminster Confession of Faith*, Chapter 11 (Free Presbyterian Church of Scotland, 1976), 56f. G. C. Berkouwer, *Faith and Justification* (Grand Rapids: Eerdmans, 1954), 84, points out that this exegesis does not lead to the conclusion that God's judgment is fictitious even though the believer is still a sinner. See Litton, *Dogmatic Theology*, 267; Schmid, *Evangelical Lutheran*, 424; C. Hodge, *Systematic Theology*, 118; Wiley, *Christian Theology*, 395, 389; Hoeksema, *Reformed Dogmatics*, 493; J. I. Packer, "Justification," *NBD*, 683; Buswell, *Systematic Theology*, 195; Pope, *Christian Theology*, 408; Thiessen, *Systematic Theology*, 186; Richardson, *Theology of the New Testament*, 233; Ladd, *Theology of the New Testament*, 445; Kuiper, *Grace Alone*, 102; Charles G. Finney, *Systematic Theology*, 382ff.

35. I agree with Berkouwer, *Justification*, 73, that Paul is not the only writer who articulates this doctrine, but that it is most associated with him perhaps because he was so often confronted with those trying to replace the gospel of grace.

just as sin came into the world through one man, and death came through sin, and so death spread to all because all have sinned" (Romans 5:12, NRSV); "all have sinned and fall short of the glory of God" (Romans 3:23, NRSV); "For we ourselves were once foolish, disobedient, led astray, slaves to various passions and pleasures, passing our days in malice and envy, despicable, hating one another" (Titus 3:3, NRSV); "For the wages of sin is death, but the free gift of God is eternal life in Christ Jesus our Lord" (Romans 6:23, NRSV). However, the death of Christ signals a change, for now his shed blood can allow one to be declared righteous: "For if while we were enemies, we were reconciled to God through the death of his Son, much more surely, having been reconciled, will we be saved by his life" (Romans 5:10, NRSV); ". . . not having a righteousness of my own that comes from the law, but one that comes through faith in Christ, the righteousness from God based on faith" (Philippians 3:9, NRSV); "And you who were once estranged and hostile in mind, doing evil deeds, he has now reconciled in his fleshly body through death, so as to present you holy and blameless and irreproachable before him" (Colossians 1:21f., NRSV).

The imputation of Christ's righteousness is the main reason for understanding δικαιόω as forensic: "Therefore, since we are justified by faith, we have peace with God through our Lord Jesus Christ" (Romans 5:1, NRSV); "And this is what some of you used to be. But you were washed, you were sanctified, you were justified in the name of the Lord Jesus Christ and in the Spirit of our God" (1 Corinthians 6:11, NRSV). The formula adopted here differs from the Trinidentine Theology. The Trinidentine Decrees (1547) of the Roman Catholic Church affirmed that justification was more than forensic since it involves a moral change. I share the view of the Reformers that this is an undue confusion of sanctification with justification.[36]

What can be said about the role of faith in justification? A. H. Strong notes that in Scripture justification is ". . . never said to be διά πίστιν = on account of faith, but διά πίστεως = through faith, or ἐκ πίστεως = by faith."[37] W. G. T. Shedd agrees with this, remarking: "Faith is the instru-

---

36. See Bavinck, *Reasonable Faith*, 459; Berkouwer, *Justification*, 94ff.; Jewett, "Salvation," 840; Packer, "Justification," 683; C. Hodge, *Systematic Theology*, 117; Strong, *Systematic Theology*, 819; L. Berkhof, *Systematic Theology*, 513; Pope, *Christian Theology*, 407. Contra Hans Küng, *Justification* (London: Burns & Oates, 1964).

37. Strong, *Systematic Theology*, 864. See L. Berkhof, *Systematic Theology*, 520f.; Berkouwer, *Justification*, 520f.; C. Hodge, *Systematic Theology*, 119.

ment, not the procuring or meritorious cause of his justification."[38] From Scripture we hear: "Let it be known to you therefore, my brothers, that through this man forgiveness of sins is proclaimed to you; by this Jesus everyone who believes is set free from all those sins from which you could not be freed by the law of Moses" (Acts 13:38f., NRSV); "For one believes with the heart and so is justified, and one confesses with the mouth and so is saved" (Romans 10:10, NRSV).

The affirmation of justification Sola-fide is in direct opposition to those espousing justification by works. Scripture proclaims: "And we have come to believe in Christ Jesus, so that we might be justified by faith in Christ, and not by doing the works of the law, because no one will be justified by the works of the law" (Galatians 2:16, NRSV); "For we hold that a person is justified by faith apart from works prescribed by the law" (Romans 3:28, NRSV); "For whoever keeps the whole law but fails in one point has become accountable for all of it" (James 2:10, NRSV). James Arminius noted this and said: "That faith and works concur together to justification, is a thing impossible."[39] This faith is not a mere intellectual exercise in futility. The Paul—James controversy has shown that faith will vindicate its comprehensiveness. Speaking theologically, it seems most proper to designate the outworkings of that faith as acts of sanctification. Perhaps this is what the staunch defender of sola fide, G. C. Berkouwer, meant when he said, "Be James' letter directed against who it may it is not aimed at Paul. For if Paul sets forth faith and righteousness of faith against works, it is against the works of the law, not works done in and out of faith."[40]

---

38. Shedd, *Dogmatic Theology*, 543. Cf. Thiessen, *Systematic Theology*, 188f.

39. Arminius, "Corollary #1 to Private Disputation 48," *Writings*, 119. See also Calvin, *Institutes* 3:11:3:382. Berkouwer, *Justification*, 112; Bavinck, *Reasonable Faith*, 450; A. A. Hodge, *Outline of Theology*, 498; Jewett, "Salvation," 845; Ladd, *Theology of the New Testament*, 448f.

40. G. C. Berkouwer, *Justification*, 137. Yet some questions linger in my mind. As Arminius, "Apology," 15(5), *Writings* 1:362, said:

> But perhaps you will say, that you do not appear before God "by the work of the law, but by works produced from faith and love." I wish you to explain to me what it is to appear by faith, and what to appear by works; and whether it can possibly happen, that a man may appear both by faith and works.

Cf. Bultmann, *Theology of the New Testament* 1:283.

Adoption

The doctrine of adoption presents few theological problems. While this phase of the ordo salutis is articulated most clearly by Paul, it would not be accurate to say that it is peculiar to him. Jesus said, "... Love your enemies and pray for those who persecute you, so that you may be children of your Father in heaven; for he makes his sun rise on the evil and on the good, and sends rain on the righteous and on the unrighteous" (Matthew 5:44f., NRSV). It was Jesus who suggested that prayer begin with the words, "Our Father in heaven, hallowed be your name" (Matthew 6:9, NRSV). The Fourth Gospel proclaims "... all who received him, who believed in his name, he gave power to become children of God" (John 1:12, NRSV) and an epistle of John expresses the same sentiment by saying "See what love the Father has given us, that we should be called children of God; and that is what we are" (1 John 3:1, NRSV). However, no writer of Scripture has crystallized this position as carefully as Paul: "But when the fullness of time had come, God sent his Son, born of a woman, born under the law, in order to redeem those who were under the law, so that we might receive adoption as children" (Galatians 4:4f., NRSV).

Similar to justification, adoption is a judicial act of God and it is concomitant with justification. In the descriptive language of Paul K. Jewett it is rightly pointed out that

> Justification is a figure to say that God frees us from the legal, penal consequence of our sin ... But adoption goes beyond that. Not only are we free, but we have the freedom to walk up to the front door of the house, as it were, with the keys in our pockets and walk right in as God's children, as his sons.[41]

Despite the claims from those of the liberal tradition, this filial relationship is not an experience shared by all humankind, for it is reserved for believers. The First Epistle of John describes a child of God as "... one who believes that Jesus is the Christ ..." (1 Jn 5:1). Paul relates children of God to faith and adds "for in Christ Jesus you are all children of God through faith" (Galatians 3:26, NRSV). Therefore, while it is true that God is the Father of all humankind, there remains a special kinship for those who believe in Jesus Christ.

---

41. Jewett, "Salvation," 860. Cf. Pope, *Christian Theology*, 13–17; Wiley, *Christian Theology*, 428–38; F. H. Palmer, "Adoption," *NBD*, 15.

There are at least six results of adoption. (1) Believers become joint heirs with Jesus Christ. Paul tells us, "Now therefore ye are no more strangers and foreigners, but fellow citizens with the saints, and of the household of God" (Eph 2:19, KJV), and again, "and if children, then heirs, heirs of God and fellow heirs with Christ..." (Rom 8:17, KJV). (2) It makes all believers family. "For this reason I bow my knees before the Father, from whom every family in heaven and on earth takes its name" (Ephesians 3:14f., NRSV). Some communities take this affirmation so pointedly that they address one another as Brother and Sister. (3) Christians are free from bondage. The Fourth Gospel describes a sinner as a "servant" of sin (Jn 8:34). The second epistle of Peter likewise says, "While they promise them liberty, they themselves are the servants of corruption; for of whom a man is overcome of the same is he brought in bondage" (2 Pt 2:19, KJV). However, it is said of the redeemed that "... you are no longer a slave but a child, and if a child then also an heir, through God" (Galatians 4:7, NRSV). (4) Children of God are promised a future inheritance. "And not only the creation, but we ourselves, who have the first fruits of the Spirit, groan inwardly while we wait for adoption, the redemption of our bodies" (Romans 8:23, NRSV). (5) Especially important is the benefit of confidence. We do not forget that God is in heaven and we are on earth, but we have a special closeness when approaching God in prayer. This is reflected by the suggested use of the intimate term Abba (Rom 8:16, Gal 4:6). Paul says, "For you did not receive a spirit of slavery to fall back into fear, but you have received a spirit of adoption. When we cry, "Abba! Father!" (Romans 8:15, NRSV). (6) The Holy Spirit testifies that believers have been received into the family of God, "When we cry, "Abba! Father!" It is that very Spirit bearing witness with our spirit that we are children of God" (Romans 8:15f., NRSV). "And because you are children, God has sent the Spirit of his Son into our hearts, crying, "Abba! Father!" (Galatians 4:6, NRSV).

Sanctification

An examination of the doctrine of sanctification is not only necessary to complete the analysis of the ordo salutis, but especially important because of the role of this doctrine in the formulation of Spirit baptism theology by Holiness Pentecostals. Unlike Keswickian Pentecostals, North American Holiness Pentecostals have traditionally defended a "second work of grace" which eradicated the Adamic nature as a prerequisite for baptism in the Spirit.[42]

It would appear that most affirmations made about sanctification are contested. I will speak to the controversial issue of the relation of justification to sanctification. This issue is of such important it is discussed in every traditional dogmatic treatment of the ordo salutis. The following table makes easy a comparison of the salient issues.

Justification	Sanctification
1. Guilt of sin removed	1. Stain of sin removed
2. Imputed righteousness	2. Imparted righteousness
3. Human acceptable to God	3. God desirable to human
4. Legal, external, objective	4. Experimental, internal, subjective
5. Relates to our standing	5. Relates to our condition[43]

The fundamental point of distinction that emerges is that justification is a forensic act of God as righteous and gracious judge while sanctification is a work of the Holy Spirit where one's disposition is actually affected.

Despite this difference between actual change and the judicial affirmation, the initial part of sanctification, which I shall call initiatory sanctification, causes many writers to make affirmations that seem to stretch paradox into contradiction. Those who use the term "positional sanctification" to explain the instantaneous past fail to realize the reality of a disposition change which is effected in the beginning of sanctification.[44] When Prior and others use this kind of terminology to express the meaning of initiatory sanctification, they are led to contradiction. Who can distinguish positional holiness (initial sanctification) from a

---

42. In the ensuing discussion the RSV and NRSV will be used in scriptural quotations unless otherwise designated.

43. This table is adapted from Donald G. Bloesch, *Essentials of Evangelical Theology* (San Francisco: Harper & Row, 1979), 2:41f., and Kenneth F. W. Prior, *The Way of Holiness* (Downer's Grove: InterVarsity Press, 1982), 55.

44. This criticism holds true for Dallas Theological Seminary theologians with whom the phrase *positional sanctification* has been especially associated. See Chafer, *Spiritual*, 107; John F. Walvoord, *The Holy Spirit* (Grand Rapids: Zondervan, 1976), 210, 213. Also contra G. Walter, "Sanctification," *NBD*, 1140; Thiessen, *Systematic Theology*, 380.

judicial affirmation of declared righteousness (justification)? In my judgment, no fine lines could be drawn between these two. The doctrine of sanctification concerns the actual change effected in humans. This being true means that the closest theological component to initiatory sanctification is regeneration. This issue will be dealt with shortly. The pressure of an implied perfectionism and the parallel to declarative righteousness in justification should not lead one to weaken the reality of scripturally defined initiatory sanctification. In the initial stages of sanctification "we have been sanctified through the offering of the body of Jesus Christ once for all" (Hebrews 10:10).

G. C. Berkouwer expresses concern about separating sanctification from justification by faith in a way that meritorious works are conceded.[45] There is a theological difference between being declared righteous and the process of working out this righteousness, but both justification and sanctification are by faith, both are continuous, and both are by God's grace. It is proper to regard justification and sanctification as distinct doctrines for the sake of understanding the teaching of Scripture. But there are some who advocate various forms of perfectionism who use this separation in a way to support their doctrine. The Roman Catholics put them together in Luther's day leading to meritorious work.[46] In that context it is important to point out that it is not proper to separate them in a way that suggests they are states into which one comes by two distinct acts of faith. According to the New Testament, the faith which justifies is the faith which breaks the power of reigning sin, to use Charles Wesley's words.

I have suggested that the essence of regeneration is as follows: (1) impartation of a new life into the natural person dead in sins (2) which ushers in a new moral disposition. The dogmatic formulation of the biblical concept of the sanctification of the believer centers on the continuing struggle between the "new person" and the "old person" whereby the believer is enabled to live victoriously by reason of the indwelling Holy Spirit. After seeing the foregoing discussion of the nature of initiatory sanctification, it seems that there is a connection with the doctrine of regeneration. In my judgment regeneration and initiatory sanctification are one and the same thing. Most dogmaticians representing historic Protestantism

---

45. Berkouwer, *Sanctification*, 63f., 93, 120, 123, 129, 107, 42. Similarly Paul K. Jewett, "Salvation," 16.

46. Paul K. Jewett, "Systematic Theology," unpublished course lectures (Pasadena: Fuller Theological Seminary, 1975), 868.

acknowledge some connection between regeneration and sanctification. Many have even referred to regeneration as the "initial stage" of sanctification.[47] Others, however, have suggested that a distinction can be made between regeneration and sanctification. But W. G. T. Shedd and those arguing this way may have in mind that phase of sanctification which follows its initiation. All in all, much of the same basic thought seems to be in the mind of the majority of the dogmaticians.[48]

Faith is the basis for sanctification. I agree with G. C. Berkouwer:

> ... progressive sanctification is compatible with a faith-connected sanctification. A deflection from a properly related justification and sanctification exists only in the view that faith—as an isolated function—is the cause of good works. Anyone who manages to maintain the full status of *Sola-fide* can speak about progressive sanctification without stumbling into the pit of legalism.[49]

Berkouwer's use of the word justification here must be understood as emphasizing the Sola-fide and not in any way compromising the forensic nature of justification. It is in the intimate connection between faith and sanctification that one best discerns the place of "good works." As Professor Berkouwer says:

> It is the works of the law not those of faith, which threaten *sola fide*. Faith is not a subjective human attitude, but a confident response in God's pity and grace, in Romans and Galatians, where justification apart from the works of the law is maintained so stoutly, we are urged to walk in the Spirit.
>
> If when the test came the faith had not been matched by works, then it would have been proved to be an incomplete faith.[50]

---

47. Strong, *Systematic Theology* 3:869–71; Jewett, "Salvation," 869; Prior, *Holiness*, 43; C. Hodge, *Systematic Theology* 3:224. L. Berkof, *Systematic Theology*, 536, says: "... regeneration is the beginning of sanctification. The work of renewal begun in the former, is continued in the latter, Phil 1:6." See Bloesch, *Essentials of Evangelical Theology* 2:42.

48. See Wiley, *Christian Theology* 2:476; Dale Moody, *The Word of Truth* (Grand Rapids: Eerdmans, 1981), 323; Hoeksema, *Reformed Dogmatics*, 520; Litton, *Dogmatic Theology*, 80; Bavinck, *Reasonable Faith*, 590; A. A. Hodge, *Outline of Theology*, 523; R. L. Dabney, *Lectures in Systematic Theology*, (Grand Rapids: Zondervan, 1972), 663.

49. Berkouwer, *Sanctification*, 107. Cf. Bavinck, *Reasonable Faith*, 485; L. Berkof, *Systematic Theology*, 537.

50. Berkouwer, *Justification*, 112, 108, 136. Lewis B. Smedes, "G. C. Berkouwer," *Creative Minds in Contemporary Theology*, ed. by Philip E. Hughes (Grand Rapids: Eerdmans, 1966), 89f., notes that Berkouwer is attempting to bring "... the entire life of man in grace

The work of sanctification is that of the true and living God. Scripture notes the involvement of the Father (1 Thess 6:23, Heb 13:21), the Son (Eph 5:25f., Titus 2:14) but especially the third divine persona (1 Cor 6:11, 2 Thess 2:13), the Spiritus Sanctus. Recognition of the believer's dependence on the Holy Spirit for his or her sanctification does not dissolve the believer's own responsibility. To assert that humans are involved in the process, however, is not to share the view that sanctification is a matter of human self moral improvement. It is extremely difficult to find a suitable way to express the relationship between God and humans in sanctification. Dogmaticians often use the word "cooperate,"[51] but this does not seem satisfactory. I am driven to a paradox: human response is important, but so is the Spirit working within. The biblical injunctions to righteousness (Rom 6:13, 19, 8:13, 2 Cor 7:1, Gal 5:16, 25) can be understood only to mean that the believer is active in the process.

Professor Bavinck points out that in the Hebrew Bible it is said that the Lord sanctifies his people (Exod 31:13, Lev 20:8, 21:8), but also that the people must sanctify themselves (Lev 11:44, 20:7, Num 11:18). In a similar fashion, the New Testament calls sanctification the gift of God (Jn 17:17–19, 1 Cor 1:2, 1 Thess 5:23), and yet believers are admonished to be perfect (Matt 5:48), to do good works (Matt 5:16, Jn 15:8), to yield their members (Rom 6:19), to be holy in their walk (1 Pt 1:15, 2 Pt 3:11), and to pursue sanctification (2 Cor 7:1, 1 Thess 3:13, 4:13, Heb 12:14).[52] Noting the Pauline analogies of the runner (Phil 3:14f.) and the wrestler (Eph 6:12), Jewett says, "... when we stand within the circle of faith, when we see salvation as a matter of God's grace, it does not follow that we are simply passive in our salvation."[53] Indeed, there is no effortless resting in God. Berkouwer rightly asserts: "... progress in sanctification never meant working out one's own salvation under one's own auspices. On the

---

into constant relationship with faith, intending to say that we are always, at every point on the way, being justified, sanctified, and preserved in and through faith." See A. A. Hodge, *Outline of Theology*, 526; Litton, *Dogmatic Theology*, 334.

51. C. Hodge, *Systematic Theology*, 226; Shedd, *Dogmatic Theology* 2:555; Pieper, *Christian Dogmatics*, 14.

52. Bavinck, *Reasonable Faith*, 476.

53. Jewett, "Salvation," 871. Shedd, *Dogmatic Theology*, 55f., calls sanctification "both a grace and a duty." Cf. Strong, *Systematic Theology*, 871; Ladd, *Theology of the New Testament*, 520.

contrary, it meant working out one's own salvation with a rising sense of dependence on God's grace."[54]

CONCLUSIONS

We now move to the final chapter which contains a summary set of conclusions that intends to draw together data from the entire study.

---

54. Berkouwer, *Sanctification*, 112.

Conclusions

Data from the canonical record and ecclesiastical history suggest that there is a specific work of the Holy Spirit which is charismatic in nature and not predetermined in action both initially and progressively. It is appropriate to relate these findings to the systematic theologian's soteriological framework. It is the raison d'être of dogmatic theology to formulate doctrines pertinent to given constituencies. As noted at the outset, the primary audience in view here are Classical Pentecostals in the industrialized West. The approach adopted, however, is such that the content should not be limited in its usefulness to this tradition alone nor this geography.

Before the foregoing examinations are cataloged into categories pertinent to systematic theology, one short commentary is needed. This centers around the age old tension between what Pentecostals mean when they refer to "receiving the Spirit" and what most other Protestants in general understand when they use this phrase or one like it.

Unfortunately, the problem on the Pentecostal side is complicated by the fact that among those without theological training there remain occasional arguments about the terms Holy Ghost and Holy Spirit. Those critical of the term Holy Spirit are most often devotees of the King James Version. This is so entrenched among some members of this group that they can be skeptical of a prophetic utterance or like phenomena if King James language does not grace the "inspired saying." But worst of all, their confusion extends into their perception of the Godhead because some think that acceptance of both terms Holy Ghost and Holy Spirit bespeaks a quadrinity!

Of course this approach is not difficult to criticize. On the basic level it is obvious that someone who holds the term Holy Spirit in disrepute because of the priority given to the King James Version has failed to realize that the King James Version incorporates both Holy Ghost and Holy Spirit. More importantly, naturally, is the fact that even a beginner's knowledge of New Testament Greek dispels this notion quickly while also debunking the revered myths. The occasional flirtation with a deviate trinitarian formula is not surprising coming from a tradition that has difficulty in correctly articulating a Triunistic concept of the divine essence. While quadrinian formulas would be held in disrepute, one might not be censored when Arian or Sabellian phrases are found on the lips of some of the Pentecostal faithful. One does not have to go far to realize that this problem is not limited to the fringe of Protestantism. The canonical investigation used lengthy quotations from an early writing by G. W. H. Lampe on the Lucan contribution to pneumatology. Lampe is widely known for *Seal of the Spirit* that came out of this period of his thinking. Both writings are considerably different than the later *God As Spirit*, which is treated elsewhere as a modern version of Spirit Christology.[1] Further, the considerable latitude taken by mainstream theologians can be easily tasted by savoring any portion of the many menus offered at the annual AAR-SBL meetings.

Given this background it may not seem preposterous that various Spirit baptism formulas adopted by Classical Pentecostals led to inferior formulations of understanding the basic concept of soteriology. At times, North American Classical Pentecostals have concluded that "Christ" is received at "conversion" and that the "full personality of the Spirit" is known only at the baptism of the Holy Spirit.[2] Ambiguity turns into chaos when the phrase "he/she received the Holy Ghost" is alternated with the phrase "baptism in the Holy Ghost."[3]

A factor contributing to this self-imposed misery is the fact that it could have been rightly said that "Pentecostal theology consists of oral tradition rather than of extensive creeds and theological tomes."[4] While this is less true today, North Americans have ignored some of its own

---

1. Harold D. Hunter, "Spirit-Christology: Dilemma and Promise."

2. See T. W. Walker, "Baptism in the Holy Spirit," *Pentecostal Doctrine*, ed. by P. S. Brewster (Greenhurst Press, 1976), Williams, *Systematic Theology* 2:233, 3:37; Hughes, *What Is Pentecost?*, 25. Cf. Bruner, *Theology of the Holy Spirit*, 60; Dunn, *Baptism in the Holy Spirit*, 107.

3. Donald T. Williams, *The Person and Work of the Holy Spirit: The Holy Spirit Effects in Us What Christ Has Done for Us* (Nashville: Broadman & Holman Publishers, 1994), 124, warns against "careless" use of the phrase "receiving the Holy Spirit."

4. MacDonald, "Pentecostal Theology," 56. See Hans-Jurgen Becken, "The Healing Ministry of the African Independent Churches," *The Future of Religion*, ed. by Gerald J. Pillay (Pretoria: Serva-Publishers, 1989), 16.

wisdom. For example, the periodical, *The Upper Room*, produced in Los Angeles by Classical Pentecostalists, had this to say in 1911:

> There is a teaching in some Pentecostal quarters that the Holy Ghost has not been received at all, except by those who has received the full Pentecostal baptism with the Bible evidence of speaking in tongues. Of course, we cannot subscribe to this for one moment. For there are (and have been through the years gone by) many, very many, precious saints of God who have received and rejoiced in the conscious indwelling presence, comfort, sanctifying power and guidance of the Holy Spirit ... Many of those who now rejoice in the full Pentecostal baptism know perfectly well that they had received Him and knew Him as the Comforter within them before they saw their fuller privilege and entered into the full blessing of Pentecost. Even so was it with the early church not many years after the Holy Ghost had first fallen on the waiting disciples in the upper room at Jerusalem. Hence to Christians at Corinth, some of whom he had to say were yet carnal, Paul wrote very plainly in 1 Cor. 3:16: "Know ye not that your body is the temple of God and that the Spirit of God dwelleth in you?" Again in 1 Cor. 6:19: "What! know ye not that your body is the temple of the Holy Ghost which is in you and which ye have of God?" Once more, in 2 Cor. 13:5: "Know ye not your own selves, how that Jesus Christ is in you except ye be reprobate?" Clearly "the Spirit of Christ" is the Holy Spirit, who is also called in other Scriptures "the Spirit of God," "the Eternal Spirit" (Heb. 9:14). In Rom. 8:11 we find, "The Spirit that raised up Jesus from the dead dwelleth in you"; in Rom. 8:9, "Now if any man have not the Spirit of Christ he is none of His." There are not several different spirits, but one Spirit, even the Holy Spirit.[5]

The loss of this remarkable insight to the movement at large reflects the depth of its theological illiteracy. Yet this insight cannot be taken for granted even today in North America. This is despite the fact that attempts of clarifying this matter multiplied through the years and was marked by contributions like Myer Pearlman's *Knowing the Doctrine of the Bible* (Springfield: Gospel Publishing House, 1937) and Ralph M. Riggs' *The Spirit Himself* (Springfield: Gospel Publishing House, 1949). One can wonder how much more advanced the Pentecostal Movement

---

5. "The Holy Ghost Received," *The Upper Room* 2:4 (January, 1911), 2. The May issue of 1911 reproduced a like article and mentions that the January article was authored by the magazine's co-editor, George B. Studd.

is on this issue while entering the last decade of this century. Recent decades have seen the "evangelicalization" and "charismatization" of the Pentecostal Movement in North America while scholarly studies of Pentecostal distinctives are frequently dominated by those who do not participate in the movement. This contrasts dramatically to the Roman Catholic Charismatic Movement which initially produced most of the highest quality pertinent materials.

The Classical Pentecostal Movement remains vulnerable in part because those outside the movement encounter great difficulty in judging the movement's juxtaposition of ethos and propositions.[6] Since the movement's praxis orientation contributes to its propensity for oral tradition, one result has been that scholarly works on pentecostal distinctives have come from those outside the movement. From at least the time of G. B. Cutten, most of these studies have been overtly negative and have made no apology for what often turned out to be defective research or ethnocentrism. It takes little more than quick scan of commentaries and church histories produced in the Nineteenth Century to realize the great difference from later commentators and historians relative to Pentecostal distinctives.

The 1980s saw scholarly opinions relative to the movement rescued from caricature. Yet, the most renowned authors remain outside the movement. The objectivity of a non-participant is important and insights can be born out of prejudged criticism. Yet, this coming decade must see a serious reckoning with the burgeoning scholarship within the Pentecostal and Charismatic Movements. There is much material being withheld from scrutiny because major publishers will not accept the manuscripts. Contributing to the paucity of published material by participating scholars is the fact that among those who are capable of such work, very few are given opportunity to fulfill their potential. Seminaries sponsored by Classical Pentecostal denominations tend to be praxis oriented to the extent that most faculty members have too many commitments to engage in scholarly publishing. If conventional hostilities are going to be reduced, distortion from any source must give way to mutual enrichment.

6. See Harold D. Hunter, "What Is Truth?" See also Harold D. Hunter, review of David Harrell's *Oral Roberts: An American Life* in *EPTA Bulletin* 5:2 (Fall, 1986); David Daniels, "Afro-American Worship: A Source for Pentecostal Theology," *The Distinctiveness of Pentecostal-Charismatic Theology*, ed. by Peter Hocken (Gaithersburg: Society for Pentecostal Studies, November 14–16, 1985).

Of the complications noted previously perhaps none of them rival the influence of Lucan priority known by the movement in the West. The earlier investigation of Lucan pneumatology noted that the book of Acts uses various phrases in tandem when describing the charismatic work of the Spirit. One passage particularly well known among Classical Pentecostals is Acts 2:38 which reads as follows in the King James Version: "Ye shall receive the gift of the Holy Ghost." Influenced by the similar phrase in Acts 19:2, it has been easy to drop the word "gift" and repeat the "biblical" question "Have you received the Holy Ghost?"

The most solid evidence clarifying the intent of the movement is that whenever a Pentecostalist embarks onto theological terrain, he or she invariably affirms the truth that all Christians know the indwelling presence of the Holy Spirit. Early formulas from this tradition concluded "Christ or the Holy Spirit" could not indwell those who had not experienced Spirit baptism with initial evidence tongues-speech. This contorted formula reflected the logical implications of their mutant unitarianism. Today, however, leaders in this segment of the movement are becoming increasingly willing to affirm the shared presence of the Holy Spirit among all believers.[7]

It seems, in fact, that most Pentecostals would be advantaged to realize that the Lucan choice of phrase reflects something of a missionary orientation. In contrast to this, the Pauline expressions are born out of theological contemplation.[8] Both approaches have their respective uses, but the current status of the Pentecostal Movement is such that it can no longer remain perplexed about a basic tenet of Scripture.

It was the express purpose of this investigation to examine the plausibility of a particular part of the Pentecostal-Charismatic distinctive pneumatology. The study has suggested that the essence of this theology is found in Scripture itself as well as most every time and place that the Christian message has been present. In order to facilitate a workable

---

7. See David Reed, "Oneness Pentecostalism," 351ff.; David K. Bernard, "Essentials of Oneness Theology" and Dan Lewis, "The Theology of the Baptism in the Holy Spirit in the United Pentecostal Church," in papers presented to *The First Occasional Symposium on Aspects of the Oneness Pentecostal Movement* (Cambridge: Harvard Divinity School, July 5–7, 1984). For current thinking look at the magazine *Spiritus: Estuidios Sobre Pentecostalism* (Mexico City: 1985 onward) edited by Manuel J. Gaxiola-Gaxiola.

8. This parallels Emil Brunner's insight (*Dogmatics* 3:283) that the phrase "repent and believe" is the missionary order while the reverse is of a theological nature. Brunner notes that both approaches are utilized in the Romans epistle.

summary of the findings, the major issues will be dealt with under nine headings.

Incidental to this inquiry has been a determination of an "initial physical" evidence of Spirit baptism. A cursory treatment is found elsewhere.[9] The actual percentage of pentecostals and charismatics that speak in tongues is much lower than many leaders imagine.[10] Classical Pentecostals will not find this satisfactory, but in the wake of works by Dunn and Bruner, it was most important to begin with the basic theological issue, namely whether one could speak of a distinct work of the Spirit—of a charismatic nature—which might be separated from one's initial experience of salvation. The answer in the affirmative means that this study should be considered a Pentecostal alternative to the likes of Dunn and Bruner.

1. A distinct work of the Spirit which is charismatic

The biblical analysis identified a work of the Spirit which is charismatic in nature that can be distinguished from other acts of God effected in the believer. The works of the Spirit in the life of the believer are manifest. The Spirit functions in calling, conversion, regeneration, justification, adoption, sanctification and Spirit baptism.

Examples taken from the biblical writers consulted have shown that the specific nature of the charismatic dimension defies classification, but encompasses all those manifestations of grace which are edifying to the body, bestowed by a sovereign God. Although the chosen Johannine Literature did not delineate the appropriate marks of the charismatic

---

9. Harold D. Hunter, "Pentecostal Pneumatology," V:A:9. A promising start has been made by Gary McGee in his edited volume entitled *Initial Evidence*. A sampling of prior explorations evidence another redefinition in process. See Gordon D. Fee, "Baptism in the Holy Spirit: The Issue of Separability and Subsequence," *Toward a Pentecostal/Charismatic Theology*, ed. by J. Rodman Williams (South Hamilton: Society For Pentecostal Studies, November 15-17, 1984); Anthony D. Palma, "The Gifts and the Fruit of the Spirit," *Conference on the Holy Spirit Digest*, ed. by Gwen Jones (Springfield: Gospel Publishing House, 1983), 1:193ff. Cf. Max Turner, *Power from on High*, 446ff. Although Frank Macchia suggests that initial evidence could be reconstructed as a sacrament, my judgment given in response to his having first suggested this in a paper read to the Society for Pentecostal Studies in the late 1980s was that Dr. Macchia's treatment of "glossolalia" avoided weighty issues presented by distinctive pentecostal pneumatological formulas.

10. The 1979 Gallup poll reported in *CT* claimed that 50%–33% of pentecostals and charismatics actually spoke in tongues. This is not surprising to those who have seen records of churches that count such things.

Spirit, Paul includes spectacular gifts (1 Cor 12:8ff.), the ability to bear weakness (2 Cor 12:9), willingness to contribute money (Rom 12:8), sacrifice of one's life (1 Cor 12:13), celibacy (1 Cor 7:7) and various institutional gifts (2 Tim 1:6f.), while Luke emphasizes tongues-speech (Acts 2:4, 10:46, 19:6), prophecy (Acts 19:7) and missionary work (Acts 2:14).

2. The term *Spirit baptism*

This study has suggested that the term Spirit baptism is appropriate for describing works of the Spirit which are charismatic in nature. There is no certain record of the use of the term "baptism in the Spirit" for an experience which was understood to be evidenced by tongues-speech alone until such a formula was developed at the Topeka Bible School run by C. F. Parham. Notable exclusions would then be patristic literature and Scripture itself.

The New Testament writers with the possible exception of Luke (Lk 3:16, Acts 1:5, 11:16) did not use the term Spirit baptism in the sense accepted here, much less as it is used by numerous Classical Pentecostals in North America. This is not to say that the phrase is not "biblical" inasmuch as there are six passages which might be taken to indicate otherwise. Rather, it is to freely admit that when speculating on the ipsissima verba of the early church, it seems likely that this was not a standard term as it is today. Especially in view is the way the term is used for the charismatic work of the Spirit, but this implies also a denial of its usage for admittance to the body of Christ. This demands caution, but not total abstinence. No sound hermeneutical principle has been violated when terms are used which are accommodating to a given generation, as long as the concepts expressed thereby are biblical.

3. Spirit baptism in relation to the classical formulation of the ordo salutis

At the turn of the century, the Protestant Movement was well grounded in a systematic treatment of salvation applied. The works produced by systematic theologians made terms famous like regeneration, adoption and calling. It is the conclusion of this study that a systematic appraisal of the biblical data relating to soteriology is favorable to understanding Spirit baptism as part of the outworking of God's grace in the believer's life.

Extreme caution should be exercised when dogmatic theology divides salvation into various works of the Spirit. To enumerate parts of the ordo salutis is to accommodate the present day church. Biblically speaking it is often difficult to distinguish clearly 'parts' of the salvation experience, but when translating the data for our own day it would appear that we are at the mercy of categories.

This means that only in extreme cases can much weight be given to the distinctions mentioned. However, such is the case when it is realized that the charismatic work of the Spirit does not always become operative immediately in the life of the believer. Luke (Acts 2:38) and Paul (1 Cor 12:13b) both seem to favor an initial experience in which one realizes all the manifold wisdom of God, but both writers (Acts 8:14–18, 9:17–19, Gal 4:6, Eph 1:13; cf. Jn 4:14, 7:37–39) seem to indicate that this is not always the case. Therefore, it seems necessary to conclude the following: the charismatic work of the Spirit can be effected subsequent to the initial salvific encounter. However, this language does not intend to violate the biblical view of the theological unity of God's saving gift.

4. Spirit baptism theology compared to traditional Protestant Pneumatology

Classical Protestant theology has been firm in rejecting any theological scheme which would challenge the unity of God's spiritual working in humans. This "one-stage" theology, as it is sometimes called, is often wrongly interpreted by Pentecostals to mean that the work of the Spirit is limited to Christian beginnings. However, this is hardly the intent of this nuance of Protestant theology. Culpepper and Pinnock have been quick to point out that pneumatic experiences are known throughout the spiritual pilgrimage. Further, Dunn and Bruner not only would agree that there is a linear dimension to all the recognizable parts of the ordo salutis, but they might concur also that this includes a charismatic work of the Spirit which is both repeated and continuous. And finally, the official responses of the major Protestant organizations to the Charismatic constituency with their own ranks, seems to recognize the essence of Spirit baptism theology as defined here.

5. Spirit baptism theology and Spirit fullness theologians

The description of Spirit baptism as a work of the Spirit which is distinct from familiar soteriological elements which are decidedly initiatory means that essentially the same thing is being said here as is argued by those Protestants who present a similar position but prefer the expression "fullness of the Spirit."

It is interesting to see how this similarity in theological intent is obscured by he semantic barrier. Spirit-fullness theologians almost uniformly deny that the term Spirit baptism is appropriate to label empowering pneumatic works. This is primarily based on 1 Corinthians 12:13a which is understood to relegate the term Spirit baptism to church initiation. Many Pentecostals, on the other hand, often obscure the issue by focusing attention on the glossocentrism of their Spirit baptism theology.[11] However, when these parts of the arguments are set aside, the resulting description of the two groups seems related. That is, both factions believe that there is a distinctive work of the Spirit which enables one to perform acts of service on the behalf of the Christian community. Again, however, a common foe is the problem of classification of Christians.

6. Spirit baptism theology compared to actualization/appropriation theology

Protestant and Roman Catholic Charismatics are agreed in saying that no quantitative improvement can be made on the reception of the Holy Spirit in the initial salvific experience. However, they are aware also that it is not always true that the completeness of the Spirit's work is immediately seen in the life of the believer. Those having experienced these spiritual breakthroughs have, nonetheless, rejected the Pentecostal idea of a "second work of grace." They have concluded that it is best to speak of a unilateral bestowal of the Spirit which occurs at one's Christian beginnings, but can be actualized/appropriated throughout one's Christian pilgrimage.

However, it does not seem possible that this scheme avoids making 'levels' of Christians, because one group can be isolated as having released God's Spirit in their lives in a way not known by others. It would seem, then, that their theological point is the same as argued here (i.e., that a

---

11. Arden C. Autry's review in *Themelios* 17:3 (April/May, 1992): 30f., of Rodman Williams' *Renewal Theology* 2 complains that the author blurs the charismatic issue by using the phrase "coming of the Spirit" rather than "filled with the Spirit."

pneumatic breakthrough can occur after one's beginnings). However, we all face together the problem of how to resolve the resulting isolationism (and often elitism) with a biblical view of spirituality.

7. Spirit baptism theology as a historical novelty

It has often been said that Pentecostal pneumatology is a historical novelty. However, the historical review has shown that the essence of this theology has been known at most stages of Christian theology. The conclusions on Scripture have been based on widely accepted methods of present day exegesis, but have then been confirmed by numerous authors from various traditions, time periods and geographical locations. This suggests that the theological deductions made here transcend, to some extent at least, cultural and philosophical influences.

8. Spirit baptism and sanctification

It is important to remember that Spirit baptism does not insure progress in sanctification. That is, πνευματικός does not equal πνευματικά. It is quite likely that the Corinthians had wrongly labeled themselves as πνευματικός, because they had experienced the πνευματικά. Whatever the particulars, Paul makes clear that the title πνευματικός rightly belongs only to those who have matured in their ethical discipleship. With regard to πνευματικά, 1 Corinthians 13 shows that one can have experienced the πνευματικά and yet not be a πνευματικός. Notice, however, that Paul does not deny the validity of the exercise of the πνευματικά. Thus, while the empowering and purifying works of the Spirit are often related, they are not inseparable.

9. The problem of spiritual classifications

The major problem with a doctrine of subsequence/appropriation/actualization is that it appears to make classes, presumably levels, of Christians. Unfortunately, this is a possible ramification of any theological scheme which attempts to take spiritual progress into account. This problem must be confronted when dealing with the doctrine of sanctification.

It would seem that real progress in sanctification leads one to a greater appreciation of God's work in us. A person who has made such progress would hardly exploit such an "advantage." Much the same is true with regard to experiencing the charismatic work of the Spirit. It would be a denial of the biblical view of spirituality for one who has experienced this work of the Spirit to believe that he or she has arrived at a spiritual plateau superior to that of others not sharing the same advantage.

The dilemma of a biblical paradox is met here, which in principle is of much the same order as that which one encounters in understanding the doctrine of election. The problem of election centers on explaining the biblical truths that God is sovereign and works in humans while at the same time a person is not passive in a Christian pilgrimage. An exact formula is difficult to develop, but at least two basic affirmations are clear: (1) a person can never take credit for any spiritual development, and (2) yet he or she cannot retire with the expectation of seeing God's work automatically accomplished throughout life. Similarly, two fundamental implications about the charismatic endowment of the Spirit seem evident. One can (1) affirm that he or she knows this special working of the Spirit, but (2) he or she can never demean as inferior one who is not in the same circle.

Bibliography

General

Barclay, William. *Promise of the Spirit*. Philadelphia. Westminster Press, 1960.
Barrett, C. K. "The Paraclete in the Fourth Gospel," *JTS* 1 (1950) 1–15.
_____. *The Holy Spirit and the Gospel Tradition*. London: SPCK, 1947.
Beasley-Murray, G. R. "Jesus and the Spirit." *Mélanges Béda Rigaus*. Pierquin: Djuclot, 1970.
Becker, J. Christian. "Aspects of the Holy Spirit in Paul." *USQR* 4:3–16.
Benjamin, H. S. "Pneuma in John and Paul." *Biblical Theological Review* 6 (1, 76) 27–44.
Bromiley, G. W. "The Holy Spirit." *Fundamentals of the Faith*. Ed. by Carl F. H. Henry. Grand Rapids: Zondervan, 1969.
Brown, R. E. "The Paraclete in the Fourth Gospel." *NTS* 13 (1966-67) 113–32.
Bruce, F. F. "Christ and Spirit in Paul." *BJRL* 59:2 (Spring, 1977) 259–85.
_____. "Was Paul a Mystic?" *The Reformed Theological Review* 34 (3, 75) 66–75.
Chevallier, Max-Alain. *Esprit De Dieu, Paroles D'Hommes*. Paris. Delachaux er Niestlé, 1966.
Christenson, Larry. *The Charismatic Renewal Among Lutherans*. Minneapolis: Lutheran Charismatic Renewal Services, 1976.
Crawford, R. G. "The Holy Spirit." *EvQ* 40 (1968) 165–72.
Dewar, Lindsay. *The Holy Spirit and Modern Thought*. London: A. R. Mowbray and Co., Ltd., 1959.
Dillistone, F. W. *The Holy Spirit in the Life of Today*. Philadelphia: Westminster Press, 1947.
Dobbin, Edmond J. "Towards a Theology of the Holy Spirit." Part I. *HeyJ* 17:1 (June, 1976) 5–19.
Dunn, James D. G. "Jesus—Flesh and Spirit: An Exposition of Romans 1:3–4." *JTS* 24 (1973) 46–68.
_____. *Jesus and the Spirit*. London: SCM, 1975.
_____. "1 Corinthians 15:45—Last Adam, life-giving Spirit." *Christ and Spirit in the New Testament*. Ed. by B. Lindars and S. S. Smalley. Cambridge: At the University Press, 1973.
_____. "2 Corinthians 3:17—'The Lord is the Spirit.'" *JTS* 21 (1970).
_____. "Spirit and Kingdom." *ExpTim* 82 (1970-71) 36–40.
Ellis, E. Earle. "Christ and Spirit in 1 Corinthians." *Christ and Spirit in the New Testament*. Ed. by B. Lindars and S. S. Smalley. Cambridge: At the University Press, 1973.
Forestell, J. T. "Jesus and the Paraclete in the Gospel of John." *Word and Spirit*. Ed. by Joseph Pleunik. Willowdale: Regis College, 1974.
Fortna, Roberts T. "Romans 8:10 and Paul's Doctrine of the Spirit." *ATR* 41 (1959) 77–84.

Gardner, Percy. *The Religious Experience of St. Paul*. New York: Williams and Norgate, 1911.

Grech, Prosper. "2 Corinthians 3:17 and the Pauline Doctrine of Conversion to the Holy Spirit." *CBQ* 17 (1955) 420–37.

Greenwood, David. "The Lord is the Spirit: Some Considerations of 2 Corinthians 3:17." *CBQ* 34 (1972) 465–72.

Hamilton, Neil Q. *The Holy Spirit and Eschatology in Paul*. Edinburgh: Oliver and Boyd Ltd., 1957.

Hendry, George S. *The Holy Spirit in Christian Theology*. Philadelphia: Westminster Press, 1965.

Hermann, Ingo. *Kyrios and Pneuma*. München: Kösel Verlag, 1961.

Hill, David. *Greek Words and Hebrew Meanings*. Cambridge: University Press, 1967.

Hoyle, R. Birch. *The Holy Spirit in Paul*. Garden City: Doubleday, Doran and Co., 1928.

Hull, J. H. E. *The Holy Spirit in the Acts of the Apostles*. London: Lutterworth Press, 1967.

Jeremias, Joachim. "The Key to Pauline Theology." *ExpTim* 76 (1964) 27–30).

Johnston, George. *The Spirit-Paraclete in the Gospel of John*. Cambridge: University Press, 1970.

Kasper, Walter. "Esprit-Christ-Eglise." *L'EXPERIENCE DE L'ESPRIT*. Ed. by Paul Brand. Paris: Beauchesne, 1976.

Lampe, G. W. H. "The Holy Spirit and the person of Christ." *Christ, Faith and History*. Ed. by S. W. Sykes and J. P. Clayton. Cambridge: At the University Press, 1972.

_____. "The Holy Spirit in the Writings of St. Luke." *Studies in the Gospels*. Ed. by D. E. Nineham. Oxford: Basil Blackwell, 1955.

_____. *The Seal of the Spirit*. London: SPCK, 1967.

Lindars, Barnabas. "Holy Spirit in Romans." *CQR* 161 (1960) 410–22.

McDonnell, Kilian. "The Holy Spirit and Christian Initiation." *The Holy Spirit and Power*. Ed. by Kilian McDonnell. Garden City: Doubleday and Co. Inc., 1975.

Moody, Dale. *Spirit of the Living God*. Philadelphia: Westminister, 1968.

Morris, Leon. *Spirit of the Living God*. London: Inter-Varsity Press, 1960.

Moule, C. F. D. "The Christology of Acts." *Studies in Luke-Acts*. Ed. by L. E. Kecker and J. L. Martyn. London: SPCK, 1968.

Mühlen, Heribert. *A Charismatic Theology*. New York: Paulist Press, 1968.

Pearson, Burger A. *The Pneumatikos-Psychikos Terminology in 1 Corinthians*. Missoula: Scholars Press, 1973.

Reicke, Bo. "The Risen Lord and His Church." *Int* 13 (1959) 157–159.

Roberts, Harold. "The Holy Spirit and the Trinity." *Doctrine of the Holy Spirit*. London: Epworth, 1937.

Robinson, H. Wheeler. The *Christian Experience of the Holy Spirit*. London: Nixbet and Co. Ltd., 1928.

Schneider, Bernardinus. *Dominus Autem Spiritus Est*. Rome: Officium Libri Catholici, 1951.

Schweitzer, Albert. *The Mysticism of Paul the Apostle*. Trans. by W. Montgomery. New York: Henry Holt and Co., 1931.

Scott, E. G. *The Spirit in the New Testament*. London: Hodder and Stoughton, 1923.

Swete, H. B. *The Holy Spirit in the New Testament*. London: MacMillan Co., 1910.

Taylor, Vincent. *The Holy Spirit in the New Testament*. London: Epworth Press, 1937.

Van Unnik, W. D. "With Unveiled Face: An Exegesis of 2 Corinthians 3:12–18." *NovT* 16 (1963) 153–69.

Vos, G. "Eschatology of the Spirit in Paul." *Biblical Theological Studies*. New York: Charles Scribner's Sons, 1912.
White, R. E. O. *The Biblical Doctrine of Initiation*. Grand Rapids: Eerdmans, 1960.
Wikenhauser, Alfred. *Pauline Mysticism*. Freiburg: Herder, 1960.
Williams, J. Rodman. *The Era of the Spirit*. Plainfield: Logos, 1971.
———. *The Pentecostal Reality*. Plainfield: Logos, 1972.
Windisch, Hans. *The Spirit-Paraclete in the Fourth Gospel*. Trans. by J. W. Cox. Philadelphia: Fortress Press, 1968.
Wood, Leon J. *The Holy Spirit in the Old Testament*. Grand Rapids: Zondervan, 1976.
Ysebaert, J. *Greek Baptismal Terminology*. Nihmegen: Dekker and VandeVegi, 1962.

Specifically Related To Spirit Baptism

Berkhof, Hendrikus. *The Doctrine of the Holy Spirit*. Richmond: John Knox Press, 1964.
Bruner, F. Dale. *A Theology of the Holy Spirit*. Grand Rapids: Eerdmans, 1970.
Christenson, Larry. *Speaking in Tongues*. Minneapolis: Dimension Books, 1972.
Cottle, Ronald D. "All Were Baptized." *JETS* 17 (1974) 75–80.
Criswell, W. A. *The Baptism, Filling and Gifts of the Holy Spirit*. Grand Rapids: Zondervan, 1977.
Dunn, James D. G. *Baptism in the Holy Spirit*. London: SCM, 1970.
Ervin, Howard, M. *These Are Not Drunken As Ye Suppose*. Plainfield: Logos, 1968.
Gelpi, Donald L. *Charism and Sacrament*. New York: Paulist Press, 1976.
———. *Pentecostalism: A Theological Viewpoint*. New York: Paulist Press, 1971.
Green, Michael. *I Believe in the holy Spirit*. Grand Rapids: Eerdmans, 1975.
Hocken, Peter. "Catholic Pentecostalism: Some Key Questions." Part I. *HeyJ* 15:2 (April, 1974).
———. "The Significance and Potential of Pentecostalism." *New Heaven? New Earth?* Springfield: Templegate Publishers, 1977.
Hoekema, Anthony A. *Holy Spirit Baptism*. Grand Rapids: Eerdmans, 1972.
Horton, Harold. *The Baptism in the Holy Spirit*. London: Assemblies of God Publishing House, 1961.
Horton, Stanley M. *What the Bible Says About the Holy Spirit*. Springfield: Gospel Publishing House, 1976.
Hughes, Ray H. *What is Pentecost?* Cleveland: Pathway Press, 1963.
Jeffreys, George. *Pentecostal Rays*. London: Henry E. Walker Ltd., 1954.
Marshall, Catherine. *Something More*. New York: Avon Books, 1974.
McDonnell, Kilian. *Baptism in the Spirit as an Ecumenical Problem*. Notre Dame: Charismatic Renewal Services, 1972.
Pettery, Richard J. *In His Footsteps*. New York: Paulist Press, 1977.
Pinnock, Clark. "An Evangelical Theology of the Charismatic Renewal." *Theological Renewal* (October/November, 1977).
Rea, John. *The Layman's Commentary on the Holy Spirit*. Plainfield: Logos, 1974.
Riggs, Ralph. *The Spirit Himself*. Springfield: Gospel Publishing House, 1949.
Roberts, Oral. *The Baptism with the Holy Spirit*. Tulsa: n.p., 1964.
Ryrie, C. C. *The Holy Spirit*. Chicago: Moody Press, 1965.
Schep, John A. *Baptism in the Spirit*. Plainfield: Logos, 1972.
Schneider, Herbert. "Baptism in the Holy Spirit in the New Testament." *The Holy Spirit and Power*. Ed. by Kilian McDonnell. Garden City: Doubleday, 1975.

Smail, Thomas. *Reflected Glory*. Grand Rapids: Eerdmans, 1975.
Smith, Oswald J. *The Spirit-filled Life*. New York: Christian Alliance Publishing Co., 1928.
Stott, John R. W. *Baptism and Fullness*. Downer's Grove: Inter-Varsity Press, 1976.
Tugwell, Simon. "Pentecostal Doctrine of 'Baptism in the Holy Spirit.'" Part I. *HeyJ* (1972).
⎯⎯⎯. "Reflections on 'Baptism of the Holy Spirit.'" Part II. *HeyJ* (1972).
Unger, Merrill F. *The Baptism and Gifts of the Holy Spirit*. Chicago: Moody Press, 1974.
Walvoord, John F. *The Holy Spirit*. Grand Rapids: Zondervan, 1958.
Wild, Robert. *Enthusiasm in the Spirit*. Notre Dame: Avia Maria, 1975.

Church History

Bouyer, Louis. "Some Charismatic Manifestations in the History of the Church." *Perspectives on Charismatic Renewal*. Ed. by Edward O'Connor. Notre Dame: University of Notre Dame Press, 1975.
Bresson, Bernard L. *Studies in Ecstasy*. New York: Vantage Press, 1966.
Bromiley, G. W. "The Charismata in Christian History." *Theology, News and Notes* 20:1. Pasadena: Fuller Theological Seminary, 1974.
Clement, C. "Speaking with Tongues of Early Christians." *ExpTim* 10.
Currie, S. D. "Speaking in Tongues." *Int* 19 (1965) 274–94.
Cutten, G. B. *Speaking with Tongues*. New Haven: Yale University Press, 1927.
Dalton, R. C. *Tongues Like As of Fire*. Springfield: Gospel Publishing House, 1945.
Dollar, George W. "Church History and the Tongues Movement." *Bsac* 22, 134–43.
Emmert, Athanasios F. S. "Charismatic Developments in the Eastern Orthodox Church." *Perspectives on the New Pentecostalism*. Ed. by Russell P. Spittler. Grand Rapids: Baker, 1976.
Estam, John E. "Charismatic Theology in the Apostolic Tradition of Hippolytus." *Current Issues in Biblical and Patristic Interpretation*. Ed. by G. F. Hawthorne. Grand Rapids: Eerdmans, 1975.
Floris, A. T. "The Charismata in the Post-Apostolic Church." *Paraclete* 3:4, 8–13.
⎯⎯⎯. "Two Fourth-Century Witnesses on the Charismata." *Paraclete* 4:4, 17–22.
Hinson, E. Glenn. "A Brief History of Glossolalia." *Glossolalia*. Nashville: Abingdon Press, 1967.
Kaasa, Harris. "Tongues: A Historical Evaluation." *Dialogue* 2, 156–58.
Kelsey, M. T. *Tongue Speaking*. New York: Doubleday and Co., 1968.
Knox, R. A. *Enthusiasm*. Oxford: At the Clarendon Press, 1954.
Lombard, Emile. *DE LA GLOSSOLALIA ET DES PHENOMENEES SIMILAIRES*. Lausanne: George Bridel and Co., 1910.
Parmentier, Martien. "Two Charismatic Movements: Montanism and Messalianism." *Theological Renewal* 3 (June/July, 1976).
Piepkorn, A. D. "Charisma in the New Testament and the Apostolic Fathers." *CTM* 42, 369–89.
Rogers, C. J. "The Gift of Tongues in the Apostolic Church." *Bsac* 122, 134–43.
Wamble, Hugh. "Glossolalia in Christian History." *Tongues*. Ed. by L. B. Dyer. Jefferson City: LeBoi, 1971.
Williams, George H. And Edith Waldvogel. "A History of Speaking in Tongues and Related Gifts." *The Charismatic Movement*. Ed. by M. P. Hamilton. Grand Rapids: Eerdmans, 1975.

Unpublished Materials

MacDonald, William G. "Problems of Pneumatology in Christology." Th.D. dissertation. Louisville: Southern Baptist Theological Seminary, 1970.

Sala, Harold J. "An Investigation of the Baptizing and Filling Work of the Holy Spirit in the New Testament Related to the Pentecostal Doctrine of 'Initial Evidence.'" Ph.D. dissertation. Greenville: Bob Jones University, June, 1966.

Waldvogel, Edith. "The 'Over-Coming Life': A Study in the Reformed Evangelical Origins of Pentecostalism." Ph.D. dissertation. Cambridge: Harvard University, April, 1977.

Wessels, Roland. "The Doctrine of the Baptism in the Holy Spirit Among the Assemblies of God." Th.D. dissertation. Berkeley: Pacific School of Religion, May, 1966.

Wright, Jr., Walter C. "The Use of Pneuma in the Pauline Corpus With Special Attention to the Relationship Between Pneuma and the Risen Christ." Ph.D. dissertation. Pasadena: Fuller Theological Seminary, May, 1977.

www.ingramcontent.com/pod-product-compliance
Lightning Source LLC
Chambersburg PA
CBHW062016220426
43662CB00010B/1352